Web Programming with Java™

by Michael Girdley,
Kathryn A. Jones, et al.

sams
.net

201 West 103rd Street,
Indianapolis, Indiana 46290

To mom and dad, who support unconditionally, c.w. liew, kas, spalding, phil lesh, and the mailing list.

—*Michael Girdley*

To Thuy

—*Brian Gloyer*

Copyright © 1996 by Sams.net Publishing

FIRST EDITION

International Standard Book Number: 1-57521-113-0

Library of Congress Catalog Card Number: 96-67954

99 98 97 96   4 3 2 1

Interpretation of the printing code: the rightmost double-digit number is the year of the book's printing; the rightmost single-digit, the number of the book's printing. For example, a printing code of 96-1 shows that the first printing of the book occurred in 1996.

Composed in AGaramond and MCPdigital by Macmillan Computer Publishing

Printed in the United States of America

Publisher and President:	*Richard K. Swadley*
Development Manager:	*Dean Miller*
Managing Editor:	*Cindy Morrow*
Director of Marketing:	*John Pierce*
Assistant Marketing Managers:	*Kristina Perry*
	Rachel Wolfe

Acquisitions Editor
Grace M. Buechlein

Development Editor
Brian-Kent Proffitt

Software Development Specialist
Cari Skaggs

Production Editor
Deborah Frisby

Copy Editors
Miriam Bishop, Fran Blauw, Stacey Houston, Kristen Ivanetich, Howard Jones, Nanci Sears Perry

Indexer
Tim Griffin

Technical Reviewer
Christopher Stone

Editorial Coordinator
Bill Whitmer

Technical Edit Coordinator
Lynette Quinn

Editorial Assistants
Carol Ackerman
Andi Richter
Rhonda Tinch-Mize

Cover Designer
Tim Amrhein

Book Designer
Alyssa Yesh

Copy Writer
Peter Fuller

Production Team Supervisor
Brad Chinn

Production
Stephen Adams, Debra Bolhuis, Michael Brumitt, Kevin Cliburn, Jason Hand, Daniel Harris, Sonja Hart, Chris Livengood, Casey Price, Laura Robbins, Bobbi Satterfield, Mark Walchle

Overview

Contents

Part II   Building a Java Applet   93

Acknowledgments

A special acknowledgment goes to Lawrence Harris for his work on the table of contents of this book. Thank you!

Thanks to Brian Proffitt and to the rest of the gang at Sams.net. Most of all, thanks to Grace Buechlein, who called me on that May afternoon to talk about this Java book. Everyone has been very kind, and it is great to be involved with a team so committed to producing quality products.

The other authors and contributors to this book also worked hard to produce a high-quality, informative book. I was responsible only for about a half of this book, but it was originally going to be only a chapter or two. My portion just kept growing and growing. This book, above all, was a team effort of authors and editors, many of whom I've never met or spoken to. The efforts from all sides to produce *Web Programming with Java* are something I have a great deal of respect for, and I appreciate all the work people did to make my 50 percent read well.

I would also like to thank Professor Liew for providing my first introduction to the Java language, along with the rest of the faculty at Lafayette, including Professor Bjorling-Sachs and Professor Collins. Kelly Anne has also been great when I was unavailable to run. My employers at Southwest Research Institute were also great, even though I walked in some mornings so bleary-eyed from late-night writing that I could barely stand. And to Mom and Dad who bought that first Apple IIe fifteen Christmases ago. And to everyone else, friends, family, grandparents: thank you.
— *Michael Girdley*

About the Authors

Michael Girdley is from San Antonio, Texas. He is currently pursuing a Bachelor of Science in computer science at Lafayette College in Easton, Pa. He is also the chief consultant at Allwilk Consulting (`http://www.allwilk.com/`), an organization specializing in Web site creation and Java programming. He is a member of the Lafayette College varsity swimming team and will earn his fourth varsity letter in 1996-1997. Michael hopes to find a job or go to graduate school after possibly graduating on time in May of 1997. He can be reached at `girdleyj@allwilk.com` and on the Web at `http://www.lafayette.edu/~girdleyj/`.

Kathryn A. Jones is a senior technical specialist in the New York office of Smith Barney, where she designs and develops NT-based client/server systems.

Jim Morey is a graduate student in pure mathematics at the University of British Columbia. He got his undergraduate degree from University of Guelph, Ontario. He is a hacker in the sense that he learns programming by hacking through other people's code. Catching the Java bug early, he hacked his way through the alpha version of Java and wrote "Pythagorus's Haven," a geometrical proof of the Pythagorean Theorem. This program won the Grand Prize in the Applet Programming Contest (`http://java.sun.com/contest/results.html`) sponsored by Sun. And recently, he won first place in the individual entertainment and games category in the Java Cup International (`http://javacontest.sun.com/winners_circle/index.html`) for CopyCat, a 3-D geometrical game. With all the computer equipment he has won, Jim will be in hacker heaven for quite some time at `morey@math.ubc.ca` or `http://www.math.ubc.ca/~morey/`.

Keith Orpen is a student of mathematics and coffee and lives in Vancouver. He can be pestered at `korpen@math.ubc.ca`, which is handy for sending him money and stuff. His favorite thing in the world is to answer Java newbie questions for free, especially if a ton of effort is involved.

Thomas Fredell is the consulting manager for the Atlanta office of Brainstorm Technologies, a leading provider of Groupware tools and consulting services. Thomas has the distinction of being the first graduate with a degree in cognitive science from the University of Virginia. His interests include software development using C, C++, and Java, and he is interested in language design and artificial intelligence. His noncomputer hobbies include skiing, sailing, squash, and chess. He can be contacted via e-mail at `tfredell @ braintech.com`.

Brian Gloyer placed first in Sun's Java Applet Programming Contest with his Dining Philosophers applet. He is currently pursuing his Ph.D. at the University of California, Irvine. His research interests include artificial neural networks, image processing, and information systems. Some of his work, along with the original Dining Philosophers applet, can be seen on his home page at `http://www.eng.uci. edu/~bgloyer`.

Richard Lesh (`rich@micros.umsl.edu`) is an instructor with the Microcomputing Program at the University of Missouri, St. Louis. He has developed a variety of applications for the Macintosh, IBM PC, and various UNIX platforms. A number of software products that he has developed are in national distribution, including PLANMaker, a business plan building product, and a number of screen-saver modules published by Now Software in Now Fun! and by Berkeley Systems in After Dark.

George Reece (`borg@imaginary.com`) holds a philosophy degree from Bates College in Lewiston, Maine. He works as a consultant with York and Associates, Inc., and as a magazine columnist for the Java Developer's Journal. He has written some of the most popular MUD software on the Internet, include the Nightmare Object Library and the Foundation Object Library. For Java, he was the creator of the first JDBC implementation, the Imaginary JDBC Implementation for mSQL. His Internet publications include the free textbooks on the LPC programming language, *LPC Basics* and *Intermediate LPC*.

Tell Us What You Think!

As a reader, you are the most important critic of our books. We value your opinion and want to know what we're doing right, what we could do better, what areas you'd like to see us publish in, and any other words of wisdom you're willing to pass our way. You can help us make strong books that meet your needs and give you the computer guidance you require.

Do you have access to CompuServe or the World Wide Web? Then check out our CompuServe forum by typing GO SAMS at any prompt. If you prefer the World Wide Web, check out our site at http://www.mcp.com.

 NOTE:

> If you have a technical question about this book, call the technical support line at
> (800) 571-5840, ext. 3668.

As the team leader of the group that created this book, I welcome your comments. You can fax, e-mail, or write me directly to let me know what you did or didn't like about this book—as well as what we can do to make our books stronger. Here's the information:

FAX: 317/581-4669

E-mail: Dean Miller opsys_mgr@sams.mcp.com

Mail: Dean Miller
         Sams Publishing
         201 W. 103rd Street
         Indianapolis, IN 46290

Introduction

by Michael Girdley

Today you went Web "surfing" (a silly name, in my opinion), and you scoped out what's there. First you loaded up your favorite site (maybe one you created) and checked it out. Seems like everything's going fine—same white background, same images, nice logo—impressive, to say the least. You make your way around and wander into some home pages, possibly from a school somewhere or from one of the multitude of Web space providers. You might see pages like the one shown in Figure IN.1.

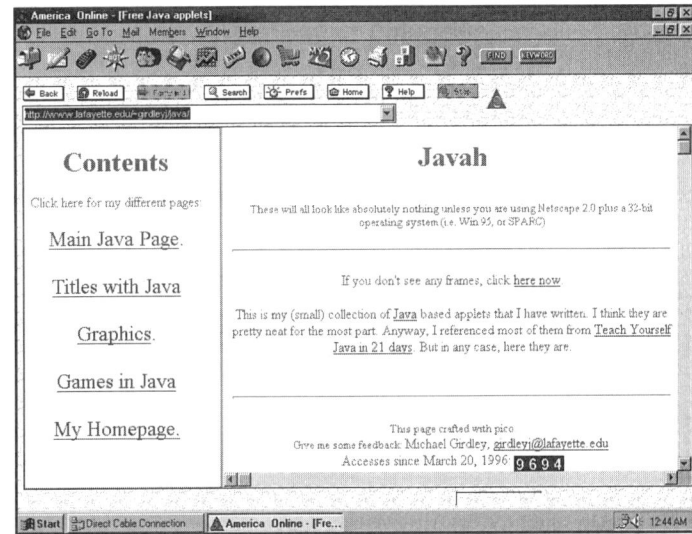

Figure IN.1.

A page you might see.

Alternatively, you might visit one of the big commercial sites like ESPNet's Sportszone. You keep seeing references to Java everywhere, and you feel you're missing out.

So you search the Web for a Java-enhanced browser and eventually find one. Then you're off. Another world opens to you. Suddenly, the Web has started coming alive. You reach Gamelan (`http://www.gamelan.com`), a compendium of links to Java resources, and an amazing number of Java's wonders present themselves.

Or again, say you've seen all the hype (when it reaches *Time* magazine, it's hype). Of course, you want to use Java in your own pages, but how?

Web Programming with Java is your guidebook to creating, designing, and using Java for and on the World Wide Web.

Who Should Buy This Book?

You might be one of the people who should buy this book if you are excited and amazed by the extension that Java provides to the World Wide Web (also called WWW or "the Web"). You might have seen the amazing Java applets out on the Internet, and you are interested in learning how to do it yourself. Perhaps you've heard or seen the hype in magazines and periodicals, and your curiosity is aroused. But you don't know how to make your own Java programs (and you are not alone—I get many e-mails from people who want to know how). You need a source that will function both as a tutorial and as a reference for you to create your own Java applets.

This book provides you the capability to make your Web pages and sites come alive.

Besides serving as a tool to teach Java, this book will help programmers who are already familiar with Java and who are interested in the application of Java to the Web. This book covers Java completely, with special attention paid to its application on the WWW.

The most basic thing that a user of this book should have is access to a computer (PC or workstation) running on a Java-capable platform, to which the Java compiler and interpreter have been ported. At the time of this writing, many platforms are Java-capable. These range from the Sun SPARC workstations to the Microsoft Windows 95 interface to Steve Job's NeXT. A complete OS/2 port has already been completed and released by IBM, though many of the bugs are still being worked out at present.

 The version of Sun's Java Developer's Kit (JDK) included in the CD-ROM that accompanies this book contains the full release of the Java language (1.x) for many different platforms.

If your platform isn't supported on the version included with this book, don't worry. Chapter 2, "Getting Started," covers the where and the how of getting the Java Developer's Kit.

 CAUTION:

> The JDK is currently not ported to run under Microsoft Windows 3.1. As such, this book and the programs included will not be useful for 3.1 users. The JDK does work under Windows 95. If you haven't looked into Windows 95, this may be one more reason to consider it.

If you have access to an appropriate system, what next? Most importantly, you should have an understanding of the major concepts of computer programming and some programming experience. As you will discover in this book, Java is an object-oriented language. Any previous experience you have in object-oriented design (OOD) will be a major bonus, though it is not necessary.

And finally, this is a book that concentrates on the use of Java on the World Wide Web. There are a number of differences between Java programming for the Web and for stand-alone Java programs. You'll see in this book that the difference between these two programming goals extends all the way to their names: stand-alone Java programs are called applications, but Java programs designed for the Web are called applets.

In conclusion, you should

1. Have a background in programming computers.
2. Have access to a computer capable of Java.
3. Be in the market to use Java on the World Wide Web.

What's in This Book?

This book covers the complete story of using Java on the Web. It contains all the information necessary to implement and create your very own Java applets and to effectively use all of the power of Java language. *Web Programming with Java* begins with an overview of the Java language and then deals progressively with more powerful and detailed concepts. Here is a summary of what each chapter contains.

Chapter 1, "An Overview of Java," is an overview of the Java language itself and some of the circumstances which prompted Sun Microsystems to create it. You will learn the *why* and *how* of Java as an object-oriented language. This object-oriented nature, you will discover, is key to the platform-independence of Java.

Chapter 2, "Getting Started," covers the major concepts you'll need to know to use Java on your platform. In this chapter, you'll learn about where to get the Java Developer's Kit and how to use it on your system. Finally, you'll see how to compile your Java programs and then view them using Sun's `AppletViewer` utility.

In Chapter 3, "An Introduction to Java Classes," you'll get a complete overview of what makes a Java class. The multiple classes and packages of classes available to you in the Java class library will all be covered. These include packages such as the `java.net` package, which enables network connections, and the `java.awt` package, which enables you to easily create GUIs.

Rounding out Part I, in Chapter 4, "Creating Your Own Objects," you'll get into creating your very own classes. You will learn how to subclass Java classes and also how to subclass your own classes. Finally, you will learn how Java handles Garbage Collection, which frees up system resources from where they are no longer needed.

Part II deals with the concept of building a complete Java applet. One of the most appealing aspects of the Web today is the graphical interaction between the user and source—the applet you create will do just that. Chapter 5, "Writing a Java Applet: The Order Entry System," begins Part II by discussing the first applet you will be creating, the Order Entry System. This chapter also describes exactly what applets entail in Java, and why.

Coverage of the Abstract Windowing Toolkit (AWT) will begin, with a description of the limits and capabilities of both applets and it. The control path of applets (init(), start(), etc.) will also be covered. Finally, you will learn exactly how to put applets into your Web pages.

Chapter 6, "The Order Entry System: Adding Features and Handling Events," begins with an explanation of the Java Abstract Windowing Toolkit, which is a package of classes that facilitate the inclusion and use of the typical user interface components, such as windows, pulldown menus, buttons, and dialog boxes. You'll look into the use and description of the AWT concepts of containers and components. Part of this chapter will cover the implementation of some of the components. The graphical components of the AWT will be covered in this chapter, while others will be left for later chapters. This chapter also covers some of the limitations of applets and compares them with Java applications.

Chapter 7, "The Order Entry System: Entry Fields, Labels, and Validation," covers the remaining components, including those specific to text input and output. There are multiple components dealing with text, including Labels, Text Fields, and Text Areas. The implementation and function of each one of these components is detailed in this chapter. This chapter also takes some more steps toward completing the Order Entry System. You will extend the System to include the components discussed in this chapter and to handle them appropriately. You will also fill in some of the "holes," such as the unfinished updateValues method, and you will activate the "Clear" button. To finish Chapter 7, you will learn the methods of password entry and identification, which are very important in the applet design business. This same section also covers data validation in the entry fields in applets.

Chapter 8, "The Order Entry System: Managing the Applet Layout," is a monster. First, you are going to further explore the concepts of containers in the Java AWT. The chapter covers how to implement the different container types and how they interact with each other. The different containers available enable you to create stand-alone window applets, and also enable you to clean up the appearance of the Order Entry System. I will also describe pop-up dialog boxes and the means to incorporate them into your applets.

Next, Chapter 8 covers the five different AWT Layout Managers. These enable you, the programmer, to place your components in containers in an orderly fashion, while still maintaining platform independence. The five layout managers are: Flow Layout, Border Layout, Card Layout, Grid Layout, and the GridBag Layout. The GridBag Layout is the layout manager you will use to reorganize the Order Entry System applet panel.

Chapter 9, "The Order Entry System: Adding Graphics and a Logo," covers some of the most exciting aspects of Java, those dealing with graphics. I will discuss the AWT Graphics class, which enables you to implement many different graphical items. These features involve drawing, displaying images, and setting colors, among others. I will discuss the Canvas class, which is a special type of component designed for use in dealing with graphics. The Order Entry System applet will also be extended further to include the concepts dealt with in this chapter.

Many languages do not have built-in capabilities to enable you to efficiently detect and deal with errors, mishaps, and events out of the ordinary. Luckily, Java includes a means to handle these exceptions to the norm simply and effectively. You will learn this process of handling exceptions and errors. In other words, although you plan on a certain progression through your code, you will also plan to implement code that will cover the instances where things don't go your way. The handling of exceptions and errors, and the command structures to implement them, will be the focus of this chapter.

Chapter 11, "Reading and Writing with Java," covers the implementation of reading and writing with Java. This process in Java is centered around the concept of streams. Just as a stream of water flows in one direction, starting and ending, so does a stream of data. Streams simply are linear paths that connect a data producer and a data consumer together to allow the serial (one chunk after another) transmission of data. Streams can connect many different things. For example, a stream can connect two independent processes together; they can connect a class to a file or even connect your class to a network. This chapter will cover in depth the usage of the multiple types of streams available in the Java-standard libraries.

Chapter 12, "Network Programming with Java," begins the third and final part of this book. Where the first part introduced the Java language, and the second part covered basic applet techniques, the chapters in this section cover more complicated and powerful applet techniques. Chapter 12 covers network programming with Java. The examples in this chapter rely extensively on the java.net package in the Java class library in order to make, manage, and utilize the network capabilities of Java. You'll learn how to have your applets and applications in Java make connections across LANs and the Internet. And most importantly, you'll learn the process of connecting from your applet to your Web server. The security limitations placed on applets will be discussed. You will develop an on-line inquiry applet, which will demonstrate these concepts.

Chapter 13, "General Purpose Classes," covers the different general purpose classes available in the Java class library and demonstrates their use. Then, Chapter 14, "Extending Java," covers extending Java to interface with other languages, including C applications. Chapter 15, "Interfacing with a Database: Catalog Applet," is about interfacing with databases in Java. It covers the process of making a network connection to a database and then creating an on-line catalog applet.

Chapter 16, "Multithreading with Java," covers one of the most important features of Java: multithreading. It is a complicated topic, which will prove to be one of the most important and powerful features of Java. Chapter 17, "Advanced Graphics: Multimedia," covers multimedia in Java applications. You'll learn how to create your own multimedia applet.

Chapter 18, "Serious Play: Game Applets," covers game programming in Java. The process of creating game elements will be discussed. You will learn about the implementation of those elements into an example applet. Finally, Chapter 19, "Security Issues," covers the future of Java and security implementations of Java.

Conventions Used in This Book

This book uses the following conventions:

○ The lines of some listings are numbered. The numbers are only for ease of reference. You do not type the line numbers into the code.

○ New terms appear in *italic.*

○ All code appears in a `monospace computer` font, as do filenames and directory names.

○ Placeholders in code appear in *`italic monospace`.*

○ When a line of code is too long to fit on only one line of this book, it is broken at a convenient place and continued to the next line. The continuation of the line is preceded by a code continuation character (➥).

 ○ The CD-ROM icon tells you that the file being discussed is included on the CD-ROM that comes with this book.

Java Basics

Chapter

1

by Kathryn A. Jones

An Overview of Java

Introduction

If you have purchased this book, you are probably planning to program with Java. There are many reasons for using Java as your programming language. You might want to learn an object-oriented programming language, and maybe you've heard that Java is simple to use. You might have come across some interesting applets while browsing the Internet (if you're using a Java-capable browser), and perhaps you want to learn to write applets of your own and add them to your Internet or intranet HTML documents. You might want to learn how to add Internet functionality to your C applications or how to use Java to write full-fledged applications that are portable. This book helps you accomplish any and all of these goals.

This overview introduces the many features of Java and explains why they are important to you, the Java programmer. It is worthwhile for you to understand the richness and usefulness of Java before getting into the specifics of the Java environment and language.

Java is an interpreted language that is similar, superficially, to C++, but different in many important ways. Java was originally intended to be an extension of the C compiler but has been completely rebuilt from the ground up to be a smaller, portable, purely object-oriented language that eliminates many of the sources of bugs and complexities common in C++.

A Brief History of Java

Java has been around since 1991, developed by a small team of Sun Microsystems developers in a project originally called the Green project. The intent of the project was to develop a platform-independent software technology that would be used in the consumer electronics industry. The language that the team created was originally called Oak.

The first implementation of Oak was in a PDA-type device called Star Seven (*7) that consisted of the Oak language, an operating system called GreenOS, a user interface, and hardware. The name *7 was derived from the telephone sequence that was used in the team's office and that was dialed in order to answer any ringing telephone from any other phone in the office. This PDA-type device was intended to be sold to consumer electronics manufacturers who would distribute the boxes under their company name. In 1993, the team, then incorporated as FirstPerson, Inc., decided to gear their technology toward a new implementation for which demand was building in the entertainment industry—interactive television. They proposed their technology to Time Warner as an operating system for set-top boxes and video-on-demand technology that would decode the data stream that Time Warner would be sending to television sets around the country. In June of 1993, Time Warner selected Silicon Graphics' technology over Sun's. A later deal fell apart and FirstPerson decided to disband. Half of the members of the original FirstPerson team continued to work with the Oak technology, however, applying it to multimedia and network computing.

Around the time the FirstPerson project was floundering in consumer electronics, a new craze was gaining momentum in America; the craze was called "Web surfing." The World Wide Web, a name applied to the Internet's millions of linked HTML documents was suddenly becoming popular for use by the masses. The reason for this was the introduction of a graphical Web browser called Mosaic, developed by NCSA. The browser simplified Web browsing by combining text and graphics into a single interface to eliminate the need for users to learn many confusing UNIX and DOS commands. Navigating around the Web was much easier using Mosaic.

It has only been since 1994 that Oak technology has been applied to the Web. In 1994, two Sun developers created the first version of HotJava, then called WebRunner, which is a graphical browser for the Web that exists today. The browser was coded entirely in the Oak language, by this time called Java. Soon after, the Java compiler was rewritten in the Java language from its original C code, thus proving that Java could be used effectively as an application language. Sun introduced Java in May 1995 at the SunWorld 95 convention.

Web surfing has become an enormously popular practice among millions of computer users. Until Java, however, the content of information on the Internet has been a bland series of HTML documents. Web users are hungry for applications that are interactive, that users can execute no matter what hardware or software platform they are using, and that travel across heterogeneous networks and do not spread viruses to their computers. Java can create such applications.

Applets

On the Internet, Java programs are called applets. Applets are Java applications that are embedded inside HTML files and can be downloaded into a Java-capable browser with the click of a mouse. Applets are different from regular Java applications. A Java application simply has a single `main()` method that indicates to the Java runtime system that it is an application. A Java applet is an application that includes several additional methods that the runtime system uses that tell it how to handle the applet, such as what to do when a user clicks an applet icon and how it looks on a page.

Before your browser's runtime Java interpreter downloads and executes the applet's code, the Java interpreter verifies the code's integrity. Java is more than a tool to help you write applets, however. It is a new, powerful programming environment.

Java's Features

Sun describes Java as a "simple, object-oriented, interpreted, robust, secure, architecture-neutral, portable, high-performance, multithreaded, and dynamic language."

Each of the features mentioned in this quotation from Sun's Web page is an important part of the Java development environment as well as a critical requirement for Web programming. The combination of these features makes Java a powerful and useful programming language that empowers you, the programmer, with the tools you need to easily create powerful programs for today's distributed environments.

Simple

Java is simple to use for three main reasons: First, Java is familiar to you if you know C. Second, Java eliminates components of C that cause bugs and memory leaks and replaces their functionality with more efficient solutions and automated tasks, so you have a lot less debugging to worry about than you would using C or C++. Third, Java provides a powerful set of pre-tested class libraries that give you the ability to use their advanced features with just a few additional lines of code.

Object-Oriented

Java is an object-oriented programming language that uses software objects called *classes* and is based upon reusable, extensible code. This means that you can use Java's classes, which are sets of variables and methods, as templates to create other classes with added functionality without rewriting the code from the parent classes or superclasses. If you plan your application's class hierarchy well, your application will be small and easy to develop. The hierarchy of classes is explained later in this chapter.

Robust

Java is robust because the language removes the use of pointers and the Java runtime system manages memory for you. The problems with pointers in C and C++ was that pointers directly addressed memory space. In a distributed environment like the Internet, when code is downloaded to diverse systems, there is no way of knowing for sure that memory space addressed by pointers is not occupied by the system. Overwriting this memory space could crash a system. Java also gives you automatic bounds checking for arrays, so they cannot index address space not allocated to the array. Automatic memory management is done using the Garbage Collector, which is explained in detail in Chapter 4, "Creating Your Own Objects."

Interpreted

Java is interpreted, so your development cycle is much faster. As you learn later when the Java interpreter is discussed, you need only to compile for a single, virtual machine and your code can run on any hardware platform that has the Java interpreter ported to it.

Secure

Java is secure, so you can download Java programs from anywhere with confidence that they will not damage your system. Java provides extensive compile-time checking, followed by a second, multilayered level of runtime checking. Java's security structure is described in detail in Chapter 19, "Security Issues."

Architecture Neutral

Java is architecture neutral, so your applications are portable across multiple platforms. Java's applications are written and compiled into bytecode for Java's virtual machine, which emulates an actual hardware chip. Bytecode is converted to binary machine code by the Java interpreter installed at the client, so applications need not be written for individual platforms and then ported from platform to platform. Java additionally ensures that your applications are the same on every platform by strictly defining the sizes of its basic data types and the behavior of its arithmetic operators. Operator overloading, the process of modifying the behavior of operators, is prohibited by Java.

High Performance

Java is "high performance" because its bytecode is efficient and has multithreading built in for applications that need to perform multiple concurrent activities. Although threads still require the use of classes, Java balances the addition of thread synchronization between the language and class levels. Java's bytecode is efficient because it is compiled to an intermediate level that is near enough to native machine code that performance is not significantly sacrificed when the Java bytecode is run by the interpreter.

Dynamic

Java is dynamic, so your applications are adaptable to changing environments because Java's architecture allows you to dynamically load classes at runtime from anywhere on the network, which means that you can add functionality to existing applications by simply linking in new classes. For example, if your applet is being run by a browser that doesn't have one of the classes included in your applet's bytecode, the browser can download the appropriate class from the server that is storing your applet, check the bytecode, and execute it. This is assuming your browser has not been configured with strict security. Chapter 19 covers browser security.

The Fundamentals of the Java Language

This chapter introduces you to the basic concepts and functions of the Java programming language and gives you brief examples to illustrate important points. The later, more advanced chapters guide you through extensive samples of code, and so the examples in this chapter are short. By the end of this chapter, you should have a basic understanding of the Java language and be ready to explore in detail Java's class libraries in Chapter 3, "An Introduction to Java Classes."

Java programming will be fairly easy for you if you have had experience with C++ because Java is designed to look and feel like C++. If you are an experienced C programmer, you will have to let go of some old habits to program Java, however, as you will discover later in this chapter. Please do not be concerned if you have little or no experience in programming—this book assumes no prior knowledge of C++. You may need to read through the chapters more slowly and carefully than an experienced programmer.

Java as an Object-Oriented Language

Java's class structure is made up of the following major components: classes, hierarchy, variables, methods, and inheritance.

Classes

The key to understanding Java's object-oriented design is understanding what classes are and what you can do with them. Classes are templates that you use to create actual objects. The instructions contained in a class are used to create one or more objects, which can be called *instances* of classes in Java. When you create an object from a class, you *instantiate* the object, which means you create an instance of the class. The words *instances* and *objects* are used interchangeably throughout the discussions of classes in this book, depending on the context of the sentence in which they're used.

In object-oriented programming, you can think of an object as you would any real-world object, for example, a rectangle. The actual rectangle would be an instance of the class `Rectangle`.

A very rudimentary declaration of a class is as follows:

```
class  classname {
//class instructions
}
```

The instructions in a class are made of two basic components: variables that hold data, and methods that manipulate the data.

Before you begin creating the classes in your application, you must design the class structure. Java's class structure is organized into a hierarchy.

Hierarchy

Classes are organized into a hierarchy to allow you to easily reuse code. When you write a Java program, first determine which objects you'll need to use in your code. Then determine what variables and methods the object's class must store. When you know what instructions your classes contain, plan your hierarchy.

Without planning your hierarchy first, you would begin creating a class for each object individually and undoubtedly would find that you are repeating instructions from class to class. In a hierarchy, instructions common to groups of objects are separated out in parent classes, or *superclasses*, and can be used by all of their *subclasses*. Therefore, when you plan your hierarchy, you would group objects by the instructions that they have in common and organize them into a hierarchy.

Superclasses are used as templates to create subclasses with variables and methods that make each subclass unique. Each superclass can be a parent to one or many other subclasses. Unlike in C++, a subclass can have only one superclass. Therefore, the Java class hierarchy looks something like the one shown in Figure 1.1.

Figure 1.1.
Java class hierarchy.

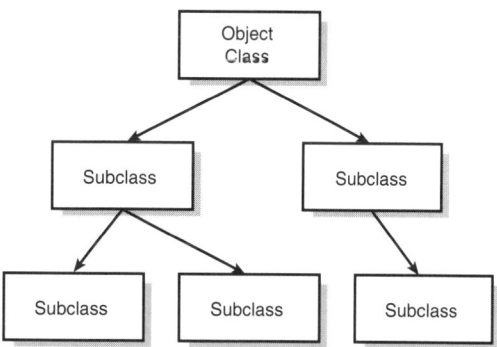

If a superclass is not defined when a class is declared, the class is automatically made a subclass of Java's Object class. Every class in a Java program is a descendant of Object. Object itself has no superclass.

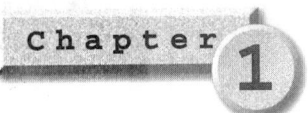

Variables

Classes store information that describe objects in *instance variables*. When objects are created from a class, they contain new instances of the class' variables. These instance variables can have values that are different from one object to the next. Values of instance variables are called *data*. When an instance variable's data is changed, it affects only the individual object. There is a way in Java to assign a variable to a class that, if changed, is changed in all instances of the class. Such a variable is called a *static variable*, which you learn about later in this chapter in the section called "Static Methods and Variables."

The basic declaration statement of a variable is this:

```
datatype variablename;
```

Two variables that might be declared for a rectangle are `length` and `width`. They could be declared in one line because they have the same data type. (You explore data types in Table 1.1 of this chapter.) Their declaration statement might be this:

```
int length, width;
```

If you created an object from a class with only these two variables declared, the object would simply hold this data. It would not know to draw lines with these values to form a rectangle. Methods must be declared to use the data in variables.

Methods

Methods are functions that must be associated with individual classes. In C and C++ and other procedural languages, functions can be placed anywhere in the code. In Java, they must be stored within classes. Instances of methods are created when instances of classes are created. Unlike variables, methods are not duplicated in objects—their code is stored only in the class.

When an object's method is invoked from its class, it uses the data of variables in the object.

Every method returns a value if it is not declared as `void`. To declare a method, you use the following statement:

```
returntype methodname (parameter list) {
    //method code
}
```

At this point in the chapter, you won't get into coding the method that draws the rectangle. After you've learned the basic coding elements of Java later in this chapter, exercises in coding methods will be more useful.

Inheritance

Variables and methods that are stored in classes in the class hierarchy are inherited by subclasses, so you do not need to re-create them. Objects created from a subclass will contain not only the instances of the variables and methods of the subclass, but also its superclass' variables and methods, as well as those of the parent of its superclass, and so on. When a variable or method is referenced in an object, it is retrieved in a specific order: Java first searches for it in the current class, then, if it is not found, it searches the parent class, and so on.

In summary, objects in your Java program are created from classes that contain variables and methods to describe the object. Classes are organized into a hierarchy in which classes inherit functionality from parent classes, which allows for reusable code. These basic concepts of the structure of Java's object-oriented programming language will become clearer to you as you read through the rest of the sections.

Basic Coding Elements

Your Java code is used to create classes, objects, interfaces, and packages. You'll learn how to create each of these in Chapter 4. This section outlines the elements of the code you need to use to create them.

Your code is written in a series of statements, which can be organized into blocks. These statements contain data and operators, which are components of expressions. You can annotate your code using comments, which makes the code more understandable.

Statements

Any line of code before a semicolon is known as a *statement* and is executed by the Java interpreter when it hits the semicolon; after executing that statement, the interpreter moves to the next statement. Each statement contains instructions for using data and operators.

Expressions

An *expression* is a part of a statement that uses data and operators to return a value.

Blocks

A *block* is a collection of statements enclosed in curly braces. Any variables that you declare and that assign values within a block are erased when the flow of execution leaves the block. The block in which the variable's value exists is called the *scope* of the variable.

Comments

Comments are used to annotate the code so that a reader can understand the purpose of certain lines and blocks of code. Comments are ignored by the Java compiler. Multiline comments are preceded by /* and are ended with */. Single line comments are preceded by //. The double slash "comments out" text only to the end of a line. A comment would appear as follows:

```
/* This declares the length variable for the Rectangle class   */
int length;
```

or

```
int length;   //Declares the length variable for the Rectangle class
```

Data Types

To represent data values in your code you use *literals*. Literals are described by types, named by identifiers, and stored in variables, which were outlined earlier in the chapter and are explored further in this section.

When you use literals in your code, they appear in their raw form rather than as a result of an expression. Several types of literals are commonly used: numbers, integers, floating points, characters, Booleans, and strings.

Table 1.1 outlines Java's strict definitions of these data types.

Table 1.1. Rules for Java literals.

Literal Type	Typename	Rule
Number	Num	Can be integer, floating point, or character.
Integer		Can be decimal, hexadecimal, or octal.
	Byte	8-bit integers between −128 and 127.
	Short	16-bit integers between −32768 and 32767.
	Int	32-bit integers between −2147483648 and 2147483647.
	Long	64-bit integers between −9223372036854775808 and 9223372036854775807 or have L or l appended to them.
	Hex	Preceded by 0x or 0X.
	Oct	Preceded by 0.

Literal Type	Typename	Rule
Floating point		Any number with a decimal point. Can be made exponential by appending an e or E, followed by the exponent.
	Float	32-bit.
	Double	64-bit.
Character	Char	16-bit integers represented by a single character and enclosed in single quotes.
		In Java, the Unicode character map is used. The following special characters must be represented by escape sequences:
		backspace \b
		backslash \\
		carriage return \r
		double quote \"
		formfeed \f
		hex number \xhh
		horizontal tab \t
		newline \n
		octal number \000
		question mark \q
		single quote \'
		vertical tab \v
Boolean	Boolean	Can only be true or false. Are not represented by 0 or 1.
String	String	Zero or more characters enclosed in double quotes.

Literals are described by *identifiers*. Identifiers are sequences of letters and digits, and can also be used to describe variables, methods, and classes. Identifiers can consist of any letter from *a* to *z*, underscore, dollar sign, digits from 0 to 9 (except as the first character); identifiers are case-sensitive.

Java has several reserved *keywords* that are its own identifiers, which cannot be used as identifiers in any way other than that defined by Java, as listed in Table 1.2. Though these words are reserved, not all are used in the most recent release.

Table 1.2. Reserved keywords.

abstract	else	int	short
boolean	extends	interface	static
break	final	long	super
byte	finally	native	switch
case	float	new	synchronized
cast	for	null	this
catch	future	operator	throw
char	generic	outer	throws
class	goto	package	transient
const	if	private	try
continue	implements	protected	var
default	import	public	void
do	inner	rest	volatile
double	instanceof	return	while

Operators

Operators are used to compare values. Java has strict definitions of *operators*. It doesn't allow for overloading, which is a C developer's common practice of changing the behavior of operators.

Java provides two types of operators: binary and unary. Binary operators are used to compare two values. Unary operators use a single value, for example:

```
a >= b
a++
```

The first example uses a binary operator, >=, which compares variables a and b. The second is a unary operator, ++, which increments the value of a by one.

All of Java's binary and unary operators can be found in Table 1.3. They are organized according to the precedence with which they are performed.

Table 1.3. Binary and unary operators.

Operator	Description
., (), []	Precedence overriding decimal, parentheses, brackets
!, ~, ++, --	Boolean negation, bitwise complement, increment, decrement
*, /, %	Multiplication, division, modulus
+, -	Addition, subtraction or unary negation
<<, >>, >>>	Left shift, right shift, zero-fill right shift
<, <=, >, >=	Less than, less than or equal to, greater than, greater than or equal to
==, !=	Equals, is not equal to
&	Bitwise or Boolean AND
^	Bitwise or Boolean XOR
¦	Bitwise or Boolean OR
&&	Evaluation AND, Logical AND
¦¦	Evaluation OR, Logical OR
?:	If…then…else
=, +=, -=, *=, /=, %=, &=, ^=, ¦=, <<=, >>=	Assignment operators
,	Comma

Declaring Variables

There are four types of statements to use for variables: declarations, assignments, initializers, and casts.

You must always declare variables before you can use them in your Java program. Variable *declarations* assign data types to variables. A declaration statement in Java consists of a data type followed by an identifier. Any of the data types listed in the previous table can be used to declare variables, for example:

```
Boolean IsReady;
float miles;
int x, y, z;
short pages;
```

Assignments are statements that assign values to variables. These, like declarations, are required before variables can be used. They are called by setting an identifier equal to a value. This value, of course, must be compatible with the data type assigned to the variable identifier. Initializers are assignment statements that are combined with the declaration statement, for example:

```
Boolean IsReady = false
float miles = 3.62
short pages = 240
```

If you want certain variable values to remain constant in your code, you can use the `final` keyword, which ensures that the variable cannot be changed by the code. Its form is this:

```
final int pages = 500
```

Casts are statements you use if you need to place a value of one type into a variable of another type. In C++, automatic coercion allows you to do this without declaring that you were aware of this change. In Java, you must explicitly call such an instruction with a cast statement. Cast statements are generally called as follows:

```
datatype identifier = (datatype) identifier
```

Java allows casts only between compatible data types.

In this section, you have learned about the data and operators that are used in expressions that are parts of statements. You now understand that statements are organized with blocks and annotated with comments. You have also examined some basic statements that deal with variable declarations. These are the fundamental elements of Java coding.

Flow of Execution

Now that you understand the basic structure and elements of the Java language, you'll see how statements flow through a Java program in this section. By default, the Java interpreter executes statements in sequential order. This section introduces you to some more complex types of statements that alter this flow of execution.

Conditionals

`if`, `if...else`, `?:`, and `switch` are four conditional statements that are used often in code. They evaluate an expression and, based on the value of the expression, they control which statements are executed.

The `if` statements consist of `if` followed by a test expression. If the test expression returns a `true` value, the statement or block of statements after the expression is executed. They are structured as follows:

```
if (test expression) statement;
```

if...else statements are similar to if statements, but include a false statement that is executed if the test expression returns a false value. They are structured as follows:

```
if (test expression) true-statement;
else false-statement;
```

The ?: is a ternary operator that allows you to assign one of two values based on the evaluation of an expression as true or as false. Its form is as follows:

```
(test expression) ? true-value : false-value
```

The switch statement evaluates an expression's value and jumps to a statement identified by the literal value of the expression. It saves coding time if there are several values in your statement. Its form is as follows:

```
switch (expression) {
    case value: statements
    case value: statements
    default: statements
}
```

Loops

Loops provide you with the ability to repeat certain statements until a condition is met. Java provides three types of loop statements: while, do...while, and for. Three other statements commonly used with loops are break, continue, and labels, but these can be used with other types of Java statements (such as conditionals) as necessary.

The while loop evaluates a condition to see if it is true, and then executes statements and checks the condition again. If the condition is still true, while executes the statements and checks again. This process continues until the condition is evaluated as false. The form is this:

```
while (expression) true-statements
```

The do...while loop is similar to while, but do...while executes statements before the condition is evaluated. When you use do...while, loop statements are always executed at least once. The form is this:

```
do statements while (expression)
```

The for loop allows you to test a range of values in your expression. Its form is generally this:

```
for (initializer; expression; increment)
statements
```

The break statement is used to exit loop and conditional statements before meeting a test condition. The continue statement directs execution back to the beginning of a loop without completing all of the loop statements. A label is used to identify a statement so execution can be directed to it with a break or continue statement. A colon (:) must be appended to a label name.

An example of a label is as follows:

```
variable declarations;
Label:
     while (test expression) {
statement;
if(test expression)  {
continue Label;
}
statement;
     }
```

Arrays

Arrays create slots that allow you to store a list of variables. Arrays are allocated using the new operator to create the array and assigning it to a variable with =. Arrays are declared as follows:

```
datatype variable[] = new datatype[number-of-slots];
```

The first half of the statement declares the variable that holds the array. Your array declarations should end in square brackets. The second half creates the array and assigns it to the variable.

The new modifier automatically initializes your array to `false` for Boolean arrays, `0` for numeric arrays, `\0` for character arrays, and `null` for all other types of arrays. You can choose to initialize the array on the same line as the declaration, as shown here:

```
datatype [] = {element1, element2, element3, etc.}
```

Using Classes, Objects, and Interfaces

Every Java application is essentially a class that contains the `main()` method. This section discusses briefly how to create and use classes, objects, and interfaces in Java applications. You'll learn about many additional elements of the Java programming language that are important to know when using classes and objects.

Creating Classes

The first step in creating an object in your application is to create its class. The following form is used to define a class:

```
class classname [extends classname] [implements interface] {
     [variable declaration;]
     [method declaration;]
}
```

In this form, the `classname` is the name of the new class; `extends` `classname` is where the parent class of a subclass would be named, after the word `extends`. The `implements` `interface` defines an interface used by the class (interfaces are covered later in the chapter). If you do not want the compiler to allow your class to be subclassed, you can precede your class statement with the word `final`. If you wish to create a class that must be subclassed, you would precede the class with the word `abstract`.

You explored variable declaration in detail in the first section. Keep in mind that variables must be initialized before being used in methods. Now you'll learn how methods are declared. Methods generally use the following form:

```
[Modifiers] return-type method-name (parameter-list) {
    [statements;]
}
```

The return type specifies the type of data or class that is returned when the method is run. The `void` return type is used when no value is returned. When naming the method, you must follow the same rules for naming classes and variables described earlier in the chapter. You must always enclose the parameter list in parentheses even if the parentheses are empty. The parameter list contains the types and variable names of all variables that you want to pass to the method. The statements are the code of your method.

Overloaded Methods

You use overloaded methods in your code when you need to call a method with different sets of parameter lists. Methods that allow flexibility in the parameters they use can be called from different parts of your program with different variables. Java's API classes, discussed in Chapter 3, use overloaded methods. To allow a different type of parameter information to be passed to your method, repeat the method in your code with the alternate parameter list included, as follows:

```
returnvalue methodname (parameter list 1)
returnvalue methodname (parameter list 2)
```

When the method is called and parameters are passed to it, Java determines which version of the method has a parameter list that most closely matches the parameters passed and executes it.

Static Methods and Variables

Static methods and variables are similar to the methods and variables already discussed, but they are a part of the class and do not require you to create an object to use them. Static variables are common to all instances created from the class they are stored in. When the value of a static variable in a class is changed, it is likewise changed for all instances of the class.

You might want to use static methods to provide utilities for the rest of your application. Statics can also be used with initializers to create constant data that is used by all instances of the class. All static statements—whether they are variables, methods, or initializers—are preceded by the word `static`.

Constructors

Constructors are methods that you use when you create objects. They take the function of initializers a step further. They have the same name as the class and return no value. A default constructor is automatically created by the Java compiler if you don't specify one in your code. It is called when an object is created without parameters. Constructors, like methods, can be overloaded.

Creating Objects

After you have a class that has variables and methods stored, you can create objects from it. You can think of an object as an area of memory that is allocated for an object's instance variables. To create the object and automatically allocate memory for it, always use the operator `new`. This `new` operator creates the object of the type specified and calls the constructor that is appropriate for the parameters passed in the parameter list. A reference is then made by Java to the new object. The form of an object creation is generally as follows:

```
classname reference-variable;
reference-variable = new classname (parameter-list)
```

The first line declares a variable that holds the reference to the object (references are explained in the next section). The second line creates a new object and assigns the variable to it. If parameters are passed, the appropriate constructor is called. If no parameters are passed, the object's default constructor is called.

References

References, which are created when objects are created, can be used to access variables and methods in other objects. References are used by other methods from other objects in the following form:

```
reference-variable.instance-variable
reference-variable.instance-method
```

Variables and methods stored in other objects are called by using the reference variable followed by a dot and the name of the foreign variable or method.

You use the reference value in comparisons. The operators used in references are `==`, `!=`, and `instanceof`. The `==` and `!=` operators can be used to tell whether two references refer to the same object or whether a reference does not refer to any object (such a case would return a `null` value).

The `instanceof` operator is used to determine whether an object was created from a certain class or one of its subclasses. If a statement comparing an object to a class using `instanceof` returns `true`, that object is in fact an instance of the specified class.

If you are a C programmer, note that pointers are replaced by references in Java. This is explained in greater detail later in the book.

Class Inheritance

When a subclass is defined, it must indicate the superclass it is being created from. This is done with the `extends` modifier. The form of a subclass declaration is this:

```
class subclassname extends superclassname {
    //new instructions
}
```

If a subclass uses a method from a superclass but adds functionality to it, it *overrides* the method. In Java, you do not need to duplicate the code in the other class. Just refer to the original method in the superclass with `super`.

null, this, and super Variables

Every class has the following three special variables: `null`, `this`, and `super`.

The `null` variable has a reference that points to nothing. You may use this reference to assign no value to a variable's identifier. `null` variables are empty containers that represent the absence of an object. To create an empty container, the following form is used:

```
datatype variablename = null;
```

The `this` variable has a reference to the actual object. A class can refer to itself using `this`. To refer to itself, a class uses the following form:

```
methodname(this);
```

The `super` variable has a reference to the superclass type of the class. You might wish to reference the superclass type when creating objects. Just precede your variables with the word `super`:

```
super (x,y)
```

Encapsulation

Encapsulation is used to hide methods and variables in your classes from being accessed from foreign methods. To encapsulate variables and methods in your classes, precede their declarations with the keyword `private`. Private variables and methods can be seen only within a class. Subclasses or external methods cannot see them.

Access Modifiers

The `private` modifier is one of three types of access modifiers that control the way foreign methods see your variables, methods, and classes. The others are `public` and `protected`.

Any foreign methods are able to access variables and methods preceded by the word `public`. There can be only one public class per source file. This class must have the same name as the source file. Applets, which are explained in detail in a later chapter, must contain at least one public class that is a subclass of the `Java.Applet` package.

Protected variables and methods can be used only within a class or its subclasses. Foreign methods cannot access protected variables and methods.

Creating Interfaces

Interfaces in Java are unlike interfaces in any other language. They provide a second form of inheritance. Because Java does not allow you to inherit from more than one superclass, Java lets you implement interfaces, which provides you with the functionality that inheritance from multiple superclasses would. Using interfaces, your object can use methods and variables from classes that are outside of its class hierarchy.

Interfaces are structured as entirely abstract classes with variables that are static and final and contain methods without code to implement them. Interfaces can inherit from an unlimited number of other interfaces. They are structured the same way in which classes are structured, except with the keyword `interface` instead of `class`:

```
interface interfacename [extends interfacename] {
    [variable declaration;]
    [method declaration;]
}
```

Interfaces are implemented by classes and can extend other interfaces. Classes that implement interfaces include the code for the methods of interfaces. These classes can implement more than one interface.

Interfaces can be used to conjoin several unrelated classes and have them respond to the same methods. For example, using interfaces, several shape classes such as `rectangle`, `triangle`, and `circle` can respond to a method called `MoveLeft()`, which would repaint the shape a certain distance to the left of the original location. In such a case, `MoveLeft()` would be declared in the interface, but its code would be stored in the class that implements the interface.

Packages

Java provides you with several libraries of classes which are called *packages*. You can use any of the classes in these packages by importing them into your application. Additionally, you may wish to package related classes you create so they can be reused in other applications. Packages are presented in detail in Chapter 3.

How Java Differs from C++

Now that you have a basic understanding of creating and working with classes, objects, and interfaces, you should be ready for Chapter 2, "Getting Started," that introduces you to the Java development environment. Before proceeding to Chapter 2, read through this section; it explains the differences between Java and C++. It is important that you understand what Java has changed and the reasons for these changes.

Java functionality differs from that of C and C++ in many ways. As I discussed earlier in this chapter, these changes are intended to create an object-oriented language that eliminates many of the opportunities for bugs and memory leaks that are common in C and C++. If you have experience in C or C++ programming, some of Java's changes may take some getting used to. The following list touches on the most important of these changes:

○ Java is an interpreted language, not a compiled language as is C++. This means that compiling is done by an interpreter before execution.

○ Java uses classes or interfaces to build composite data types instead of structures and unions, as in C++. This ensures portability.

○ There are no `#defines` in Java because the development team felt that using `#defines` advocates coding that is hard to read.

○ Command-line arguments are different in Java. They are arrays of strings that contain the arguments. Through a mechanism known as *varargs*, C++ allows you to provide a variable number of arguments to a function. This mechanism is not supported by the Java language.

○ Java has no header files. Instead, Java uses interfaces that show only the methods and final, or constant, variables instead of the entire structure.

○ Pointers, one of the primary features that introduce bugs and memory leaks into programs, are removed in Java. By getting rid of structures and encapsulating arrays through references, Java has attempted to get rid of the original reasoning behind pointers. Java does not allow you to construct a reference to anonymous memory, so it produces robust, efficient code much less prone to bugs, memory leaks, and corruption.

○ Java has replaced multiple inheritance by interfaces to avoid problems with fragile superclasses.

○ To ensure a purely object-oriented structure, there are no individual functions in Java. Functions must be encapsulated in a class.

○ While Java retains `goto` as a reserved word, it is not implemented or supported by the Java language.

○ Java has strict definition of operators. It doesn't allow for operator overloading.

○ Automatic coercion, which is a common cause of inaccuracy in C++, would allow you to place an incompatible variable into another without declaring that you were aware of this change. In Java, in order to store a variable of one type in a variable of another type, you must explicitly call it with a cast statement.

○ Java programs crash reliably and obviously, whereas crashes in C and C++ programs are not as apparent.

○ Java implements a new function called automatic garbage collection. The Java runtime system keeps track of all references to an object until the object is no longer needed. When there are no more references to an object, it makes it available for garbage collection.

○ Java also implements automatic memory management and thread controls. Although threads still require the use of classes, Java balances the addition of thread synchronization between the language and class levels. For example, garbage collection is run as a background process (or low-priority thread). It remains quiet until there is either a sufficient pause in the execution of foreground threads for it to run, or the system explicitly requires the use of memory which is taken up by unreferenced classes.

○ The Java language provides a `finally` statement for use with Java exceptions. The `finally` statement delimits a block of code used to release system resources and perform various other cleanup operations after the `try` statement.

○ Java strings are first-class objects. They are a class provided in the `java.lang` package. This provides consistency and predictability in string functions.

Summary

This concludes the introduction to the Java language. As you read through the rest of this book, you may need to refer to some sections in this chapter to be sure you understand the basic elements of Java that have been outlined for you. In the next chapter, you'll learn about Java's packages in detail, as well as more complex programming elements that these packages make easier.

Chapter 2

by Kathryn A. Jones

Getting Started

Obtaining the Java SDK

 This book helps you accomplish any and all of the goals outlined in the last chapter with the help of the Java Developer's Kit (JDK) and a Java-capable Web browser, which you will need to install on your computer. The JDK includes all of the primary tools of the Java development environment: the compiler, interpreter, debugger, and AppletViewer. You'll need the browser to run applets from pages on the Internet. Consequently, you must have a TCP/IP connection to the Internet for your browser to take advantage of Java's networking capabilities. You can install the JDK from the CD-ROM included with this book.

 `http://java.sun.com`

or

 `http://www.javasoft.com`

If you do not have a CD-ROM drive, you can download the JDK from the Java Web site or the Java FTP site. To download from the Sun Java home page, connect to the following URL:

`http://java.sun.com.`

The Java home page of Sun Microsystems lists several links. Two of the links are Developer's Corner and Downloads. You should be able to navigate through either of these links to get to the JDK page. This page provides you with detailed instructions for downloading and installing the JDK on your platform.

 `ftp://java.sun.com/pub/`

or

 `ftp://www.blackdown.org/pub/Java/pub/`

To download from the FTP site, FTP to the following:

`ftp://java.sun.com/pub/`

Download the JDK for your platform using binary transfer mode and follow the detailed instructions for installing the JDK on your platform.

You need to configure your particular system after downloading the JDK. The most important step after downloading and extracting the JDK is setting the class path. If you are a Windows 95 user, you need to insert into the following line into your autoexec.bat file:

`set classpath=.;c:\java;c:\java\lib\classes.zip`

This method is also assuming that the JDK is installed on your C drive. On NT, you have to go into the Control Panel, then choose System, and then in User Environment Variables, under the dialog box, enter the name of the new variable in the Variable text area, as follows:

```
Path=c:\java
```

If you have any trouble downloading from Sun, try one of the Java mirror sites that are listed on the Java home page.

http://www.gamelan.com

http://www.javasoft.com

NOTE:

Java's home page is one of your most valuable sources of information on Java. Because Java is still evolving as a network programming language, you should regularly check that home page for news on releases, bugs, fixes, and information on third-party Java product development. You might also find the Frequently Asked Questions (FAQs) sections useful. Here are a couple of other Web sites among a rapidly growing number of Java sites that are worth exploring:

```
http://www.gamelan.com
http://www.javasoft.com
http://www.io.org/~mentor/jnIndex.html
http://www.marimba.com
http://www.javaworld.com
```

Currently, three 32-bit Web browsers support Java applets: Netscape Navigator 2.0 or greater, Microsoft Internet Explorer 3.0, and Sun HotJava. At the time of this writing, Netscape Navigator 2.0 (or later) and Microsoft's Internet Explorer 3.0 are the only Web browsers capable of working with applets created with the latest JDK tools. Sun's Web browser, HotJava version 1.0 preBeta1, is compatible with the FCS applet API. HotJava is worth downloading because it is currently one of the largest applications written in Java, and it includes source code. Be sure to check the Java home page for updates on the release of HotJava and the JDK.

You can download HotJava from the Sun Java home page. FTP sites are listed there for downloading the JDK.

http://www.netscape.com

Until the next release of HotJava, Netscape Navigator 2.0 or later is necessary for your Java development efforts. You can download Netscape Navigator from the Netscape home page at:

```
http://www.netscape.com
```

Be sure to follow Netscape's installation instructions for your platform.

You might also want to use third-party development tools that will ease your development efforts. In August 1996, four products with visual development environments are available for Java: Microsoft's Visual J++, SunSoft's Java Workshop, Borland Latte (these also include tools for compiling and debugging Java applications), and Symantec Café. In the near future, undoubtedly several more development environments and tools will be available to you to make Java programming easier.

You'll find information about the Java Workshop on Sun's Java home page. You can explore the Borland and Symantec Java home pages for information regarding their products:

```
http://www.borland.com/Product/java
http://cafe.symantec.com/
```

Be sure to keep an eye out for new tools that will help you program with Java. Because Java is such a new technology, the race is on for software companies to offer Java tools and integration.

NOTE:

The only tools that you need to use this book are the JDK and Netscape Navigator 2.0 (32-bit) or later.

The Java Development Environment

The Java Developer's Kit provides you with four basic tools that help you write, compile, debug, test, and run Java code. These tools are the Java compiler, the Java interpreter, the Java debugger, and the Java AppletViewer. Java's other tools, such as the Java API documentation generator (javadoc), the Java disassembler (javap), and the Java header and stub file creator (javah) are included in the JDK, but they are not necessary for the purposes of this book. The Java tools, combined with Java libraries of utility classes and methods, form the complete Java system.

The following section describes the basic Java tools that you will use and explains how they are useful.

Your Text Editor

You can write your Java source code using any standard text editor, such as Notepad, Write, or Edit for Windows NT/95 users and TextEdit for Solaris users. A variety of text editors more suitable for development can be found on the Internet. You might want to use a text editor that comes with a development application, such as Visual C++. Java source code is generally saved with the extension .java.

The Java Compiler

Your Java source code can be compiled using `javac`, the Java compiler. It compiles source code into bytecode for the interpreter to execute. Compiled Java code is automatically given the extension `.class` by the compiler.

One important change that the Java team made from C was in compiling. C is a compiled language. It outputs binary machine code, which can be run only on the machine for which it is compiled. Compiled C code executes quickly, but it is architecture-dependent. As stated before, one of the important features of Java is that it is architecture-neutral. Java accomplishes architecture independence by splitting the compiling function across two tools: the Java compiler and the Java interpreter. The Java compiler outputs *bytecode*, similar to machine code but written for the *Java virtual machine*, which doesn't exist. The interpreter verifies this bytecode, converts it into machine code of the hardware platform it is installed on, and executes it. Source code must only be written for one machine: the virtual machine. The interpreter takes care of the rest. Therefore, the Java language is both compiled and interpreted.

The Java Interpreter

Java's interpreter is called `java`. It converts the bytecode output from the `javac` compiler to machine code and executes it.

Java is unlike purely interpreted languages, which generally interpret source code before execution, sacrificing performance. Another important feature of Java that Sun boasts is high performance. Execution by Java's interpreter is near to the speed of binary executables produced by compiled languages. The reason for this is that Java code is compiled to an intermediate stage where the file is still architecture-neutral, but close enough to machine code that it can run efficiently. In addition, Java's multithreading feature can improve performance by moving interpreter operation to the background. Multithreading is discussed in Chapter 15, "Interfacing with a Database: Catalog Applet."

In addition to architecture-independence, the other advantage of using the Java interpreter is security. The interpreter can evaluate classes to ensure that the bytecodes being interpreted do not violate any language constraints or perform illegal activities on the system or memory. This can prevent many viruses from spreading.

The interpreter runs outside the browsing environment. It provides the programmer with the ability to run stand-alone applications that have nothing to do with the Internet but that are portable and platform-independent.

The Java Debugger

You can debug your code using the Java debugger, called `jdb`. It helps you find and fix bugs in Java code.

The Java debugger provides a command-line debugging environment for Java programs. Debugging can be done on a local or remote Java interpreter.

The Java AppletViewer

You can test your applets using the Java applet viewer, called AppletViewer. It provides a programmer with a way of testing applets outside of a full-blown Web browser.

Although Netscape Navigator has Java functionality and can be used to view applets, its security features prevent it from loading applets from the local drive. It also doesn't have the networking capabilities of the Java AppletViewer. Therefore, the AppletViewer is the best tool for full applet capability.

Compiling with Java

When using the JDK, the process of compiling is currently performed in a command line (shell environment). This section describes in detail how you use the Java tools; it steps you through creating and compiling your first Java program.

The first step is to run the text editor of choice and create the classic HelloWorld program. Type the following lines of source code exactly as written here:

```
// HelloWorld.java
class HelloWorld {
    public static void main (String args[]) {
    System.out.println("Hello World!");
    }
}
```

Save the file as HelloWorld.java in the classes directory. Don't be concerned at this point with what this code means. The next chapter explains the fundamentals of the Java language, and this program's syntax becomes clear to you.

javac/javac_g

After saving your source code with the extension .java, you can compile it using the Java compiler, javac. To run the javac compiler, execute it with the following syntax. (Note that javac expects an extension after the file name.)

```
javac [ options ] filename.java
javac_g [ options ] filename.java
```

For your example, run the following command:

```
javac HelloWorld.java
```

If the code compiles correctly, you will see two files in your classes directory: `HelloWorld.java` and `HelloWorld.class`. The `.class` file has now been converted to bytecode.

The following error message might result if you mistyped the `javac` commands. Retype the command carefully if you receive this error:

```
For Windows NT/95:  bad command or file name
For Solaris:  /bin/sh: javac: not found
```

The next error means that an expression is mistyped in your source code. Check your source code for errors if you receive this message:

```
Invalid expression statement
```

The following error means that either the `javac` command or your Java file cannot be found. If you receive this error, make sure that your path includes the directory containing the Java tools so you are able to run the tools from any directory without an explicit mapping to them. Also, make sure you are running the command from the same directory as your `HelloWorld.java` file.

Error message for Windows NT/95:

```
 Bad command or file name
```

Error message for Solaris:

```
 /bin/sh: javac: not found
```

When you run the compiler, you can feed it certain options that change its behavior. Table 2.1 provides a list of all of the command-line options that you can feed `javac` and a description of each option.

Table 2.1. Command-line options for javac.

Option	Function
`-classpath path`	Sets path where `javac` looks for classes it needs. Directory list is colon-delimited.
`-d directory`	Specifies the root directory for creating a directory tree for a hierarchy of packages.
`-g`	Turns on debugging tables in code generation for later debugging of bytecodes.
`-nowarn`	Suppresses warnings that the compiler produces.
`-O`	Optimizes code produced by inlining static, final, and private methods.
`-verbose`	Prints messages about the source file and classes.

`javac_g` is a non-optimized version of `javac` that is suitable for use with debuggers such as `jdb`.

java/java_g

You can use the Java interpreter to verify and execute your code. To run the Java interpreter, enter the executable name, options, class name (without the file name extension, unlike `javac`), and arguments as outlined here:

```
java [ options ] classname args
java_g [ options ] classname args
```

For our example, run the following command:

```
java HelloWorld
```

This should produce the following output:

```
Hello World!
```

Ordinarily, you compile source code with `javac` and then execute it using Java. However, Java can be used to compile and run bytecode when the `-cs` option is used. As each class is loaded, its modification date is compared to the modification date of the class source file. If the source has been modified more recently, it is recompiled and the new bytecode file is loaded. Java repeats this procedure until all the classes are correctly compiled and loaded.

`java_g` is a non-optimized version of Java that is suitable for use with debuggers such as `jdb`.

There are several options that you can feed the interpreter that change its behavior. Table 2.2 lists all of the command-line options for the Java interpreter.

Table 2.2. Command-line options for Java.

Command	Function
`-cs`, `-checksource`	Recompiles any class whose .java source file is later than its .class file.
`-classpath` *path*	Overrides the CLASSPATH environment variable.
`-mx` *x*	Sets maximum size of memory allocation pool to *x*. Pool must be larger than 1,000 bytes and a k or m must be appended to the number to indicate size. The default is 16MB.
`-ms` *x*	Sets the size of the memory allocation pool to *x*. Pool must be larger than 1,000 bytes and a k or m must be appended to the number to indicate size. The default is 1MB.
`-noasyncgc`	Turns off asynchronous garbage collection. The only time garbage collection occurs is when the program calls for it or runs out of memory.

Command	Function
-ss x	Sets the maximum stack size for C threads to x. Must be greater than 1,000 bytes and a k or m must be appended to the number to indicate size.
-oss x	Sets the maximum stack size for Java threads to x.
-v, -verbose	Prints a message to stdout when a class is loaded.
-verify	Uses verifier on all code.
-verifyremote	Uses verifier only on classes loaded with classloader.
-noverify	Disables verifier.
-verbosegc	Prints a message when garbage collector frees memory.
-t	Prints trace of an instruction being executed. Only available with javag.
-debug	Allows jdb connection to current session of Java interpreter. Displays password when debugging session is started.
-DpropName=newVal	Enables user to change values at runtime. Requires the full packaging extension to the class variable.

jdb

If the compiler returns errors related to your code, you can use the Java debugger to debug your code. The most common way to start jdb on local classes is using the following syntax:

```
jdb classname [parameters]
```

To run the debugger, you are substituting the command for Java with jdb. This starts the Java interpreter with the class to be debugged and any specified parameters, and stops before executing the class's first process.

If you need to run jdb with Java interpreter already running, you can connect to the interpreter using the -host and -password options. In order to be able to retrieve the password from the Java interpreter session, it must have been invoked using the -debug option. When you start Java using the -debug option, it provides a password with which the jdb can be started.

You can feed the Java debugger several command-line parameters that change its behavior. These parameters can be listed using jdb's help parameter. Table 2.3 lists all of these commands.

Table 2.3. Command-line parameters for the jdb.

Option	Function
catch *classID*	Breaks for the specified exception.
Classes	Lists currently known classes.
clear *classID:line*	Clears a breakpoint.
Cont	Continues execution from breakpoint.
down [*n frames*]	Moves down a thread's stack.
dump ID [*ID..*]	Prints all object information.
exit (or quit)	Exits debugger.
help (or ?)	Lists commands.
ignore *classID*	Ignores the specified exception.
list [*line number*]	Prints source code.
load *classname*	Loads class.
locals	Prints all local variables in current stack frame.
memory	Reports memory usage.
methods	Lists methods in a class.
print ID [*ID..*]	Prints an object or field.
resume [*threadID..*]	Resumes threads. Default is all.
run class [*args*]	Starts execution of a loaded class.
step	Executes current line.
stop in *classID.method*	Sets a breakpoint in a method.
stop at *classID:line*	Sets a breakpoint at a line.
suspend [*threadID..*]	Suspends threads. Default is all.
threads *threadgroup*	Lists threads.
thread *threadID*	Sets default thread.
threadgroups	Lists threadgroups.
threadgroup *name*	Sets current threadgroup.
up [*n frames*]	Moves up a thread's stack.
use [*path*]	Displays or changes source path.
where [*threadID*] or all	Dumps a thread's stack.
!!	Repeats last command.

Table 2.4 lists the command-line options for jdb that are used when accessing a running interpreter.

Table 2.4. Command-line options for the jdb.

Command	Function
-host <hostname>	Sets the name of the host machine on which the interpreter session to attach to is running.
-password <password>	Logs in to the active interpreter session. This is the password printed by the Java interpreter. The password prints when invoked by the -debug option.

AppletViewer

You can use the AppletViewer to test applets in a runtime environment. The AppletViewer takes HTML files that refer to the applet and displays them. The only option for AppletViewer is -debug. This starts the AppletViewer in the jdb.

To invoke the AppletViewer, change to the directory of the HTML file in which the applet is embedded and type the following command:

```
appletviewer filename.html
```

The AppletViewer program has a few menu options that you can use while it is running. Its menu also allows you to set network and security properties for appletviewer. Table 2.5 lists the AppletViewer menu options and their descriptions.

Table 2.5. Applet menu options.

Option	Function
Restart	Runs the loaded applet again.
Reload	Reloads the applet from disk. Useful if the class has changed since it was loaded.
Clone	Creates a new window based upon command-line arguments for the first.
Tag	Shows the applet tag used in the HTML document to start the applet.
Info	Provides any information about the applet that is available.
Properties	Allows the different configurations to be set for AppletViewer.

AppletViewer's properties are outlined in Table 2.6. They provide the network and security options of AppletViewer.

Table 2.6. AppletViewer properties.

Option	Property
HTTP proxy server	required
HTTP proxy port	required
Firewall proxy server	required
Firewall proxy port	required
Network access	Several levels—no access, only access to applet's host, unrestricted access
Class access	restricted or unrestricted

Summary

These tools, in combination with the Java class libraries that you will learn about in Chapter 3, "An Introduction to Java Classes," are everything you'll need to program with Java. Graphical development environments incorporate all of the tools I have discussed in this chapter, but make using them even easier.

by Keith Orpen

An Introduction to Java Classes

`http://java.sun.com/JDK-1.0/api/packages.html`

Programmers in most other languages have to re-invent the wheel repeatedly to accomplish basic tasks. In contrast, Java comes with several standard packages of ready-made classes to handle basic functionality. These carefully designed packages are a joy to use: you'll find that quite often a few lines of Java can accomplish what it takes a C programmer dozens of lines of mostly tedious code to do. This chapter describes the classes found in the standard Java packages. The programming interface is listed online at `http://java.sun.com/JDK-1.0/api/packages.html`. Chapter 4, "Creating Your Own Objects," describes how you can use these classes as the foundation on which to build your own custom classes.

As described in Chapter 1, "An Overview of Java," a *class* in Java is a description of how to create and operate on a certain kind of program object. An *object* is a chunk of computer memory with various values stored in it, which the program knows how to access and use. These program objects only really exist when your applet or Java application is actually running, but you as the programmer have to tell the compiler how to use them.

If you're a C or C++ programmer, keep in mind as you learn Java that every variable of class type is actually a *reference* to the class object. In C a variable can be an entire `struct`, which is different from being a *pointer* to `struct`. This isn't the case in Java. For example, comparing variables of class type in Java (using the relational operators `==` or `!=`) is actually a comparison of references, not values (but see the `equals()` method of `java.lang.Object`). Internally this is like comparing memory addresses, but references aren't exactly pointers: you cannot access those addresses. Assigning and copying in method arguments is always the copying of a single reference value for each object, never a field-by-field copy as in C. This is no limitation, and it actually saves you grief.

If you're an Eiffel programmer, then of course you're right at home!

The standard Java classes are organized into packages, and also by inheritance. *Packages* are a way of grouping related classes to avoid potential naming conflicts, while inheritance provides the economy of expression that makes object-oriented programming powerful. The standard Java packages are

```
java.lang
java.awt
java.applet
java.awt.image
java.awt.peer
java.io
java.net
java.util
```

The standard Java classes are often quite minimal implementations, designed to be subclassed by you, the programmer. In this way, you get the best compromise between having to write the same code over and over, and having to live with libraries that are cluttered and too "fat." Perhaps best of all, you can be certain that the code you share with others has the same core of basic classes to draw upon. This makes your applets smaller and hence more "internet friendly." These classes are intended to be reliable and efficient, and some may even use platform-dependent native code behind the scenes. So it is often impossible to write a more efficient routine in Java alone. Java is a relatively "small" language, and most of these packages are not strictly required by the language definition, with the exception of the `java.lang` package.

Packages in Java

In Java, a *package* is a collection of classes that are in some way related, and are to be compiled in their own name space. Typically, all the classes in a package are designed together by the same person or team. Thus, name conflicts between classes within the package can be avoided by design. To avoid name conflicts across different packages, the package name of a class is prepended to the class to distinguish it from classes of the same name that may exist in other packages.

For example, the fully qualified name of the Java `Button` class is `java.awt.Button`, since this class is defined in the `java.awt` package. If you like being confused, you can even write your own class called `Button` that does something completely different from the Java `Button` class. Then you can still access the predefined class by using its long name, `java.awt.Button`.

If no name conflicts exist, you may *import* the name `java.awt.Button`, or indeed the entire package if you choose. Imported names may be used in their short form (i.e. `String` rather than `java.lang.String`). For example, to import the entire `java.awt` package, as well as the single class `java.util.Vector`, put these two lines at the top of your source file:

```
import java.awt.*;
import java.util.Vector;
```

The `java.lang` package is automatically imported into every Java compilation.

`http://java.sun.com/JDK-1.0/knownbugs.html#Compiler`

CAUTION:

In theory, packages establish separate name spaces, but see `http://java.sun.com/JDK-1.0/knownbugs.html#Compiler` for some known bugs.

Packages also provide new levels of access control. The default rule for access control (when no access control specifier is present) is *not* the same as `public`: it makes the class or field visible to any class inside the package and invisible outside the package. This is sometimes called "friendly"

access control. Packages must explicitly declare classes and fields to be `public` if they are to be visible from other packages. The special access specifier `private protected` makes a field accessible to subclasses in the same package only. Subclasses from other packages do not see a `private protected` field.

java.lang

The `java.lang` package contains the various classes that are essential to the definition of the Java language or that, by their nature, need to access the internals of Java in a way that most classes cannot do. For example, the string class `java.lang.String` is part of the language definition, and `java.lang.Thread` is used to control concurrent threads of execution in Java. The `java.lang` package contains the primordial class `Object`, of which every Java class is a subclass. It also contains wrapper classes for the various primitive types, which allow you to treat an `int`, for example, as a bona fide Java object (instance of a subclass of `Object`), by instantiating a `java.lang.Integer`. You need to do this in order to store integers in a vector array (`java.util.Vector`), for example. Objects belonging to these wrapper classes are freely convertible into the corresponding primitive type.

NOTE:

Think about why the `String` class is so special. It is impossible to write it yourself. It has a special form of constructor call: the double-quoted string literal actually results in the construction of a `String` object. This lexical tie-in requires special compiler design and makes the compiler depend on the class design!

Object

One of the most important classes in Java, the `Object` class implements the basic methods that every class must have. Every Java class inherits from this class; `Object` is the only Java class with no superclass. Every method in the `Object` class is available to every object in Java (though another, intermediate base class may override some methods). The `Object` class includes utility methods to generate hash codes and to create clones, and the method `equals()`, which tests two objects for equality. There are also some thread synchronization primitives (`notify()`, `notifyAll()`, `wait()`), a way to interrogate objects about their run-time class (`getClass()`), and the `finalize()` method, which you can override to specify some code that is performed before the object is garbage-collected. For example, here you may close any open files that are created by the object.

A reference to `Object` can reference any Java object at runtime. For example, an array of `Objects` can hold references to many different types of object; all these types are subclasses of `Object`. This is a completely type-safe way to get beyond the "casting void pointers" trick, which every C programmer is familiar with.

CAUTION:

Be careful when using the `finalize()` method. Merely dropping all references to an object does not guarantee that it is ever garbage-collected. The garbage collector can decide not to bother, if memory is plentiful. So don't rely on `finalize()` to be called in a timely way. See Chapter 4 for more on garbage collection.

The `equals()` method

The `equals()`Object method is used this way:

```
public class Thing extends Object
{
    static Thing Fred;
    ...
    public boolean sameAsFred( Object o )
    {
        return o.equals( Fred );
    }
}
```

Note that `equals()` is supposed to be a different kind of test than comparing references. Equals is a comparison of the two given objects *by value,* which means they can be equal even if they are different objects so long as they have the same type and are functionally equivalent objects. That is, every instance variable that represents a part of the state of the external object being modeled is equal in the two objects. This is a recursive definition since the instance variables may themselves be class objects. So this kind of test is relatively more expensive than comparing references. The predefined library classes each override the `equals()` method to mean something sensible. However if you want this method call to be meaningful, you generally override it in your own objects. This is especially true if you are inheriting directly from the `Object` class since the `equals()` method in the `Object` class does nothing except compare references. And remember that even if your class has no explicit superclass (empty `extends` clause), your class has `Object` as its implicit superclass. The following segment is a typical example of overriding the `equals()` method:

```
public class MyClass
{
  String name;
  int serialno;

  /* other methods ... */

  public boolean equals( MyClass o )
  {
    return name.equals(o.name) && serialno==o.serialno;
  }
}
```

If you are strict about using inheritance to express *is–a* relations, rather than *has–a* relations, then your equals() method is like the above, albeit with different instance variables. A Manager *is–an* Employee; any further instance variables a Manager may have are not part of its identity as an Employee, so Manager need not override Employee's equals() method at all.

Now suppose you need to express the idea of a *workgroup*. If you assume that a workgroup always has one manager, it is certainly tempting to make the WorkGroup class extend the Manager class. However, you run into problems: a workgroup just isn't a special kind of manager. When you try to write the equals() method, you are compelled to write ugly code such as the following:

```
public class WorkGroup extends Manager
{
  /* This is an example of how NOT to do this! */

  String groupname;

  /* other methods ... */

  public boolean equals( WorkGroup o )
  {
    return super.equals( o ) && groupname.equals(o.groupname);
  }
}
```

This code is Object ugly because you must explicitly call on the superclass to find whether the two workgroups have the same manager. This is nonsense! Moreover, this class is not easy to modify. Next week, the boss may tell you that a workgroup can have two managers. A much better way to express the idea of a workgroup is to make a WorkGroup class (extending Object) having instance variables to specify the Manager and the other Employees (a workgroup has a manager, and so forth).

Generally speaking, if your class inherits directly from Object, you override the equals() method, making it compare corresponding instance variables. If your class extends a subclass of Object, then you must decide what semantics are appropriate, although by being consistent you can often avoid this decision.

The toString() method

The Object class defines the toString() method, which returns a String that represents the value of the object. The Object class itself cannot do more than a rudimentary job at this. You should therefore override this in your own classes whenever such a conversion is meaningful. The string representation may be incomplete; there is no requirement that the object be recoverable from the string.

The clone() method

The clone()Object method creates a "clone" of the object, and returns it. By default, this is a "shallow" clone: instance variables that are references of class type are not cloned recursively. Rather, the reference value is copied. This means that the clone may reference some of the same objects as the original. If you prefer different behavior, you must override this method in your own objects.

Objects that specifically do not want to be cloned may throw a `CloneNotSupportedException` from their `clone()` method to complain about it.

Wrappers for Basic Types

The classes `Boolean`, `Character`, `Double`, `Float`, `Integer`, and `Long`, defined in the package `java.lang`, are full-fledged Java objects whose purpose is to represent the values of primitive types. They all work in about the same way, so let's look at `Boolean` as an example.

You can use a `boolean` value to construct a `Boolean` object:

```
Boolean b = new Boolean( true );
```

To get `boolean` values back out of a `Boolean` object, use the `booleanValue()` method:

```
if ( b.booleanValue() ) System.out.println( "yes" );
```

The `Boolean` class also provides both constant `Boolean` values as class variables:

```
if ( b.equals( Boolean.TRUE ) )
  flag = Boolean.FALSE;
```

Similarly, each of the various wrapper classes provides class variables to delimit its range of legal values. The abstract class `java.lang.Number` is also provided as a superclass for the numerical classes `Double`, `Float`, `Integer`, and `Long`. The `Number` class merely specifies the four abstract methods `intValue()`, `longValue()`, `floatValue()`, and `doubleValue()`; this guarantees that any instance of a subclass of `Number` (say a `Double`) can be converted into any of the four representations (possibly with rounding).

Strings in Java

Java provides a smart implementation of character strings. A `String` object holds a fixed character string. Since these objects are read only, the implementation of `String` can be clever and return shared references into a pool of unique strings if it chooses to (you can use the `intern()` method to guarantee this). An object provides an array in which to manipulate string data; it grows as required when new data is appended or inserted.

A `String` is typically constructed using a double-quoted string literal:

```
String s = "My String";
```

However, `String`s can also be constructed from arrays of `char` or `byte`:

```
char s_data[] = { 'M', 'y', ' ', 'S', 't', 'r', 'i', 'n', 'g' };
String s = new String( s_data );
```

Or from a `StringBuffer`:

```
String s = new String( my_strbuffer );
```

There are many useful methods for scanning strings and for extracting substrings:

```
String ring = "My String".substring(5, 9);      // extract substring "ring"
```

Notice how the indices start at 0, and notice that the lower bound is inclusive, the upper exclusive. Then the length of the substring is easily calculated as 9–5 = 4.

The `length()` method gives the length of a string.

The `String` class also has several static `valueOf()` methods that know how to convert various types into string representations. The notation is quite mnemonic:

```
String five = String.valueOf(5);
```

and so on. For more general objects, the method call `String.valueOf(Object)` uses the object's `toString()` method to perform the conversion. `StringBuffer` objects hold string data of variable length. You can `append()` any `Object` on the end, and the result is to append the string representation of that object to the `StringBuffer` (typically, you append a `String` anyway). You can `insert()` an `Object` at any index, and the string representation is inserted at that point, moving the rest of the buffer to make room. Although `StringBuffer` objects are handy for working with string data, all of the useful scanning methods are in the `String` class, so usually `StringBuffer` objects are an intermediate step to constructing a `String`. You can convert a `StringBuffer` to a string using the `toString()` method, or the constructor `String(StringBuffer)`. Conversion of `StringBuffer`s into `String`s is smart: the array of character data is not copied unless and until a subsequent operation via a `StringBuffer` reference tries to alter the data, and then a copy is made transparently.

You can concatenate a `String` with another `String` or `StringBuffer` by using the + operator. Indeed, so long as one operand of the + operator is a `String`, then the other is converted into a `String` and the result is the concatenation of the two `String`s:

```
String myaddress = 1234 + ' ' + "Birch St.," + ' ' + "Birchville";
```

Math

The class `java.lang.Math` is a class with only static methods and no instance variables. There are no instances of this class, so it requires no constructors. It is a collection of mathematically useful functions, together with the two constants `Math.PI` (an approximation of π, the circumference of a circle divided by its diameter) and `Math.E`, which is approximately Euler's number e, the base for natural logarithms.

```
// how many times does this angle wrap around
double q = Math.floor( angle / (2*Math.PI) );
// bring the angle into the range 0..2*PI
angle -= q * 2 * Math.PI;
```

The trigonometric functions always measure angles in radians (180 degrees equals [pi] radians; equivalently, a radian is the angle subtended by a circular arc of length 1 on a circle of radius 1), and the exponential and log functions use Math.E as the base. Some Math functions throw an ArithmeticException if their argument is absurd. Try Math.sqrt(-1.0) to see this happen. Interestingly, although the tangent of a right angle is undefined, Math.tan(Math.PI/2) does not result in an exception; rather, a very large number is returned. Due to roundoff, Math.PI/2 is never exactly a right angle.

Cloning Objects: the Cloneable Interface

Besides overriding the clone() method in java.lang.Object, a class may implement the interface Cloneable to indicate that it makes sense to clone this type of object. The interface is an empty one. You don't need to supply any methods to conform to Cloneable, although you may want to override the default clone() method. Other classes can tell whether a class implements Cloneable by examining its class descriptor (an instance of the class Class).

Threads of Execution

In Java, a program or applet can be busy with several things at once. This means your classes must be able to create and control threads of execution. The java.lang classes Thread, ThreadGroup, and the interface Runnable provide this control. A Thread represents a single thread: a context of sequential execution. What gets executed is the run() method of the Thread, or of a Runnable that is designated as the Thread's *target*. A ThreadGroup can hold several Threads and ThreadGroups, which is handy in case you want to organize your Threads into a tree structure and operate on whole subtrees of Threads at once. Moreover, Threads are prohibited from accessing the parent of their ThreadGroup. So by using ThreadGroups, you can be sure a rogue thread isn't going to suddenly suspend or kill a thread you don't want it to. Chapter 16, "Multithreading with Java," explains multithreaded Java programming.

Exceptions and Errors

Java contains an elegant exception-handling mechanism. When a method cannot complete normally, there are three choices. You can return a nonsensical value, never ever return, or throw an exception. The first choice is not usually acceptable, and the second is downright antisocial. Applets want to take particular care that this doesn't happen. What's left? Throwing an exception transfers control non-locally to a block of "rescue" code defined in some currently executing method that called on your method, perhaps indirectly (for example, to a context perhaps several frames up the execution stack, but in the same thread). This rescue code is called a "catch block." The objects that get "thrown and caught" are of class Exception, Error, or any class that implements the interface Throwable. These thrown objects describe the exceptional condition and the context in which it occurs. An Exception indicates that a method can't complete its stated mission because of bad arguments or unavailable resources. An Error is more serious and indicates a condition that is abnormal and unexpected. In the Java API these are heavily subclassed to provide more and less specific "flavors" of exception. Chapter 10, "The Order Entry System: Exception Handling and Browser Interaction," explains exception handling in more detail.

The Runtime Environment

The java.lang package provides access to the external system environment by way of the related classes Runtime and System. External processes are manipulated by way of class java.lang.Process, and security policy is set by an object of type java.lang.SecurityManager.

Compiler

The java.lang.Compiler class provides a way to access an embedded Java compiler, which is loaded at startup if the java.compiler system property is defined. The value of the property should be the name of a dynamically linked library implementing the compiler. There is no predefined compiler; you must provide one.

Runtime

You can't construct a Runtime instance yourself. A Runtime object is obtained by calling the static method Runtime.getRuntime(). By using a Runtime instance, you can

- Execute a subprocess.
- Exit the program.
- Load a dynamically linked library.
- Run the garbage collector or finalize objects.
- Estimate free memory.
- Control program tracing.
- Localize streams (make them translate from Unicode to the local character set).

A Runtime object can be used to execute another system process by way of the exec() method (in four flavors) that returns a java.lang.Process object. The Process instance is useful for attaching to the standard input, output, and error streams of the new process. You can also kill the subprocess, wait for it to terminate, and retrieve its exit code, all by way of the Process object. The process exists outside the Java virtual machine. It is not a Thread but a separate system process, and some aspects of its behavior may be system-dependent.

You can use a Runtime object to load a dynamically linked library. This is necessary in order to use native methods in Java. Procedures for loading dynamic libraries are covered in Chapter 14, "Extending Java."

The methods traceInstructions() and traceMethodCalls() request that the Java virtual machine print trace information about each instruction or each method call that gets executed, respectively. Where the output ends up or whether tracing is supported at all is implementation-dependent.

While you can use a Runtime object to run the garbage collector or finalize any outstanding objects (gc() and runFinalization() methods), this should not normally be necessary, since the Java environment runs a separate thread whose purpose is to finalize and garbage collect when necessary (see Chapter 4). Furthermore, although the exit() method can be used to exit the program, it should normally be avoided, except to specify an exit code upon normal termination of a stand-alone program. Low-level methods and applets generally throw exceptions instead.

System

While the Runtime functionality is accessed through an actual instance, the System class provides some similar functions by way of static methods and class variables. There are no instances of the System class. The System class allows you to

- ○ Access the standard input, output, and error streams.
- ○ Exit the program.
- ○ Load a dynamically linked library.
- ○ Run the garbage collector or finalize objects.
- ○ Access system Properties.
- ○ Access the SecurityManager.
- ○ Perform system-dependent array copy and time-check operations.

The standard input, output, and error streams of your Java application or applet are accessed as System.in, System.out, and System.err. These class variables are PrintStream objects (see java.io, below), allowing your application to perform the usual UNIX-style I/O. That's not much use in a finished applet, since an applet embedded in a web page is typically disallowed from doing anything useful with these streams. They are handy for debugging in appletviewer, and also in stand-alone Java applications.

Java also maintains some *system properties*, accessible through the System class. These take the place of environment variables and anything else in the system that is relevant to the Java environment. The static method getProperties() returns a java.util.Properties object describing the system properties. For example, the properties can be listed by a little program such as the following:

```
public class Props
{
    public static void main( String args[] )
    {
        System.getProperties().list(System.err);
    }
}
```

This program results in a list of system properties:

```
-- listing properties --
java.home=/mnt2/java
java.version=1.0
file.separator=/
line.separator=

java.vendor=Sun Microsystems Inc.
user.name=korpen
os.arch=sparc
os.name=Solaris
java.vendor.url=http://www.sun.com/
user.dir=/nfs/grad/korpen/www/java
java.class.path=.:/home/grad/korpen/www/java:/mnt2/ja...
java.class.version=45.3
os.version=2.x
path.separator=:
user.home=/homes/staff/korpen
```

Use the static method `getProperty()` to get individual properties by name.

SecurityManager

By extending the abstract class `java.lang.SecurityManager`, you can specify a security policy for the current Java program. Any code loaded over the Internet by your program is then subject to that policy, for example. A Java program has only one `SecurityManager`. You can look up the current `SecurityManager` by calling `System.getSecurityManager()`. This method returns `null` to indicate that the default security policy is being used. The default policy is rather lax. However, you can install a custom security manager. This allows you to do the following, among other things:

○ Prevent Java code from deleting, writing, or reading certain files.

○ Monitor or disallow certain socket connections.

○ Control which `Threads` may access which other `Threads` or `ThreadGroups`.

○ Control access to packages, and to system properties.

For example, the method call that checks whether the calling code is allowed to delete a certain file is declared:

```
public void checkDelete( String file );
```

The method must either return quietly, or throw a `SecurityException`. This is typical of the `public` methods in class `SecurityManager`.

To provide a custom security manager, write a subclass of `SecurityManager` and override some of its check methods. Although the `SecurityManager` class is abstract, none of its methods are abstract. You still want to override a fair number of them, though, since the check methods inherited from `SecurityManager` always throw a `SecurityException`. You don't have to call on these methods yourself for the security manager to be effective. Once the security manager is installed, various library methods call on it to check for security clearance. To install your `SecurityManager`, create an instance of it, and call `System.setSecurityManager()`. Here is a little program (SMDemo.java) that demonstrates how to use a custom security manager. You should create files named DELETEME and KEEPME before running the program:

```java
import java.io.File;

class MySecurityManager extends SecurityManager
{
  public void checkDelete( String file )
  {
    // Only allow the file "DELETEME" to be deleted.
    if ( !file.equals( "DELETEME" ) )
      throw new SecurityException( "cannot delete: " + file );
  }

    // Override many more checkXXX() methods here...
}

public class SMDemo
{
  public static void main( String argv[] )
  {
    MySecurityManager m = new MySecurityManager();
    File deleteme = new File( "DELETEME" );
    File keepme = new File( "KEEPME" );

    System.setSecurityManager( m );

    deleteme.delete();  // Should be OK.
    keepme.delete();    // Should get a SecurityException.

    System.exit(0);
  }
}
```

After you execute the program, you should see that the file DELETEME is gone and the KEEPME file is still there, the program having triggered a `SecurityException` upon trying to delete it.

The security manager can only be set once in a program. So by setting it yourself, you know that untrusted code isn't busy installing its own super-lenient policy. See Chapter 19, "Security Issues," for more details on security issues.

Applets are not usually allowed to set the security manager.

Classes at Runtime

Even at runtime, it is possible to access certain features of a class. This is done by way of the class `Class`, which implements a class descriptor object for a Java class. You can get a class descriptor from an existing class either by using the `getClass()` method of `java.lang.Object` or by calling the static method `Class.forName()`:

```java
Class stringClass = Class.forName("String");
```

Using a class descriptor, you can find out:

○ The class name

○ The superclass

○ Whether the class is actually an interface

○ Which interfaces the class implements

○ Which ClassLoader originated this class

There is also a way to instantiate new objects from the class descriptor: the newInstance() method. This has the limitation that no arguments can be passed to the constructor, so it fails unless the class has an accessible constructor which takes no arguments. There also doesn't seem to be any way to use the class descriptor to produce a valid operand for the right-hand side of instanceof.

Class java.lang.ClassLoader is meant to provide a way to load classes at runtime from a user-defined source. It is an abstract class. A subclass must implement the loadClass() method to load an array of bytes from somewhere and then convert it into a class descriptor by calling resolveClass() and defineClass().

java.awt

The java.awt package is a uniform interface to various windowing environments (AWT stands for Abstract Window Toolkit). The various classes in this package make it easy to create graphical user interface (GUI) elements such as scrollbars, text fields, buttons, checkboxes, and so on. Internally, these classes bind to a native windows toolkit in the local implementation. Your applet does not have to know which toolkit is actually being used since the same method calls have functionally equivalent results in any implementation, be it X Window, MacOS, OS/2, or Windows NT/95. You'll find that programming in java.awt is easier and more elegant than native windows programming anyhow. Future versions of Java reportedly will incorporate still more powerful coordinate-based drawing functions, making Java unbeatable for writing portable GUI, driven programs.

The interface between java.awt and the native windows toolkit is provided by the java.awt.Toolkit class and the package java.awt.peer, which is discussed later.

The framework for any GUI application is provided by the java.awt.Component class and its subclasses. Every GUI element (except menus) corresponds to a subclass of Component. Menus have slightly different requirements and they subclass the java.awt.MenuComponent class.

Many of the components are demonstrated in the included Java program AWTDemo.java, together with some nifty event-handling tricks. Figure 3.1 shows some Checkboxes, a Choice, three Labels, a TextField (subclassed to accept only numbers), a Scrollbar and a Button. These classes are all explained in the following sections.

Figure 3.1.

The sample program
AWTDemo.java: first screen.

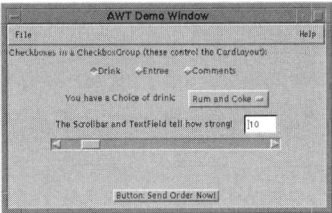

Component

The Component class represents a GUI component that has size, font, and color attributes, can redraw itself, and handle events (such as a mouse click) which occur within the component's display area, as well as perform various other functions. An example of a simple component is java.awt.Button, which displays a rectangular button with a string label and responds to click events. Components size themselves using java.awt.Dimension objects. These are simple objects with two instance variables: width and length.

Some of the handiest methods from java.awt.Component include the following:

hide()—Hide the component.

show()—Show the component. Most components are visible by default, but Windows are initially invisible, and must be shown. Showing a Window also brings it to the front.

disable()—Disable the component so a button has its text grayed out, for example.

enable()—Enable a disabled component again.

paint()—Here the component paints itself. When inheriting from another component, you typically override this. You shouldn't call this method directly. Call repaint().

repaint()—Asks the runtime system to paint the component as soon as possible.

handleEvent()—You can override this method to provide specific responses to user events.

createImage()—Create images from an ImageProducer. This is described later in this chapter as part of the package java.awt.image.

validate()—Verify that the component is *valid,* which means that the peer has been created and displays properly (see java.awt.peer, below), and that the component is properly laid out.

A word about validation: components are validated automatically before they are drawn for the first time. But if you add() new components to a container after it has already been shown, you need to call the validate() method of the container explicitly (anyway, it never hurts to do so). The validate() method is recursive. It validates all components contained in the validated component, as well as the component itself.

Container Components

Container components contain other components. All containers belong to a subclass of the `java.awt.Container` class which knows how to `add()` and `remove()` components to or from the container and how to `layout()` the various components using a layout manager. Every component that is not a top-level window (instance of `Window` or a subclass) *must be added to a container* to be visible on screen.

Of course containers can contain containers, so a GUI is nothing but a hierarchy of components organized by containers. This can be several levels deep. Every component is either a top-level window or else has a parent container (accessible by way of the `getParent()` method in `java.awt.Component`).

Containers are either `Panels` or `Windows`. A `Panel` (`java.awt.Panel`) is a general purpose container that sits inside a parent container on your screen. An applet is a `Panel`, for example. A `Window` (`java.awt.Window`) occupies its own top-level window on your screen. By default, a `Window` is very plain without borders, title, or pulldown menus. These added features are provided by a special class of window, `java.awt.Frame`. The `AWTDemo.java` program uses a `Frame` as its top-level window (see Figure 3.1). A handy method that is special to `Window` subclasses is the `pack()` method. This method resizes the `Window` so that every component in it can be laid out at its preferred size.

TIP:

You should call a `Window`'s `resize()` or `pack()` method before showing it for the first time, to give it a definite size.

The remaining container classes are `Dialog` and `FileDialog`, which are each a kind of `Window`. A `Dialog` object implements a window that is optionally modal (a *modal* dialog grabs the input focus so the user is forced to provide input before proceeding) and that vanishes when the parent `Frame` is iconified. These are properties that a dialog box should have. A `FileDialog` provides a standard type of modal dialog box that allows the user to select a file on the local filesystem for saving or loading. The sample program `AWTDemo.java` shows a `FileDialog` when you select `Load...` from the `File` menu. Use a `java.io.FilenameFilter` object to filter the filenames that are displayed in the dialog.

Buttons and Other Components

Let's take a look at some of the standard components that comprise a user interface. For the details of how to handle the various events, see the next section, "Event Handling."

Button

A `Button` component is a simple pushbutton that displays a string label and responds to mouse presses from the user. Pressing a button triggers an action event. See Figure 3.1 for a picture of a typical `Button`.

Canvas

A `Canvas` is a blank area suitable for drawing in. You can use a `Graphics` object to put polygons or images on the `Canvas`. Because a `Canvas` has no predefined responses to events and because its appearance is completely arbitrary, a `Canvas` is a good place to start when designing custom components that look unlike the standard components.

Checkbox

A `Checkbox` is a small box with two states: either it's checked or unchecked. Clicking the mouse over an enabled `Checkbox` toggles its state. A `Checkbox` can have a string label. Figures 3.1, 3.2, and 3.3 all have `Checkboxes`. Notice how they look different when in a `CheckboxGroup`.

CheckboxGroup

You put `Checkboxes` in a `CheckboxGroup` in order to make them exhibit "radio button" behavior: when one is checked, the others become unchecked. Only one `Checkbox` from the group can be checked at any time. The `CheckboxGroup` does not act as a container for the `Checkbox` component; it only tells some of the `Checkboxes` to uncheck themselves when necessary. `Checkboxes` can be placed in a group on creation or by calling their `setCheckboxGroup()` method.

Choice

A `Choice` component allows the user to specify one of a short list of choices, which appear on a little popup menu next to the current choice. The choices on the list are identified by a string name. Figure 3.1 shows a `Choice` component.

Label

A `Label` component displays a line of text. The text can be aligned to the left, right, or center of the `Label`. The user isn't allowed to edit the text in a `Label`. Use a `TextField` for that. Figure 3.1 shows several `Labels`.

Figure 3.2.
The sample program
AWTDemo.java: second screen.

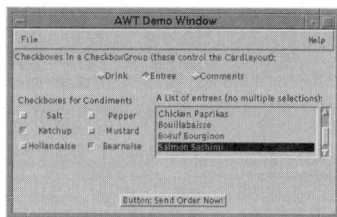

List

A List presents a scrollable list of items, identified by string names. Use this instead of a Choice when multiple selections are meaningful or when there may be too many items to conveniently display on a single popup menu. Figure 3.2 shows a typical list. Lists can allow or disallow multiple selections.

Scrollbar

Most Scrollbar components are automatically generated when required by List or TextArea components. If you want to create your own scrollbars, you can do so. The orientation is specified by the constants Scrollbar.HORIZONTAL and Scrollbar.VERTICAL. Take a look at the horizontal scrollbar in Figure 3.1.

The Scrollbar reports its current position via the getValue() method. To make the values meaningful, set the minimum and maximum values, together with the line and page increment values, using either the full five-argument constructor or the setValues() method.

There are five basic operations on a Scrollbar: line up, line down, page up, page down, and absolute positioning. Corresponding to these, there are five scrollbar event types. You don't have to discriminate between these very often. The event argument is always the integer value reflecting the new scrollbar position. Unless you want real-time response to Scrollbar actions, it is not necessary to handle Scrollbar events at all.

TextField

A TextField component holds a single line of text in a little window. The text is allowed to be longer than the window, in which case only part of it shows. By default, the user is allowed to edit the text. You can also set a TextField to be read only using setEditable(false). This method is from class TextComponent, the abstract superclass of both TextField and TextArea. The NumberField shown in Figure 3.1 is a customized form of TextField.

TextArea

A TextArea is a pane containing lines of text. Like a TextField, it can be editable or not. Figure 3.3 shows a TextArea in action.

Figure 3.3.
The sample program
AWTDemo.java: third screen.

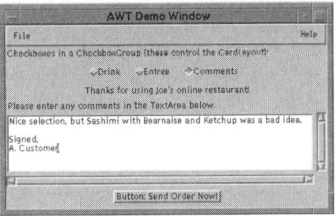

Event Handling

Programs that use a graphical user interface are inherently event-driven, at least in part. An *event* refers to something the user causes to happen using the mouse, keyboard, or other input device. An event-driven program typically just sits in an infinite loop that goes something like "wait for event, handle event, repeat." In Java, you don't have to code this behavior; it is taken care of by the AWT. You override the event handling methods in the Component class in order to perform specific actions in response to user events.

When an event occurs within a GUI component, it is the native windows toolkit that first receives the event. The event is then passed to the AWT class that represents the component (the native widget corresponding to the AWT component is said to be the *peer* of the component). For example, when a Button is pressed, what really happens is that the *peer* of the button receives the event, creates a java.awt.Event object to describe it, and sends it to the java.awt.Button object corresponding to that button. The handleEvent() method of the Button object is invoked. By default, this method is inherited from the Component class and it decodes the event and calls on the various short form event-handler methods of the Button.

The short form event-handler methods are largely self-explanatory:

```
mouseDown(), mouseDrag(), mouseUp(), mouseMove(), mouseEnter(), mouseExit()
keyDown(), keyUp()
action()
```

The action() method means that an "action" has occurred. This depends on which type of component received the event. For example, for a Button, this represents a press. The default versions of all these methods do nothing and then return false. The boolean return value of all these methods (and of handleEvent()) indicates whether the event is fully handled. Return true only when you wish no further action on this event.

Among its instance variables, each Event object has an *event type*, a *target*, and an arbitrary *argument*. The event type is one of the predefined constants describing roughly what has happened: Event.ACTION_EVENT, Event.KEY_PRESS, and so on. The target is the component in which this event has occurred, and the argument is an arbitrary Object that further specifies the event. For example, for Scrollbars, it is an Integer which is the new slider value.

Until the Event is fully handled by some event handler, it continues to propagate up the container hierarchy, passing from each component to its parent container. If the event emerges from a top-level container such as Window or Frame and is not fully handled, then it is passed back to the native windows toolkit to be handled in the usual way.

http://java.sun.com/tutorial/ui/components/peer.html

CAUTION:

In fact, mouse events can't be intercepted correctly for some components in the JDK release 1.0: see http://java.sun.com/tutorial/ui/components/peer.html

There are a few ways you can intercede in this process to provide custom behavior (using Button as an example):

- ○ Override a short form event-handler function in a Container which contains the Button.
- ○ Override the handleEvent() method of a Container which contains the button.
- ○ Subclass Button and override an event handler.

For example, a TextField object generates keyboard events. Usually, you want the default behavior: the characters typed appear normally in the TextField. By subclassing TextField, you can intercept the keyboard events and provide alternative behavior such as putting all input characters in lowercase. You achieve this by *altering* the event as it passes up the hierarchy but is still returning false so that the changed event is returned to the native text field widget. On the other hand, returning true in response to some keyboard events ensures that those events are ignored.

See the example program AWTDemo.java for an idea of how to do this. The TextField shown in Figure 3.2 is actually an instance of class NumberField (defined in AWTDemo.java), which extends TextField and overrides the handleEvent() method. You can only type numbers in this component.

If you override both handleEvent() and one of the short-form event handlers in the same component, be aware that the short-form handler is never called, unless your handleEvent() explicitly does so, or else calls on the superclass's handleEvent() method to do so. The easiest way to do this is to make your handleEvent() method like this:

```
public boolean handleEvent( Event e )
{
    if ( e.id == Event.ACTION_EVENT ) {
        // do some stuff ...
        return true;     // this event was fully handled
    }
    // perhaps more stuff...

    return super.handleEvent( e );     // refer this event to a higher authority
}
```

If you are consistent with this practice, you can be sure that the superclass knows how to decode the event and call on your short-form event handlers.

Getting Painted

To do any special drawing operations that change the look of your component, you need to override the paint() method and put the drawing code there. The single argument to paint() is a Graphics object through which you can draw images, lines, text, and so forth. The AWT calls on your paint() method when the component needs to be redrawn.

All paint requests occur in a single high-priority thread. This guarantees that they happen in the proper order and quickly. This also means that you never call the paint() method of a Component directly. Call the repaint() method instead when you wish a Component to be redisplayed. Many built-in methods automatically result in a repaint(), but you may need to call repaint() yourself in certain situations.

The repaint() method actually results in a call to the component's update() method. The default update() method clears the display area of the component to the current background color and then calls paint(). This can create excessive flicker for some applications so you may want to override the update() method to prevent the background from getting cleared. See Chapter 17, "Advanced Graphics: Multimedia," and Chapter 18, "Serious Play: Game Applets," for examples of advanced painting techniques including animation and double-buffered graphics.

Events propagate up the component hierarchy but paint requests propagate *down*. The top-level windows are drawn first, and then their immediate children, and so on. This ensures that the children show up on top of their parent container.

Menus

The AWT includes support for pulldown menus. The various components that implement the menus are not of class Component, but rather of class java.awt.MenuComponent. This reflects the "popup" nature of menus: they don't occupy space in a parent container, but pop up on top of other windows when required.

A menu is represented by a java.awt.Menu object. It can only be displayed on a menu bar (java.awt.MenuBar). In turn, a menu bar must be associated to a Frame in order to be useful. So a Frame can have a MenuBar, a MenuBar contains Menus, and a Menu contains MenuItems.

A MenuItem is a choice on a menu which is labeled with a string. CheckboxMenuItem extends MenuItem and has a string label with a checkbox gadget beside it. Selecting the item toggles the checkbox. The Menu class itself extends MenuItem, so a menu can be an item on another menu, that is to say, a submenu.

AWT menus support separators and tear-off functionality. A tear-off menu can be dragged onto the desktop where it occupies a new top-level window. A separator is a menu item with the special name "–". A tear-off menu is created by calling the constructor with a second, `boolean` argument set to `true`:

```
Menu my_menu = new Menu( "My Menu", true );  // create a tear-off menu
```

A menu bar can have a designated *help menu* which is distinguished from the other menus in some way. For example, it is often placed at the extreme right end of the menu bar. See the sample program `AWTDemo.java` for examples of menus on a menu bar including a help menu, separators, and a submenu.

Layout Managers

When you add components into a container, it is the layout manager of the container which determines the actual size and location of each component. The two argument forms of `add()` allow you to specify a placement argument which is interpreted by the layout manager. The `java.awt` classes implementing layout manager policies are described here. They all implement the interface `java.awt.LayoutManager`.

All containers have a default layout manager, but you can designate whichever layout manager has your favorite policy by passing a new instance of the `LayoutManager` to the container's `setLayout()` method. You can also provide custom layout managers by implementing the `LayoutManager` interface yourself. The sample program `AWTDemo.java` demonstrates many of the layout managers in action.

TIP:

To give hints to the layout manager about your component's preferred or minimum size, override the `preferredSize()` and `minimumSize()` methods in class `Component`.

BorderLayout

The possible placements are "North," "South," "East," "West," and "Center." They are identified by the string names. The components around the edges are laid out first and the center component gets the leftover room. This can make some components larger than necessary since they are stretched out to meet the edges of the container. Put the components inside a `Panel` to avoid this.

CAUTION:

Always use the two argument form of `add()` when using `BorderLayout` (for example, `add("North," myButton)`); the single argument version is ignored.

CardLayout

This layout manager lets several components occupy the same space, with only one visible at a time. Think of the components as lying on "cards," which are shown one at a time. You need a way for the user to flip through the cards. Typically this is a Choice or a series of Checkboxes in a CheckboxGroup. You can also have next/back Buttons.

In the sample program AWTDemo.java, there are three "cards" in a CardLayout, and the user switches between them using Checkboxes. The three cards are shown in Figures 3.1, 3.2, and 3.3.

FlowLayout

This is one of the simpler layout managers. Components are arranged left to right in a row until no more fit. Then a new row is begun. Each row is centered in the parent component by default. This is the default layout for Panels.

GridLayout

A GridLayout arranges components in a grid of rectangular cells, all the same size. The contents of each cell are resized to fill the cell so you may want to put them on a panel in some of the cells and let them take their natural size. The Checkboxes in Figure 3.2 are laid out using a GridLayout.

As you add components to a GridLayout, the cells are populated in reading order: from left to right in each row and then down to the next row.

GridBagLayout

The most flexible layout manager provided by java.awt is the GridBagLayout. Like a GridLayout, it is based on a rectangular array of cells. However, each component may occupy a rectangular area covering several cells. There is no requirement that the child components have the same size. Each child component has an associated GridBagConstraints object to give hints to the layout manager about its minimum size and preferred position in the container.

Graphics and Images

The java.awt package includes some classes to help you draw custom graphics and images. You typically want to draw either in a Canvas, or an off-screen Image (for double-buffered graphics see Chapter 17). Drawing operations are usually performed in the paint() or update() methods of the component you want to draw in.

Graphics

An instance of `java.awt.Graphics` is the single argument to `paint()` and `update()`. This object provides access to a drawable area as well as a graphics "context": a current drawing color, font, and drawing mode. Here are just a few of the methods in the class `Graphics`:

```
drawLine()

drawPolygon()

drawRect()

drawOval()
```
—A misnomer because it really draws an ellipse.

```
drawImage()
```
—Draw a bitmap `Image`, perhaps scaling it first.

```
drawString()
```
—Draw a `String` in the current font.

```
fillPolygon()

setColor()

setFont()

getFontMetrics()
```

To assist in these coordinate-based drawing operations, there are the `java.awt` classes `Point`, `Polygon`, and `Rectangle`.

Image

An `Image` object references a bitmapped image. Applets can load images from a URL. If you have an `ImageProducer` handy, you can call `createImage()` in either class `Component` or `Toolkit`. It's also possible to load an image using the `getImage()` method of a `Toolkit` object which can load from a URL or a file. The Java AWT has built-in support for the GIF and JPEG formats. See `java.applet` and `java.awt.image` for more on producing `Image`s.

An `Image` is not displayed on-screen automatically. You must paint it in a component using the `drawImage()` method in `java.awt.Graphics`. You can also perform arbitrary drawing operations in an `Image` by getting a `Graphics` object for the `Image` from the `getGraphics()` method.

When loading images, the `java.awt.MediaTracker` class can come in handy. A `MediaTracker` provides a way to wait for one or several related images to finish loading before doing anything further.

Color

You can mix a color from red, green, and blue light. This is the RGB Color Model. It's important in Java since most of the time you draw onto a computer monitor which represents colors this way. RGB is the default color model for `java.awt.Color` objects which represent colors in Java.

A `Color` object is constructed from three intensity values in the range 0–255, one for each primary color: red, green, and blue. Alternatively, a single `int` can hold the 24 bits that serve to define any RGB color. Colors can also be converted between RGB and another color model, the HSB color model (Hue, Saturation, Brightness). The *saturation* of a color is a measure of how vibrant or intense the hue appears. Color with zero saturation is just a shade of gray while a color with saturation equal to 1 is as vibrant as the color can be. *Brightness* controls whether green looks more like forest green or lime green, for example. The HSB color model is useful for some operations such as desaturating a color image or changing the brightness only.

There are many convenient class variables for common colors. Thus, `Color.red` denotes red, `Color.white` denotes white, and so forth.

Fonts

If you get sick of looking at your system's default font or if you want extra large titles and such, you can create a `java.awt.Font` instance to represent a font which is available on your system. For example, to specify italic, 18-point Helvetica:

```
Font helv18i = new Font( "Helvetica", Font.ITALIC, 18 );
```

You then use this as an argument to `setFont()` in class `Graphics` or `Component`. You probably want to stick to well-known font names because each font you load must be available on the user's system. Use the `java.awt.Toolkit` method `getFontList()` to read off the locally available font names:

```
import java.awt.*;

    public class Fonts
    {
        public static void main(String args[])
        {
            Toolkit t = Toolkit.getDefaultToolkit();
            String fonts[] = t.getFontList();
            for (int i = 0; i < fonts.length; i++)
                System.err.println( fonts[i] );
            System.exit(0);
        }
    }
```

To provide the measurements necessary for basic typesetting, a `FontMetrics` object can be retrieved for each font. There are methods in both classes `Graphics` and `Toolkit` which provide a `FontMetrics` instance, but you can construct one from the font directly:

```
FontMetrics helv18i_m = new FontMetrics( helv18i );
```

The `FontMetrics` object provides you with such arcane knowledge as the ascent, leading (rhymes with bedding!), descent, and character widths of the font. Unless you already love typesetting, try your best to use a standard text component and avoid accessing font metrics directly. If you love typesetting, then be aware that you can't do any high-powered typesetting with these objects in any case. The `Font` and `FontMetrics` classes don't seem to have any idea about kerning pairs and ligatures, for example. A `FontMetrics` object provides enough information to display screen fonts readably.

java.applet

Java applets are one of the main attractions of programming in Java. The `java.applet` package provides some methods that are very useful for programming applets. Some of these methods are shortcuts. They can be done using the other standard Java classes but only with a fair amount of work. Would you rather load an image over the Web by opening your own socket connection, speaking `http` to a Web server and parsing the header and image data, or by doing this?

```
public class MyApplet extends java.applet.Applet
    {
        Image my_image;

        public void init()
        {
            try {
                my_image = getImage( new URL( getCodeBase(), "myimage.jpg" ) );
            } catch (MalformedURLException e) {}
        }

        // More stuff ...
    }
```

Similar support exists for loading audio and even for directing the host browser to load a new Web page.

Applet

Every applet is defined by a public class extending `java.applet.Applet` which extends `java.awt.Panel`. The `Applet` class provides the four basic methods which embody the life cycle of an applet:

> `init()`—Called to initialize the applet after loading.
>
> `start()`—Called when the applet is displayed.
>
> `stop()`—Called when the applet is no longer being displayed.
>
> `destroy()`—Called when the applet is about to be unloaded.

Don't call these methods yourself. The host environment calls them automatically in response to user actions.

Each of these four methods should be fast. In particular, don't make the mistake of putting a lengthy or infinite loop into the start() method. If you have a lot of work to do (such as I/O or animation), use the start() method to start a new Thread which does the real work. You can even give your applet a run() method and declare that it implements Runnable; then pass in the applet itself as the target of the new thread:

```
public class BusyApplet extends Applet implements Runnable
    {
        Thread t;

        public void run()
        {
            // Get busy ...
        }

        public void start()
        {
            t = new Thread(this);   // Thread t executes my run() method
            t.start();
        }

        public void stop()
        {
            t.stop();
            t = null;
        }

        // etc ...
    }
```

Use the init() method to initialize any local variables and load external resources such as images and audio clips. You may think that these operations are time-consuming and should therefore have a separate thread but the routines described below for images and audio already function asynchronously. They return immediately after starting separate threads, as required.

Some of the handy multimedia-related methods in class Applet include the following:

getAppletContext()—Get a handle to the current context (host browser or applet viewer).

getAudioClip()—Get an audio clip from a URL.

getImage()—Get an image from a URL.

play()—Play an audio clip directly from a URL.

showStatus()—Show a message on the status line of the host browser.

The interfaces AppletContext and AudioClip are provided as a system-independent way of accessing the objects returned by getAppletContext() and getAudioClip(). You can use an AppletContext instance to find other applets on the same page or to direct the browser to visit a new URL.

When an applet is included in a Web page using the APPLET tag, the page designer can specify certain applet parameters which are string names with associated string values. You can access these values using the getParameter() method and use them to modify the behavior of your applet.

java.awt.image

The java.awt.image package allows device-independent loading and filtering of bitmapped images.

Color Models

A color model is a way of representing colors numerically. The abstract class java.awt.image.ColorModel provides a uniform superclass for various color models. The subclasses have to know how to convert their representation into the default RGB values together with transparency information (an *alpha* value). An alpha of 0 is transparent; 255 is opaque.

Two predefined types of color model in java.awt.image are DirectColorModel and IndexColorModel. A DirectColorModel encodes red, green, blue, and alpha channel values but possibly with less than eight bits per channel and the channel masks can be arbitrarily ordered within a 32-bit integer. An IndexColorModel works by looking up colors on a color table of red, green, blue, and alpha values. The maximum number of bits in each value is arbitrary up to a point; you never need more than eight per channel. The color table can have any length.

Producing Images

The java.awt.image package provides a black-box type protocol for loading image data. The interfaces ImageConsumer, ImageProducer, and ImageObserver allow objects to declare that they are interested in the following:

❍ Receiving image data (ImageConsumer)
❍ Producing image data (ImageProducer)
❍ Being notified of progress in loading or preparing images (ImageObserver)

An ImageConsumer registers itself with the ImageProducer. The producer loads the image data from "somewhere" which depends on the exact implementation of the interface, and sends the data to the consumer by calling the consumer's setPixels() methods. What the consumer receives is the raw pixel data in an array. For example, the java.awt.image class PixelGrabber is an ImageConsumer which grabs a rectangular sub-image of a given Image.

Any `Component` or `Toolkit` instance can use its `createImage()` method to create an `Image` object when given an `ImageProducer`. You've seen how to load images in an applet and from a `java.awt.Toolkit` object. Further sources for `Image`s include:

> `MemoryImageSource`—Produces an `Image` from an array of RGB values.
>
> `FilteredImageSource`—Produces an `Image` from an existing `ImageProducer` and an `ImageFilter` (see the section "Image Filters," later in this chapter).

Both of these classes implement the `ImageProducer` interface. Also, every `Image` can supply an `ImageProducer` (via the `getSource()` method) which reproduces the image itself.

The interface `java.awt.image.ImageObserver` requires the single method `imageUpdate()`. This method is called if the `ImageObserver` is supplied as an argument to an `Image` method such as `getWidth()` and the status of the image suddenly changes (the unknown width becomes known, for example). The `java.awt.Component` class uses this mechanism to redraw components automatically as their images load.

Image Filters

As image data passes from producer to consumer it can be filtered. The `java.awt.image` class `ImageFilter` implements an image filter which does nothing. It is the superclass for all image filters. The `RGBImageFilter` class extends `ImageFilter` and provides a shortcut for writing filters which only want to manipulate RGB color data. To write a custom image filter, you subclass one of these.

Using an `ImageFilter` is a matter of instantiating a `FilteredImageSource` with it and the original image. Then you can create the new image from the `FilteredImageSource` by the usual `createImage()` method.

Possible uses for custom image filters include rotating existing images, adjusting their brightness and contrast, blurring images, or doing other special effects. The predefined `CropImageFilter` is an `ImageFilter` which extracts a specific rectangular sub-image.

java.awt.peer

Every `java.awt.Component` object has a *peer*. Essentially a peer is an object in the native windows toolkit together with an interface to it. A `Toolkit` instance knows how to create peer objects. In Java programming it is very seldom necessary to do anything relating directly to the peer objects; but it's nice to know they are there. The `java.awt.peer` package is nothing but a collection of interfaces to these peer objects, one for each AWT component. This includes `ButtonPeer`, `CanvasPeer`, `CheckboxPeer`, and so on. Each interface provides the basic methods which the AWT uses to manipulate the peer in a toolkit-independent way. You should not attempt to call these methods directly. In fact, unless you are writing your own toolkit, you don't need to know this package at all.

java.io

The Java model for I/O is entirely based around streams. A *stream* is a one-way flow of bytes from one place to another. Files, pipes, and sockets are places to attach streams to. The many flavors of stream classes defined in the java.io package are organized by inheritance to avoid duplication of methods. A stream class throws an IOException when things go awry.

Of course, java.io also provides methods for accessing files on a local file system. As far as possible this is made system-independent.

The predefined PrintStreams, System.out, and System.err are useful for printing diagnostics when debugging Java programs and applets. The standard input stream System.in is also available; it is of class InputStream.

Basic Streams

The most basic stream classes don't provide buffering, and they don't structure their data at all. They provide nothing but a pathway for bytes. The differences between them lie in the mechanical question of where the bytes are to be found: in a file, in memory, or on a pipe. You generally use one of these classes only as a step toward instantiating a more useful form of stream.

InputStream, OutputStream

These are the base classes for all the other stream classes. They allow you to read() and write() arrays of byte. InputStream objects can declare that they support *mark and reset* behavior. This means that the input stream can be marked at some point and repositioned there subsequently. This is handy if you try to parse an input stream. The OutputStream class has a flush() method which writes any bytes that may be saved in a buffer (however, an instance of OutputStream is not required to buffer bytes).

FileInputStream, FileOutputStream

These classes attach streams to File and FileDescriptor objects which correspond to files on a local file system. They extend InputStream and OutputStream and provide the same basic functionality. You can get a FileDescriptor object referencing the stream by calling the getFD() method.

ByteArrayInputStream, ByteArrayOutputStream

The class ByteArrayInputStream extends InputStream and reads out of an array of bytes rather than from a file or socket. This is useful when you have the data already in memory but you need to pass it to a method which expects a stream.

Likewise, `ByteArrayOutputStream` writes into a buffer of bytes which grows as required. You can access the written data as an array of bytes by calling the `toByteArray()` method or as a `String`, using `toString()`.

StringBufferInputStream

A `StringBufferInputStream` is an `InputStream` which reads from a `StringBuffer`.

PipedInputStream, PipedOutputStream

These streams correspond in pairs: every `PipedOutputStream` needs to write to a `PipedInputStream`, and vice versa. This arrangement can be thought of as a pipe between the thread writing the `PipedOutputStream` and the thread reading the `PipedInputStream`. In this way, you can create `Runnable` objects which act as stream filters, for example (but also see `FilterInputStream` and `FilterOutputStream`, below).

These streams provide the same basic read/write functionality as `InputStream` and `OutputStream`, above.

SequenceInputStream

This class extends `InputStream` and allows the transparent concatenation of several `InputStreams` into a single stream. When one stream hits end-of-file, the `SequenceInputStream` automatically begins reading from the next one in sequence.

The constructor takes either two `InputStreams` or else a `java.util.Enumeration` of `InputStreams`.

Filtered Streams

Just moving bytes is not enough. Various forms of improved functionality are needed so often that embedding them into the stream object itself makes sense. All these improved or filtered stream classes extend `FilterInputStream` or `FilterOutputStream`. You can think of them as filters because they have an input and an output, and the output is the input but transformed in a useful way.

FilterInputStream, FilterOutputStream

These are the base classes for streams which extend the basic I/O operations of `InputStream` and `OutputStream`. They are intended to be subclassed. You can't instantiate them because the constructor is `protected`.

A `FilterInputStream` is constructed from a single `InputStream` which then becomes an instance variable. Now `FilterInputStream` extends `InputStream` so it implements all the methods of `InputStream` but only as trivial wrappers which access its actual, protected `InputStream`. Additional methods providing the extended functionality are to be supplied in subclasses.

The same setup applies to `FilterOutputStream`.

BufferedInputStream, BufferedOutputStream

The class `BufferedInputStream` extends `FilterInputStream` and you use it like an `InputStream`. The difference is that a `BufferedInputStream` is more efficient. It saves up bytes in a large buffer until you need them. This means that most `read()` requests don't actually cause an I/O operation.

Class `BufferedOutputStream` does the same only for output streams.

LineNumberInputStream

This class acts like an `InputStream` with the added methods `getLineNumber()` and `setLineNumber()` which let you keep track of line numbers.

PrintStream

A `PrintStream` is a special kind of `OutputStream` with the added methods `print()` and `println()`. These methods print the string representation of any object (as per `String.valueOf()` or `toString()`) onto the output stream. The `println()` method appends a newline character while `print()` does not. Even though a `char` is 16 bits wide, only the lower eight bits of each character are written.

Upon creation, you can specify whether the stream should flush itself every time a new line is written.

PushbackInputStream

This is an `InputStream` which allows you to `unread()` a single byte into a pushback buffer. You may not `unread()` another byte until the pushback byte is read again. This is useful for parsing strings since you often need to peek at the next byte without necessarily accepting it as input.

Data I/O

Streams read and write bytes but quite often you want to send other primitive Java types. The interfaces `DataInput` and `DataOutput` specify that a class knows how to read and write the various primitive Java types in a machine-independent way. The most useful methods in `DataInput` and `DataOutput` are shown in Tables 3.1 and 3.2. All of the `DataOutput` methods in Table 3.2 return `void`.

Table 3.1. Useful `DataInput` methods.

Method	Description
`boolean readBoolean()`	Read a single `boolean`.
`byte readByte()`	Read a single `byte` (8 bits).
`char readChar()`	Read a single `char` (16 bits).
`float readFloat()`	Read a single `float` (32 bits).
`double readDouble()`	Read a single `double` (64 bits).
`int readInt()`	Read a single `int` (32 bits).
`long readLong()`	Read a single `long` (64 bits).
`short readShort()`	Read a single `short` (16 bits).
`int readUnsignedByte()`	Read a `byte` and interpret as an unsigned integer.
`int readUnsignedShort()`	Read a `short` and interpret as an unsigned integer.
`void readFully(byte b[])`	Read bytes into an array until it is full.
`void readFully(byte b[],int,int)`	Read bytes into a sub-array until full.
`String readUTF()`	Read a UTF-encoded string.
`String readLine()`	Read a sequence of bytes terminated by new line.

All but one of these input methods throws a `java.io.EOFException` if the end of the input stream is reached before all the bytes in the specified object can be read. The lone exception is `readLine()`. It returns `null` to indicate that EOF occurred before a new line was seen.

Table 3.2. Useful `DataOutput` methods (all return void).

Method	Description
`writeBoolean(boolean)`	Write a single `boolean`.
`write(int)`	Write a single `byte` (8 bits).
`writeByte(int)`	Write a single `byte` (8 bits).
`write(byte[])`	Write a sequence of `bytes`.
`write(byte[],int,int)`	Write a sequence of `bytes` from a sub-array.
`writeChar(int)`	Write a single `char` (16 bits).
`writeFloat(float)`	Write a single `float` (32 bits).
`writeDouble(double)`	Write a single `double` (64 bits).

continues

Table 3.2. continued

Method	Description
writeInt(int)	Write a single int (32 bits).
writeLong(long)	Write a single long (64 bits).
writeShort(int)	Write a single short (16 bits).
writeUTF(String)	Write a String in UTF-encoded format.
writeBytes(String)	Write a String as a sequence of bytes.
writeChars(String)	Write a String as a sequence of chars.

Using these methods, you can read and write primitive Java types with ease. Your classes can use these methods to write themselves onto a stream by writing each instance variable.

 CAUTION:

Beware of the difference between byte and char. A String which is written using writeChars() must be read as a sequence of char. Don't use readLine() or readBytes() for this. In fact, avoid doing this altogether. Use writeBytes() or writeUTF() instead.

If you are willing to let the new line character delimit the end of all your strings, you can read them using readLine(). A convenient way to do this is to make the corresponding output stream be a PrintStream and use the println() method to write the String. However, this method creates problems if your strings contain embedded new line characters.

To read and write more general strings, there are at least two options. Either the receiving end knows the length of the string in advance, in which case you may use writeBytes(), or else you need a scheme for terminating strings reliably. The easiest way to achieve this is also the most flexible way to read and write strings: by using readUTF() and writeUTF(). These methods read and write strings in a modified UTF-8 format. UTF is an ISO standard format which translates Unicode characters into streams of bytes in such a way that the normal ASCII bytes in the stream (encoded as 0x00-0x7f) always correspond to actual ASCII characters, while the non-ASCII bytes encode non-ASCII characters. A big advantage to using readUTF() and writeUTF() is that there is no need for you to send the length of the string or to add a terminator character. The UTF formatting takes care of that.

DataInputStream, DataOutputStream

These stream classes extend FilterInputStream and FilterOutputStream and provide a concrete implementation of the interfaces DataInput and DataOutput. They are two of the most useful stream classes in java.io, particularly for network applications.

Using Files

Although applets are seldom allowed to access the local file system, stand-alone Java programs can do so. The java.io package provides some classes to try and make this as system-independent as possible. Conventions about path separator characters and such are loaded from the system properties (see java.lang.System).

File

A java.io.File object represents a file name which may correspond to a file on an external file system. Using a File object, you can test whether such a file exists (exists() method). You can check permissions with canRead() and canWrite(). If the file is a directory (isDirectory()), you can list its contents by calling list(). You can use a java.io.FilenameFilter to restrict which files get listed. The File class includes several handy methods to create directories, rename files, check modification times, and so forth.

To open the file for reading or writing, instantiate a FileInputStream or a FileOutputStream.

FileDescriptor

A FileDescriptor is an opaque handle to an open file on the local system. You can use it to instantiate FileInputStream and FileOutputStream objects. File descriptors for the standard input, output, and error streams are accessible as static class variables in, out, and err (for example, FileDescriptor.out is the standard output).

RandomAccessFile

Class RandomAccessFile is the most flexible way to access a local file. This class implements both DataInput and DataOutput and provides a seekable file pointer. It is a suitable base class for classes which want to store fixed-length data records in a file. A RandomAccessFile may be opened in read-only or in read-write mode.

Interface FilenameFilter

The FilenameFilter interface has a single method, accept(), which decides which files to include in a listing of a given directory. FilenameFilters are used in the list() method of java.io.File and in java.awt.FileDialog.

StreamTokenizer

This is a base class for writing lexical analyzers. It scans an InputStream and breaks it into a sequence of tokens of predefined types.

java.net

The `java.net` package handles network-related functions: URLs, World Wide Web connections, and sockets for more general network interaction. Chapter 12, "Network Programming with Java," explores some possible applications of these classes in client/server applets.

Addressing the Web: URLs

A URL is a Uniform Resource Locator, an address which references a "resource" on the World Wide Web. While a resource is often just a web page sitting in an HTML file, it can be more, such as a search engine query or a CGI script, for example. A URL contains more information than just the internet address of the WWW server. The protocol for connecting to the server and the location of the resource on the server are all embedded in the URL. A typical URL reads:

```
http://www.myserver.com/~me/myFile.html
```

Here, the *protocol* is `http` (HyperText Transfer Protocol), the *server* is `www.myserver.com`, and the *virtual path* is `/~me/myFile.html`. Schematically, a URL has a format like:

```
protocol://server:portNumber/virtualPath#referenceInfo
```

This is a fairly general form of URL. Most of the elements are optional. Missing elements are interpreted in the context where the URL is defined. For a web page or applet to refer to a URL with the same protocol on the same server and port number, it is enough to have only the virtual path.

An *absolute* URL is one whose virtual path begins with `/` or `~user` (the WWW home directory of a particular user). This includes any URL which specifies a server. A URL which isn't absolute is *relative*. A URL may also have reference information after a hash sign (#). The interpretation of this reference depends on which protocol is being used. For `http` it is the name of a hypertext anchor in the named HTML file. The browser is requested to jump directly to that position in the file.

The default port number for `http` is 80. Other typical protocols you may see include `gopher`, `telnet`, `nntp`, `file`, and `ftp`.

URL

Java provides the `java.net.URL` class which encodes a URL in a convenient and uniform way. After you create a URL, you can't alter its value. Here are some ways to construct URLs:

```
URL u1 = new URL( "http", "www.myserver.com", 80, "/myFile.html" );
URL u2 = new URL( "http", "www.myserver.com", "/myFile.html" );
URL u3 = new URL( "http://www.myserver.com" );
URL u4 = new URL( u3, "myFile.html" );
```

The first three forms expect you to know an *absolute* virtual path to the resource (a virtual path beginning with / or ~). The last example is different. A URL is created by resolving the second argument, a String, as a URL *in the context of* the first URL. If the String is a relative URL, the return value is the complete absolute URL to the same resource, where the string is interpreted as being relative to the first URL. If the second argument already represents an absolute URL then it is returned (unchanged).

Applets often need to create URLs relative to their *code base* (the URL of the directory containing their class file). For this, use the getCodeBase() method of java.applet.Applet:

```
URL my_image_url = new URL( getCodeBase(), "myImage.gif" );
```

In creating URLs, you usually have to catch the exception java.net.MalformedURLException.

The URL class has the methods getProtocol(), getHost(), getPort(), getFile(), and getRef() to save you the trouble of parsing the URL. getRef() gets the reference information after the hash sign. You can also use openConnection() to open a URLConnection to the object at that URL or getContent() to return a Java object representing the content of the URL. If you wish to read the contents as raw data, use the openStream() method to get an InputStream to the URL.

For applets, URLs are perhaps most useful for calling the getImage() and getAudioClip() methods.

URLConnection

There may be times when you want to have the possibility of more flexible interaction with a Web server. For example, you may want to use the POST method to send information to a CGI script. A URLConnection represents a connection to a given URL and allows a richer interaction than just the URL object. You can open an OutputStream to a URL, get various http header fields, and so on. It is possible to set certain properties of the connection before connecting so as to restrict the types of interaction allowed. Class URLConnection also has the methods getContent() and getInputStream() which do the same thing as getContent() and openStream() in the class URL.

URLEncoder

To pass string arguments to a CGI script (such as a search engine), you have to put a query on the end of the URL by appending a question mark and a series of argument definitions:

```
http://www.myserver.com/cgi-bin/myscript.cgi?name=JoeBlow
```

Here, the value of the name argument is "JoeBlow." In general, to cope with whitespace and other weird characters, the argument values must be translated into a format corresponding to a special MIME type. The class java.net.URLEncoder exists just to provide this translation, by way of its lone static method, encode(). For example:

```
String s = URLEncoder.encode( "William Thornhump \003" );
System.out.println( s );
```

(notice that the string contains a Control+C character with value 3). This code results in the output:

```
William+Thornhump+%03
```

URLStreamHandler

A URLStreamHandler knows how to handle a particular type of protocol over a stream connected to a URL. Unless you are interested in embedding new protocols into your Java program, you don't have to bother with these low-level objects. Use the methods in the classes URL and URLConnection instead. A URLStreamHandler for a given protocol is instantiated once when the protocol name is first encountered in creating a URL instance. This is an abstract class.

The java.net package includes the interface URLStreamHandlerFactory. A class implementing this interface knows how to create a URLStreamHandler from a given protocol name, by way of the createURLStreamHandler() method. To provide a custom URLStreamHandler for a new protocol, you first have to subclass the abstract class URLStreamHandler, overriding methods as appropriate (at the very least, you must implement the openConnection() method). Next, write a class implementing URLStreamHandlerFactory, whose createURLStreamHandler() method understands the new protocol name, and set it as the URLStreamHandlerFactory for your application:

```
URL.setURLStreamHandlerFactory( myFactory );   // a static method in class URL
```

Your new URLStreamHandlerFactory doesn't have to worry about decoding the standard protocols. If the createURLStreamHandler() method returns null, the standard factory is consulted. This also allows you to override the standard protocol definitions, if you wish. A Java program can only set the URLStreamHandlerFactory once.

Content Handlers

As URLStreamHandlers are to protocol types, so ContentHandlers are to *content* types of a URL. An object in the abstract class java.net.ContentHandler knows how to read a given URLConnection and turn the input into an Object. Again, unless you are interested in extending the different content types understood by your Java program, you don't need to bother with this class. The different ways of encoding the content of a URL are known as MIME types, so you need a ContentHandler for each MIME type you wish to be able to access. To make a custom ContentHandler which corresponds to a new MIME type, you need to implement the single method getContent(). To make it work with the existing routines in classes URL and URLConnection, you must also install a new ContentHandlerFactory, using the static method setContentHandlerFactory() in class URLConnection. A ContentHandlerFactory is an object which implements the interface java.net.ContentHandlerFactory by providing the method createContentHandler() which turns the string name of a MIME type into a ContentHandler.

Sockets and Internet Addresses

A *socket* is one endpoint of a two-way network connection. In Java, sockets come in three flavors: `Socket`, `ServerSocket`, and `DatagramSocket`. The actual implementation of all three of these kinds of socket is accomplished by the class `SocketImpl` which provides a fairly standard set of socket calls. To work with fancy setups like firewalls and proxies, you may have to provide your own socket implementation by subclassing `SocketImpl` and setting your own `SocketImplFactory`.

InetAddress

An `InetAddress` object holds an internet address and is essential for using sockets. You can get an `InetAddress` by calling the static method `InetAddress.getByName()` with a host name or an IP address in standard string format:

```
InetAddress a = InetAddress.getByName( "www.myhost.com" );
InetAddress b = InetAddress.getByName( "123.45.67.89" );
```

To refer to the local host, you can pass in `null`.

ServerSocket

A `ServerSocket` is created on a local port and then it listens for incoming socket connections. The `accept()` method blocks until there is a connection and then returns a corresponding `Socket` object. The new connection is a stream connection, as described below under `Socket`. The `ServerSocket` continues to listen until closed.

CAUTION:

The constructor is called as `ServerSocket(int port)` or as `ServerSocket(int port, int max)`. The optional second argument is the maximum number of pending connections to hold in a queue before refusing further new connections. It is *not* the number of seconds to wait for a connection, as stated in the Java API 1.0.

Socket

A `Socket` object represents a standard stream socket. This means that data passes along the connection in sequence and is reliably delivered. The stream socket is a layer of socket functionality which uses a more primitive packet interface behind the scenes, transparently resending bad packets as required (as long as the connection remains open). This type of socket can have an `InputStream` or an `OutputStream` connected to it, or both. These streams are accessed by way of the `getInputStream()` and `getOutputStream()` methods. (In fact, you can specify with an optional constructor argument that a `Socket` should be a datagram socket—not a stream socket—but it's not clear why this is a good idea, since there is a datagram socket class already.)

A Socket is created using an address and port number to which a connection is attempted immediately. If there is a socket listening at that port (Java ServerSocket or otherwise) and it is willing to accept the connection, then the Socket is constructed and may be used immediately. Otherwise, the constructor throws an exception.

Datagram Sockets

Datagram sockets bind to a local port where they send and receive datagram packets. A datagram packet is a short sequence of bytes, addressed to a particular host and port. Unlike a stream socket, a datagram socket does not maintain a connection with a remote socket. Packets may be sent to any host and port at which a datagram socket is waiting to receive one. It is the packet, not the socket, which knows to whom it is addressed.

In Java, datagram sockets are implemented by the class java.net.DatagramSocket. A DatagramSocket can send() and receive() datagram packets which are represented by class java.net.DatagramPacket. The packets are not guaranteed to arrive in sequence or even to arrive at all.

java.util

The java.util package is explored in Chapter 13, "General Purpose Classes." It contains some utility classes and useful data structures, described briefly here.

Dictionaries, Hashtables, and Properties

A Dictionary lets you create an association between *keys* and *values*. These can be any Java objects. In a real dictionary, the key is a word, and the associated value is the definition of that word. The key-value pairs are stored in the Dictionary using the put() method. The values are retrieved by the get() method, given the corresponding key. The keys() and elements() methods return an Enumeration of the keys or the elements of the Dictionary.

A Hashtable is an efficient form of Dictionary which relies on a hashing function, which generates an integer hash code for each key and uses standard hashing techniques to ensure speedy access. This relies on proper implementations of hashCode() and equals() in the objects used as keys. In particular, the hash codes should not be too "predictable."

Class java.util.Properties extends Hashtable, and adds the load(), save(), and list() methods for writing and reading the key-value pairs to and from streams. The convenience method getProperty() performs an explicit type cast operation on the returned element for you, from Object to String. The system properties are stored in a Properties object.

Stacks and Vectors

Arrays in Java are already far nicer objects than in many programming languages, however, they are most appropriate for storing items up to a fixed maximum number. A `java.util.Vector` object is like an array which automatically allocates more storage as required. The elements of the `Vector` are stored in sequence, indexed by integers starting from 0. The `size()` method returns the current number of elements. Any Java object can be stored in a `Vector`. You can insert an element into a position in the `Vector` and the existing elements roll over to make room. When you remove an element, the objects to the right roll back and fill the space. So you normally can't rely on an object staying at a fixed index in the `Vector`.

The `Vector` class is flexible enough to serve as a base class for various stack and queue type data structures. The class `java.util.Stack` extends `Vector` and provides a basic pushdown stack of objects (Last In, First Out or LIFO). You can `push()` an element onto the top of the stack and you can `peek()` at the top element or `pop()` it off the stack.

Counting Things: Enumerations

There are many situations where you have a collection of elements and you want to iterate over the collection, visiting each element once. If they are already in some particular ordered structure such as an array or `Vector`, you can do this with a simple `for` loop. A more flexible way is provided by the interface `java.util.Enumeration`. For example, an `Enumeration` can iterate over the elements in a hash table using the `hasMoreElements()` and `nextElement()` methods. To get the `Enumeration`, call the `elements()` method of the `Hashtable` (or `Vector`, `Stack`, and so on).

Observers and Observables

Sometimes an object needs to become an *observer* which monitors the condition of a second, *observable* object. For example, a spreadsheet must monitor changes in its cells and respond by recalculating the spreadsheet values. This is particularly important in a multithreaded environment. Java offers a uniform approach to the observer model by way of the base class `java.util.Observable` and the interface `java.util.Observer`. An `Observable` keeps a list of `Observers` which have registered their interest in watching changes in the `Observable`. When an observable change occurs, the `Observable` object calls its `notifyObservers()` method. This results in calls to the `update()` method of each `Observer`.

Other Utility Classes

You may think that Java has everything except the kitchen sink, but here it is: the kitchen sink department. Java provides additional classes to handle those tricky functions which everybody needs at some point but which are a real headache to code. The `java.util` classes `BitSet`, `Date`, `Random`, and `StringTokenizer` offer bit-string logical operations, time and date functions, random number generation, and string-splitting capability, respectively.

Summary

In this chapter, you learned what each of the standard Java packages can do, and you at least heard mention of just about every different kind of class contained in them. These classes play a huge role in reducing the amount of boring code you need to write, and consequently they help to cut down on bugs. You get to have more spare time for surfing (the ocean or the Internet, as applicable). The next chapter (Chapter 4, "Creating Your Own Objects") deals with the mechanics of coding subclasses of these classes tailored to your own needs.

Chapter

4

by Kathryn A. Jones

Creating Your Own Objects

- Creating Objects from Java Classes
- Creating Your Own Classes
- Creating Interfaces
- Using the Garbage Collector

This chapter builds on the fundamentals of object-oriented programming covered in Chapter 1, "An Overview of Java." It explains how to create actual objects, classes, and interfaces. First, you will learn to create objects from the classes in Java's packages, which are covered in Chapter 3, "An Introduction to Java Classes." Second, you will learn to write your own classes and methods; and third, you'll learn how to create and use interfaces. After you master these concepts, you will be ready to move onto all the fun chapters that show you how to create Java applets and applications.

As you know, an *object* is an instance of a class that has variables that describe it and methods that modify it. The Java applications you will write will continuously create objects from classes. Objects you create interact with other objects created in your application by invoking methods to perform actions on the other objects. So, essentially, all you'll need to know in order to write a Java application is how to create objects from classes and how to create methods to manipulate them. Using methods to combine the functionality of individual objects, you can create applications that can do practically anything. You can animate graphics, create interactive games, or create an on-line order-entry system that records and processes information a user enters into on-line forms. Later in the book, you will learn how to write each of these types of applications from beginning to end. This chapter provides shorter examples to introduce you to creating and using objects, classes, and interfaces.

Creating Objects from Java Classes

The next section teaches you how to create your own class. This section uses the classes from Java's built-in packages to concentrate on creating objects. As you learned in Chapter 3, Java provides several basic libraries of classes that have been tested and are thread-safe. You will want to use many of these utilities provided by Java's packages in your code in order to save time.

The operator you will use in your code to create new objects is called, appropriately, new. When you call the new operator in your code, you follow it by the name of the class from which you want to instantiate the object. Java automatically allocates a portion of memory to store instances of the variables declared in the class. This portion of memory is the *object*. After allocating an object, you will use methods in the object's class to send messages to it. You also can send messages to the object from methods in other classes.

You can use several pieces of code to create an object in Java in addition to the new operator. When new creates the object from the specified class, it automatically calls a *constructor* to build it. The constructors you create enable parameters to be passed to the object. You can create your own constructors for objects, but it is not a requirement. Java calls a default constructor if new is called without parameters. You can create one or many constructors for the object, each with different parameters, or you can let Java assign a default constructor. When new is called with parameters, Java selects the constructor you created that has the matching parameters.

When you create an object, you typically declare a reference variable that will hold the object's *reference*. Java creates a reference automatically whenever new instantiates an object in order to locate the object in memory when necessary. You will need a *reference variable* that stores the reference in order to refer to the object in your code. The reference variable is a name you assign to the object.

The very rudimentary form of an object creation follows:

```
classname reference-variable = new classname (parameter list);
```

Here, classname represents the class you use to create the object. reference-variable is the name you use to refer to the reference Java creates so that Java's runtime system can locate it. The new operator followed by classname actually instantiates the object from the class. The parameter list is the part of the object creation that specifies which of the constructors stored in the class are used to create the object.

The following example creates a new Rectangle object from the Rectangle class in the java.awt package:

```
Rectangle ThisRect = new Rectangle();
```

This example of the creation of a new Rectangle object accomplishes four tasks in one line of code: it declares the reference variable ThisRect, creates a new Rectangle object, assigns the Rectangle object to the reference variable ThisRect, and initializes the object.

These tasks can be separated into two lines in the following form:

```
classname reference-variable;  //variable declaration
reference-variable = new classname (parameter list); //creation, assignment,
➥initialization
```

In the Rectangle example, you could create the Rectangle object in two lines, as this code shows:

```
Rectangle ThisRect;
ThisRect = new Rectangle();
```

Declaring the Reference Variable

Rectangle ThisRect is a simple variable declaration, much like the object-variable declarations covered in Chapter 1. This declaration tells the compiler that the reference variable ThisRect refers to an object for which the class is Rectangle. When you think about it, the class in the declaration of an object-reference variable is very similar to the data type in the declaration of a variable in a class. Recall that the data type explained in Chapter 1 was declared as the following:

```
data-type variable-name;
```

The data types used to declare object variables basically are predefined Java classes with states and behaviors just like any other class, except that data types are classes that cannot be subclassed. Therefore, you can think of the declaration of a reference variable to hold an object just as you would the declaration of a variable to hold a value of a data type.

Creating the Object

Declarations do not instantiate objects. `Rectangle ThisRect` does not create a new `Rectangle` object; it just creates a variable named `ThisRect` to hold a `Rectangle` object. To instantiate the `Rectangle` object, you assign the reference variable to the object-creation sequence, which consists of the `new` operator followed by the class name and its constructor parameters.

The `new` operator returns a reference to the newly created `Rectangle` object, which is stored in the `ThisRect` reference variable.

Initializing the Object

Constructors are special methods provided by each Java class to initialize new objects from a class. The `new` operator creates the object, and the constructor initializes it.

Here's an example of using the `new` operator with parameters for a constructor to build a `Rectangle` object with a width of 4 and a height of 2:

```
new Rectangle(4, 2);
```

`Java.awt.Rectangle` provides several constructors. In the example, `Rectangle(4, 2)` calls the constructor that exists in `Java.awt.Rectangle` that has arguments that match the number and types of parameters specified in the initialization statement. The 4 and 2 parameters match the number and type of the width and height arguments of the following `Java.awt.Rectangle` constructor:

```
public Rectangle(int width, int height);
```

A class may provide multiple constructors to perform different kinds of initializations on new objects. When looking at the implementation for a class, you can recognize the constructors because they have the same name as the class and have no return type. In a class with multiple constructors, they all have the same name but different arguments. Each constructor initializes the new object in a different way. In addition to the default constructor used to initialize a new `Rectangle` object and the `Rectangle` constructor used earlier for `ThisRect`, `Rectangle` can use a different constructor, as shown in this code:

```
Rectangle ThisRect = new Rectangle(3, 3, 4, 2);
```

This creates a `Rectangle` object at point 3,3 of width 4 and height 2, using the following constructor from `Java.awt.Rectangle`:

```
public Rectangle(int x, int y, int width, int height);
```

Using the Object

After your object is instantiated, you can change its behavior by using methods to change the values of its variables or by directly assigning new values to the variables. Using methods to change variables is a more consistent way to manipulate objects. This section examines both these procedures.

You can access an object's variables directly from another object by adding a period (.) to the end of the reference-variable name and appending the name of the object variable, as shown in this example:

```
reference-variable.variable;
```

To access the `width` variable in one of the `Rectangle` objects created in the preceding section, you can use the following reference:

```
ThisRect.width;
```

To change the value of the `width` and `height` variables in the `ThisRect` object, you simply set them equal to new values in the following statements:

```
ThisRect.width = 5;
ThisRect.height = 3;
```

To get the `width` variable from the `ThisRect` object, you can refer to it as the following:

```
Width = ThisRect.width;
```

You can call an object's methods by adding a period (.) to the end of the reference-variable name and appending the name of the object method, followed by parameters to the method enclosed in parentheses:

```
Reference-variable.methodName(parameters);
```

To invoke the `Java.awt.Rectangle.reshape` method on the `ThisRect` object, you use this statement:

```
ThisRect.reshape(5, 3);
```

This statement reshapes the object by modifying its `height` and `width` variables. It has the same effect as the direct variable assignments used earlier in this section:

```
ThisRect.width = 5;
ThisRect.height = 3;
```

The `reshape()` method in the `Java.awt.Rectangle` package is declared void, so it doesn't return a value. All methods that are not declared as void do evaluate to some value. You can use the value returned by a method in expressions or as variable values.

Creating Your Own Classes

Although you can create functional applications by creating and using objects with Java's built-in classes, you undoubtedly will want to know how to create your own classes, constructors, methods, and variables to add additional functionality to your applications. This section explains how you can accomplish these tasks.

Writing the Class

When you create your own class, you usually will want it to be a subclass of a built-in Java class. Most basic functionality is provided by the classes in Java's packages. By restricting your class creations to subclasses of Java classes, you ensure the portability of your application. You know for sure that every user of your application will have Java's built-in classes available in his runtime system.

Remember that the primary advantage of subclassing is that it enables you to reuse code. You create subclasses as extensions of existing classes to create new objects with properties that are enhancements of existing objects. These subclasses use the existing methods and variables of the superclass and add methods and variables that make each subclass unique.

You learned the basic form of a class structure in Chapter 1. An example of how you can create a subclass called `Square` from the `Rectangle` class follows:

```
public class Square extends Rectangle {
//new variable and method declarations
}
```

`Square` is the name of your subclass. The name of your class must be a legal Java identifier and should begin with a capital letter. The `extends Rectangle` part is where the `Rectangle` class is identified as the superclass. This allows the `Square` class to use any variables or methods defined in `Rectangle`. If a superclass is not specified, Java assumes that the `Java.lang.Object` class is the superclass. The `Square` class' unique variables and methods are declared next.

The `class Square` statement uses the `public` access modifier to allow all other classes and subclasses to access it. You can precede a class name or method name with the word `final` if you do not want the compiler to allow it to be subclassed or overridden, or by the word `abstract` if you want to require that it be subclassed.

Your subclass inherits variables and methods from its superclass that are declared `public` or `protected` by the superclass. If variables and methods are declared `private`, they are not inherited. If no access modifier is specified, only classes within the same package can inherit methods and variables.

Within your subclass, you can hide the superclass' variables by using the superclass' variable names for subclass variables, and you can override methods inherited from the superclass. Although the subclass does not inherit the superclass' hidden variables and may override the superclass' methods, the subclass always can access these variables and methods as they appear in the superclass by using the keyword `super`, as this example shows:

```
ThisHeight = super.height;
```

This statement refers to the value of height as it is stored in the superclass.

You create all the methods and variables of the class, enclosing them in curly braces ({}). The collection of methods and variable declarations within the braces are called the *body* of the class. The variables typically are declared first.

Declaring the Member Variables

The class member variable declaration is much like the reference variable declaration in an object creation:

```
type variable-name;
```

The difference is that member variables exist in the body of the class, but are declared outside of methods, object creations, and constructors. In the following example of the Square class, the area variable is declared:

```
class Square extends Rectangle {
    int area;
    // methods
}
```

Typically, a member variable is not capitalized. It must be a legal Java identifier. No two member variables within a class can have the same name.

The member variable declaration offers several optional modifiers, as shown in this code:

```
[access-modifier] [static] [final] [transient] [volatile] type variable-name;
```

The access modifier public, private, or protected restricts access in the same way it does for methods and classes. static defines the variable as a class variable rather than an instance variable. This means that when the variable value is changed, it is changed in all instances. An instance variable is specific to the instance only. final indicates that the variable is a constant. Constant variables typically are written in all uppercase letters. They cannot be changed. transient indicates that the variable is not part of the persistent state of the object and will not be saved when the object is archived. volatile indicates that the variable is modified asynchronously by concurrently running threads.

Creating the Methods

As you learned in Chapter 1, a *method* returns a value unless it is declared as void. The method name is preceded by a return type to inform Java of how to interpret the value returned. It is followed by an optional list of arguments enclosed in parentheses. Like classes and member variables, the method declaration can be preceded by an access modifier. The following code shows how the method declaration is structured:

```
[access-modifier] returnType methodName([arguments]) {
    //statements
}
```

If you include arguments when you write a method, you can call it with matching parameters. Parameters pass information to the method.

Using the fundamentals you learned in the previous chapters of Part I about statements, expressions, operators, and variables, you can create methods to manipulate your objects.

The following sections explain several types of methods available in Java: `Class` and `Instance` methods, constructors, and `finalize()` methods.

Using Instance Members versus Class Members

Members—a word for the variables and methods in a class—can be specific to the class or to the instance of the class, depending on how you write them and where you place them in your code. This is an important concept to learn, because variable values may differ when you define them as class variables rather than instance variables, and vice versa. Different rules apply to instance and class members as well, so you will be prone to compile errors if you are not mindful of these concepts.

Member variables can be class variables or instance variables. *Class variables* are declared using the `static` modifier. When Java's runtime system loads the class, the class variables are allocated in memory only once. When instances of the class are created, the class variables are not copied but instead are shared by all the instances. No additional memory is allocated for these variables because only one copy exists. Class variables can be accessed from any instance or from the class. Because class variables are shared by instances, the values assigned to them are the same for all instances of the class. When class variables are changed, they are changed universally for all instances that refer to them.

If no modifier is specified, variables are instance variables by default. Unlike class variables, all *instance variables* are copied and allocated memory by the Java runtime system each time an instance is created. An object's instance variables can be accessed only from an object—not from the class. If you want to access the instance variables of object A from your class, for example, you cannot refer to it directly. You must create a new object B that refers to it. The value of an instance variable is specific to the object. Other objects created from the same class can have different values assigned to their instance variables.

Member methods can be class methods or instance methods. *Class methods* also are declared using the `static` modifier. They have no access to the instance variables of the objects. They are invoked on the class and do not require any instance to be created in order to be called.

Instance methods, on the other hand, have access to the instance variables of the object, other objects, and the class variables of their class. They can be run only when an object is created.

You will want to use class variables in your code when you need only one copy of an item that must be accessible by all objects created from the class. Using class variables saves memory. You will want to use class methods for security reasons—to restrict access to the objects' instance variables.

Creating the Constructors and the Finalize() Methods

Constructors and `finalize()` methods are special methods you can use in your class. As you have learned, constructors are used to build objects when they are instantiated. You can use the `finalize()` method to destroy objects.

As you know, classes can store multiple constructors (all with the same name) with different arguments that are called when the `new` operator instantiates an object with parameters. If no parameters are passed, Java assigns a default constructor. The default constructor for the `Rectangle` class, for example, is `Rectangle()`. Constructors use the same access modifiers as methods and classes.

Many of Java's built-in classes provide multiple constructors. The `Java.awt.Rectangle` class that you have been using in this chapter, for example, provides the following constructors:

```
public Rectangle();
public Rectangle(int x, int y, int width, int height);
public Rectangle(int width, int height);
public Rectangle(Point p, Dimension d);
public Rectangle(Point p);
public Rectangle(Dimension d);
```

In your class, you may want to create multiple constructors if you will be passing different parameters when creating new objects. The Java compiler decides which constructor to use based on the number and type of parameters passed. If you create a new rectangle with the following statement, for example, Java selects the second constructor:

```
new Rectangle(3, 3, 4, 2);
```

When you write your constructors, keep in mind that each name must be the same as the name of its class, and each constructor must have arguments that are different in number or in type. Unlike regular method declarations, you do not define return types.

Constructors are not limited to single-line declarations. They can declare variables and methods like a regular method does. Although they can look much like regular methods, you will be able to spot constructors when you read through Java code, because they do not specify a return type and have the same name as the class.

If you need to access the constructors in your `Square` class' superclass, for example, you can do so by using the keyword `super` before the declaration:

```
super.Rectangle()
```

This line invokes a constructor provided by `Rectangle`, which is the superclass of `Square`. Typically, the superclass constructor is invoked first in the subclass' constructor.

When objects no longer are needed in an application, they must be cleaned out of memory. Java provides an automatic Garbage Collector to find unused objects and reclaim their memory. The Garbage Collector runs a `finalize()` method just before clearing an object from memory. You can override Java's `finalize()` method in your code. This `finalize()` method, provided by the `Java.lang.Object` class, releases system resources, such as open files or open sockets, before the object is collected. The last section of this chapter describes in detail how garbage collection works. For now, it is enough to know that the Garbage Collector is responsible for automatically clearing unused objects from memory.

You have the option of using the `Object` class' `finalize()` method or overriding it by creating your own `finalize()` method for your class. The structure of a `finalize()` method declaration follows:

```
protected void finalize() throws throwable{
//statements
}
```

In the body of this special method, you will close files and sockets after determining that they are no longer in use.

To call a `finalize()` method specified in your superclass, precede the name `finalize()` with the keyword `super` and a period (.). It is a good idea to call the superclass' `finalize()` method after your class' `finalize()` method, in case the object has obtained resources through methods that it inherited. Such a `finalize()` method looks like this:

```
protected void finalize() throws Throwable {
// clean up statements
super.finalize();
}
```

Creating Interfaces

At this point, you know how to create classes, to define their member variables and methods, and to instantiate objects from them. You will be able to create some small applications with this knowledge. Java's strict class hierarchy rules limit a subclass you create, however, to inherit only from the classes in its hierarchy. To create more complex applications, you undoubtedly will need to inherit from classes outside your class' hierarchy. In Java, you access methods and variables from classes outside your class' hierarchy by implementing multiple interfaces in your class. These interfaces must be defined in the foreign classes that you are accessing. You also can make portions of your class available to other classes that cannot inherit from it by defining interfaces in your class.

Interfaces always are abstract. Their variables can be used only as constants; they always are static and final. Their methods are `abstract` and `public`. An interface declares a set of methods and constants without specifying the implementation for any of the methods. When a class implements an interface, it provides implementations for all the methods declared in the interface.

As you learned in Chapter 1, interfaces are implemented by a class in the class declaration:

```
class classname implements [interface-list] {
}
```

The form of an interface declaration for a class follows:

```
[public access-modifier] interface Interface-name extends [interface-list]{
    //methods and constants
}
```

The `public access` modifier is the only modifier supported in the latest release of Java for interfaces. It can be used before an interface declaration to allow all other classes and packages to use it. If `public` is not declared, only the classes within its package can use the interface. The keyword `interface` is followed by the name of the interface, which typically is capitalized. The `extends interface-list` part is similar to a class extending a superclass, but it can list multiple interfaces that it extends. This list is comma-delimited.

Like inheritance in a subclass, an interface inherits all constants and methods from the interfaces it extends unless the interface hides an inherited constant by declaring a variable of the same name or overrides a method with a new method declaration.

There is no need to use any of the following modifiers in an interface, because they are invalid:

```
private
protected
synchronized
transient
volatile
```

Here is an example of an interface declaration:

```
interface Movable {
    void moveLeft(int x, int y);
    void moveRight(int x, int y);
}
```

This is an example of the implementation of the `Movable()` interface in a class:

```
class Rectangle implements Movable {
    public void moveLeft(3, 1) {
    //code for moving object
    }
}
```

Using the Garbage Collector

Now that you have learned to subclass objects, you might wonder how the memory they are allocated is managed. If you're a C++ developer, you might think that I missed some memory-management steps in my subclassing explanation. In Java, memory management is performed automatically with a utility called a Garbage Collector. When an object that has been instantiated by your application finishes performing its task, it is destroyed and Java's automatic Garbage Collector reclaims its memory.

The Java team made its most important improvement over C++ in automatic memory management and thread controls. Through the use of an automatic, threaded garbage-collection utility, Java removes the burden of memory management from the shoulders of the programmer yet retains high performance standards. Additionally, it eliminates the many bugs commonly caused by the use of pointers in C++ applications without sacrificing performance. This section describes what garbage collection is and how it uses multithreading to maintain the performance of your application.

Understanding Garbage Collection

Garbage collection is Java's answer to automatic memory management. This section on garbage collection begins by explaining why the management of memory in a multithreaded application should be automated, and how Java automates explicit memory management tasks of C-type languages, and how garbage collection works.

In C and C++, creating multithreaded applications is possible through explicit memory management. Programmers manage memory by using memory-management libraries to allocate memory, free memory, and keep track of which memory is available to be freed and when. Explicit memory management has proved to be a common source of bugs, crashes, memory leaks, and performance degradation in C++ applications. The need to free programmers from the encumbrance of memory management is evidenced by the fact that most bugs in C++-type code are caused by misuse of pointers and freeing of objects that are allocated in memory. If memory management is automated, programmers can spend most of their time worrying about the functionality of their applications instead of wasting it by debugging memory problems.

Pointers, pointer arithmetic, `malloc`, and `free`, which are used for memory management in C++, automatically are incorporated into Java's environment. Pointers are replaced by references. As you discovered earlier in this chapter, Java has a `new` operator, which is used to allocate memory for objects. There is no `free` function, however, that a programmer can invoke in code to clean up the memory space when the object no longer is needed. There is, in fact, no need to deallocate or free memory explicitly in Java.

Java generally automates memory management by tracking the use of objects that are created as your application runs. The interpreter automatically marks objects to be freed from memory when they no longer are in use. Such automatic memory management is performed by Java's Garbage Collector.

The purpose of Java's Garbage Collector is to ensure that memory is available when it is needed. When the Garbage Collector executes, it searches, discovers, marks, clears, and compacts unused memory, increasing the likelihood that adequate memory resources are available when required by the user.

More specifically, when an object is instantiated from a class, it is given a unique reference, which is used by the Garbage Collector. The Garbage Collector sets the reference counter to 1 when the object is allocated. It keeps track of all the references to objects instantiated in an application by incrementing the counter each time an object is referenced and decrementing it when the reference is gone. The Garbage Collector searches for reference counters that are equal to 0, meaning that there are no more references to the object. After discovering that a counter is set to 0, the Garbage Collector marks the unused object for removal, making it a candidate for garbage collection.

Java ensures that certain objects integral to the system will never be freed, such as the Object class.

After an object is cleared from memory, it leaves a hole the size of the object that can be reused. The Java Garbage Collector searches memory for fragments and reorganizes it by compacting it. When the Garbage Collector *compacts* memory, it consolidates the objects that have references into a contiguous group, making one large area of unallocated memory available for use by new objects as necessary.

Java provides for situations in which a long chain of object references comes full circle, back to the originating reference, leaving the counts for unused objects at 1 and the memory uncleared. Java avoids this problem by marking root objects, searching all references to objects, marking them, searching those objects' references, and so on until no other references exist. The Garbage Collector then removes all unmarked objects and compacts memory.

The effect of compacting objects is that they are moved to different areas of memory. In Java, references to objects that have moved are not lost, because these references are not pointers to specific areas of memory but instead are handles that are maintained in an *object index*, which maps them to actual objects. When an object is moved, only its references in the object index must be repaired.

You might wonder how such activities possibly can run throughout the execution of an application without degrading performance. The following section explores that question.

Looking At the Garbage Collector's Effect on Performance

The Garbage Collector's processes, described in the last section, would normally be very CPU-intensive—incrementing and decrementing counters for vast quantities of references to objects, searching them for 0 values, compacting memory, and remapping references in the object index. Java's Garbage Collector is not CPU-intensive, partly because it provides some additional tricks, such as designating objects that do not need to be referenced and saving work for the Garbage Collector, but mostly due to the fact that it runs as a separate, low-priority thread.

The Java Garbage Collector takes advantage of the user's behavior when interacting with Java applications. When a user pauses while using an application, when the system pauses, or when the system requires the use of memory taken up by defunct classes, the Java runtime system runs the Garbage Collector in a low-priority background thread and frees unused objects from memory. Because the Garbage Collector utility is effective only because it runs in a multithreaded environment, this section briefly explains what multithreading means.

Multithreading is an innovation that makes applications more interactive and faster. *Single-threaded* applications only have the capability to execute one process at a time. While a process is executing, all other processes are stalled. Because every application is a separate process, you have the option of switching between applications in such an environment, pushing one application's processing to the foreground; this pauses all other applications, however. When a process polls the operating system for events and requests an event, the operating system checks to see whether any other processes are performing any event processing and gives them time to complete. The operating system then passes the event to the process and allocates time for it to execute. With several application processes given time to execute, the user perceives that they are running simultaneously. They are not executing their tasks simultaneously, however. If one of these processes is lengthy, it monopolizes the system's resources and other processes do not run.

Such an application would be fine for small tasks but would not be practical for Internet applications, which may need to run several applets at once or perform tasks while the user is doing something else.

Multithreaded applications have the capability to maintain multiple concurrent paths of execution. While the user is performing some action in an application, other applications can perform other tasks. These paths of execution are called *threads*.

Java is a multithreaded application. It balances thread synchronization between the class level (performed at runtime) and the language level (performed when code is written). The runtime Java interpreter runs the Garbage Collector as a low-priority background thread while executing an application's code without disturbing the performance of the application. You will see how to create multithreaded applications with the Java language in Chapter 16, "Multithreading with Java."

Java's automatic garbage collection makes programming in Java easier, eliminating many potential bugs that would arise if you managed memory explicitly. It generally provides better performance than you will find in most applications created with explicit memory management.

Summary

In this chapter, you learned to create objects, classes, and interfaces; and to declare their variables and methods. If you understand the concepts outlined in this chapter, you will have no problem moving onto the chapters in the rest of the book. In the rest of the chapters, you will have the opportunity to practice putting these concepts to work while creating actual applications.

Part

II

Building a
Java Applet

Chapter

5

by Michael Girdley

Writing a Java Applet: The Order Entry System

In the preceding four chapters, you have had an introduction to Java as an object-oriented language. You will see, as the book continues, that this is what makes Java so powerful and easy to use. In Chapter 3, "An Introduction to Java Classes," you were given an introduction to the `java.applet` and `java.awt` classes. You extend your knowledge of those classes over the next six chapters as we build the Order Entry System applet. This construction of the Order Entry System and the concepts behind it will span almost all of Part II. Finishing up Part II of this book, Chapter 11, "Reading and Writing with Java," covers reading and writing with Java.

In this chapter, the Order Entry System is described. It is constructed over the next seven chapters as you explore the implementation and dynamics of the Java language and class libraries. You explore the basic concepts behind Java applets and the Abstract Windowing Toolkit (AWT), which allows you to construct a useful applet for entering and submitting orders. By the end of Chapter 10, "The Order Entry System: Exception Handling and Browser Interaction," you will have a fully functioning system, along with the knowledge necessary to customize and maintain it.

The Sample Applet: The Order Entry System

The World Wide Web (WWW) is evolving from being a means to communicate static scientific documents in its early days to becoming an interactive and alive medium. Currently, both individuals and businesses use it as a medium for their messages to reach a worldwide audience. Java is changing the Web from being a static means of communicating. The future of the WWW, as many people predict, is to be a unique medium involving active interaction, motion, and multimedia expression.

The Order Entry System functions in this interactive capacity. It includes graphical user interface (GUI) components such as buttons, scrolling lists, and text entry fields for use by someone viewing your Web site. This chapter covers the techniques of password entry and validation in Java Applets in order to limit access to your applet. It also checks the data to make sure that the data is appropriate for entry.

The Order Entry System functions as a stand-alone window, complete with a menu bar, and has all of the functions of a working window common to operating systems, such as Windows 95, X Window, and others. This functionality is accomplished through the use of Java frames and the layout managers provided in Java; the functionality is covered in Chapter 8, "The Order Entry System: Managing the Applet Layout." The layout of the GUI components is managed using the GridBagLayout Managers to ensure a clean interface. You will be aiming to produce a professional-looking and clean-running applet in both appearance and function. In keeping with this goal, you will also add graphics-based text and figures, and a logo to the applet. Figure 5.1 shows the Order Entry System GUI.

Figure 5.1.

The Order Entry System GUI.

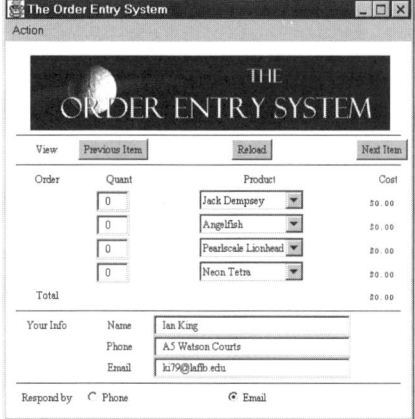

The Order Entry System takes user input from the keyboard and mouse. This is handled using code based on the concept of *events*, which are happenings that require some kind of reaction from a Java program using the AWT. For example, one such event requires the browser to command the Web browser to change its current focus to another HTML document. The concept of events in Java will be covered in the upcoming chapters. This enables the user to view, in the case of the Order Entry System, different Web documents containing descriptions of the different products available. Finally, this chapter covers the means to get the order back to you, either through e-mail or through use of CGI scripting.

You will build the Order Entry System block by block, adding more function and capability as you progress through Java concepts and their implementations. Each chapter covers an additional group of Java's capabilities and applies those to the System. But first, I need to cover some necessary concepts.

The Java AWT

Essential to Java is platform independence. As even those with just a little experience in programming know, porting programs between platforms is often a daunting task. Take, for instance, the question of how many bytes are required to store an integer type. Many systems, such as UNIX-based machines, use four bytes to store an integer. Intel machines use two. This inconsistency in changing platforms suggest what kinds of problems are posed to developers wishing to create machine-independent code. The designers of Java have attempted to circumvent these problems through careful planning.

The Java Abstract Windowing Toolkit (AWT) is the means by which GUIs are implemented in the Java language. It provides the programmer with the means to create windows utilizing buttons, text entry fields, and all of the typical elements you expect in windows systems. It allows the Java programmer to design windowing programs that can be used on any machine in which a Java bytecode interpreter and an AWT have been implemented. Above all, the AWT is important because it allows you to easily produce high-quality interactive and efficient Java applications and applets.

NOTE:

Applets, as you have seen in Chapter 3, are a special type of Java program designed to be incorporated into HTML documents. Applications are stand-alone Java programs. Their differences are covered more in depth later on in this chapter.

An important characteristic of the Java AWT is that it has been designed to be event-driven. By this, I mean that actions are delivered to your program based on the AWT, and your program handles them from there. The AWT has standardized those actions to make handling them very easy.

Also important to the portability of the AWT across different platforms and operating systems is how it handles the layout of different components. In many window systems, such as Microsoft Windows, the programmer must specify exact coordinates to specify the position of each different component of the window. This is, obviously, a problem when you are trying to design with platform-independence as a goal. What happens when you design an applet for a screen size of 1024×768 and someone tries to view it on a screen of much lower resolution? An applet that once filled the entire screen cleanly is now a mess. The AWT is designed to circumvent this problem by not specifying exact layouts for a window; instead, it uses various different lay out managers in the class library, managers that function based on general rules to lay out the components in a window. This is covered in depth in Chapter 8.

NOTE:

The AWT is designed to produce windows to appear exactly like the native windows in any system. This way, your programs are not distinctively Java when run on different platforms. They blend cleanly into the local windowing system with little or no discontinuity.

The Organization of the Java AWT

The Java AWT is designed based on the concepts of components and containers. Components are the building blocks of AWT-based applets and applications. A diagram of the inheritance hierarchy of some of the AWT is shown in Figure 5.2.

Figure 5.2.
The partial inheritance
hierarchy of the AWT.

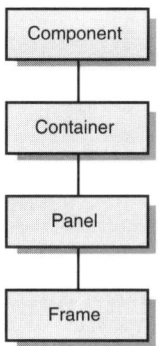

You should notice that the vast majority of the other classes of the AWT are subclasses of the class `Component`.

One subclass of the component class is containers. Containers are AWT components that function to contain other components. Containers allow you, the programmer, to break down your GUI into smaller and smaller sections until each is laid out exactly the way you want it. This is accomplished easily because containers themselves are derived from components. Because each container can apply a specific layout to the components that it is housing, the programmer has much more control.

The type `Component` can be conceptually divided into three major categories: containers, user interface components, and windowing components.

Containers

Containers hold other components, including containers themselves. The container type you see most often is the `Panel` class. Panels are the general container class that function just to hold other components. They don't do much else, but they are indispensable in the overall design goals for the AWT.

User Interface Components

User interface components are the buttons, scrolling lists, and text entry fields that you should be familiar with in dealing with any windows-based interface. Here is a list of the major interface components provided by the AWT:

Labels
Buttons
Radio buttons
Checkboxes
Lists
Choices

Text fields
Text areas
Scrollbars
Menus
Canvases

NOTE:

Canvases are special components that are, as their name implies, drawing surfaces. You are not limited to drawing just on canvases. You can also draw on panels, but as you see in later chapters, drawing on panels can lead to complications in layout and portability.

These different types of interface components, their form and their functions, are detailed in depth in the chapters to come as you build the Order Entry System.

Windowing Components

Windowing components are the components that function to produce stand-alone windows and menus in your Java applets and applications. Although these are technically a type of container, they are more easily understood if they are placed in a separate grouping aside from general containers. The major types of windowing components are frames and dialogs. Frames are the means by which you can create stand-alone windows outside of your browser; you also use frames when creating your own windowed application. Frames can include menu bars. Dialogs are limited windows. The most common type of dialog is the "OK" window, which presents a message to a user and then gets an OK to continue. Chapter 8 explores two types of dialogs: modal and non-modal. The difference between the two types is that modal dialogs allow input from the user only to its window, and no others, while it is active.

The Order Entry System contains almost all of the different components available. The System GUI is shown in Figure 5.3.

supersimple AWT-Based Applet Example

This simple applet isn't going to do much except incorporate a button and a comment field into an applet. This example is useful for you to get a feel for the basic Java applet constructors before you move on to more complex examples. In any case, here it is:

```
1.  import java.awt.*;
2.
3. public class supersimple extends java.applet.Applet
4. {
5.  public void init()
6.      {
```

```
7.          add(new Button("Order"));
8.       TextArea CommentArea = new TextArea(5,25);
9.                    CommentArea.insertText("Hal Bialeck",0);
10.        add(CommentArea);
11.     }
12.}
```

<u>Figure 5.3.</u>
The components in the
Order Entry System interface.

Frame
Menu
Canvas
Label
Button
Text field
Choice
Radio buttons

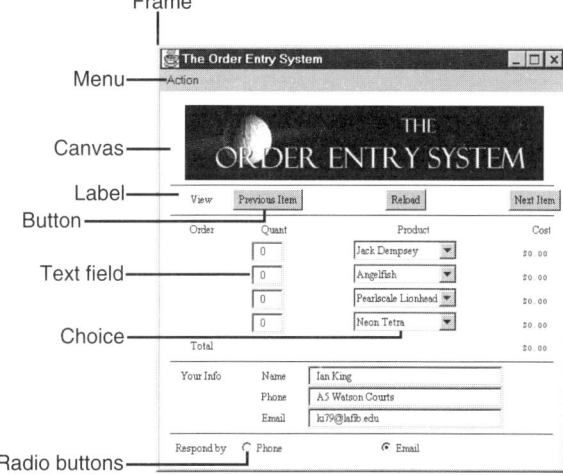

NOTE:

All applets in this book are included on the book's companion CD-ROM.

CAUTION:

Java requires that your applets are saved in the same file name as the class name. For example, if your class is named dinky, it must be saved in a file called dinky.java. You will otherwise receive an error when you try to compile it.

Line 1 imports all of the classes in the Java.awt package. Earlier chapters covered the process of importing other classes into your classes. If you are not familiar with this process, go back and review that section. You can view applets simply as classes you write to extend and modify the framework of the java.applet.Applet class. This process is specified in the class declaration in line 3.

As for the rest of the code, here is an explanation in brief (don't worry much about understanding it all now). Line 5 declares the new function init(), which overrides the method imported in the Java.applet.Applet class. Line 7 creates and inserts a button with the text Order on it. Lines 9 and 10 create a text area and insert the text Hal Bialeck in the beginning of the area. Finally, line 11 inserts the text area.

This example gives you a feel for the flow of Java applets.

Figure 5.4 shows this applet when displayed in the AppletViewer utility from the JDK.

Figure 5.4.

The supersimple AWT example applet.

NOTE:

As you found out in previous chapters, applets must be imbedded in an HTML document before they can be viewed by a Java-enhanced browser or the AppletViewer utility. How to place applets in your Web pages is covered later in this chapter. You learn how to design the HTML document to display this example.

This chapter has covered what makes up the framework of classes to produce Java-based GUIs. Next is the concept of *applets*, which are Java programs specially designed to be downloaded across the Internet and included in an HTML document displayed by a Java enhanced browser.

Applets

Applets are designed to bring the Web alive. They function to add animation, sound, and eventually complete multimedia into HTML documents. Java is also part of the future of interfacing with virtual-reality environments implemented via VRML. At present, Java is limited only by the capabilities of the Internet itself.

For more information on VRML, the Virtual Reality Markup Language for the Web, visit VRML's home at `http://www.vrml.org`.

`http://www.vrml.org`

The most important feature of applets on the Web, however, is the fact that applets change the Web from being a static medium to one based on interactivity with users. At present, Java is limited only by the capabilities of the Internet itself. As the Internet grows in data transmission, Java is ready to expand with it.

Applets are capable of commanding and interacting with the Web browser executing them.

TIP:

Remember that not everyone can view applets that you might put on your Web pages. At the time of this writing, only HotJava, Microsoft Internet Explorer, Netscape Navigator 2.0 (and above) and a number of others are Java-capable. Also, Navigator 2.0 for Microsoft Windows 3.1 does not support Java, though the current release of Navigator 3.0 for 3.1 does support it. You should, therefore, use applets merely to enhance a Web page or site, not to be the centerpiece. This limitation will change in the future as Java-capable browsers become the standard, just as browsers capable of displaying images have become the standard today. (Of course, someone will always insist on using Lynx, a text-only browser; you can't do much about these folks.)

Technically, applets are subclasses of the panel container of the AWT. They derive much of their function and form from panels. But just as the process of imbedding container upon container makes panels so powerful, the same is true about the versatility of applets. The diagram of the inheritance path of the class implementing applets, `java.applet.Applet`, is shown in Figure 5.5.

Figure 5.5.

The inheritance path of applets.

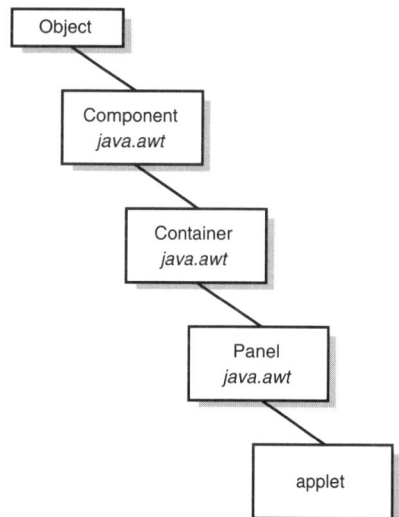

Java Applets versus Java Applications

Java programs are divided into two types: applets and applications. As I have discussed previously, applets are Java programs that are specialized for use over the Web. Applications are stand-alone Java programs that can be run via a Java interpreter, and when run in that manner they appear just as any compiled C++ or Basic program would. Since this book focuses on Java programming for the WWW, I will concentrate on applets when examining the Java language.

As you will find out in Chapter 12, "Network Programming with Java," networking with Java is powerful and easy. As Java was designed to be a networking language, many of the problems with network programming in other languages have been removed. Both Java applications and applets have access to these networking capabilities, but applets are limited in scope to where they can connect and to where they can perform input/output tasks.

Applet Limitations

As of the 1.0.2 release of Java from June of 1996, applets are limited in order to ensure the security of the user. When you are designing applets, you should be aware of limitations in the areas of read/write access, connectivity, and native language library access.

Read/Write Limitations

Applets cannot read or write to the local file system. If applets were able to access the local file system, there would be little to stop an evil applet from searching the local files for valuable information and then sending that information back to its originating server. Nothing would stop a programmer from writing an applet to reformat a hard drive or spread a virus. Obviously, allowing Java applets to have read/write privileges on local machines would be disastrous.

Connectivity Limitations

Applets cannot make connections and transfer data except from the machine from which they were downloaded. For example, say an applet was written to post form data or send e-mail messages. Although allowing this kind of access would be advantageous, it is obviously dangerous. Suppose someone wrote an applet that would send a threatening e-mail message to the President (president@whitehouse.gov) each time someone viewed a page on the Web. Allowing this kind of access would be disastrous in that no one browsing the Web would be able to trust applets they are downloading across the Internet. By their nature, applets are untrusted by Web browsers. In fact, if you run the Order Entry System you are constructing over the next six chapters in Netscape Navigator 2.0, you will be presented with a large label informing you that you are viewing an "Untrusted Applet Window." This is to keep an unscrupulous programmer from writing an applet that would disguise itself as a trusted application and prompt the user for a password that it would return to its server. This distrust of Java applets is becoming less common as more people and developers accept Java.

Native Library Access

Java has the capability to access native libraries from other languages such as C++. Applets are restricted from this feature. If this was allowed, there would be nothing to keep applets from calling native language methods that would perform some evil action. By limiting the applet's library access, the ability for a programmer to write some evil methods in another language and circumvent Java's security measures by using them in an applet is removed.

Process Limitations

Java applets are also restricted from executing any code on a local machine. This includes forking processes on UNIX systems. These limitations are entirely necessary. Say, for instance, an evil applet spawned a process to search (grep'ed in UNIX) your file system for the word *address* or *password*, and then sent an e-mail message containing the results back its server. This would be disastrous.

Hopefully, as the Internet and Java develop, the tight leash around applets will loosen. For the present day, however, you have to live with these constraints in order to take advantage of the capabilities of Java.

NOTE:

There are also other notable security concerns and solutions to these problems. They are detailed in Chapter 19, "Security Issues," which deals with security issues and Java.

The Applet Life Cycle

Applets follow a set life cycle during their execution. They are initialized, started, stopped, and destroyed. Initially, the Java bytecodes are run through a security check by an object running in the browser. Then, to start execution, the Java runtime calls the init() method of your applet.

The init() Method

The init() method is where your applet does much of its setup, such as defining its layout, parsing parameters, or setting the background colors. As with all of these methods, if you do not override the default methods provided in the java.applet.Applet class, they are called and do their normal duty. In the case of the init() method, if it isn't overridden, nothing goes on. In any case, it is still called.

If you noticed in the supersimple example discussed earlier, you utilized the init() method to set the initial layout for the applet. For the other three methods standard in the life cycle of Java applets, you simply used the default methods in the Applet class.

The start() Method

The start() method is used mainly when implementing threads in Java. You will learn more about threading in Java in Chapter 16, "Multithreading with Java," which covers threading and multithreading. If you have no clue as to what threads are, it might be helpful to glance at the beginning of that chapter.

In Java, threading is most helpful when performing audio playing or animation. In these cases, or if you want your program to be able to stop and restart, it is helpful to override the start() method and implement your own. But if this isn't the case, you can just utilize the start() method in the Applet class.

The stop() Method

The stop() method is used to do what its name suggests: stop what is going on. In it, you usually stop() the threads that you initiated in the start() method. As is the case with the start() method, if you aren't doing anything that is threaded, you do not have to worry about implementing this method in your applet.

TIP:

When a viewer leaves a page, by default, the applet continues running. Utilizing the stop() method ensures that whatever you have started in your applet stops to free up system resources.

The destroy() Method

As with the previous three methods, the destroy() method is as simple as its name. When it is called, the applet is told to free up system resources. In most general cases, you probably won't need to override this method, although there are some very special cases in which you might want more control on applet shutdowns.

Figure 5.6 is a diagram of the call path of these methods used to control Java applets.

Figure 5.6.
The life cycle of applets.

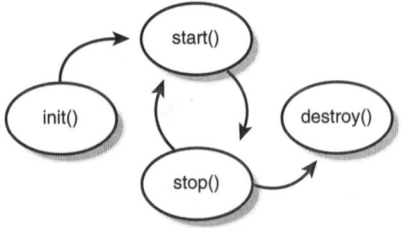

It is important to note that applet design should include multiple calls to `start()` and `stop()`; `init()` and `destroy()`, however, are never called more than once.

NOTE:

Different browsers act differently when reloading applets. Netscape Navigator 2.0 simply recalls the `start()` method of an applet when a viewer returns to a page that he or she has already visited. The AppletViewer included in the Java Developer's Kit instead reloads the entire applet from scratch. (This was a frustrating lesson learned late in one night of programming.) For this reason, you will probably always use the AppletViewer utility when testing your applets. You will need to use trial and error to figure out how your specific browser functions.

Ideally, I would have liked to include an example demonstrating the life cycle of a Java applet. However, to do so would mean incorporating threading, and that would complicate things more than helping. For the present time, keep these applet characteristics in mind as you develop the Order Entry System in the chapters to come.

Adding Applets to Web Pages

This section covers the HTML codes specific to Java applets and how to include them in your Web pages. You should have a small amount of familiarity with the way HTML works before going through this section. If you don't, it would be best if you looked at one of the many books or Web documents available to teach HTML. A good source of information is Laura Lemay's *Teach Yourself HTML in a Week*. Many good Web documents teach HTML. Many of them are available on-line.

This section familiarizes you with how two browsers utilize Java: Netscape Navigator version 2.0 and above, and Sun's HotJava. This section covers the tags for declaring an applet in a Web page, parameters, and other features of HTML code for implementing applets. You will be, if nothing else, entirely comfortable with the process of putting not only your own applets into your pages, but also those written by programmers (those who give you permission, of course).

Netscape Navigator and Applets

Netscape has pushed long and hard to continue developments above and beyond its competition in the Web browser arena. By releasing its software for free, Netscape has attracted millions of new users and continues doing so through technical advances. The 1.0.2 version of Java is included in the JDK on the CD-ROM with this book. Most surveys report that the Navigator is far and away the dominant browser on the market today.

NOTE:

You can assume that most of the other browsers on the market today will follow the Netscape format of applet inclusion in HTML documents. This is the same for Microsoft Internet Explorer and IBM's releases of its Web Explorer.

NOTE:

Navigator 2.0x currently supports Java only when run in operating systems that easily support multithreading, such as Windows 95 and X Windows for UNIX machines. It is also supported under the MacOS on Power Macs and Windows NT. Sadly, this leaves Windows 3.1 users unable to view Java applets under Navigator 2.0. However, the 3.0 test release of Navigator, currently named "Atlas," does include Java support for Windows 3.1.

HTML Coding for Applets in Netscape

The initiating tag for inserting an applet in an HTML document is the `<APPLET>` tag. It is followed later by the `</APPLET>` tag, which signifies that all HTML code between the two tags is focused on the applet.

NOTE:

Note that only the HTML code between the tags is related to the applet, not the text inside of the two tags. This enables you to place text on a page just for people using browsers not enhanced for Java.

The `<APPLET>` tag follows this format:

```
<APPLET CODE = "yourclass.class" WIDTH = 200 HEIGHT = 100>
```

This tells the browser the following:

- ○ That it should place an applet on the page
- ○ The name of the applet
- ○ The size it should allocate for display of the applet

By default, the browser looks in the directory in which it finds the HTML document to find the applet. However, there is another parameter available, the `CODEBASE` parameter, that allows you to specify where the browser should look to find your applet code. Here is an example of this feature:

```
<APPLET CODEBASE = "myapplets" CODE = "king.class" WIDTH = 10 HEIGHT = 0>
</APPLET>
```

You can also specify your code to be loaded from another site in the following manner:

```
<APPLET CODEBASE = "http://coolapplets.com/java/"
    CODE = "theirapplet.class"
    WIDTH = 100 HEIGHT = 50>
</APPLET>
```

This code says to the browser: "I want you to insert an applet named `theirapplet.class` and you can find it at `http://coolapplets.com/java`. Make it a width of 100 pixels and a height of 50 pixels." To sum it up, the `CODE` parameter tells the browser what applet to get, and the `CODEBASE` parameter specifies where to look for it.

Parameters and Applets

Java programs can be written to accept parameters specified in between the `<APPLET>` and `</APPLET>` tags. The following HTML code demonstrates this feature.

```
<APPLET CODEBASE = "http://discus.com/fish/and/Java"
    CODE = "angelfish.class"
    WIDTH = 100
    HEIGHT = 50>
<PARAM NAME = betta value=1>
<PARAM NAME = cichlid value = "Jack Dempsey">
</APPLET>
```

This code does the same as the previous example except it also provides some variables for the applet to access. Chapter 10 covers how to handle these parameters in our applets.

Aligning the Applets

Just as with images, you are able to specify in your HTML code how you want to align your applets relative to other items on your page. Here is an example of the HTML declaration of an applet that included alignment of the applet:

```
<APPLET CODEBASE = "http://phil.com/gd/java/"
    CODE = "lesh.class"
    WIDTH = 100
    HEIGHT = 500
    ALIGN = ABSMIDDLE>
</APPLET>
```

If the terms `ABSMIDDLE` and `BASELINE` aren't familiar to you, I would strongly suggest reviewing alignment in HTML documents. Wise and proper alignment is the key to producing professional quality HTML pages, with or without Java.

NOTE:

| Just as HTML is case-insensitive, so are these applet-specific HTML codes.

Feature Focus

There are three other notable parameters available to you: HSPACE, VSPACE, and NAME. By setting the HSPACE and VSPACE values, you can specify the horizontal and vertical space, respectively, that the browser places between your applet and text. The NAME parameter allows you to give your applet a name that can be used when creating applets. The name is used when two different applets on the same page wish to communicate with each other.

Displaying the supersimple Example Applet

As promised earlier in this chapter, here is the full HTML code for placing the supersimple applet:

```
1. <HTML>
2. <HEAD>
3. <TITLE>The supersimple Applet</TITLE>
4. </HEAD>
5. <BODY BGCOLOR = #FFFFFF>
6. This is the supersimple Example Applet:
7. <APPLET CODE = "supersimple.class" WIDTH = 100 HEIGHT = 50 ALIGN = ABSMIDDLE>
8.   <hr>
9.   Your browser does not support Java.
10. Go get a real one.
11.   </APPLET>
12.</BODY>
13. </HTML>
```

This HTML document, viewed through the AppletViewer utility, is shown in Figure 5.7.

Figure 5.7.

This HTML code when displayed by the Appletviewer.

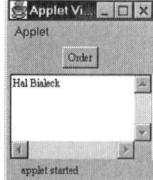

This code simply inserts the supersimple applet onto an HTML document with a white background. On a Java-capable browser and through the AppletViewer utility, this all comes out fine. However, on a browser not able to display applets, the text inside is displayed. Figure 5.8 shows what happens when viewed from a non-Java enhanced browser.

Figure 5.8.
The above HTML viewed through Netscape 2.0 for Windows 3.1.

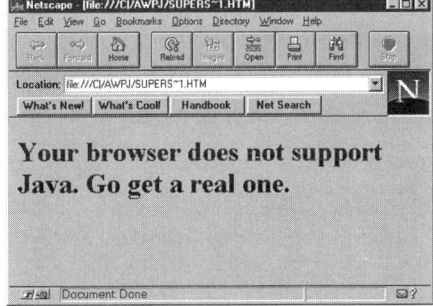

TIP:

When including applets on your Web site, you can specify alternate text in the <APPLET> declaration for people viewing your site without browsers capable of Java. To do this, just put the text after the <APPLET> tag and before the </APPLET> end tag. Browsers with Java capabilities concentrate on the applet and parameters, while those without Java features ignore everything but the text and display it accordingly. You can also include ALT = "*your alternate text here*" in the <APPLET> tag to specify alternate text, although simply adding HTML between the tags works on many more browsers.

Applets and HotJava

The HotJava browser released by Sun was actually written with the Java language. HotJava, being written in Java itself, demonstrates the capabilities of the Java language. However, there is a big catch in using it: HotJava currently supports only an earlier alpha release of the Java language. Sadly, browsers capable of the beta release and later releases, such as Netscape Navigator, are not compatible with these alpha release applets. For now, the vast majority of applets are being written and compiled in Java 1.0 beta and later. As of the time of this writing, Java is in the 1.0.2 release.

NOTE:

In fact, the Java compiler was also written in Java. You may ask yourself how this might work—how could they compile the compiler without a compiler? It was originally written in C.

As of the time of this writing, HotJava is in pre-beta release. By the time you read this, it should be available in full release to handle the Java 1.02 release.

For a comprehensive listing of applets on the Web, a good place to start is Gamelan at `http://www.gamelan.com/`.

 `http://www.gamelan.com/`

However, numerous alpha 3 release applets are available. If you are looking to see everything that's out there, it would be wise to fire up HotJava at least once and go looking for alpha-based applets. A good place to start is Gamelan at `http://www.gamelan.com/`.

Here is the form for including alpha 3 release Java applets in your Web pages:

```
<APP CODE = yourapplet NAME1 = "a value" NAME2 = 456 . . . >
```

In this example, `NAME1` and `NAME2` are replaced by the names of your parameters to your applet. There is no limit to the number of parameters. Also, note that the `CODE` parameter does not require you to place `.class` after your applet name. Finally, there is no `</APP>` tag, so including alternate text is impossible in the alpha 3 release.

Get the latest version of Java, HotJava, and related information at `http://java.sun.com/`.

 `http://java.sun.com/`

If you want to go all out, you can write your applet both in the alpha release and in the later releases. To include both, simply insert the `<APP>` tag in between the `<APPLET>` tag and the `</APPLET>` tag. This displays your alpha 3 release applet for HotJava and the Java beta applet for browsers that support that release. Remember, you can always get the latest version of Java, HotJava, and related information on the Web at `http://java.sun.com/`.

What's Been Done So Far

This chapter has covered some key ideas to Java and how you are going to apply those ideas in constructing the Order Entry System applet. This chapter has discussed what applets are; how they are born, live, and die; and how applets differ from full-blown Java applications. This chapter also covered what you can and cannot do with applets. It covered a sample applet and gave you a feel for the flow and layout of Java programs.

This chapter has also discussed what the Abstract Windowing Toolkit (AWT) is, and its power and implementation. The insertion of applets into HTML documents was also covered for both the alpha 3 and later releases. Hopefully, this chapter has successfully managed to cut through all of the fluff and get down to the important concepts of Java applets and the Java language itself.

What's Coming Up

Here is a brief summary of what is going to be covered in the rest of Part II.

Chapter 6, "The Order Entry System: Adding Features and Handling Events," covers the inclusion of AWT components into your applets and into the Order Entry System. It also covers how user actions, which are events in the AWT, are handled and how your program deals with them.

Chapter 7, "The Order Entry System: Entry Fields, Labels, and Validation," deals with including more of the AWT components including text entry fields and data validation. Where Chapter 6 dealt with the inclusion of graphical AWT components, the components in this section deal with text focused components such as labels, and text areas.

Chapter 8, "The Order Entry System: Managing the Applet Layout," describes why and how to manage the layout of the applet. The chapter also covers the concepts of frames, which permit stand-alone windows in your applets, and also menu bars. This chapter also covers the multiple layout managers in the AWT and how and when to use them.

Chapter 9, "The Order Entry System: Adding Graphics and a Logo," handles two concepts of images and graphics in the Order Entry System and how to use those ideas in other projects. This chapter improves the appearance of the Order Entry System. It also covers the MediaTracker class, which enables you to control the loading of images.

Finally, Chapter 10, "The Order Entry System: Exception Handling and Browser Interaction," covers the process of Java exceptions and error-handling. It also deals with communicating with the browser displaying your applet. And to finish it up, it covers how to get the order back to you.

At the end of it all, you will have a fully functioning and good-looking applet in the Order Entry System. It will be able to take an order from across the Internet and get it back to you. Best of all, by the end of this part, you will have the knowledge necessary to customize the Order Entry System and also to create your own quality applets for the Web.

Chapter

6

by Michael Girdley

The Order Entry System: Adding Features and Handling Events

This chapter looks into the use and description of the java.AWT concepts of containers and components. Part of this chapter covers the implementation of some of the components. The graphical components of the AWT are covered in this chapter, while others are left for later chapters. Here is a list of the components that are covered in this chapter:

> Buttons
> Checkboxes
> Radio buttons
> Choice menus
> Lists
> Scrolling lists
> Sliders and scrollbars

NOTE:

Notice that the component Canvas is left out of this chapter. It is a graphic component, but for organizational purposes it is included in Chapter 9, "The Order Entry System: Adding Graphics and a Logo."

This chapter also covers the implementation of handling user inputs, or *events*. This concept is touched on in the preceding chapter, but to sum it up, events are basically what their name says, "something happening." Some events are mouse clicks, keyboard presses, and events created by your own program to "fake" an event. All these events are covered in the "Handling Events" section of this chapter.

Finally, this chapter applies the concepts of components, applets, the AWT, and events to the Order Entry System. In building the Order Entry System applet, this chapter exercises these features in the process of coding a larger program. This is the area in which many instructional books are lacking.

But first, I'll get into some components.

Graphical Components

If you remember from the preceding chapter, the component class is the keystone to the AWT. The vast majority of the available classes in the AWT derive from this class. This includes the container class, which is one of the subclasses of the component class. This is the main reason that you can place components in containers, and so on. This feature is useful when you manage the layout of the Order Entry System in Chapter 8, "The Order Entry System: Managing the Applet Layout," but for now, just appreciate the power of components and the AWT as a whole.

Components come in many shapes and sizes. As I stated before, this chapter covers the components that are graphics-oriented. Of course, all the components are graphical in nature. They are drawn just as any other GUI item is, but the components covered in this chapter are those that are not text-oriented, meaning not designed for the output or input of text. Placing all the components in one large section may seem to be the most logical, but dividing them into two groups keeps you from being bombarded by 12 explanations at once and also facilitates reference use of the book. Text-oriented components are covered in Chapter 7, "The Order Entry System: Entry Fields, Labels, and Validation."

The simplest components are buttons, which are covered next.

Buttons

In the AWT, buttons are like the buttons found on virtually every GUI system. Listing 6.1 is an applet that demonstrates the insertion of buttons in an applet.

Listing 6.1. The heyabutton applet code.

```
1.// Import all of the java.awt package and the applet package.
2. import java.awt.*;
3. import java.applet.*;
4. // Declare the heyabutton class.
5. public class heyabutton extends Applet
6.     {
7.
8.      // Create a variable aButton of the Button class.
9.     private Button aButton;
10.        // Overriding the default init() method.
11.      public void init()
12.            {
13.             // Allocate space for the Button.
14.              aButton = new Button("Longhorn");
15.             // Add the button to the Applet panel.
16.              add(aButton);
17.            }
18.    }
```

The heyabutton class, when viewed from the AppletViewer utility, is shown in Figure 6.1.

Figure 6.1.

The heyabutton applet
when viewed from the
AppletViewer utility.

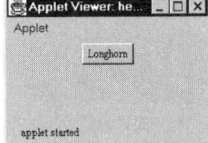

Line 1 makes all the classes from the `java.awt` package available to you. Line 2 does the same with the applet package. Line 3 says that this program extends the applet class in the library. In other words, it is a subclass of the applet class and shares all functionality of it. You are, of course, overriding some of the inherited methods with your own declarations. In this applet, the code in line 6 is doing just that. This line declares a void that overrides the standard `init()` method with your own code.

But before that, line 5 declares a `private` button, which means that, for the purposes of object-oriented design and data encapsulation, the variable is local to this class and not accessible from outside. The `button` type is contained in the file `java.awt.Button`.

Line 8 uses the `new` method, "make `aButton` a new instance of the `Button` class." Now, `aButton` is your very own instance of the `java.awt.Button` class from the library.

So what do you do with it? You have a button; now add the component to the applet using Java's `add()` method. The method `add()` is common to all containers that place a component in the container. (Exactly where it goes is covered with the applet layout in Chapter 8.) For now, it's enough to know that it puts its parameter in the container from which it is called. Here's an example:

```
add(aPanel);
```

This line adds the `aPanel` component to the current container. The following code adds the `aButton` component to the container `somecontainer`:

```
somecontainer.add(aButton);
```

That is the end of the functional part of the applet and the coverage of buttons and how to add components.

TIP:

After you have a good bit of Java knowledge, it's a good idea to go into the libraries and check out the contents. If you have experience with object-oriented design programs, such as C++, the library structure should be familiar. If not, Java is a good language to start with when you are trying to get into object-oriented design.

The process of looking at the methods, looking at the data structures, and going through the implementation does a great deal for your debugging and code design efforts.

Checkboxes

A *checkbox* is like its name sounds: it's a box you put a check in. Checkboxes are either on or off, selected or unselected. The mouse click (or a tab down) on the checkbox toggles its value, making a checked box unselected and vice versa. You use checkboxes when you are creating an interface that needs to get data that is either yes or no. For example, "Would you like to be included on our mailing list?"

Checkboxes are created using the class java.awt.Checkbox of the AWT.

NOTE:

| The line numbers in the following example are for ease of reference only.

Here is the standard constructor for creating a checkbox:

```
1. private Checkbox aCheckbox;
2. aCheckbox = new Checkbox();
```

Of course, you can combine these two statements:

```
1. Checkbox aCheckbox = new Checkbox();
```

Checkboxes, like most classes implemented in Java, are overloaded to be able to accept different combinations of input. This is a feature shared with C++ and some other languages designed to facilitate object-oriented programming.

To create a checkbox and set the label, use the following format:

```
Checkbox aCheckboxpluslabel = new Checkbox("Label here!");
```

To set the checkbox's initial value, you can include another parameter:

```
Checkbox anotherCheckbox = new Checkbox("Label here!", null, true);
```

In this constructor, the first parameter is the label, and the third parameter is the initial starting value. The second parameter places the checkbox into a CheckboxGroup. This is used to create radio buttons, which are a group of checkboxes in which only one of them can be selected at the same time. Listing 6.2 is an applet that creates and inserts four checkboxes into an applet.

Listing 6.2. The heysomecheckboxes applet code.

```
1. import java.awt.*;
2. import java.applet.*;
3. public class heysomecheckboxes extends Applet
4.    {
5.        // Override the initialize method.
6.        public void init()
7.            {
8.                // Declare the four checkboxes and set their labels.
9.                Checkbox JonBox = new Checkbox("Jon");
10.               Checkbox IanBox = new Checkbox("Ian");
11.               Checkbox NateBox = new Checkbox("Nate");
12.               Checkbox MichaelBox = new Checkbox("Michael");
13.               // Add the four checkboxes to the applet panel.
14.               add(JonBox);
15.               add(IanBox);
16.               add(NateBox);
17.               add(MichaelBox);
18.            }
19.    }
```

Lines 1 through 6 do the same standard stuff: declare the applet and import classes, for example. Lines 9 through 12 create four checkboxes, each with a different label. In this case, four different names are used. This is helpful if you use an applet (or application) to report work done on a project and you need to say who has worked on or contributed to the project. Lines 14 through 16 add these boxes to the applet. Figure 6.2 shows this applet displayed in the AppletViewer utility.

Figure 6.2.

The `heysomecheckboxes` applet when viewed from the AppletViewer utility.

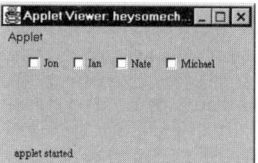

There are four checkboxes with corresponding labels on the applet. Easy enough, right? Sometimes, though, you may want only one checkbox in a group of checkboxes to be true at any one time. This situation is covered in the section on radio buttons.

Here are some of the methods available for controlling instances of checkboxes:

`getState()`	This method is a function that returns the current state of the calling instance of a checkbox. Remember, the state of checkboxes is either true or false.
`setState(boolean)`	This method allows you to set the state of the calling instance.
`getLabel()`	This method returns the label of an instance of the checkbox class. The label is of type `String`.
`setLabel(string)`	This method allows you to set the label of a checkbox to a new string.

Coordinated Checkboxes: Radio Buttons

The preceding section covered the addition of checkboxes to applets. The preceding example had the checkboxes operate independently of each other. But often you want only one checkbox to be true at a time. This behavior is characteristic of radio buttons in Java.

There isn't a specific type of `RadioButton`. Instead, radio buttons are created by creating a group of checkboxes and specifying the initial checkbox to be selected. This group is defined by a class called (surprisingly) `CheckboxGroup`. The class `CheckboxGroup` allows you to group checkboxes and then manages the states of each checkbox in the group so that only one is selected at a time. Here is a sample declaration of a `CheckboxGroup`:

```
private CheckboxGroup NameBoxGroup;
NameBoxGroup = new CheckboxGroup();
```

The process of adding checkboxes to the group is easy. When you declare a checkbox, you add the group name as another parameter. For example, you declare a checkbox and want to include it in the group declared above, NameBoxGroup. You also want it to be the box that starts with its value as true. Here is how you do it:

```
JonBox = new Checkbox("Jon", NameBoxGroup, true);
```

Do this for each checkbox you want in the group and you're ready to go. Listing 6.3 takes the previous example, the heysomecheckboxes applet, and extends it to include the four names to act as radio buttons. The new applet is the HeyaCheckBoxGroup applet.

Listing 6.3. The HeyaCheckBoxGroup applet code.

```
1.  // import all of the classes in the java.awt and applet packages
2.  import java.awt.*;
3.  import java.applet.*;
4.  // declare the class HeyaCheckBoxGroup.
5.  public class HeyaCheckBoxGroup extends Applet
6.     {
7.         // Overriding the standard init() void.
8.         public void init()
9.            {
10.               // Declare the NameGroup as a CheckboxGroup().
11.                  CheckboxGroup NameGroup = new CheckboxGroup();
12.               // Declare the JonBox as a new Checkbox(), and
                     do the same for  four more boxes.
                  // Also, set the JonBox to be initially true while
                     the rest are false.
13.               Checkbox JonBox = new Checkbox("Jon",NameGroup,true);
14.               Checkbox IanBox = new Checkbox("Ian",NameGroup,false);
15.               Checkbox NateBox = new Checkbox("Nate",NameGroup,false);
16.               Checkbox MichaelBox = new Checkbox("Michael",NameGroup,false);
17.
18.                // Add all of the Checkboxes to the applet panel.
19.               add(JonBox);
20.               add(IanBox);
21.               add(NateBox);
22.               add(MichaelBox);
23.            }
24.     }
```

This applet declares an instance of CheckboxGroup in line 10. Lines 13 through 16 declare four checkboxes and insert them into the NameGroup with the JonBox being set initially true. Then the four boxes are added to the applet using the add method in lines 19 through 22. Figure 6.3 shows this applet.

Figure 6.3.

The HeyaCheckBoxGroup applet when viewed from the AppletViewer utility.

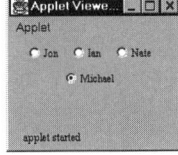

Other methods are available in checkboxes that deal with checkbox groups:

`getCheckboxGroup()`	This allows you to get the group to which a checkbox belongs.
`setCheckboxGroup(CheckboxGroup cbg)`	This allows you to change the group to which a checkbox belongs. It takes an instance of `CheckboxGroup` as a parameter.

Also, the `setCurrent(Checkbox)` and `getCurrent()` methods of the `CheckboxGroup` class allow you to set and get the currently chosen checkbox.

Pop-Up Choice Lists

Pop-up choice lists allow you to combine many different choices into one area. A large number of radio buttons can become unwieldy, so this type of choice list puts many different choices into one compact area. Figure 6.4 is an applet that features a pop-up choice list viewed from the AppletViewer utility:

Figure 6.4.

A choice list.

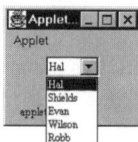

Choice boxes come from the `java.awt.Choice` class. To declare a new choice box, you can use the following code:

```
Choice names = new Choice();
```

To insert items into the list, you use the `addItem()` method of the `Choice` class. The `addItem()` method takes a string as a parameter. Here is the code to place the four names—Jon, Ian, Nate, and Hal—into the choice list called `names`:

```
names.addItem("Jon");
names.addItem("Ian");
names.addItem("Nate");
names.addItem("Hal");
```

The items are listed in the pop-up choice list in the order in which they are added. The selection in the box is the current selection of the choice list. To change it, use the method `select()`. It is overloaded to accept both integers and strings. Should you want to select the third choice in a list initially, use the code:

```
names.select(3);
```

To choose the string `"Jon"`, you use the following:

```
names.select("Jon");
```

The `getItem()` method allows you to get the string at a certain position if you know the index. Simply give it an integer, and it returns the string at that position. Also, after you put an item in the list, it is there for good; there is no way to get it out.

Scrolling Choice Lists

On some occasions, you want to have all the selections available for viewing at one time. You can do so by using scrolling lists. They allow more than one item to be selected at a time. Figure 6.5 shows an applet that contains a scrolling list.

Figure 6.5.

A scrolling choice list.

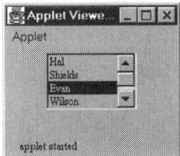

Lists are declared using the following constructors:

`List()`	This is the default constructor. Only one choice may be selected at a time.
`List(int, boolean)`	This creates a scrolling list of the size defined in the integer parameter, and the `Boolean` flag sets the ability to have multiple selections. `True` means that it can have multiple selections; `false` means it can't.

Here is an example construction of a list that specifies six items able to be viewed at one time and allows multiple selections at one time:

```
List Names = new List(6, true);
```

As with pop-up choice lists, you use the `addItem()` method of lists to insert items into the list:

```
Names.addItem("Hal");
Names.addItem("Nate");
Names.addItem("Evan");
```

Another instance of the `addItem` method allows you to set where you want the next item inserted in the list. Here is an example that places another name at position four in the list:

```
Names.addItem("Ignacio",4);
```

You can also use the `select()` method to set which items you want initially selected. The following two lines set the first and fourth items in the list to be highlighted:

```
Names.select(1);
Names.select(4);
```

Figure 6.6 shows the preceding declaration, plus a few more, added into an applet viewed through the AppletViewer utility.

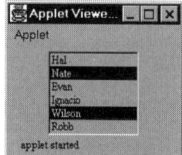

Figure 6.6.

The `ScrollListExample`
applet viewed through the
AppletViewer utility.

Listing 6.4 shows the `ScrollListExample` applet code.

Listing 6.4. The `ScrollListExample` applet code.

```
1. // import all of the classes in the java.awt and applet packages
2. import java.awt.*;
3. import java.applet.*;
4. // declare the class HeyaCheckBoxGroup.
5. public class ScrollListExample extends Applet
6.     {
7.         // Overriding the standard init() void.
8.         public void init()
9.             {
10.                 List Names = new List(6,true);
11.
12.                 Names.addItem("Hal");
13.                 Names.addItem("Nate");
14.                 Names.addItem("Ignacio,4");
15.                 Names.addItem("Yi");
16.                 Names.addItem("Wilson");
17.                 Names.addItem("Robb");
18.                 Names.select(1);
19.                 Names.select(4);
20.                 add(Names);
21.             }
22.}
```

A number of other useful methods are available in the `List()` class:

`clear()`	This removes all the items from the list.
`getItem(integer)`	This returns the string at the index specified by the parameter.
`countItems()`	This returns an integer specifying the number of items currently in the list.
`replaceItem(string, integer)`	This replaces the item at the index specified by the integer with the string.

getSelectedIndex()	This returns an integer specifying the position in a list of the selected item.
getSelectedIndexes()	This returns an array of integers, each of which specify the indexes of all the selected items.
getSelectedItems()	This returns an array of strings that are all the selected items at the current time.
getSelectedItem()	This returns the string that is currently selected.

Scrollbars

Scrollbars are common to every graphical user interface system. In the AWT, they are used to scroll areas such as lists and sliders, which are a graphical means to set values. Figure 6.7 shows a small applet that includes a slider.

Figure 6.7.
An applet with a slider.

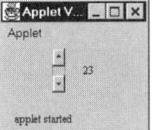

As sliders, scrollbars are used to input a value to the program from the user. The programmer can set the initial minimum value, the maximum value, the orientation, and the visible area of the scrollbar. You also can set how the scrollbar changes per different user actions. This activity is described later in this chapter when the process of handling events in the AWT is covered.

This section covers the construction of instances of the Scroll() type and their implementation. Chapter 8 covers using scrollbars to scroll through a window. There are two major ways to construct a scrollbar.

Scrollbar(*int*) constructs a scrollbar and sets the initial orientation (vertical or horizontal) of the scrollbar. The *int* you send in is either Scrollbar.HORIZONTAL or Scrollbar.VERTICAL. These are the only values currently available to you. You can then later use the setValues(*int initial, int visiblearea, int min, int max*) method to set the initial value, the visible area of the window, the minimum value, and the maximum value for the scrollbar, respectively.

Scrollbar(*int orientation, int visiblearea, int initial, int min, int max*), takes five parameters (in this order): the orientation (either Scrollbar.HORIZONTAL or Scrollbar.VERTICAL), the visible area value, the initial value, the minimum value, and the maximum value.

The page value is the amount that the value of the scrollbar changes when a user clicks on the area between the end arrow and the current position. To set the page increment value, use the setPageIncrement(*int pageincrement*) method, which takes an integer parameter and makes that value the page value.

The line increment is the amount that the scrollbar changes when a user clicks on the end arrow of the scrollbar. The method to change or set this value is the `setLineIncrement(int lineincrement)` method of the `Scrollbar` class. As with the `setPageIncrement(int pageincrement)` method, this method accepts an integer.

Listing 6.5 is a sample applet that contains two scrollbars, using both of the `Scrollbar()` constructors discussed previously.

Listing 6.5. The `TwoScrollBars` applet code.

```
1. import java.awt.*;
2.
3. public class TwoScrollBars extends java.applet.Applet
4.      {
5.         public void init()
6.             {
7.                // Declare the Vertical Bar as a horizontal scrollbar.
8.                Scrollbar VertBar = new Scrollbar(Scrollbar.VERTICAL);
9.                // Set the values to be: initial value 25,
10.                  visible, area to 35, min to 0, max to 200.
11.                VertBar.setValues(25, 25, 0, 200);
12.                    // Add the scrollbar to the applet panel.
13.                add(VertBar);
14.
15.                // Declare the HorizBar as a horizontal scroll bar,
16.                  with initial 16. value 10, visible area of 50,
17.                //minimum of 0, and maximium of 200.
18.                Scrollbar HorizBar = new Scrollbar
19.                 (ScrollBar.HORIZONTAL, 10, 50, 0, 200);
20.                 // Add the HorizBar to the applet panel.
21.                add(HorizBar);
22.                }
23.}
```

Lines 1 through 6 do the standard stuff: declare the applet and import classes. Line 8 declares the scrollbar and sets the initial orientation of the `VertBar` variable. Then the `setValue()` method is used to set the initial value, the visible area, the minimum value, and the maximum value. The scrollbar is then added to the applet panel. In lines 15 through 21, basically the same thing happens, except that all the setup done in setting and adding the HorizBar is done in lines 18, 19, and 21.

NOTE:

There are actually more constructors for creating scrollbars. However, in the end, they all produce the same product and are just as easy. By providing you with the "all in one" constructor that takes five parameters, and also including a minimalist constructor that takes only one parameter, I hope that you are getting a feel for the whole range of constructors.

Here is a summary of the `Scrollbar` methods and declarations:

`Scrollbar(int orientation, int visiblearea, int initial, int min, int max)`   The parameters set the orientation, visible area, initial value, minimum value, and maximum value respectively.

`setPageIncrement(int)`   As discussed previously, this sets the page increment. This is the amount that the scrollbar changes when the user clicks between the current position and the endpoint.

`setLineIncrement(int)`   As discussed above, this sets the line increment. The line increment is the amount that the scrollbar changes when the user clicks on the end arrow of the scrollbar.

`setValues(int initial, int visible area, int min, int max)`   This is the method to set the initial value, the visible area of the window, the minimum value, and the maximum value for the scrollbar respectively.

`int getValue()`   This returns the current value, an integer, of the scrollbar. This is the main method used later when making scrollbars active.

In any of the examples discussed in this chapter, you may notice that something is wrong. The insertion and setup of these different components of the AWT are covered except how to handle them when something happens with them. For example, nothing happens when you click on the buttons that have been created. Handling user actions like button selection is covered later in this chapter. But first, let's get started on creating the Order Entry System.

Getting Started on the Order Entry System

This section covers how to create and insert the different components to be used onto the applet panel. Don't worry about the positioning of the buttons. This is taken care of when you manage the applet layout in Chapter 8. For now, just worry about creating the components and slapping them down.

Also, notice that the Order Entry System exists as a stand-alone window. This also is covered in Chapter 8. Finally, the logo is left out for now because it is covered in Chapter 9.

Ideally, you want to use every component to give yourself a feel for them. So give it a shot, even though it may complicate matters. For the time being, you are going to implement the components covered in this chapter.

To start off, import all the AWT classes and also the Applet package as follows:

```
import java.awt.*;
import java.applet.*;
```

And then declare the applet class like this:

```
public class OrderEntrySystem extends Applet {
```

The customary place to initialize and set up your applet is in the `init()` method. So, declare the `init()` method and insert and declare your first component, a button that reads Submit. Here is the code segment that declares the button and inserts it onto the applet panel:

```
Button SubmitButton = new Button("Submit");
add(SubmitButton);
```

Continue doing the same tasks for two more buttons labeled Quit and Clear, in the same manner. Next, insert a checkbox that asks if the person using the system is a repeat customer:

```
Checkbox RepeatCustCheckBox = new Checkbox("Repeat Customer?");
add(RepeatCustCheckBox);
```

You also should query the users as to how they are to be contacted. The choices are phone, e-mail, or U.S. mail. A radio button setup is ideal for this query since you want only one button to be active at one time. The first step in creating radio buttons is to create an instance of the `CheckboxGroup` class that coordinates the behavior of all the instances of the `Checkbox` class. Add the following:

```
private CheckboxGroup ContactMethodGroup;
ContactMethodGroup = new ContactMethodGroup();
```

Next, create the buttons you're going to put in the group, using the declaration method specified previously:

```
Checkbox EmailBox = new Checkbox("Email",ContactMethodGroup,true);
Checkbox PhoneBox = new Checkbox("Phone",ContactMethodGroup,false);
```

And so on for the rest of the buttons. Because you'd rather e-mail, set the Email button to be initially true while the rest are false. Also, remember to `add()` all the buttons. There are a number of products to choose from in the applet, so set a means to choose from a number of products. Chapter 11, "Reading and Writing with Java," touches on how you could read in a file that contains all the products and prices. For now, set all the products in the program. First, construct the `ProductList` class as an instance of the `List` class and add some of the products.

```
List ProductList = new List(4, false);
ProductList.addItem("Oscar");
ProductList.addItem("Lionhead");
ProductList.addItem("Jack Dempsey");
ProductList.addItem("Angelfish");
.
.
```

The first parameter sets the list to have four items visible at a time. The second sets the list so that only one item may be selected at a time. There's also a pop-up choice box to let the user select the size of the product (in this case, fish) that he or she wants. To declare a choice box, you use much the same code as above.

Finally, the last component to add is a slider. This is used to allow the user to input the amount of each product that he or she wants to order. Here is the declaration for the slider:

```
Scrollbar OrderAmountSlider = new Scrollbar(Scrollbar.VERTICAL, 0, 0, 0, 100);
add(OrderAmountSlider);
```

The scrollbar is declared to be vertically oriented, with a visible area of zero, an initial value of zero, a minimum of zero, and a maximum of 100.

Listing 6.6 is the complete code listing, showing what you should have so far in building the Order Entry System.

Listing 6.6. The `OrderEntrySystem` applet code so far.

```java
import java.awt.*;
import java.applet.*;
public class OrderEntrySystem extends Applet {
     public void init()
        {
          // Add and create three buttons.
             Button SubmitButton = new Button("Submit");
          add(SubmitButton);
          Button ClearButton = new Button("Clear");
          add(ClearButton);
           Button QuitButton = new Button("Quit");
          add(QuitButton);
          // Add and create the repeat customer checkbox.
           Checkbox RepeatCustCheckBox = new Checkbox("Repeat Customer?");
          add(RepeatCustCheckBox);
          // Declare the CheckboxGroup, and allocate space.
          CheckboxGroup ContactMethodGroup;
          ContactMethodGroup = new CheckboxGroup();
          // Create some checkboxes to put in the group.
            Checkbox EmailBox = new
            Checkbox("Email",ContactMethodGroup,true);
          Checkbox PhoneBox = new
            Checkbox("Phone",ContactMethodGroup,false);
          Checkbox MailBox = new
            Checkbox("US Mail",ContactMethodGroup,false);
          // Add the checkboxes into the applet panel.
          add(EmailBox);
          add(PhoneBox);
          add(MailBox);
          // Create the list, 4 items visible, no multiple
          // selections.
          List ProductList = new List(4, false);
          // AddItems to the List.
          ProductList.addItem("Oscar");
          ProductList.addItem("Lionhead");
          ProductList.addItem("Jack Dempsey");
          ProductList.addItem("Angelfish");
          // Add the List to the Applet panel.
          add(ProductList);
          // Create the Choice box.
          Choice SizeChoice = new Choice();
          // AddItems to the List.
          SizeChoice.addItem("Jumbo");
          SizeChoice.addItem("Large");
          SizeChoice.addItem("Medium");
          SizeChoice.addItem("Small");
          // Add the Choice to the Applet panel.
```

continues

Listing 6.6. continued

```
        add(SizeChoice);
        // Create a vertical slider, initial value of 0,
        // minimum value of 0, maximum value of 144.
          Scrollbar OrderAmountSlider = new
          Scrollbar(Scrollbar.VERTICAL, 0, 0, 0, 100);
        // Insert the slider to the Applet panel.
        add(OrderAmountSlider);
          }
}
```

Figure 6.8 shows what you see when you view this applet through the AppletViewer utility.

Figure 6.8.

The start of the Order
Entry System applet.

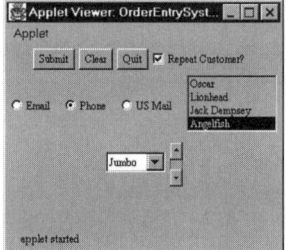

What's Wrong with the Order Entry System?

If you run the Order Entry System applet so far, you will notice something a little peculiar: nothing happens. You can click on the buttons, move the slider, and whatever else, and nothing happens. These user actions are called *events* in the Abstract Windowing Toolkit. Your program has to be able to deal with these events and give the proper response. For example, if a user clicks the up arrow on a slider, your program has to react and increment a variable. If a Clear button is clicked, your program has to reset all the data that has been input to default values. The next section covers the implementation and concepts behind events and handling them. It also deals with the specialized action() method used for different types of component events. And after that, it sets up much of the dealing with events in the Order Entry System. Also, you may think, "It looks terrible." Well, you're right. Hold on because the solutions are coming up in future chapters.

Dealing with Events

Some events in the AWT are mouse drags, window resizing, and slider. Your programs that use the AWT are set to react to each event. This makes programs based on the AWT very different from typical programs. When you're creating a windowing system, one of the tasks you do is enable your system to act on an event-by-event basis as opposed to a linear basis. The AWT takes this responsibility out of your hands.

Events in Java are declared using the Event class. Different types of events are identified by a different constant held in Event.id. Each different type of event, such as mouse clicks and window resizing, is identified by a different constant. For example, if a mouse button is pressed, an event is generated whose id is equal to the constant MOUSE_DOWN. Table 6.1 explains all the mouse and keyboard event types. Table 6.2 contains events related to windows. Table 6.3 contains the miscellaneous events such as the event ids specific to the List class and scrolling events, and Table 6.4 lists the different values contained in instances of the Event class.

Table 6.1. The keyboard and mouse event id types.

ID Constant	Meaning
KEY_PRESS	Generated when a key is pressed.
KEY_RELEASE	Generated when a key is released.
MOUSE_UP	Mouse button is released.
MOUSE_DOWN	Mouse button is pressed.
MOUSE_ENTER	Mouse enters the window area.
MOUSE_EXIT	Mouse exits the window area.
MOUSE_MOVED	Mouse is moved.
MOUSE_DRAG	Mouse is dragging something.
HOME, PGDN, PGUP, etc.	Action key is pressed.
F1 .. F12	The function keys.
LEFT, UP, RIGHT, etc.	Arrow key pressed.
ACTION_EVENT	An action event occurs.

Table 6.2. The event id types for window events.

ID Constant	Meaning
WINDOW_DESTROY	Destroy button pressed on window.
WINDOW_ICONIFY	Window told to minimize.
WINDOW_EXPOSE	Window told to "expose" itself.
WINDOW_MOVED	Window moved.

Table 6.3. Miscellaneous event types.

ID Constant	Meaning
SCROLL_LINE_UP, SCROLL_PAGE_DOWN, and so on	The different scroll events for different user inputs on scrollbars.
SCROLL_ABSOLUTE	Scrollbar is moved.
LIST_SELECT, LIST_DESELECT	An item in the list selected or deselected.
LOAD_FILE, SAVE_FILE	A saving file event, for example.
GOT_FOCUS, LOST_FOCUS	A component gets or loses the focus.

Table 6.4. The different values contained in instances of the Event class.

Name	What It Is
Object target	Which component generates the event.
long when	A time stamp.
int id	A constant that says what kind of event it is.
int x	The x coordinate of the event.
int y	The y coordinate of the event.
int key	The key that is pressed.
int modifiers	Which modifier key is used (ALT, for example).
clickCount	The number of consecutive click counts (2 for a double-click, 0 if it isn't set, for example).
Object arg	An arbitrary argument used for customization.

NOTE:

A few more event constants than these are available. However, the event.ids covered in this chapter are effective for almost all purposes.

Also, the when member of the Event class is used for time stamping. You generally don't worry about this because the vast majority of programs you deal with are event-driven and not linear.

The `handleEvent()` Method

After an event occurs, the Java runtime constructs an instance of the Event class and sets its id field appropriately. It then sends that instance to the `handleEvent()` method of your Java program that overrides the default `handleEvent()` method. This method deals with the event appropriately.

The `handleEvent()` method is a Boolean function. Three possible results can be returned: `true`, `false`, or `super.handleEvent(Event)`. A returned `true` value signifies that your `handleEvent()` method has taken care of the event. A `false` value signifies that your event has not been handled. This is not desirable. The proper path for events to be handled is first through a class and then through its parent. A `false` value has the event sent to the parent container, and you don't want that. Instead, return `super.handleEvent(Event)`, which sends the event to a parent of a class (the class it has been derived from) to be dealt with. To summarize, either return `true`, saying that your `handleEvent()` took care of the event, or return `super.handleEvent(Event)` to show that you didn't handle the event and your parent class should.

Dealing with the `action()` Method

Notice that some events are missing in the previous lists. What about events resulting from instances of the Choice class? Well, these kinds of events are more easily handled with a Java method called the `action()` method. With the `action()` method, events work a little differently. The `action()` method deals with events that are generated by the AWT components themselves. The different components all create specific action events that your AWT programs can override to deal with specific events. The `action` method has the following structure:

```
public boolean action(Event InEvent, Object SomeObject) {
    if (InEvent.target == AButton)  {
        . . .
    } return . .
}
```

The `action` void returns, like the `handleEvent()` method, either `true` or `false` depending on whether the method has handled the event. Each different component calls the `action` method in a different way, using different parameter values in place of the SomeObject parameter. The InEvent parameter in the event is the calling component, and the SomeObject parameter can be anything (because basically everything in Java derives from an Object). When the `action` method is called for button presses, the argument is the string label of the button. When it is called from an instance of the Choice class, the argument is the selected string.

There are also specialized methods that handle very specific events. You can use them to simplify your other event-handling methods. Table 6.5 is a summary of these specialized event-handling methods.

Table 6.5. The different types of `action` and related methods.

Method	When Called
`action(Event InEvent, Object SomeObject)`	The standard action method.
`keyUp(Event InEvent, int key)`	Mouse button is released.
`keyDown(Event InEvent, int key)`	Mouse button is pressed.
`mouseUp(Event InEvent, int xpos, int ypos)`	Mouse button is released.
`mouseDown(Event InEvent, int xpos, int ypos)`	Mouse button is pressed.
`mouseMove(Event InEvent, int xpos, int ypos)`	Mouse is moved.
`mouseDrag(Event InEvent, int xpos, int ypos)`	Mouse is dragging.
`mouseEnter(Event InEvent, int xpos, int ypos)`	Mouse has entered the component.
`mouseExit(Event InEvent, int xpos, int ypos)`	Mouse has left a component.

In summary, user actions in Java can be categorized into those that are handled by the `handleEvent()` method and those that are handled by the different types of `action` methods. There is a large amount of overlap. It is easy to use the `handleEvent` method to deal with many of the component events covered by the `action` method. To do this, test for the `ACTION_EVENT` event `id` and then act based on the value of `Event.target`.

However, using both the more specific `action` methods and the `handleEvent` method ensures that your code is easier to read, design, and maintain. Of course, as with many languages, Java allows you many ways to do things, and with experience you will develop your own style.

Listing 6.7 is a sample applet that deals with handling events using both the `action` method and the `handleEvent` method.

 TIP:

Cases and syntax are very important in Java, especially when you're dealing with overriding methods and inheritance. For example, if you declare a `HandleEvent()` method and execute your Java program expecting it to override the `handleEvent()` method in the AWT, nothing happens. When in doubt, look for these kinds of errors.

Listing 6.7. The `Event` applet code listing.

```
1. import java.awt.*;
2. import java.applet.Applet;
3.
4. public class EventExample extends Applet {
5.
6.     // Declare a local variable, AList of the List type.
7.     private List AList;
8.     // Declare a local variable, AButton of the Button type.
```

```
9.      private Button AButton;
10.
11.     // Override the default init() method.
12.     public void init() {
13.             /* Allocate space for the AList.  Set it to show four
14.                 items visible at one time and turn off the ability
15.                 for the user to make multiple selections with the
16.                 false boolean parameter. */
17.             AList = new List(3, false);
18.
19.             // Add four items to the List class and initially select item #1..
20.             AList.addItem("Blue");
21.             AList.addItem("Yellow");
22.             AList.addItem("Green");
23.             AList.addItem("Red");
24.             AList.addItem("Purple");
25.             AList.addItem("Orange");
26.             AList.select(1);
27.             // Add the list class to the applet panel.
28.             add(AList);
29.
30.             // Allocate space for the AButton.
31.             AButton = new Button("Click Me");
32.
33.             // Add the button to the applet panel.
34.             add(AButton);
35.
36.     }
37.
38.     /* Overriding the default HandleEvent method.  Here we will
39.         write code to receive Events from the Java run time. */
40.     public boolean handleEvent(Event inEvent) {
41.
42.             /* Check to see what kind of Event we're given, if
43.                 it is an Event where the user selects an item in
44.                 our list, then we're going to deselect that item
45.                 and reselect number 1. */
46.             if (inEvent.target == AList)
47.             {
48.                 if (inEvent.id == Event.LIST_SELECT)
49.                     {
50.                     /* Make the first item in the list the
51.                         selected item. */
52.                     AList.select(0);
53.                 }
54.         }
55.         return super.handleEvent(inEvent);
56.     }
57.
58.     public boolean action(Event InEvent, Object  SomeObject) {
59.             if (InEvent.target == AButton)
60.             {
61.                 // Set the label equal to the selected list item.
62.                 AButton.setLabel(AList.getSelectedItem());
63.                 return true;
64.             } else
65.             return false;
66.     }
67. }
```

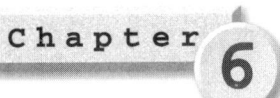

Figure 6.9.

Screen shot of the
`EventExample` applet.

What's Going On in the `EventExample` Applet

If you try out this applet, you'll notice that it is a little frustrating. No matter what you choose, it always selects back to `Blue`. This is accomplished by the `handleEvent()` method declared starting in line 34. The method only checks the `Event` to see if its `id` is equal to that of having something selected in a list, `LIST_SELECT`. If it is, line 52 sets the selected member of the list to item number 0. Eventually, Java comes back and repaints the applet window and the list component itself.

Then line 55 tells the default method to handle the event. This way, it still does tasks like window resizing in stand-alone windows and customizes your own `handleEvent()` without having to cover all the rudimentary and mundane tasks.

Line 58 is the place where the `action` method is declared. It is used for a couple of reasons. One, it is an aspect of Java you should know about. Two, it is much easier to use the `action` method instead of the `handleEvent()` method to handle events from components like choices. In any case, line 59 checks to see if the `Event` is generated by the `AChoice` choice, and if it is, sets the button label to the currently selected item in the list. As is customary, the `action` method returns a `true` if it handled the event; it returns `false` if it did not.

NOTE:

The Shift, Alt, Ctrl, and Meta keys are all supported by Java. For example, if you are testing for the Alt+PgDn combination being pressed, the code is the following:

```
public boolean handleEvent(Event InEvent)
{
    if (InEvent.id == Event.KEY_PRESS)
        {
          if (InEvent.key == Event.PGDN) &&
            (Event.ALT_MASK & InEvent.modifiers) != 0)
            {
              // Do what you wanna do.
            }
        }
}
```

The only thing new here is dealing with the most interior `if` statement. This statement checks to see if the key pressed is PgDn and also to see if the modifier contained in the event signifies the Alt key.

The Steps in Creating Event-Based AWT Programs

The following are basically all the general guidelines to follow when creating an AWT-based program that is event driven.

First, figure out what you want. If you want buttons, declare them. In your applet (preferably in your `init()` method, although it doesn't have to be there), set up the panel layout. Add your components, and as covered in Chapter 8, manage the applet layout.

Second, design your method to handle the events you receive. In the `handleEvent` (along with the `action` method if you want), test the `Event.id` to see what kind of event you are given. For each `id` type you want to recognize, check it against the constants such as `MOUSE_DOWN` and react accordingly. For instance, if the `Event.id` equals `KEY_PRESSED`, then you want to check your instance of `Event.key` to see which key has been pressed.

Third, set the `handleEvent()` method to return the proper value: `true` if you have handled the event properly or `super.handleEvent(Event)` if you want the applet's immediate parent to handle the event.

Handling Events in the Order Entry System

You need to set up the framework to handle events in the Order Entry System. To do this, write the `handleEvent()` method and add it to the applet that you have developed so far. Also, add some of the variables that are local to the applet.

First, you handle the events of the Clear button being pressed, as follows:

```
if (InEvent.target == clearButton)
    {
      // Reset all of the variables and settings .
        .
        .
    }
```

Do the same for each of the other buttons, and put the respective code for their functions in as you go along. You aren't able to code the Send button's function completely until later in the book.

You don't need to do anything to make the Repeat Customer? checkbox active. When the data is collected and sent under the Send button's actions, the checkbox value is checked and sent. You can also accomplish this with the radio button group, checking each checkbox when the send-off time comes.

You may have noticed in the figures of the Order Entry System in Chapter 5, "Writing a Java Applet: The Order Entry System," that the applet keeps a running total and subtotal of the items currently selected to be ordered. You need to declare some internal variables: one for each subtotal being calculated and one for the grand total. Here are the declarations for these variables:

```
private double SubTotalOne = 0,0;
private double Total = 0.0;
```

For now, you are going to enter only one product and the size for that product. Each product has a base price and a price modifier depending on the size. The subtotal is calculated by multiplying the base price, the number of items desired, and the price modifier together. The total is calculated as the sum of all the subtotals. Here are the local variables used for computing price:

```
private double multiplierSmall = 0.5;
private double multiplierMedium = 1.0;
private double multiplierLarge = 1.5;
```

For now, hardwire the prices and the different products into the applet. Later in Chapter 14, "Extending Java," you learn techniques to read files from your server and then use the data in your applets. The following constants are the base prices for each product:

```
static double ProdOneBaseValue = 1.0;
static double ProdTwoBaseValue = 1.33;
static double ProdThreeBaseValue = 1.75;
static double ProdFourBaseValue = 8.75;
static double ProdFiveBaseValue = 0.33;
```

You have to override the `action` method in the applet to handle most of the events coming from the components. You don't need to deal with the radio buttons and the checkboxes in the applet because their immediate values don't have an effect on the function of the component. The `action` method handles the events generated by the choice box. Here is the code section from inside the `action` method that modifies the subtotal and total variables when a new product choice is made:

```
public boolean action (Event InEvent, Object SomeObject) {
.
.
if (InEvent.target == SizeChoice) {
    updateValues();
}
.
.
```

The `updateValues()` function is a `void` that is declared locally to update all the totals. It is implemented later in the book.

This is all that is taken care of in the `action` method as opposed to the `handleEvent()` method, which covers everything. You still have to update the totals and the multipliers when the list selection (for example, what the size chosen is) is made. To do this, add some code to the `handleEvent()` method to call the `updateValues()` function when a new list selection is made. It is handled in the same way as the list has been handled in the previous `EventExample`.

Finally, you need to updateValues() when the slider is changed. The code to do this is placed in the handleEvent() method. Here, you are checking to see if the current event is one of either line up or line down (for example, someone presses the end arrow).

```
public boolean handleEvent(Event InEvent) {
.
.
if (InEvent.id == Event.SCROLL_LINE_UP ||
    InEvent.id == Event.SCROLL_LINE_DOWN)
    {
       updateValues();
}
```

And that covers the events in everything that's been added so far. Listing 6.8 is this chapter's final version of the Order Entry System applet.

Listing 6.8. The Order Entry System code listing.

```
import java.awt.*;
import java.applet.*;
public class OrderEntrySystem extends Applet {
    // The subtotal and total variables.
    private double SubTotalOne = 0.0;
    private double Total = 0.0;
    // The price multipliers for each different product size.
    private double multiplierSmall = 0.5;
    private double multiplierMedium = 1.0;
    private double multiplierLarge = 1.5;
    // The local constant base prices.
    static double ProdOneBaseValue = 1.0;
    static double ProdTwoBaseValue = 1.33;
    static double ProdThreeBaseValue = 1.75;
    static double ProdFourBaseValue = 8.75;
    static double ProfFiveBaseValue = 0.33;
    // Declare all of the variables we'll use.
      private Button SubmitButton;
    private Button ClearButton;
    private Button QuitButton;
    private Checkbox RepeatCustCheckBox;
    private Checkbox MailBox;
    private Checkbox EmailBox;
    private Checkbox PhoneBox;
    private List ProductList;
    private Choice SizeChoice;
    private Scrollbar OrderAmountSlider;
    // Initialize the Applet.
    public void init()
        {
        // Add and create three buttons.
           SubmitButton = new Button("Submit");
        add(SubmitButton);
         ClearButton = new Button("Clear");
        add(ClearButton);
          QuitButton = new Button("Quit");
        add(QuitButton);
```

continues

Listing 6.8. continued

```
          // Add and create the repeat customer checkbox.
            RepeatCustCheckBox = new Checkbox("Repeat Customer?");
          add(RepeatCustCheckBox);
          // Declare the CheckboxGroup, and allocate space.
          CheckboxGroup ContactMethodGroup;
          ContactMethodGroup = new CheckboxGroup();
          // Create some checkboxes to put in the group.
            EmailBox = new Checkbox("Email",ContactMethodGroup,true);
           PhoneBox = new Checkbox("Phone",ContactMethodGroup,false);
           MailBox = new Checkbox("US Mail",ContactMethodGroup,false);
          // Add the checkboxes into the applet panel.
          add(EmailBox);
          add(PhoneBox);
          add(MailBox);
          // Create the list, 4 items visible, no multiple selections.
          ProductList = new List(4, false);
          // AddItems to the List.
          ProductList.addItem("Oscar");
          ProductList.addItem("Lionhead");
          ProductList.addItem("Jack Dempsey");
          ProductList.addItem("Angelfish");
          // Add the List to the Applet panel.
          add(ProductList);
          // Create the Choice box.
          SizeChoice = new Choice();
          // AddItems to the List.
          SizeChoice.addItem("Jumbo");
          SizeChoice.addItem("Large");
          SizeChoice.addItem("Medium");
          SizeChoice.addItem("Small");
          // Add the Choice to the Applet panel.
          add(SizeChoice);
          // Create a vertical slider, initial value of 0,
          // minimum value of 0, maximum value of 144.
            OrderAmountSlider = new Scrollbar(Scrollbar.VERTICAL, 0, 0, 0, 100);
          // Insert the slider to the Applet panel.
          add(OrderAmountSlider);
        }
    public boolean handleEvent(Event InEvent) {
        if (InEvent.id == Event.SCROLL_LINE_UP ¦¦
          InEvent.id == Event.SCROLL_LINE_DOWN)  {
            updateValues();
        } else
        if (InEvent.target == ClearButton) {
                // Reset all of the variables and settings .
        } else
        if (InEvent.target == QuitButton)  {
        // Quit the applet.
        } else
        if (InEvent.target == SubmitButton) {
         // Submit the order.
        }
        return super.handleEvent(InEvent);
```

```
    }
    public boolean action (Event InEvent, Object SomeObject) {
        if (InEvent.target == SizeChoice) {
            updateValues();
        return true;
        } else return false;
    }
    private void updateValues() {
        // Empty for now.
    }
}
```

The Order Entry System So Far

You've made great steps forward with the Order Entry System in this chapter. You started with nothing, and now it has an initial layout along with a framework for functionality. There is, however, still a good amount wrong with the applet. First, the totals, subtotals, and scrollbar values are not placed on the applet panel. You fix this in the next chapter, where the AWT components that deal with text input and output are covered. How to place text on the applet to better organize it is also covered in the next chapter. Finally, where's the text input? It is coming in the next chapter, "The Order Entry System: Entry Fields, Labels, and Validation."

Chapter 7

by Michael Girdley

The Order Entry System: Entry Fields, Labels, and Validation

The preceding two chapters covered the basic concepts behind applets and many of the components in the AWT. This chapter covers the remaining components, including those specific to text input and output. There are multiple components dealing with text including labels, text fields, and text areas. The implementation and function of each one of these components are detailed in this chapter.

In this chapter, you also take some more steps toward completing the Order Entry System. This chapter extends the system to include the components discussed in this chapter and handles them appropriately. The chapter also fills in some of the "holes," such as the unfinished `updateValues` method, and activates the Clear button.

Finally, the chapter covers the methods of password entry and identification, which are very important in the applet design business. This same section also covers data validation in the entry fields.

Text-Oriented Components

The AWT components covered in this chapter deal with text, both input and output. The generic AWT text output components are labels. They are simply unformatted text that can be added to a container.

NOTE:

There are also other means to insert text into AWT programs. These are, however, graphical and are covered in Chapter 9, "The Order Entry System: Adding Graphics and a Logo." If you want to do this, look for the `drawString()` method in the index. Since these methods function to draw graphics onto components and are not components themselves, they are saved for later.

Labels

Labels are simple components. You provide a string, and it gets placed onto an applet or your panel. Labels are used to label your other components or features in your panel. Since labels do nothing, there is no need to handle events generated by them. As such, you will notice that there are no `Events` related to labels in the preceding chapter. Labels are limited in their ability to change fonts and their plain unattractiveness when placed together.

Adding labels to your AWT programs is simple. In fact, doing so is almost embarrassing because it is so easy. The following line adds a component containing the string `"It's so easy."` to a container:

```
add(new Label("It's so easy."));
```

Of course, if you want to have the ability to change the string displayed on your label at a later time, you declare a variable of the `label` type and then add it to your container using `add`. The following lines do just that:

```
Label ALabel = new Label("It's so easy."));
add(ALabel);
```

The following are the three major constructors for creating labels:

```
ALabel = new Label();
BLabel = new Label("The String You Want");
CLabel = new Label("The String You Want", AlignConstant);
```

In the first constructor, `ALabel` is allocated to be an instance of `Label` with no string or alignment set. In the next two constructors, the first parameter is the string you want to have displayed. In the third constructor, the `AlignConstant` is one of `Label.LEFT`, `Label.RIGHT`, or `Label.CENTER`. Each different constant sets the alignment of the text in the label component. Default alignment is left.

There are some useful methods when dealing with instances of the `Label` class. The most important is the `setText` method. The `setText` method takes a parameter of a string and then changes the text on the label to the string. The following line changes the text of an instance of the `Label` class:

```
ALabel.setText("This is how we do it.");
```

That's it. You can also get the text of a label with its `getText` method. It returns an instance of the `String` class, as follows:

```
AString = ALabel.getText();
```

You can also do the same with the alignment of a label. The `setAlignment` and `getAlignment` methods allow this. The `setAlignment` method accepts one of the alignment constants in the `Label` class (`Label.LEFT`, `Label.RIGHT`, `Label.CENTER`). The `getAlignment` method returns one of these same constants.

The code for the `CrazySimpleLabel` applet is shown in Listing 7.1.

Listing 7.1. The `CrazySimpleLabel` applet code.

```
import java.awt.*;
import java.applet.*;
public class CrazySimpleLabel extends Applet {
    private Label LabelA;
    private Label LabelB;
    private Label LabelC;
    public void init() {
        // Allocate a new Label.
        LabelA = new Label();
        // Set the label string.
        LabelA.setText("  I want this text.");
        // Set the label alignment.
        LabelA.setAlignment(Label.RIGHT);
```

continues

Listing 7.1. continued

```
        // Add the Label
        add(LabelA);
        // Allocate a new Label.
        LabelB = new Label(" I want this text. ");
        // Set the label alignment.
        LabelB.setAlignment(Label.CENTER);
        // Add the Label
        add(LabelB);
        // Allocate a new Label, set the text and alignment.
        LabelC = new Label("I want this text.    ", Label.LEFT);
        // Add the Label
        add(LabelC);
    }
}
```

This small applet creates and inserts three different labels onto the applet panel. Each one is aligned differently. Figure 7.1 shows the output from this applet when viewed with the AppletViewer.

Figure 7.1.

The output from the
CrazySimpleLabel applet,
which demonstrates the
Label class of the AWT.

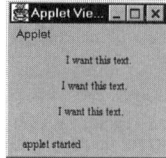

You may question the extra spaces in some of the label definitions here. Well, I cheated a little to make a point. Otherwise, making the alignment stand out distinctly is tough. But if you remove the spaces from the strings in Listing 7.1, you can see a very small difference—though it is not immediately apparent.

Text Fields

Text fields allow text input from the user. They allow the full mouse editing capabilities to which you are accustomed on Windows-based systems. This includes the cutting and pasting specific to each platform. Text fields have a limited width. However, text fields do scroll to follow where the cursor is. There are four constructors for the TextField class. The following creates a text entry field with a width of zero characters:

```
ATextField = new TextField();
```

The following creates a text entry field of WidthInChar (an int) characters wide:

```
BTextField = new TextField(WidthInChar);
```

The following line creates a text field of size zero with the initial text InitialText (an instance of the String class):

```
CTextField = new TextField(InitialText);
```

The following line constructs a text field with the initial text `InitialText` and of size `WidthInChar`. It is the one you will find most convenient to use.

```
DTextField = new TextField(InitialText, WidthInChar);
```

There are also a number of useful methods when dealing with `TextFields`. Most important is the `getText()` method, which follows. It returns the text in the field as an instance of the `String` class.

```
String AString = ATextField.getText();
```

To set the text in a text field, you do the same thing as with labels

```
ATextField.setText(AString);
```

where `AString` is an instance of the `String` class. You can also check the width of an instance of the `TextField` class with the `getColumns()` method. This function returns the width of the text field in characters as an integer.

Also, when users are editing the text in the field, you can set the selected text for them. On most systems, this is some kind of highlight, such as inversion of the text and background colors. Either way, the AWT provides two methods to select the text in an entry field. The `selectAll()` method selects all the text in a field. The `select(StartPos, FinishPos)` method allows you to specify the beginning and ending integers between which you want to have the text selected.

The `setEditable(ABoolean)` and `IsEditable()` functions in the `TextField` class allow you to set and test the editability of the text field. If `IsEditable()` returns `true`, then the user is able to make changes in the field. However, if it returns `false`, the text is "locked" in the field and not changeable. To set what `IsEditable()` returns, use the `setEditable` method, which takes a variable of type `boolean` as its only parameter.

Events and Text Fields

The `textField` class generates a call to your `action` method when the user presses the Enter or Return key when the user's focus is on the text field. Other than that, no events are generated by the `textField` class. To handle the events generated by text fields, your `action` method should contain code of the following format:

```
public boolean action(Event InEvent, Object InArgument) {
.
.
    if (InEvent.target == YourTextField) {
        // Do what you want here. . .
        return true;
    } else . . .

}
```

This format is included in the `TextFieldCrazy` applet code, which uses text fields as shown in the Listing 7.2. The corresponding output is shown in Figure 7.2 (remember that the line numbers are for reference only).

Listing 7.2. The `TextFieldCrazy` applet code.

```
1. import java.awt.*;
2. import java.applet.*;
3.
4. public class CrazyTextField extends Applet {
5.
6.     // A text field of width 10 with the initial text set.
7.     private TextField ATextField = new TextField("ABC", 25);
8.     // A label with the text set.
9.     private Label ALabel = new Label("Type ABC in field.");
10.        // The string we will be checking against.
11.     private static String AString = new String("ABC");
12.
13.     public void init () {
14.         // Add the label to the applet panel.
15.         add(ALabel);
16.         // Select the text between indexes 5 and 8.
17.         ATextField.select(5, 8);
18.         // Add the text field to the applet panel.
19.         add(ATextField);
20.
21.     }
22.
23.     public boolean action(Event InEvent, Object InParam) {
24.         if (InEvent.target == ATextField) {
25.             if (AString.equals(ATextField.getText())) {
26.                 ATextField.setEditable(false);
27.             }
28.           return true;
29.         } else return false;
30.     }
31.}
```

Figure 7.2.

The `CrazyTextField` applet,
which demonstrates handling
events generated by the
`TextField` class.

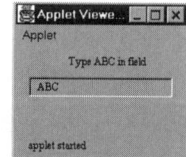

What's going on? The `init()` class does all the usual stuff—adding the components to the applet panel and doing the major setup tasks. Line 14 selects the text between the fifth and eighth characters in the text field. Then the `action` method of the applet is called when the `TextField` generates an `Event`. It first checks, in line 24, to see if the event target (the event that initiated the event) is the text field. If so, then it checks to see if the text in the field is the text `ABC`. If this is true, then it sets the field so that the user cannot further edit the text contained within it.

TIP:

A note on the `private` modifier: Java is highly object oriented. One major characteristic of object-oriented programming is the idea of data encapsulation. This means that data and variables inside of a class should not be accessible by those outside the class (like other classes who import them). Declaring things to be `private` ensures that those variables aren't accessible except by methods inside the class to which they belong, even if someone wants to try to access them.

You can also set your methods and classes to be `final`. When they are labeled as such, they are unable to be extended or overridden by other classes. Use this when possible because it reduces errors and also increases program efficiency.

`TextFields` are great, but what if you want to edit more than one line? That's the place where the `TextArea` class comes in.

Text Areas

Text areas in the AWT allow editing of multiple lines of text. They share many of the characteristics of `TextFields`, except they are extended to facilitate editing large areas of text. There are three major constructors for the `TextArea` class. The following creates an empty `TextArea` of width and height zero:

```
ATextArea = new TextArea();
```

You set the width and height of the field before inserting it. To set the width and height while declaring the field, use the constructor

```
BTextArea = new TextArea(WidthInChars, HeightInChars);
```

where both of the parameters are integers. To set the initial text along with the width and the height of the text area, use the constructor format

```
CTextArea = new TextArea(TextString, WidthInChars, HeightInChars);
```

where the first parameter is an instance of the `String` class and the remaining two parameters are integers.

There are a number of useful functions to use with the `TextArea` class. The two simplest are the `getColumns()` and `getRows` functions. They each return an integer value representing either the width of the text area in characters or the height in characters.

The `insertText` and `replaceText` methods are a little more useful. The `insertText` method takes the following format:

```
ATextArea.insertText(AString, PositionInt);
```

The preceding line inserts the text contained in the string `AString` at position `PositionInt`. The `replaceText` method takes the following format:

```
ATextArea.replaceText(AString, StartInt, EndInt);
```

The preceding line replaces the text between positions `StartInt` and `EndInt` with the text in `AString`. The `appendText` method appends a string (passed as a parameter) at the end of the current text in the text area.

When you're dealing with the user selecting text, you can use a number of other methods. For instance, if you ask a user to highlight a portion of text that he or she likes the best, you can find the start and end positions of the selection `getSelectionStart()` and `getSelectionStop()` methods. These methods each return integers representing the first and last positions of the selected text. If you want to get the selected text itself, use the `getSelectedText()` method, which returns an instance of the `String` class. The following line of code sets the string `AString` equal to the selected text in a text area:

```
AString = ATextArea.getSelectedText();
```

You can also set the selected text in a text area. The following method does just that:

```
ATextArea.select(StartPos, EndPos);
```

where both parameters are integers. To select all the text in the text area, you use the `selectAll()` method, as follows:

```
ATextArea.selectAll();
```

TIP:

It is risky to count on users to be able to perform the cutting and pasting of text for a couple of reasons. One, on many systems such as X Window, cutting and pasting text aren't intuitive. Two, many of the individuals using the Web these days are new to computers, so they may not know how to cut and paste.

Events and Text Areas

Perhaps the most difficult task when you're dealing with components in the AWT is not creating them, but getting them active. Text areas and text fields differ in their dealings with events. Text areas do not generate any calls to an `action` method. Instead, they generate events that are usually dealt with by your program's `handleEvent` method. Two events that you will find useful are `Event.SELECT` and `Event.DESELECT`. A complete listing of the `Event.ids` that deal with the `List` class are included in Chapter 6, "The Order Entry System: Adding Features and Handling Events." In most cases, you associate an event generated by another component such as a button or a list.

If you want, the Order Entry System can associate a selection in the product list with inserting new text about that product into the text area. Or a button labeled "Clear" can empty the text area when its event is handled in the action method.

To deal with text areas in your programs, include coding of the following format in your `handleEvent` method:

```
if (InEvent.target == YourTextArea) {
    if (InEvent.id == WhatYouAreCheckingFor) {
        // Do what you want. . .
    }
}
```

Adding These Concepts to the Order Entry System

Now that some more AWT concepts have been covered, it's time to include a couple more features in the Order Entry System. First, add some labels in order to help organize the applet panel into an orderly and easy-to-follow layout. Also, incorporate some text fields and a text area into the system. Finally, construct the framework to handle events from these new components.

First, to add labels, include the following code:

```
add(new Label("Name: ");
```

Since most of the labels are static and don't need to be changed after adding them, you don't generally need to declare variables of the `Label` component class. Instead, allocate a new `Label` and then insert it onto the applet panel. You will add multiple labels in this same way.

There are a couple of labels that you need to change during the running of the applet. The total, subtotal, and price per item need to be displayed via labels. As different choices about sizes and products are made, these labels need to be updated. To do this, call the `updateValues` method, which was discussed last when events were generated by these components. The `updateValues` method updates all the internal values to match current settings and choices. This method is implemented in this section.

Also, since labels need to display strings, you need to convert the integers to an instance of the `String` class. To do this, use a method of the `Integer` type of Java. The following code sets a label to show a value of 20:

```
ALabel.setText(Integer.toString(20));
```

This is applicable to the variable containing the amount of an item to be ordered. However, some of the other variables and constants are of the type `Double`. But, you are in luck because the same conversion is possible with `Doubles`.

TIP:

If you can't find something that you want to do, check out the source code for the Java library. They are in the SRC directory of your installed developer's kit. All the classes included are well documented and easy to follow. And if it looks like Greek, then at least you tried, right?

To add a text field, you need to declare an instance of it as a variable in the applet. This line creates a new instance of `TextField` that is 25 characters in width:

```
Private textfield nameentryfield = new textfield(25);
```

By declaring it `private`, you disable any access outside the applet to the variable. This isn't necessary but is good coding practice. You also declare the same type of text fields to enter other user information such as city or contact information.

The Order Entry System includes a text area to allow the users to enter any comments they may have. To declare an instance of the `TextArea` that is 25 characters wide, 4 rows tall, and with no starting text, use this line:

```
private TextArea CommentTextArea = new TextArea(4, 25);
```

With both this text area and the other components, you include their addition to the applet panel in the `init` method.

You don't need to deal with any events generated by the labels in the applet since the `Label` class doesn't generate any events. However, you want to set the framework for handling events from text entry fields. To do this, add the following code segment to the `action` method for each text field that you want to deal with:

```
if (InEvent.target == NameEntryField) {
    // What we want to do here . .
    return true;
    } else
```

Of course, the inside of the `if` statement is different for each text field in the applet. For example, the name text entry field calls a method to check to see that there is actually a name included.

For functionality, you don't need to handle any events from the comment text area. A method called `resetValues` is also added; it resets all internal values in the applet.

The `updateValues` method does the real work of the applet. In a sense, you can look at the rest of the program as an interface for it. It takes the input data and computes the necessary output. The way `updateValues` works is simple. First, it declares all the variables that it needs to use. It finds the indexes of the different choices and lists. It uses the input from the slider to compute the different output values such as the subtotal and the total. It changes the text in the corresponding labels on the applet panel to match the new values. And then the runtime comes along, and when it updates the applet panel, it changes the appearance to be what the method just set it to.

Listing 7.3 shows the code for the Order Entry System so far. Figure 7.3 shows the resulting Order Entry System with these additions.

Figure 7.3.

The Order Entry System with
text-oriented components
added.

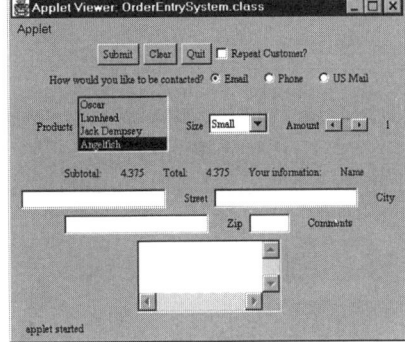

Listing 7.3. The Order Entry System code with text-oriented components added.

```
import java.awt.*;
import java.applet.*;
public class OrderEntrySystem extends Applet {
    // The subtotal and total variables.
    private double SubTotalOne = 0.0;
    private double Total = 0.0;
    // The price multipliers for each different product size.
    private double multiplierSmall = 0.5;
    private double multiplierMedium = 1.0;
    private double multiplierLarge = 1.5;
    private double multiplierJumbo = 2.25;
    // The local constant base prices.
    static double ProdOneBaseValue = 1.0;
    static double ProdTwoBaseValue = 1.33;
    static double ProdThreeBaseValue = 1.75;
    static double ProdFourBaseValue = 8.75;
    // Declare all of the variables we'll use.
    private Button SubmitButton;
    private Button ClearButton;
    private Button QuitButton;
    private Checkbox RepeatCustCheckBox;
    private Checkbox MailBox;
    private Checkbox EmailBox;
    private Checkbox PhoneBox;
    private List ProductList;
    private Choice SizeChoice;
    private Scrollbar OrderAmountSlider;
    // The labels which will be variable and change when
    // the other selections are changed.
    private Label SubTotalLabel = new Label("$0.0 ");
    private Label TotalLabel = new Label("$0.0 ");
    private Label AmountLabel = new Label("$0.0 ");
    private Label PricePerItemLabel = new Label("$0.0 ");
    // The entry field for the user to enter their name.
```

Listing 7.3. continued

```java
private TextField NameEntryField = new TextField(25);
private TextField ZipEntryField = new TextField(5);
private TextField StreetEntryField = new TextField(25);
private TextField CityEntryField = new TextField(25);
// The comment entry area.
private TextArea CommentTextArea = new TextArea(4, 25);
// Declare the init method.
public void init()
    {
    // Add and create three buttons.
      Button SubmitButton = new Button("Submit");
    add(SubmitButton);
    Button ClearButton = new Button("Clear");
    add(ClearButton);
     Button QuitButton = new Button("Quit");
    add(QuitButton);
    // Add and create the repeat customer checkbox.
     Checkbox RepeatCustCheckBox = new Checkbox("Repeat Customer?");
    add(RepeatCustCheckBox);
    // Add a label to the ContactMethodGroup.
    add(new Label("How would you like to be contacted? "));
    // Declare the CheckboxGroup, and allocate space.
    CheckboxGroup ContactMethodGroup;
    ContactMethodGroup = new CheckboxGroup();
    // Create some checkboxes to put in the group.
      Checkbox EmailBox = new Checkbox("Email",ContactMethodGroup,true);
    Checkbox PhoneBox = new Checkbox("Phone",ContactMethodGroup,false);
    Checkbox MailBox = new Checkbox("US Mail",ContactMethodGroup,false);
    // Add the checkboxes into the applet panel.
    add(EmailBox);
    add(PhoneBox);
    add(MailBox);
    // Label the item list.
    add(new Label("Products"));
    // Create the list, 4 items visible, no multiple
    // selections.
    ProductList = new List(4, false);
    // AddItems to the List.
    ProductList.addItem("Oscar");
    ProductList.addItem("Lionhead");
    ProductList.addItem("Jack Dempsey");
    ProductList.addItem("Angelfish");
    // Add the List to the Applet panel.
    add(ProductList);
    // Add a label to the choice of sizes.
    add(new Label("Size:"));
    // Create the Choice box.
    SizeChoice = new Choice();
    // AddItems to the List.
    SizeChoice.addItem("Jumbo");
    SizeChoice.addItem("Large");
    SizeChoice.addItem("Medium");
    SizeChoice.addItem("Small");
    // Add the Choice to the Applet panel.
    add(SizeChoice);
    // Add a label to the slider.
```

```
        add(new Label("Amount:"));
        // Create a vertical slider, initial value of 0,
        // minimum value of 0, maximum value of 144.
          OrderAmountSlider = new
                Scrollbar(Scrollbar.HORIZONTAL, 0, 0, 0, 144);
        // Insert the slider to the Applet panel.
        add(OrderAmountSlider);
        // Insert the label which says how many are set to be ordered
        // of the item.
        add(AmountLabel);
        // Add the subtotal label and a label saying that it is the subtotal.
        add(new Label("Subtotal: "));
        add(SubTotalLabel);
        // Add the total label and a label saying that it is the total.
        add(new Label("Total: "));
        add(TotalLabel);
        // Insert a label to signify that this
        // is the personal information (address,etc.)
        // section and also insert text fields to prompt for that information.
         add(new Label("Your information: "));
         add(new Label("Name:"));
        add(NameEntryField);
        add(new Label("Street:"));
        add(StreetEntryField);
        add(new Label("City:"));
        add(CityEntryField);
        add(new Label("Zip:"));
        add(ZipEntryField);
        // Add a label to the comment text area.
        add(new Label("Comments:"));
        // Add the comment box.
         add(CommentTextArea);
        // Method which resets all of the internal values.
         resetValues();
            }
// This method will be called when the user presses the "Clear" button and
// also when the applet is initialized in the init() method.
public void resetValues() {
    // Reset all of these labels to zero.
    SubTotalLabel.setText("$0.0 ");
    TotalLabel.setText("$0.0 ");
    AmountLabel.setText("0 ");
    PricePerItemLabel.setText("$0.0 ");
    // Clear all of the lists and choices.
    ProductList.select(0);
    SizeChoice.select(0);
    OrderAmountSlider.setValue(0);
    // Clear all of the text fields.
    NameEntryField.setText("");
    StreetEntryField.setText("");
    CityEntryField.setText("");
    ZipEntryField.setText("");
}
//   Method which will deal with some of the events
//generated during execution
// of the applet.
public boolean handleEvent(Event InEvent) {
    // Check to see if the Slider was changed.  If so,
```

Listing 7.3. continued

```
        // update the values in the applet.
        if (InEvent.id == Event.SCROLL_LINE_UP ||
            InEvent.id == Event.SCROLL_LINE_DOWN)  {
            updateValues();
        } else
        // If the list of products was changed then update the applet values.
        if (InEvent.target == ProductList) {
            updateValues();
        } else
        // If the clear button was pressed, reset all of the applet values.
        if (InEvent.target == ClearButton) {
            resetValues();
        } else
        if (InEvent.target == QuitButton)  {
        // Quit the applet.
        } else
        if (InEvent.target == SubmitButton) {
         // Submit the order.  To be completed later.
        }
        // Let the parent handle the event. . .
        return super.handleEvent(InEvent);
    }
// The rest of the Events will be handled here. . .
public boolean action (Event InEvent, Object SomeObject) {
        // If the event was generated by the size choice field
        // then update all of the display.
        if (InEvent.target == SizeChoice) {
            updateValues();
        // Yes, we handled the event..
        return true;
        }
        else
        // If the event was generated by the NameEntryField. . .
        if (InEvent.target == NameEntryField) {
            /* Is the field empty?  If so, we will later add a pop-up dialog
               box to alert the user that they have not entered their name.
             */
        return true;
        } else
        // Otherwise, say that we didn't handle the event. .
        return false;
    }
/* This void will change all of the values to match any changes
   in the input settings. First, it declares a number of
   variables local to the method.  Then, it sets a modifier
   variable and a base price variable depending on which items
   are selected in the choice box, the list, and the slider.
   Then, it inserts those values onto the applet panel.
*/
private void updateValues() {
// The index of the selected size.
        int WhichChoice = SizeChoice.getSelectedIndex();
// The amount of items desired.
int AmountSelected = OrderAmountSlider.getValue();
// The index of the selected product.
```

```
int WhichProduct = ProductList.getSelectedIndex();
/* The initial base price and modifier.  Remember,
   the modifier is the amount the base price is
   multiplied by to get the price per item.
*/


double CurrentBasePrice = 0.0;
double CurrentModifier = 0.0;
/* This switch statement compares the index of the
   product list, held in WhichProduct,
   and sets the inital BasePrice accordingly.
*/
switch (WhichProduct) {
                case 0:
                CurrentBasePrice = ProdOneBaseValue;
                break;
    case 1:
                CurrentBasePrice = ProdTwoBaseValue;
                break;
    case 2:
                CurrentBasePrice = ProdThreeBaseValue;
                break;
    case 3:
                CurrentBasePrice = ProdFourBaseValue;
                break;
        }
/* This switch statement compares the WhichChoice
   variable (which is the selected index in the
   sizeChoice choice box) to the different indexes.
   And then sets the modifier accordingly.
*/
switch (WhichChoice) {
                case 3:
                CurrentModifier = multiplierSmall;
                break;
    case 2:
     CurrentModifier = multiplierMedium;
     break;
    case 1:
                CurrentModifier = multiplierLarge;
                break;
               case 0:
                CurrentModifier = multiplierJumbo;
                break;
        }
    // Insert the number on the slider to the applet.
    AmountLabel.setText(Integer.toString(AmountSelected)+ " ");
    // Compute the priceperitem and insert it onto the applet panel.
    double PricePerItem = (CurrentBasePrice*CurrentModifier);
    PricePerItemLabel.setText(Double.toString(PricePerItem)+ " ");
    // The subtotal is the number ordered times the price per item.
    double SubTotal = (CurrentBasePrice*CurrentModifier*AmountSelected);
    // Insert the subtotal onto the applet panel.
    SubTotalLabel.setText(Double.toString(SubTotal)+ " ");
    /* Since the total is the same as the subtotal
       (cause we only have one item to be ordered
```

continues

Listing 7.3. continued

```
      at a time), we can simply use the value in the subtotal.
   */
   TotalLabel.setText(SubTotalLabel.getText());
   }
}
```

The Order Entry System So Far

Don't you find it interesting how fast these programs grow? If this information seems unclear, use the comments to follow what's going on. Here's the general flow of the applet. First, all the internal variables are declared, and then the Java runtime calls the `init()` method. The `init()` method allocates many of the variables and defines the layout of the applet panel. Then the user does something to create an event. When an event does arise, the `handleEvent` and `action` methods handle the event. Different methods and actions are taken based on the event that is generated and on which components are targeted. For example, when the Clear button is pressed, the `clearValues` method is called.

The Order Entry System takes some more great strides in this chapter. Complete functionality has been added to almost all the components in the applet. The slider now functions completely, and the value it sets is now used to compute the correct subtotal and total based on the choices the user makes. In these ways, the Order Entry System is doing great. However, there are two major items wrong with the Order Entry System.

First, you may look at the applet shown in Figure 7.3 and think something along the lines of "This looks terrible." Well, you're right. All the pieces to the applet have been added, but they still haven't been ordered correctly. You do this in the next chapter when the concepts of containers and layout managers are covered. The applet looks like a jumbled mess now, but it improves in the next chapter, "The Order Entry System: Managing the Applet Layout."

Second, there is still some functionality missing. The applet should exist as a stand-alone window. The process of implementing this feature is included in the next chapter. There are also some instances in which pop-up dialogs should be included in the applet. For example, if a user does not enter his or her name, a window should pop up and alert the user that he or she has not entered information correctly. Stay tuned, more to come.

Data Validation

Data validation, in terms of this book, is the process of checking data to see if it is correct. As it relates to the Order Entry System, it is checking text entered through text fields to see if they are what you want. For example, if you have a field that accepts a phone number, you should check to see that the text entered contains 10 integers.

When you want to validate data entered in fields, follow these steps:

1. Write a `boolean` function that returns a `true` or `false` when supplied the text from the field. The function returns a `true` when the string is acceptable; `false` otherwise. To write this function, parse the string. Java contains a number of useful functions for parsing strings; they are covered in Chapter 3, "An Introduction to Java Classes."

2. Next, add to your `action` method an `if` statement that calls the method written in step 1 if the `Event.target` is the text field that you are trying to validate. If the result of the function in step 1 is `true`, keep on going. If it is `false`, alert the user or do what you want to do.

That's all you have to do. If you noticed, the framework for this feature is set up in the Order Entry System. After some more topics are covered in the next chapter, code is enabled such that when the `NameField` generates an event (that is, when the user presses Enter or Return while the cursor is in the text field) and sends it to the `action` method, it calls the `CheckName` function, which returns a Boolean. Then, if the `CheckName` function returns a `false` value, an OK dialog box is set out to alert the user that the name entry field is empty. If the function returns `true`, then you go on your merry way. And that covers it all.

Dealing with Passwords

While the Order Entry System applet does not use password entry, it is worth covering. When you're prompting someone for a password, it is customary to echo a different character than what is typed. This character is usually an * or a blank space.

To have a text field echo another character, use the `setEchoCharacter` method of the `TextField` class. For example, to set the characters that are echoed to ! when text is typed into a field, you can use the following code line:

```
ATextField.setEchoChar('!');
```

You can use a couple more methods in conjunction with the `setEchoChar(char)` method. The `getEchoChar()` function returns the echo character. Also, the `echoCharIsSet()` Boolean function returns whether an echo character is set. It returns an instance of the `boolean` variable.

Summary

In this chapter, you learned about a number of important Java AWT components. They included all those that deal with the plain input and output of text. Then you learned how to use these components by incorporating them into the Order Entry System. I discussed the Order Entry System and looked ahead to improving it in the chapters to come. I discussed the process of data validation in AWT programs and how you could incorporate that into the Order Entry System.

The next chapter covers some of the most important features of the AWT. You will learn how to manage the layout of your AWT programs so that they maintain platform independence while looking good. You will then apply those techniques to the Order Entry System as you take more steps to improve it.

Chapter

by Michael Girdley

The Order Entry System: Managing the Applet Layout

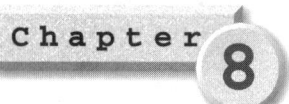

This chapter is going to cover much information. First, it further explores the concepts of containers in the Java AWT. It covers how to implement the different container types and how they interact with each other. Remember, containers are components which function to contain other components. The different containers available allow you to create stand-alone window applets, and also clean up the appearance of the Order Entry System. The chapter also describes pop-up dialog boxes and the means to incorporate them into your applets.

Second, the chapter covers the five different AWT layout managers. These allow you, the programmer, to place your components in containers in an orderly fashion while you still maintain platform independence. The five layout managers are: `FlowLayout`, `BorderLayout`, `CardLayout`, `GridLayout`, and `GridBagLayout`. The `GridBagLayout` is the layout manager that is used to reorganize the Order Entry System applet panel later in this chapter.

More About Containers

The first concept to understand is the idea that containers are components. Containers are components and they also hold components. Containers can hold other containers. When you embed containers inside of containers, you are subdividing the applet (or application) display area. By doing this, you can apply different layouts to each separate subdivision of the display face.

It is beneficial to have different groups of components laid out in different ways. This way, you don't have to settle on a layout that is mediocre for all of your components. Instead, you can choose the layout that is best and apply that to each subdivision (container) of the applet face. This process is how you create appealing interfaces and still maintain platform independence. This concept is covered again when you add to the Order Entry System later on in this chapter.

The simplest containers are panels. In terms of simplicity, they are to containers what labels are to interface components. But in terms of power, the `Panel` class is infinitely more powerful and useful than the `Label` class.

Panels

Panels are AWT components that hold other components. By themselves, panels are basically nothing. One usually expects a container as known in the real world to have some visible form; however, panels are invisible. They have no visible boundaries or characteristics to visually separate them from other components or containers. If you try to display an empty instance of the `Panel` class you get what you expect when you display something that is made completely of nothing: nothing. In a nutshell, panels are classes whose sole purpose is to group other components together.

To declare a panel, use the following code:

```
Panel APanel = new Panel();
```

To insert components, including other containers, into a panel, use the same method that you use when inserting components onto applet faces, the add method. To insert a component named SomeComponent into your new panel declared above, use the following code:

```
APanel.add(SomeComponent);
```

The add method takes an instance of the Component class as a parameter. Each container, including Applet, has an add method. This is inherited from the java.awt.Container class found in the AWT package. To insert a component into another container, you should do what you did above, call the container's add method and include the component as a parameter. To simply insert something onto the main panel, such as you do with the Applet class, simply add(SomeComponent) without specifying it as a method of another container.

The add method has so far appeared in two seemingly unrelated sections of the book (inserting components into an applet and also into a container). This should raise some questions in your head. If you look back at the inheritance hierarchy of the java.awt.Applet class in Chapter 5, "Writing a Java Applet: The Order Entry System," you see that the Applet class is actually a subclass of the Panel class. This is why the chapter refers to the applet face as the "applet panel." This is because applets themselves are actually specialized Panels that have included more methods so they are able to be executed in an HTML document by a Web browser. Here is the inheritance path of the java.awt.Applet class in Figure 8.1. Pay attention to the fact that applets are themselves subclasses of the Panel class.

Figure 8.1.
The inheritance path of the
java.awt.Applet class.

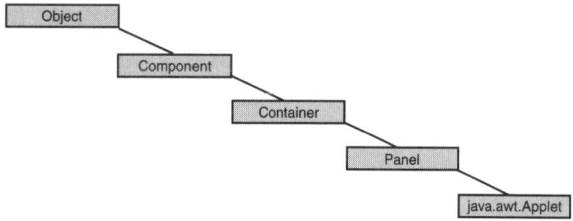

Later, the chapter covers the concept of layout managers in the AWT. These layout managers can be applied to set the layout inside of Panels and other containers.

Frames

Frames are another subclass of java.awt.Container. They share the same two major operators: add and a method to be named later (sounds like baseball), and also do quite a bit more. Frames arc the means by which you can incorporate stand-alone windows into your Java applets or create windowing Java applications.

NOTE:

java.awt.Frame and java.awt.Dialog (covered in the next section) are both actually subclasses of the Window class. The Window class is the means to implement a stand-alone window in Java. However, it is non-functional for our purposes. While the Panel class can be readily embedded inside of other containers, the java.awt.Window class generally is not. For this reason, the children of the Window class are separated to ease explanation and understanding because of the functional difference.

To create a new instance of a Frame, there are two constructors you will find useful. They are of the format as follows:

```
Frame AFrame = new Frame();
Frame BFrame = new Frame("This one has a title, man.");
```

Both constructors declare instances of the Frame class and then allocate space for them. The difference is that the BFrame frame is declared to have a title from the start. You can also set the title of the AFrame frame. If you want to set the title of the AFrame frame to be the String "So do I.", use the setTitle() method:

```
AFrame.setTitle("So do I.");
```

The setTitle method takes an instance of the String class to be its parameter which it then sets to be the title of the window.

In the AWT, the sizing of windows is not done by measurement or proportion of the screen. Instead, it is accomplished through counting the number of pixels in a direction. To set the size of a frame in pixels, use the resize method of instances of the Frame class. To set AFrame to be 100 pixels wide by 150 pixels high, you can use the following declaration:

```
AFrame.resize(100, 150);
```

The resize method accepts two integers: the width first, and then the height in the second parameter position.

CAUTION:

You must call the resize method on your frames. Otherwise, the default is a height of zero and a width of zero which means you get absolutely nothing when you display them unless the resize method is called with non-zero values.

Listing 8.1 is a small application, FrameCrazee, that displays a frame from inside an application.

Listing 8.1. The FrameCrazee application code.

```
1.  import java.awt.*;
2.  import java.applet.Applet;
3.
4.  public class FrameCrazee extends Object {
```

```
5.
6.    public static void main(String[] arg) {
7.
8.    Frame AFrame = new Frame();
9.    Frame BFrame = new Frame("This one has a title, man.");
10.
11.   // Set the title of the AFrame.
12.   AFrame.setTitle("So do I.");
13.
14.   // Resize the BFrame to width of 300 pixels,
15.   // And a height of 250 pixels.
16.   BFrame.resize(300, 250);
17.
18.    // Display the BFrame.
19.    BFrame.show();
20.
21. }
22.
23. }
```

Figure 8.2 is the output resulting from this application when run using the java command-line interpreter.

Figure 8.2.

Output from the
FrameCrazee application in
Listing 8.1.

CAUTION:

Notice that this is a Java application and not an applet. If you try to do this with an applet and expect it to work, you will be a little surprised. Instead, you have to do a little dancing to get frames incorporated with applets. This is covered a few pages further on.

Lines 1 through 6 do the typical stuff you expect in a applet. But remember, this is an application, so we can simply execute it using the Java interpreter included in the JDK.

Lines 8 and 9 declare and initialize two instances of the Frame class using the constructors described previously. Line 12 sets the title for the AFrame frame and line 16 resizes the BFrame frame to be 300 pixels wide by 250 pixels high. And finally, line 19 displays the BFrame using the show method of the frame class. But where is the AFrame declared and initialized in line 8? All you can see is the BFrame frame displayed in the output in Figure 8.2. The show() method of the frame isn't invoked to set it visible.

But importantly, why is this an application and not an applet like all of the others? Isn't this a book focusing on the creation of Java programs for the Web? Well, the problem is that instances

of the `Frame` class are not allowed to be owned by a derivative of the `Applet` class. Instead, you have to override the `Frame` class and then use that class when defining frames in your applets. Otherwise, you discover that frames owned by applets usually appear, but functionality disappears. Using frames in applets is covered after the next section on the `show()` method.

Showing and Hiding Frames

The `show()` method of the `Frame` class is the means by which you set a frame to show itself to the world and be active. To set a frame named `CFrame` to display itself, use the following code:

```
CFrame.show();
```

If defined correctly, the `CFrame` is displayed. The opposite of the `show()` method is the `hide()` method. It is called in the same manner as the `show()` method except it causes the frame to become invisible again.

Frames and Applets

As noted before, frames cannot belong to applets directly. Instead, you have to sidestep this a bit. The process to do so is not difficult. It involves the following process.

In your applet, after you close your last "}", declare another class called something like `FrameJr`. Set this class to `extend` the frame class. Inside of the class body, you declare that you want to construct the `FrameJr` class. Constructors are covered in Chapter 7, "The Order Entry System: Entry Fields, Labels, and Validation." Constructors function to set the properties and do some initial setup when called. To set the `FrameJr` class, use the following declaration:

```
class FrameJr extends Frame {

 FrameJr (String InTitle) {
  super(InTitle);
  .
    .
 }
}
```

When an instance of your class `FrameJr` is declared in your applet using the following statement,

```
Frame AFrameJr = new FrameJr(Title);
```

the constructor of your `super` class (which is your class's parent, the one it extended) is called and your `Frame` is created just like normal. You can also include any other setup tasks you wish to deal with inside of the constructor for your class. For example, you might want to add an "!" to the end of your title before constructing it. To do this, change your `InTitle` string before you call the super of your class.

CAUTION:

Notice that there is no constructor with which you can build an instance of `FrameJr` with no title. If you wish for this to work, you must declare another constructor inside of the class declaration which accepts no parameter and then calls `super()` with no parameter.

TIP

This method of reconstruction of your classes is not limited to frames. It works for any class. For example, you might want to create a version of the `String` class whose constructor accepts a string and removes all of the capital letters. You can write a class to extend the `String` class and then in the constructor remove all of the capitals before you call the `super()`, which is the string's original constructor.

Allowing User Resizing of Frames

Another important method you can use with the `Frame` class is the `setResizeable(boolean)` method. This method either turns on or turns off the capability for the user to change the size of the frame being displayed. If you send a value of `false` to the method, the user is no longer permitted to change the size of the frame. A `true` value allows resizing of the window. The default setting when a frame is initialized is `true`, indicating that the user can resize the window.

Setting the Frame's Icon

One of the most interesting features of frames in the AWT is the capability to set the icon of the frame. This is accomplished using the `setIconImage(AnImage)` method, which accepts a parameter which is of the Java type `Image`. This type is covered in the next chapter, which covers Java-based graphics. At that time, the Order Entry System logo is set to be the icon.

Frame Menu Bars

Menu bars attached to frames are the typical pull-down menus customarily attached to windows on almost every window-based system, including those which are text-based along with the typical graphical-based systems. If you've used Microsoft Windows, X Window, or MacOS, you should be familiar with the typical format of including pull-down menus across the top of a window border. Frame menus are implemented using the `MenuBar` class. There is one major constructor for the `MenuBar` class:

```
MenuBar AMenuBar = new MenuBar();
```

You must then set your Frame to have its menu bar as the `AMenuBar`. This is done using the `SetMenuBar()` method of the `Frame` class. To set the `AMenuBar` as the menu bar of the `AFrame`, use the following code line:

```
AFrame.setMenuBar(AMenuBar);
```

Each individual item along the menu bar is constructed from the `Menu` class. There are two major constructors for the `Menu` class:

```
Menu AMenu = new Menu("One");
Menu BMenu = new Menu("Two", true);
```

Both constructors accept the first parameter as a string which sets what the text label for each menu is across the top of the frame. The second constructor adds another parameter of the Boolean type. If the parameter is `true` then the menu is removable. If it is `false` then it is not. The default is `false`.

The following line adds the `AMenu` class from above to your menu bar:

```
AMenuBar.add(AMenu);
```

This code adds an option labeled "One" to your menu bar. You can also add menu items to your instance of the `Menu` class as well as adding other menus. It is also possible to add checkboxes to your menus. To do so, declare a checkbox as in Chapter 6, "The Order Entry System: Adding Features and Handling Events." Then, insert it into the menu where you wish it to belong. Also in the same fashion as in Chapter 6, handle the events that the checkbox generates either in the `action` or `handleEvent` method of your program.

To add menu items to your menus, you can declare instances of the `MenuItem` class. The `MenuItem` constructor accepts a string parameter which is the text label of the item when it appears on the menu:

```
MenuItem AMenuItem = new MenuItem("Hey!");
```

You can also add text only to your menus as choices. The format for doing this is:

```
Menu.add("A choice!");
```

If you are going to do this, be prepared to use the `action` method to facilitate handling the event. If you're set on using `handleEvent`, then use just the `MenuItem` class.

Menus in a Nutshell

Menus aren't always easy to grasp because of the multiple classes. To summarize, the whole menu bar starts with an instance of the `MenuBar` class. This instance is then set to be the menu bar for a frame using the `setMenuBar` method of the frame.

Then, menus are added to the menu bar. (Menus are the list that falls down when you click on a label contained in the menu bar.) Menus can be added to other menus or to instances of the class

`MenuItem`. Menu items function as text labels. Their purpose as separate variables is to give you a target if you decide to use the `handleEvent` method.

To create a menu bar, follow these steps:

1. Create an instance of the `MenuBar` class.
2. Set your frame's `MenuBar` to be the instance declared above.
3. Create multiple `Menus` to be in your menu bar.
4. Add and create each `MenuItem` and sub-menu you wish to include.
5. Add all of the pieces in Step 4 to their corresponding `Menu` in Step 3.
6. Add your menus to the instance of `MenuBar`.

To visually help you grasp the organization of menu bars, Figure 8.3 is a typical menu hierarchy of insertion.

<u>Figure 8.3.</u>
A typical menu hierarchy of insertion.

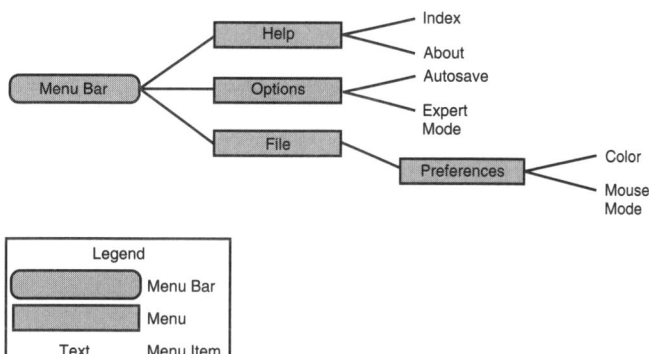

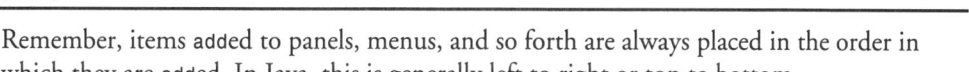

TIP:

Remember, items `added` to panels, menus, and so forth are always placed in the order in which they are `added`. In Java, this is generally left to right or top to bottom.

Events and Menus

Handling events generated by menus is most easily done in the `action` method of your AWT programs. When an instance of the `MenuItem` class fires a call to the `action` method, the first parameter is the `Event` itself. The second parameter is the string of the menu item generating the event. This can be used for advanced tasks, if need be, such as receiving menu items generated without declaring a `MenuItem` first. Once you have experience, you can use items like the `instanceof` operator to simplify your handling of events. But for the time being, going for the simple way is a good idea.

The following `if` statement block works in either event handling method:

```
if (evt.target  == SomeMenuItem)  {
 // Do whatcha like . .
 } else . . .
```

If you are using a checkbox or other component in the menu, you can use the same format with a different target.

Setting the Frame Cursor

This is, in my opinion, one of the coolest things about the `Frame` class. You have the capability of changing the appearance of the cursor of the frame. There are a number of different cursors available. Table 8.1 is a list of the cursor constants that you can use to set the cursor. To find this information, look at `java\src\awt\Frame.java`.

Table 8.1. The multiple cursor constants available to set the cursor of frames.

Cursor Constants
DEFAULT_CURSOR
CROSSHAIR_CURSOR
TEXT_CURSOR
WAIT_CURSOR
SW_RESIZE_CURSOR
SE_RESIZE_CURSOR
NW_RESIZE_CURSOR
NE_RESIZE_CURSOR
N_RESIZE_CURSOR
E_RESIZE_CURSOR
W_RESIZE_CURSOR
S_RESIZE_CURSOR
HAND_CURSOR
MOVE_CURSOR

To set the cursor of a frame, use the `setCursor` method. To set the cursor of the frame `AFrame` to the crosshair cursor, use the following code segment:

```
AFrame.setCursor(CROSSHAIR_CURSOR);
```

There is also a `getCursor` method which returns an integer which is one of the above constants. You can use this function to check which cursor is being used. The available `Frame` class methods are summarized in Table 8.2.

Table 8.2. Frame methods.

Method	Description
`String getTitle()`	Returns a `String` which is the title of the window.
`setTitle(String)`	Accepts a `String` parameter that is then set to be the title of the window.
`Image getIconImage()`	Returns an instance of `Image` (see next chapter) that is the icon used on the window.
`setIconImage(Image)`	Accepts an instance of `Image` that is then set as the icon for the window.
`MenuBar getMenuBar()`	Returns the menu bar for the window.
`setMenuBar(MenuBar)`	Sets the menu bar for the window.
`remove(MenuComponent)`	Removes the specified menu bar from the window frame.
`dispose()`	Gets rid of the frame and frees all of the resources it is using.
`boolean isResizeable()`	`true` or `false` depending on whether the dialog is set to be resizeable.
`setResizeable(boolean)`	Sets the ability for the user to resize the dialog window.
`setCursor(integer)`	Accepts an integer which is one of the cursor constants listed previously.
`integer getCursorType();`	Returns an integer which is one of the cursor constants listed previously.

Using Applets as Applications

Web browsers incorporate a Java interpreter to interpret the Java bytecodes to be able to execute applications. The executable called "java" included in the JDK does this also. To execute a Java application, use the command line `"Java YourClassHere"`. To convert your applets to run as stand-alone applications, there are two major methods.

Method one is the simplest of the two. The process involves creating a `public void main(String arg[])` in your applet. Then, create a new instance of the `Frame` class, initialize it and call the applet `init()` and `start()` methods, and then `add` your applet to the frame. Then, show the `Frame` containing the applet. The following code demonstrates this technique inside an applet called `AApplet`.

```
public void main(String arg[]) {

  // Create the new instance of the Frame class.
  Frame AFrame = new ("Morrissey Fan-Club");

  // Initialize the frame and the applet.
  AFrame.resize(300, 300);
  AApplet.init();
  AApplet.start();

  // Add the applet to the frame.
  AFrame.add(AApplet);

  // Show the frame.
  AFrame.show(AApplet);
}
.
.
```

Method two is tough, but you should use it if you want to keep up the efficiency level. First, change the class from extending the `applet` class to extending the `Frame` class. Then, modify your applet to run with the knowledge that the `main(String arg[])` function is the only one called by the Java runtime. The `init()`, `run()`, etc. methods are no longer called because those are specific to the applet class. You, however, can set your `main` method to call the `init()` method.

Unless you have a complete understanding, you should probably stick to method one.

Dialogs

Dialogs are another subclass of the `java.awt.Window` type. They are used for simple alerts, information providing to the user, or simple data entry. You see these every time your windows system can't find a file or the system wants to know what file you want. In fact, the AWT provides a predefined file dialog for your use. Of course, in writing applets it isn't of much use since applets can't load or save local files. But remember, applications do have unlimited local access to the file system.

There are two key states dialogs can be in. In one state, a dialog can demand that it receives attention enough to finish its tasks before any other window is allowed to be active. An applet in this state is typically called "Modal." There are multiple other ways to refer to a window that doesn't demand attention in this manner ranging from non-modal to modeless to unmodal. This book refers to them as non-modal.

Dialogs are declared in the `java.awt.Dialog` class. As stated before, dialogs are a subclass of the `java.awt.Window` class. As such, dialogs are "siblings" with the frame class. The two classes share the features of having a title, and of either being resizeable or not. They share these characteristics and you can use the same methods to set their characteristics (`setTitle(String)`, `isResizeable()`, and so on).

The `Dialog` class is dependent on the `Frame` class. When you declare a dialog, you must attach it to an instance of the `Frame` class. There are two major constructors for the `java.awt.Dialog` class. The following two lines construct and create two different instances of the `Dialog` class, `ADialog` and `BDialog`:

```
Dialog ADialog = new Dialog(AFrame, ABoolean);
Dialog BDialog = new Dialog(AFrame, TitleString, ABoolean);
```

Both of these declarations construct new instances of the `Dialog` class. The first parameter in each is the frame to which the dialog box belongs. The second constructor takes a string parameter which the system sets to be the dialog box title. And the final parameter in each is a Boolean value or variable which sets the modality of the dialog box. A true value indicates that the dialog box is modal (demands attention and resolution of its desires before any other window is permitted attention) and a false value indicates otherwise.

Dialogs share much with frames in terms of methods. As mentioned before, both the `Frame` class and the `Dialog` class use the `getResizeable()` and `setResizeable(boolean)` methods. They also share the `resize(integer, integer)` method which sets the window size.

Table 8.3 summarizes the methods available in the `Dialog` class.

CAUTION:

Remember, for every class which is a descendant of the `Window` class (including `Frame`, `Dialog`, and `FileDialog`), you must specify the window size using the `resize(integer width, integer height)` method. Otherwise, you get a window of zero width and zero height, which results in a non-existent and invisible window.

Table 8.3. Dialog methods.

Method	Description
`boolean isModal`	`true` or `false` depending on whether the dialog is modal.
`String getTitle()`	Returns a string that is the title of the dialog.
`setTitle(String)`	Sets the dialog title to the `String` parameter.
`boolean isResizeable()`	`true` or `false` depending on whether the dialog is set to be resizeable.
`setResizeable(boolean)`	Sets the ability for the user to resize the dialog window.

Dialog Example Applet

The applet in Listing 8.2 attaches two dialogs to an instance of the `Frame` class.

Listing 8.2. The `DialogCrazee` applet code.

```java
import java.awt.*;
import java.applet.Applet;

public class DialogCrazee extends Applet {

// Define and initialize your main frame window.
Frame AFrame = new FrameJr("Dialog Crazee");

// Define an untitled modal dialog.
Dialog ADialog = new Dialog(AFrame, true);

// Define a titled, non-modal dialog.
Dialog BDialog = new Dialog(AFrame, "I've gotta title!", false);

public void init () {

  // Resize the AFrame to width of 100 pixels,
  // And a height of 150 pixels.
  AFrame.resize(100, 150);

  // Resize each of the dialogs so you can see them.
  ADialog.resize(100,100);
  BDialog.resize(200,200);

  // Add a label to each of the dialogs.
  ADialog.add(new Label("I am ADialog."));
  BDialog.add(new Label("I am BDialog."));

  // Display the AFrame.
  AFrame.show();
 }

}

class FrameJr extends Frame {

 FrameJr (String InTitle) {
  super(InTitle);
 }
}
```

What occurs in this applet is relatively simple. The initial coding declares the different variables. Then, they are set up in the `init()` method. And finally, the `AFrame` is told to appear.

But if you execute this applet, you are in for a surprise. Where are the dialogs you have worked to create? Well, they haven't been told to show themselves.

Since dialogs are usually set to appear when some event happens, such as the user wishing to load a file, that prompts the program to display it. This fits in great with the idea of handling events in the AWT. You connect the appearance of each one of the dialogs with an action that takes place in the frame.

To generate these actions in the original AFrame, you create two buttons in the original frame labeled "A" and "B", then set the handleEvent method to display the respective dialog when the user presses the buttons.

The first step is to add a couple of new buttons to the AFrame frame. To do this, use the constructor in Chapter 6:

```
new AButton = new Button("A");
new BButton = new Button("B");
```

Then, insert these buttons into the AFrame using the add method. The handleEvent method in the previous example also needs to be created. Insert two if blocks to check and see if one of the buttons is the originator of the event.

The improved DialogCrazee applet follows as Listing 8.3. The output from the DialogCrazee applet appears in Figure 8.4.

Listing 8.3. The improved DialogCrazee applet code.

```
import java.awt.*;
import java.applet.Applet;

public class DialogCrazee extends Applet {

    // Define and initialize our main frame window.
    Frame AFrame = new FrameJr("Dialog Crazee");

    // Define an untitled modal dialog.
    Dialog ADialog = new Dialog(AFrame, true);

    // Define a titled, non-modal dialog.
    Dialog BDialog = new Dialog(AFrame, "I've gotta title!", false);

    // Define the two new buttons to go into the frame.
    Button AButton = new Button("A");
    Button BButton = new Button("B");

    public void init () {

        // Resize the AFrame to width of 100 pixels,
        // And a height of 150 pixels.
        AFrame.resize(100, 150);

        // Resize each of the dialogs so you can see them.
        ADialog.resize(100,100);
        BDialog.resize(200,200);

        // Add a label to each of the dialogs.
        ADialog.add(new Label("I am ADialog."));
        BDialog.add(new Label("I am BDialog."));

        // Add the two buttons to the frame.
        add(AButton);
        add(BButton);
```

continues

Listing 8.3. continued

```
        // Display the AFrame.
        AFrame.show();
    }

    public boolean handleEvent(Event InEvent)  {

        if (InEvent.target == AButton)  {
            ADialog.show();
        } else

        if (InEvent.target == BButton)  {
            BDialog.show();
        }

        return super.handleEvent(InEvent);
    }

}

class FrameJr extends Frame {

    FrameJr (String InTitle) {
        super(InTitle);
    }
}
```

NOTE:

Ideally, you want the dialogs which belong to a frame to be declared inside of that frame. Then, when you handle an event, you call a public method of the FrameJr (or whatever you call it) class which then shows the dialog. However, this seems simpler. It is not difficult to place your dialogs inside your frame constructor so plan on doing that. Even though the code is a little choppier, it is sound coding practice.

Figure 8.4.

The output from the DialogCrazee applet.

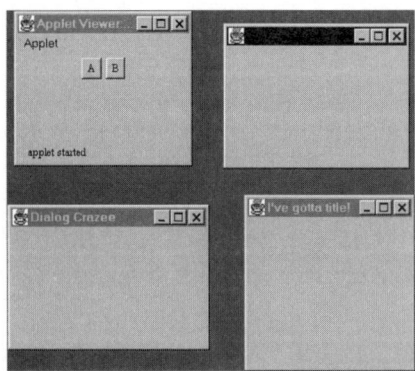

CAUTION:

If you run this applet and then try to close the frame window, you notice that nothing happens. To make the close button functional, you need to add a `handleEvent()` method to the declaration of an instance of the `Frame` class since it doesn't include functionality for this feature as a default. If you are creating an application which is an extension of the `Frame` class, place the `handleEvent()` method in the class declaration itself. If you are using the method described here to place frames into applets, place the `handleEvent()` method inside of that class declaration.

To accomplish this inside of your secondary class (for example, one such as the `FrameJr` class), include the following `if` block inside of a `handleEvent()` method for your frames:

```
if (InEvent.id == Event.WINDOW_DESTROY)
 {
   dispose();
 }
```

File Dialogs

A special dialog subclass is dedicated to saving, loading, and dealing with files. Each implementation of the AWT for each different windowing system mimics that system's standard native file dialog. If you implement the `FileDialog` class in X Window for example, you get the typical X Window file dialog.

There are two major constructors for the `FileDialog` class:

```
FileDialog AFileDialog = new (AFrame, AString);
FileDialog BFileDialog = new (AFrame, AString, AInteger);
```

For both of the constructors, the first two parameters are the same. Just as with the general dialog class, you must specify a frame to which the dialog belongs. You also need to specify the title for the dialog. The second constructor takes a parameter which is one of either `FileDialog.LOAD` or `FileDialog.SAVE`. This constant determines whether the dialog is a load file dialog or a save file dialog.

If the first constructor is called, an open file dialog is created. So, in summary, to open a file, use the first constructor. To save a file or load a file, use the second constructor with the different constants available. There is **no** constant called `FileDialog.OPEN`; you must use the first constructor.

The `FileDialog()` class uses many of the same methods common to descendants of the AWT Window class, and some others. Here is a summary of the file dialog methods in Table 8.4.

Table 8.4. Some available file dialog methods.

Method	Description
int getmode()	Returns an integer constant that is one of the different constants signifying load, open, and so forth.
String getDirectory()	Returns a string that is the directory of the file dialog's focus.
void setDirectory	Sets the current directory focus to the String directory.
void setFile(StringTheFile)	Sets the current file for the dialog.
String getFile()	Returns a string that is the file name of the current file in focus.
FilenameFilter getFilenameFilter()	Returns the current filter of the file listing.
setFilenameFilter	Sets the current file name filter.

Window-to-Window Data Exchange, or Connecting the Object-Oriented Way

In some cases, you run into problems in terms of connecting the two different classes together. For example, you want to send some data that you get in one window to another window. Or your dialog box asks for information and you wish to allow your frame to use it.

A similar dilemma arises when dealing with other classes. You have to "hardwire" the connection between the two classes. This is contrary to one of the primary goals of object-oriented programming which is the re-usability of code. Making one frame class so that it can only send data back to an instance of the Applet class means that you need to rewrite and recompile the sender each time you want to use it with a different class. And also, you have to have a different copy of each version of your class around for every other class it connects with.

The solution to this problem is the idea of interfaces. Interfaces are classes which have not had any method implemented. In other words, instances of interfaces are, except for local constants, a big empty. However, they allow the user to create linkages between classes without having to worry about the different implementations. To use an interface in your applet, you must declare an instance of it. For example, if you want an interface which allows you to relate a value of an integer to another class that uses the interface, declare the following interface:

```
interface MyInterface {
  abstract public int AnInteger;
}
```

You can also declare methods inside of your interfaces by using the same `abstract public` format. Though the `abstract` isn't needed for methods since it is the only state that methods in an interface are allowed to be. In essence, you are declaring variables and methods with concern for what they do, but saving the "how" for another class to take care of. To create a class which takes care of the implementation of your interface, you use the following class declaration:

```
class AFrame extends Frame implements MyInterface {
 .
 .
 .
}
```

The method described first in this section "hardwires" the connection between the two classes. You can also do the following when you want to use information contained in the class which implements the interface:

```
((MyInterface) getParent()).AnInteger
```

You can also do the same with methods by being able to call the methods which were declared in the interface and then implemented in the other class:

```
((MyInterface) getParent()).AVoid();
```

What is happening in each of these statements is that the result of the function `getParent()` (which returns the immediate parent of an object) is cast to be an instance of the interface type. Then, the method or variable of the interface, which is implemented by the other class, is accessed.

Well, can't you avoid all of this trouble and hardwire it in? Yes, but there are two reasons you don't want to. For one, Java compilers aren't very fast at the moment. A five hundred line program can take a minute to compile. If you have to rewrite one line of one five hundred line class to get it to connect with another class and then compile it for five different connections, it is going to take time.

Finally, the reason this is included in this section is that it is very useful in terms of the AWT and its windowing capabilities. You want to write your dialogs to be able to be reused with different frames you create.

Adding to the Order Entry System

It is time to apply some of the new concepts covered in this chapter to the Order Entry System. The first topic to cover is the code changes necessary to make the Order Entry System function as a stand-alone window. This includes inserting a button in the applet panel which the user can press to call up the order window. Also, some pop-up dialogs are incorporated into the applet. You want a dialog to appear specifically when the user leaves the name field empty. It is also simple to incorporate other dialogs to appear in response to other events.

Making the Order Entry System a Stand-Alone Window

Using the concepts covered earlier in this chapter, this section covers the method to convert the Order Entry System to a stand-alone window. You add a button to the applet panel which the user can press to bring up the window. Then, the user can fill in the form on the window.

To have a frame belong to an applet, you first have to declare another class inside of the applet file which extends the `Frame` class. This is because frames cannot belong directly to applets. Instead, sidestep this by declaring your own class which overrides the `Frame` class. The name for the new class type is called the `OrderEntryFrameType`. The declaration for this class type is as follows:

```
class OrderEntryFrameType extends Frame {

 FrameJr (String InTitle) {
  super(InTitle);
  }
 .
 .
 .
}
```

But instead of adding the components and setting up variables as in the original Order Entry System in the applet's `init()` method, you need to create a method in the OrderEntryFrame which accomplishes all of the component insertion and setup done in the applet's `init()` method. To do this, you copy the corresponding code in the `init()` method to a method you create in the `OrderEntryFrameType`. Call this method `setup()`. So, the format for the `OrderEntryFrameType` class declaration is as follows:

```
class OrderEntryFrameType extends Frame {

 FrameJr (String InTitle) {
  super(InTitle);
  }

 public void setup() {
  // The init() code body goes here. . .
  .
  .
 }
}
```

The components that were once added to the applet panel in the applet's `init()` method are now added to the frame itself. Also all of the variables that are used in the Order Entry System are placed into the frame itself. The full code cost listing of this is included in the complete listing of the applet coming up.

Since these variables are moved into another class, shut them off from being accessed by parent classes. Follow this practice of data encapsulation. All accesses to the data contained in the `OrderEntryFrameType` are done through methods and functions declared in the class itself.

Almost all of the methods of the original applet are moved to the frame class itself. The function of the system is encapsulated. This makes it easy to actually run the system as an application if need be.

The newly changed Order Entry System follows as Listing 8.4. Here are the major improvements as of this iteration:

1. The majority of the function is now transferred to a separate frame. This frame is declared in a separate class in the applet file. All of the functions and variables which had been in the applet are moved to the frame itself. Notice that the applet code is translated to an instance of the Frame class which belongs to the applet class. The action and handleEvent methods are also transferred. The new frame instance is completely independent of the applet. (In fact, *two* instances of the OrderEntryFrameType can just as easily be declared and both of them implemented.)

2. Also, a button is added to the applet face. The user's activation of this button results in the initialization and display of the frame and also deactivates the button so that another order entry frame cannot be activated.

Listing 8.4. Another iteration of the Order Entry System.

```
import java.awt.*;
import java.applet.*;

public class OrderEntrySystem extends Applet {

// Declare an instance of your frame class defined later in the // file.
OrderEntryFrameType OESFrame;

// Declare and initialize the button which will be on the applet
// face and the user can click to activate the order frame.
Button Order = new Button("Click to Order");

public void init() {
   add(Order);
 }

public boolean handleEvent(Event InEvent) {
 if (InEvent.target == Order) {

   // Disable the order button.
   Order.disable();

   // Construct the OESFrame.
   OESFrame = new OrderEntryFrameType("Order Entry System");

   OESFrame.resize(340,400);

   // The setup method which initializes the frame face and
   // the components in it.
   OESFrame.setup();
```

continues

Listing 8.4. continued

```
   // Display the order frame.
   OESFrame.show();
 }

 // Let the parent handle the event.
 return super.handleEvent(InEvent);
 }
}

/* This class declares the new extension of the frame class which
   will allow you to utilize a frame in the applet.  */

class OrderEntryFrameType extends Frame {

 // This is the constructor for your new class.
 OrderEntryFrameType (String InTitle) {

  // Call the Frame constructor.
  super(InTitle);

  // Set the layout of the frame (this has to be done to make things work).
  // This concept will be covered later on in this chapter.
  setLayout(new FlowLayout());
 }

 // This method does the construction of the frame panel.
 public void setup() {

    // Add and create three buttons.
    SubmitButton = new Button("Submit");
    add(SubmitButton);
    ClearButton = new Button("Clear");
    add(ClearButton);
    QuitButton = new Button("Quit");
    add(QuitButton);

    // Add and create the repeat customer checkbox.
    Checkbox RepeatCustCheckBox = new Checkbox("Repeat Customer?");
    add(RepeatCustCheckBox);

    // Add a label to the ContactMethodGroup.
    add(new Label("How would you like to be contacted? "));

    // Declare the CheckboxGroup, and allocate space.
    CheckboxGroup ContactMethodGroup;
    ContactMethodGroup = new CheckboxGroup();

    // Create some checkboxes to put in the group.
    Checkbox EmailBox = new Checkbox("Email",ContactMethodGroup,true);
    Checkbox PhoneBox = new
  Checkbox("Phone",ContactMethodGroup,false);
    Checkbox MailBox = new
  Checkbox("US Mail",ContactMethodGroup,false);

    // Add the checkboxes into the applet panel.
    add(EmailBox);
```

```
add(PhoneBox);
add(MailBox);

// Label the item list.
add(new Label("Products"));

// Create the list, 4 items visible, no multiple
// selections.
ProductList = new List(4, false);

// Add items to the List.
ProductList.addItem("Oscar");
ProductList.addItem("Lionhead");
ProductList.addItem("Jack Dempsey");
ProductList.addItem("Angelfish");

// Add the List to the Applet panel.
add(ProductList);

// Add a label to the choice of sizes.
add(new Label("Size:"));

// Create the Choice box.
SizeChoice = new Choice();

// Add items to the List.
SizeChoice.addItem("Jumbo");
SizeChoice.addItem("Large");
SizeChoice.addItem("Medium");
SizeChoice.addItem("Small");

// Add the Choice to the Applet panel.
add(SizeChoice);

// Add a label to the slider.
add(new Label("Amount:"));

// Create a vertical slider, initial value of 0,
// minimum value of 0, maximum value of 144.
  OrderAmountSlider = new Scrollbar(Scrollbar.HORIZONTAL, 0, 0, 0, 144);
// Insert the slider to the Applet panel.
add(OrderAmountSlider);

      // Insert the label which says how many are set to be ordered
      // of the item.
      add(AmountLabel);

      // Add the subtotal label and a label saying that it is
      // the subtotal.
      add(new Label("Subtotal: "));
      add(SubTotalLabel);

      // Add the total label and a label saying that it is the total.
      add(new Label("Total: "));
      add(TotalLabel);
```

continues

Listing 8.4. continued

```
    // Insert a label to signify that this is the personal information
// (address, etc.) section and also insert text fields to prompt
    // for that information.
      add(new Label("Your information: "));
      add(new Label("Name:"));
    add(NameEntryField);
    add(new Label("Street:"));
    add(StreetEntryField);
    add(new Label("City:"));
    add(CityEntryField);
    add(new Label("Zip:"));
    add(ZipEntryField);

    // Add a label to the comment text area.
    add(new Label("Comments:"));

  // Add the comment box.
   add(CommentTextArea);

 // Method which resets all of the internal values.
  resetValues();


 }

// The subtotal and total variables.
private double SubTotalOne = 0.0;
private double Total = 0.0;

// The price multipliers for each different product size.
private double multiplierSmall = 0.5;
private double multiplierMedium = 1.0;
private double multiplierLarge = 1.5;
private double multiplierJumbo = 2.25;

// The local constant base prices.
static double ProdOneBaseValue = 1.0;
static double ProdTwoBaseValue = 1.33;
static double ProdThreeBaseValue = 1.75;
static double ProdFourBaseValue = 8.75;

// Declare all of the variables you'll use.
private Button SubmitButton;
private Button ClearButton;
private Button QuitButton;
private Checkbox RepeatCustCheckBox;

private Checkbox MailBox;
private Checkbox EmailBox;
private Checkbox PhoneBox;

private List ProductList;
private Choice SizeChoice;
private Scrollbar OrderAmountSlider;
```

```
// The labels which will be variable and change when
// the other selections are changed.
private Label SubTotalLabel = new Label("$0.0 ");
private Label TotalLabel = new Label("$0.0 ");
private Label AmountLabel = new Label("$0.0 ");
private Label PricePerItemLabel = new Label("$0.0 ");

// The entry field for the user to enter a name.
private TextField NameEntryField = new TextField(25);
private TextField ZipEntryField = new TextField(5);
private TextField StreetEntryField = new TextField(25);
private TextField CityEntryField = new TextField(25);
// The comment entry area.
private TextArea CommentTextArea = new TextArea(4, 25);

private void updateValues() {

        int WhichChoice = SizeChoice.getSelectedIndex();
        int AmountSelected = OrderAmountSlider.getValue();
        int WhichProduct = ProductList.getSelectedIndex();
        double CurrentBasePrice = 0.0;
        double CurrentModifier = 0.0;


        switch (WhichProduct) {
            case 0:
                CurrentBasePrice = ProdOneBaseValue;
                break;
            case 1:
                CurrentBasePrice = ProdTwoBaseValue;
                break;
            case 2:
                CurrentBasePrice = ProdThreeBaseValue;
                break;
            case 3:
                CurrentBasePrice = ProdFourBaseValue;
                break;

        }

        switch (WhichChoice) {
            case 3:
                CurrentModifier = multiplierSmall;
                break;
            case 2:
                CurrentModifier = multiplierMedium;
                break;
            case 1:
                CurrentModifier = multiplierLarge;
                break;
            case 0:
                CurrentModifier = multiplierJumbo;
                break;
        }
```

continues

Listing 8.4. continued

```
        AmountLabel.setText(Integer.toString(AmountSelected)+ " ");
        double PricePerItem = (CurrentBasePrice*CurrentModifier);
        PricePerItemLabel.setText(Double.toString(PricePerItem)+ " ");
        double SubTotal = (CurrentBasePrice*CurrentModifier*AmountSelected);
        SubTotalLabel.setText(Double.toString(SubTotal)+ " ");
        TotalLabel.setText(SubTotalLabel.getText());
    }

// This method will be called when the user presses the "Clear" button and
// also when the applet is initialized in the init() method.
public void resetValues() {

  // Reset all of these labels to zero.
  SubTotalLabel.setText("$0.0 ");
  TotalLabel.setText("$0.0 ");
  AmountLabel.setText("0 ");
  PricePerItemLabel.setText("$0.0 ");

  // Clear all of the lists and choices.
  ProductList.select(0);
  SizeChoice.select(0);
  OrderAmountSlider.setValue(0);

  // Clear all of the text fields.
  NameEntryField.setText("");
  StreetEntryField.setText("");
  CityEntryField.setText("");
  ZipEntryField.setText("");
}

public boolean handleEvent(Event InEvent) {
  if (InEvent.id == Event.SCROLL_LINE_UP ||
      InEvent.id == Event.SCROLL_LINE_DOWN)  {
    updateValues();
  } else
  if (InEvent.target == ProductList) {
      updateValues();
  } else
  if (InEvent.target == ClearButton) {
            resetValues();
  } else
  if (InEvent.target == QuitButton)  {
  // Quit the applet.
   System.exit(0);
  } else
  if (InEvent.target == SubmitButton) {
   // Submit the order.
  }
  return super.handleEvent(InEvent);
}

public boolean action (Event InEvent, Object SomeObject) {
  if (InEvent.target == SizeChoice) {
   updateValues();
   return true;
  }
```

```
  else
  if (InEvent.target == NameEntryField) {
  // Is the field empty?  If so, we will later add a pop-up dialog
  // box to alert the users that they have not entered their name.
   return true;
   } else
   return false;
 }
}
```

The Order Entry System is still growing. Next, the ability to display a dialog box in response to a user action is added. Notice that the framework for this ability is built in the `action` method of the `OrderEntryFrameType` class that has been created.

Figure 8.5 is the Order Entry System when viewed from the `Appletviewer` utility.

Figure 8.5.

The Order Entry System from the `Appletviewer` utility.

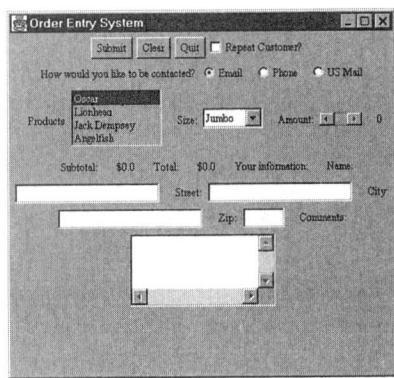

The disable() and enable() Methods

These two methods allow you, the programmer, to deactivate and activate your components. It is used in the latest version of the Order Entry System to disable the button which calls the Order Entry System window. You can use these methods to enable and disable your components when you wish.

Adding Pop-Up Dialogs to the Order Entry System

Adding a pop-up dialog to the Order Entry System is simpler than converting to a stand-alone window. The framework for displaying the dialog window is already completed. Now, create a new class which extends the `Dialog` class as you create a new class to create the `OrderEntryFrameType`. Then, declare an instance of your new dialog box type and implement it in the frame type.

When the name text field creates an event, it is handled by the action method. The action method is set to recognize this event, except it is not set to do anything when it gets the event. You are going to change this.

The first step is to declare an extension of the Dialog class.

```
class WarningDialog extends Dialog {

 private Button OkButton = new Button("OK");
 private Label ALabel;

 WarningDialog(Frame HostFrame, String Message)  {
  super(HostFrame, "Warning!", false);

  ALabel = new Label(Message);
  resize(180,100);

  setLayout(new FlowLayout());
  add(ALabel);
  add(OkButton);
 }

 public boolean action (Event InEvent, Object Param)  {
  if (InEvent.target == OkButton)  {
   hide();
  }
  return true;
 }
}
```

Add this class declaration to the Order Entry System class declaration file. Then, declare an instance of it inside of the OrderEntryFrameType:

```
WarningDialog WDialog = new WarningDialog(this, "You have not entered a name. ");
```

To display the warning dialog, call the show() method, which is inherited from the dialog class when the dialog class is extended:

```
WDialog.show();
```

Figure 8.6 shows what happens when the user of the Order Entry System leaves the name field blank.

Figure 8.6.

The Order Entry System with
the WarningDialog class
included.

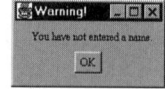

The new extension of the Dialog works great, but look at what happens when the dialog box window is resized in Figure 8.7.

Figure 8.7.

The WarningDialog box resized.

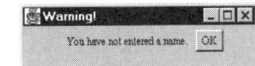

The layout of the components in the dialog box is at fault. For now, the default layout (which is the FlowLayout manager) has been used. But it is obvious that this isn't going to work. The next section covers the different AWT layout managers and applies one to the Order Entry System.

TIP:

The this keyword is very useful in Java. It refers to the current class. For example, you want to attach a dialog to a frame and declare that dialog in the frame. You say,

```
Dialog D = new Dialog(this, "Sample", true);
```

Layout Managers in the AWT

AWT layout managers are the means by which you, the programmer, can give a set of general rules to determine how your components in a container are arranged. Remember, applets are standard with an initial panel incorporated so you can set the layout of your applet face.

In other windowing systems such as Microsoft Windows, the programmer specifies actual coordinates for different components of the window to be arranged. However, this is impossible in Java since the goal is platform independence. The window you create under Solaris should work on a Macintosh, a DEC Alpha, and an NeXT. This goal of independence makes some tasks more difficult. As for the layout of components in general, it is one of the tougher concepts in Java. It is much easier to set the exact coordinates like other systems. While container layout is difficult, it has been designed to be powerful and relatively convenient to implement.

In any case, the following sections outline the five Java AWT layout managers.

FlowLayout

The FlowLayout manager is the default layout manager for applets. If you look back, you notice that the applets constructed earlier follow a general layout pattern. Components are inserted left to right until the end of a row is reached. Then, the same process begins on the next line until that row is filled also. If an attempt is made to place too many components in a panel, the ones that didn't fit are left out.

To set the layout manager you wish to use, the setLayout() method is available. The following code line sets the layout in a panel APanel to the FlowLayout manager:

```
APanel.setLayout(new FlowLayout());
```

There are multiple options you can use with the `FlowLayout` manager. First, the manager allows you to specify the alignment of the layout. There are three constants available in the `FlowLayout` class: `FlowLayout.LEFT`, `FlowLayout.CENTER` (the default), and `FlowLayout.RIGHT`.

You can also set the vertical and horizontal "padding" between different components. This is done in one version of the `FlowLayout` constructors. The default value for this padding is 5 pixels vertical and 5 pixels horizontal.

Table 8.5 summarizes the `FlowLayout` constructors.

Table 8.5. The constructors for the `FlowLayout` class.

Constructor	Effect
`FlowLayout()`	Default constructor.
`FlowLayout(align)`	align is one of `FlowLayout.LEFT`, `FlowLayout.CENTER`, or `FlowLayout.RIGHT`.
`FlowLayout(align, HPad, VPad)`	HPad and VPad are integers specifying the horizontal and vertical padding between components in terms of pixels.

The following r code declares a panel, sets the internal panel layout, and adds a component to that panel:

```
Panel P = new Panel();
P.setLayout(new FlowLayout(FlowLayout.RIGHT, 10, 15);
P.add(new Label("Text."));
```

BorderLayout

The `BorderLayout` manager divides a container into five different segments. These are "North," "South," "Center," "West," and "East." Of course, the "North" segment of a container is the top, the "West" is the left and so on. There are two major constructors for the `BorderLayout` manager:

```
BorderLayout BLayout = new BorderLayout();
BorderLayout BLayout2 = new BorderLayout(10, 15);
```

The second constructor sets the horizontal and vertical padding just like in the `FlowLayout` manager. To add components to a container using this manager, you must specify the region which the component occupies like this:

```
add("West", AComponent);
```

This inserts the `AComponent` into the western (left) region of the container.

The following applet declares an instance of the `BorderLayout` class and then adds one button to each of the five areas. The code is in Listing 8.5.

Listing 8.5. The `BorderExample` applet code.

```java
import java.awt.*;
import java.applet.*;

public class BorderExample extends Applet {
 public void init()  {
  BorderLayout BLayout = new BorderLayout(5, 5);
  setLayout(BLayout);

  add("West", new Button("west"));
  add("East", new Button("east"));
  add("North", new Button("north"));
  add("South", new Button("south"));
  add("Center", new Button("center"));
 }
}
```

Figure 8.8.

The `BorderExample` applet when viewed from the `Appletviewer` utility.

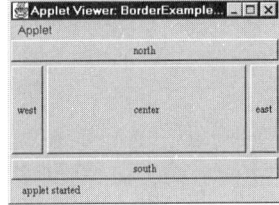

The output from this applet is Figure 8.8.

Notice that the different buttons expand to fill the area they are given under this layout manager.

CardLayout

The `CardLayout` manager is unique among the different layout managers in the AWT. Instead of placing all of the components next to each other, it allows components to be positioned behind each other. Basically, the idea is that you can define a couple of component groups and then when certain actions occur, you can switch between those groups on the same display area.

To put the `CardLayout` manager into use, first define an instance of the `CardLayout` manager in your applet. Then, `setLayout` of your applet to the instance you just declared. For each separate card you want to have, create a `Panel` and place in it what you want. Finally, add each of the new panels using the `add` method.

Table 8.6 shows the methods available for use in the `CardLayout` manager.

Table 8.6. The available `CardLayout` manager methods.

Methods	Effect
first(AContainer)	Display the first card inserted. The parameter is the name of the parent container which implements the `CardLayout` manager.
last(AContainer)	Same as `first` except showing the last item in the layout.
next(AContainer)	Display the next card inserted. The parameter is the name of the parent container which implements the `CardLayout` manager.
show(Acontainer, AString)	Display the card.

Overall, this manager isn't as functional as it can be. Ideally, the tabbed card layouts found in systems such as Windows 95 can be implemented. However, this isn't possible with the current AWT. Hopefully, the carding features of the AWT will be a feature which is extended in future development of Java.

GridLayout

The `GridLayout` manager divides a container into uniformly sized rows and columns. Imagine drawing a grid over a container and then each component filling a grid square as you `add()` them to the container. The placement continues from left to right and top down. There are two major constructors for the `GridLayout` manager class:

```
GridLayout GL1 = new GridLayout(IntRows, IntColumns);
GridLayout GL2 = new GridLayout(IntRows, IntColumns, HPad, VPad);
```

In the first constructor, the two parameters specify the number of grid rows and columns to divide the container into. The second constructor also accepts the number of pixels of horizontal and vertical padding between the grid squares. This manager isn't great for larger layouts, but useful when applied to smaller containers involved in subdividing a large display.

 NOTE:

The "grid" discussed in this section is not represented on the container as any lines or borders. Rather, it is a means to mentally picture the dividing of the container into uniform squares.

The `GridBagLayout` manager extends the basic idea behind the grid layout manager. The main difference lies in that the components can be different sizes in terms of occupying multiple grid spaces. Where components can only occupy one grid space in the container, there are also a number of parameters to align the components inside of the grid. You are also capable of setting component padding and the anchoring of the components inside of the grid square. This is all great and powerful, but unlike many of the other features of Java, not very intuitive.

To implement the grid bag layout, you need to declare an instance of the `GridBagLayout` class. Then, set the layout of the container to this variable where `GBL` is the local instance of the `GridBagLayout` class:

```
GridBagLayout GBL = new GridBagLayout();
setLayout(GBL);
```

The multiple parameters, such as anchoring, alignment, grid position, and so forth are declared in a class called `GridBagConstraints`. To complete any of these settings for a component, you first declare an instance of the `GridBagConstraints` class. Then, you change the constants representing these parameters in the instance of the constraints class. For example, if you want to set the anchoring of the component inside the grid space, you say:

```
Constraints.anchor = GridBagConstraints.NORTH;
```

where `Constraints` is an instance of the `GridBagConstraints` class. To associate these constraints with the component when you add it to your container, you use the following code:

```
GBL.setConstraints(AComponent, Constraints);
add(AComponent);
```

And you continue this process for each component you want to add using this layout manager.

Setting the Layout Constraints

As stated previously, for each component you wish to insert, you must set the current constraints under which that component is inserted. This has been demonstrated before when the `setConstraints` method is used to set the constraints for a component which is then inserted.

There are a large number of settings for you to set in the instance of the `GridBagConstraints` class. The primary fields of the constraints class are the `gridx` and the `gridy` fields. These specify the x and y coordinates of the grid space in which you wish for your component to appear. Note that the grid squares begin at 0,0 (the upper-left corner of your grid).

There are two ways to insert components into the grid. One way is to specify the actual coordinates in which you want your component to appear. The second way, and the way intended by Java's designers, is to specify both of these constants to be the value of `GridBagConstraints.RELATIVE`. The idea is that you begin placing components into the grid and they are placed left to right, in adjacent squares. Finally, when you want to move down to the next line, you specify the `gridx`.

Use the second method. Placing components in this manner means that you also need to say when you want to go to the next row to place the next component. To do this, set another of the constraints to a different constant. These settings are the `gridwidth` and `gridheight` settings in your instance of the `GridBagConstraints` class.

`gridwidth` and `gridheight` set the amount of grid cells that a component occupies when it gets placed. For example, a `gridheight` of 2 means that the component occupies two grid cells in terms of height. And if you want the component to occupy three cells in width, set the `gridwidth` to 3. Your instance of the constraints in the Order Entry System is called `Constraints`. To set the component to occupy three grid cells in width, use the following line:

```
Constraints.gridwidth = 3;
```

The default for these values is 1. Leave them alone until you are ready to begin placing components on a new row. To do this, set the `gridwidth` to equal `GridBagConstraints.REMAINDER`. This signals the layout manager that this component is the last on this row.

That takes care of the general placing of the components in the grid. There are also a number of other constraints which allow you to place the components inside of the grid space they are occupying.

The first of these is the `anchor` value of the `GridBagConstraints`. This tells the layout manager where the component is positioned inside of the grid box it is occupying. The acceptable values are `GridBagConstraints.SOUTH`, `GridBagConstraints.NORTHEAST`, `GridBagConstraints.WEST`, and so forth. All of the eight directions are covered.

The `fill` parameter tells the layout manager how components such as buttons fill the grid box that they are in. There are four possible settings. These are demonstrated in Table 8.7.

Table 8.7. The four `GridBagConstraints` settings.

Setting	*Effect*
`GridBagConstraints.NONE`	No expansion.
`GridBagConstraints.HORIZONTAL`	Expand to fill horizontally.
`GridBagConstraints.VERTICAL`	Expand to fill vertically.
`GridBagConstraints.BOTH`	Expand to fill both vertically and horizontally.

The `weightx` and `weighty` settings determine the sizes of the different components relative to each other. This is used to have your components spread out to fill the container. Otherwise your components all cluster in the center of the container. The weights are all relative to each other. A component with a `weightx` of 3 has a size three times that of a component having a `weightx` of 1.

If you want to add some pixels around a component to separate it from the other components surrounding it, use the `ipadx` and `ipady` settings in the constraints variable. Whatever number you set each of these values to is the number of pixels that the layout manger places as an empty area around your component.

Recipe for Implementing the `GridBagLayout` Manager

The following steps outline the steps in implementing the `GridBagLayout` manager for a container:

1. Declare an instance of the `GridBagLayout` manager and an instance of `GridBagConstraints` in your program.

2. Set the layout of your container to be the instance of the `GridBagLayout` manager you defined in Step 1.

3. For each component you wish to add, either declare a new instance of the constraints or modify an old one.

4. For the constraints made available in Step 3, set the values in that instance. For example, set `gridwidth` equal to `GridBagConstraints.REMAINDER` if you want to say that you are finished filling this row. Also set other constraints such as the `weightx` or `fill`.

5. `setConstraints` for the layout manager using the component name as the first parameter and the second parameter as the constraints.

6. `add` the component to the container, sending the first parameter as the constraints from Step 4 and the second as the name of the component.

7. Repeat Steps 3 through 6 until you are finished.

Fixing the Layout of the Order Entry System

Now you take what there is so far in the Order Entry System and organize its appearance. The plan is to "divide and conquer" the regions of the entry interface that you have already begun constructing. The entire window face is designed with this goal in mind. The primary layout (the layout manager which is used on the window panel itself) is going to be the `GridBagLayout` manager. As shown, it is by far the most powerful in terms of getting components where you want them. There are a number of sub-panels in use. Each subdivides the main frame window, whose layout is managed by the `PrimaryLayout` which is an instance of the `GridBagLayout` class. Each individual sub-panel is named by function, such as `InfoPanel` which is the sub-panel that gets the user information. Each sub-panel which uses the `GridBagLayout` manager also has an instance of the `GridBagConstraints` class to help manage it. A complete inspection of the code isn't really necessary. The most important concept to understand is the process of subdividing the containers to get the layout that you want. While it is tedious (as you can tell from the length of the code), it is the solution to provide both pretty layouts *and* platform independence. Figure 8.9 is what you end up with after it is all over.

Figure 8.9.

What the Order Entry System looks like after it is completed with this section.

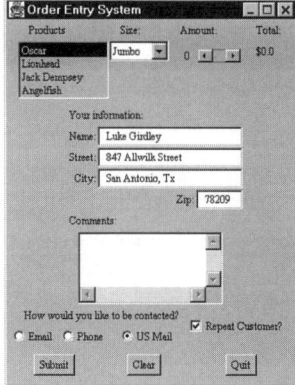

Listing 8.6 is the revised `setup()` and constructor implementation. It now implements the different AWT layout managers to control the placement of the components in the container.

Listing 8.6. The `OrderEntryFrameType` class code.

```
class OrderEntryFrameType extends Frame {

 OrderEntryFrameType (String InTitle) {
  super(InTitle);

 }

 WarningDialog WDialog = new WarningDialog
     (this, "You have not entered a name. ");
public void setup() {

     // Set the initial grid bag layout for the frame.
     GridBagLayout PrimaryLayout = new GridBagLayout();
     setLayout(PrimaryLayout);

     // Set the constraints for the Product Panel, which will contain product
     // choices, sizes, etc.
     GridBagConstraints ProductPanelConstraints = new GridBagConstraints();

     // The Product Panel will take up the rest of the space on this line.
     ProductPanelConstraints.gridwidth = GridBagConstraints.REMAINDER;

     // Declare and initialize the Product Panel.
     Panel ProductPanel = new Panel();

     // Set the layout for the Product Panel and set the constraints for
     // the components inside of the Product Panel.
     GridBagLayout ProductPanelLayout = new GridBagLayout();
     GridBagConstraints InProductPanelConstraints =
         new GridBagConstraints();
ProductPanel.setLayout(ProductPanelLayout);
```

```
        // Here we will set the list panel, which will hold the
        // list choice method and insertion.
        Panel ListPanel = new Panel();
        ListPanel.setLayout(new BorderLayout());

        Label ProductLabel = new Label("Products");
        ListPanel.add("North", ProductLabel);

        // Create the list, 4 items visible, no multiple
        // selections.
        ProductList = new List(4, false);

            // Add items to the List.
            ProductList.addItem("Oscar");
            ProductList.addItem("Lionhead");
            ProductList.addItem("Jack Dempsey");
            ProductList.addItem("Angelfish");

            // Add the List to the list panel.
            ListPanel.add("Center",ProductList);

            // Add the embedded panel to the Product Panel.
            InProductPanelConstraints.anchor = GridBagConstraints.NORTH;
            ProductPanelLayout.setConstraints(
                    ListPanel, InProductPanelConstraints);
ProductPanel.add(ListPanel);

            // Another panel which will be embedded in the Product Panel.
            Panel SizePanel = new Panel();
            SizePanel.setLayout(new BorderLayout());


            // Add a label to the choice of sizes.
            SizePanel.add("North", new Label("Size:"));

            // Create the Choice box.
            SizeChoice = new Choice();

            // Add items to the List.
            SizeChoice.addItem("Jumbo");
            SizeChoice.addItem("Large");
            SizeChoice.addItem("Medium");
            SizeChoice.addItem("Small");

            // Add the Choice to the Applet panel.
            SizePanel.add("Center",SizeChoice);

            // Add the embedded panel to the Product Panel.
            ProductPanelLayout.setConstraints(SizePanel,
            InProductPanelConstraints);
ProductPanel.add(SizePanel);

            // Another panel which will be embedded in the Product Panel.
            Panel AmountPanel = new Panel();
            AmountPanel.setLayout(new BorderLayout());
```

continues

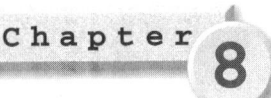

Listing 8.6. continued

```
        // Add a label to the slider.
        AmountPanel.add("North", new Label("Amount:"));

        // Another embedded panel which will contain the slider and
        // the output label.
        Panel SliderPanel = new Panel();
        SliderPanel.setLayout(new FlowLayout());

        // Insert the label which says how many are set
        // to be ordered of the item.
SliderPanel.add(AmountLabel);

            // Create a vertical slider, initial value of 0,
            // minimum value of 0, maximum value of 144.
            OrderAmountSlider = new
            Scrollbar(Scrollbar.HORIZONTAL, 0, 0, 0, 144);
            // Insert the slider to the Applet panel.
            SliderPanel.add(OrderAmountSlider);

            AmountPanel.add("Center", SliderPanel);

    // Add the embedded panel to the Product Panel.
    ProductPanelLayout.setConstraints(AmountPanel,
        InProductPanelConstraints);
ProductPanel.add(AmountPanel);

            // The last panel which will be embedded in the Product Panel.
            Panel TotalPanel = new Panel();
            TotalPanel.setLayout(new BorderLayout());

            // Add the subtotal label and a label saying
            // that it is the subtotal.
TotalPanel.add("North", new Label("Total: "));
            TotalPanel.add("South",TotalLabel);

            ProductPanelLayout.setConstraints(TotalPanel,
            InProductPanelConstraints);
ProductPanel.add(TotalPanel);

    ProductPanelLayout.setConstraints(TotalPanel,
        InProductPanelConstraints);
// Add the embedded panel to the Product Panel.
    ProductPanel.add(TotalPanel);

    // Set the constraints for the Product Panel's insertion.
    PrimaryLayout.setConstraints(ProductPanel, ProductPanelConstraints);
    // Add the Product Panel to the frame.
    add(ProductPanel);

    // The second panel to be embedded in the frame is the Info panel.
    // This panel gets the information about the user.
    GridBagLayout InfoPanelLayout = new GridBagLayout();
    Panel InfoPanel = new Panel();
    GridBagConstraints InfoPanelConstraints = new GridBagConstraints();
    InfoPanelConstraints.gridwidth = GridBagConstraints.REMAINDER;
    ProductPanelLayout.setConstraints(InfoPanel, InfoPanelConstraints);
    InfoPanel.setLayout(InfoPanelLayout);
```

```
                GridBagConstraints InInfoConstraints = new GridBagConstraints();
                InInfoConstraints.gridwidth = GridBagConstraints.REMAINDER;
                InInfoConstraints.anchor = GridBagConstraints.WEST;
                Label InfoLabel = new Label("Your information: ");
                InfoPanelLayout.setConstraints(InfoLabel, InInfoConstraints);
                InfoPanel.add(InfoLabel);

        // The name entry field area.
                Panel NameFieldPanel = new Panel();
                NameFieldPanel.setLayout(new BorderLayout());
                NameFieldPanel.add("West",new Label("Name:"));
                NameFieldPanel.add("East",NameEntryField);
                InInfoConstraints.anchor = GridBagConstraints.EAST;
                InfoPanelLayout.setConstraints(NameFieldPanel,
                    InInfoConstraints);
InfoPanel.add(NameFieldPanel);

        // The Street entry area implementation.
                Panel StreetFieldPanel = new Panel();
                StreetFieldPanel.setLayout(new BorderLayout());
                StreetFieldPanel.add("West",new Label("Street:"));
                StreetFieldPanel.add("East",StreetEntryField);

                InfoPanelLayout.setConstraints(StreetFieldPanel,
                    InInfoConstraints);
                InfoPanel.add(StreetFieldPanel);

                Panel CityFieldPanel = new Panel();
                CityFieldPanel.setLayout(new BorderLayout());
                CityFieldPanel.add("West",new Label("City:"));
                EntryFieldPanel.add("East",CityEntryField);
                InfoPanelLayout.setConstraints(CityFieldPanel,
                    InInfoConstraints);
InfoPanel.add(CityFieldPanel);

        // The zip entry field implementation.
                Panel ZipFieldPanel = new Panel();
                ZipFieldPanel.setLayout(new BorderLayout());
                ZipFieldPanel.add("West",new Label("Zip:"));
                ZipFieldPanel.add("East",ZipEntryField);
                InfoPanelLayout.setConstraints(ZipFieldPanel,
                    InInfoConstraints);
InfoPanel.add(ZipFieldPanel);

        // The comment label.
                InInfoConstraints.anchor = GridBagConstraints.WEST;
                Label CommentLabel = new Label("Comments: ");
                InfoPanelLayout.setConstraints(CommentLabel,
                    InInfoConstraints);
                InfoPanel.add(CommentLabel);

        // Add the comment box.
                InInfoConstraints.anchor = GridBagConstraints.CENTER;
                InfoPanelLayout.setConstraints(CommentTextArea,
                    InInfoConstraints);
InfoPanel.add(CommentTextArea);
```

continues

Listing 8.6. continued

```
PrimaryLayout.setConstraints(InfoPanel, InfoPanelConstraints);
// Add the info panel to the frame layout.
add(InfoPanel);


// Add and create the repeat customer checkbox.
    Panel ContactPanel = new Panel();
    ContactPanel.setLayout(new BorderLayout());

// Add a label to the ContactMethodGroup.
ContactPanel.add("North",new
        Label("How would you like to be contacted? "));

// Declare the CheckboxGroup, and allocate space.
CheckboxGroup ContactMethodGroup;
ContactMethodGroup = new CheckboxGroup();

// Create some checkboxes to put in the group.
Checkbox EmailBox = new Checkbox("Email",ContactMethodGroup,true);
Checkbox PhoneBox = new
    Checkbox("Phone",ContactMethodGroup,false);
Checkbox MailBox = new
    Checkbox("US Mail",ContactMethodGroup,false);

// Add the checkboxes into the applet panel.
ContactPanel.add("West",EmailBox);
ContactPanel.add("Center",PhoneBox);
ContactPanel.add("East",MailBox);

// Sets the constraints for the Contact panel.
    GridBagConstraints ContactPanelConstraints = new GridBagConstraints();
    ContactPanelConstraints.gridwidth = 2;
    GridBagConstraints.RELATIVE;
    ContactPanelConstraints.weightx = 2.0;
    PrimaryLayout.setConstraints(ContactPanel, ContactPanelConstraints);
    add(ContactPanel);

// Insert the different checkboxes into the panel.
GridBagConstraints CustCheckBoxConstraints =  new GridBagConstraints();
CustCheckBoxConstraints.weightx =1.0;
CustCheckBoxConstraints.gridwidth = GridBagConstraints.REMAINDER;
Checkbox RepeatCustCheckBox = new Checkbox("Repeat Customer?");
PrimaryLayout.setConstraints(RepeatCustCheckBox, CustCheckBoxConstraints);
add(RepeatCustCheckBox);

GridBagConstraints ButtonConstraints = new GridBagConstraints();
ButtonConstraints.gridx = GridBagConstraints.RELATIVE;

// Spreads the buttons out across the window.
ButtonConstraints.weightx = 1.0;
ButtonConstraints.weighty = 1.0;

// Declare, set, and add the "Submit" button.
SubmitButton = new Button("Submit");
PrimaryLayout.setConstraints(SubmitButton, ButtonConstraints);
add(SubmitButton);
```

```
// Declare, set, and add the "Clear" button.
ClearButton = new Button("Clear");
PrimaryLayout.setConstraints(ClearButton, ButtonConstraints);
add(ClearButton);

// Set the constraints and insert the Quit button.  This button
// due to the REMAINDER setting will be the last on the line.
GridBagConstraints LastButtonConstraints = new GridBagConstraints();
LastButtonConstraints.gridwidth = GridBagConstraints.REMAINDER;
QuitButton = new Button("Quit");
PrimaryLayout.setConstraints(QuitButton, LastButtonConstraints);
add(QuitButton);

// Method which resets all of the internal values.
resetValues();
}
```

Summary

In this chapter, you covered a good amount of ground. First, you saw the specifics of a number of the different containers available in the AWT, such as the Frame class and the Panel class. You also saw how the Applet class is a descendant of the Panel class. You learned how to manipulate windows from inside your programs and also how to set the menu bar in those windows. Next, you saw how to create dialog boxes using the AWT, and you included these boxes in the Order Entry System. Finally, you learned how to use the different layout managers in the AWT, and you included those in the Order Entry System.

Perhaps the most recognized fact about Java is that it can bring the Web alive. Many lay people believe that Java is "just the motion on the Web." This fact says something about Java and its appeal: graphics and animation. The next chapter covers the basic graphical functions of Java and takes the first steps toward creating animation, covered in depth later in this book.

In the next chapter, the graphical functions and capabilities of Java are added to the Order Entry System, and an imported logo is placed upon the head of the frame. These capabilities are used to incorporate some graphics into the Order Entry System interface.

Chapter 9

by Michael Girdley

The Order Entry System: Adding Graphics and a Logo

Currently, some of the most exciting aspects of Java are those dealing with graphics. This chapter covers these features. First, this chapter covers the AWT Graphics class, which allows you to implement many different graphical items. These features involve drawing, displaying images, and setting colors, among others. This chapter also discusses the Canvas class, which is a special type of component designed for use in dealing with graphics in AWT programs. The Order Entry System is also extended in this chapter as you include the concepts dealt with in this chapter in the applet.

The AWT Graphics Class

The AWT graphics class is an abstract class that is the basis for all graphical constructions in Java. You cannot implement this class directly. To utilize it, you must copy another instance of the Graphics class or have a component generate it. The Graphics class enables you to drawLines, implement boxes and 3-D boxes, use different fonts, and implement different colors. A number of functions in the Graphics class implement these capabilities.

The paint and update Methods

You use the paint and update methods to implement the features in the Graphics class in your programs. You use the following code line to declare the paint method:

```
public void paint(Graphics g)  {
```

Note that the paint method accepts one parameter, an instance of the Graphics class. Here's what happens in the paint method: Your paint method is sent an instance of the Graphics class, which defines the current status of the segment of the display that your class is responsible for. Next, your paint method modifies that state using the methods in the Graphics class and those implemented in other classes. Then the Java runtime modifies the display to eventually match those changes once the execution of your paint method is completed. Then the whole process begins again. Understanding this process is key to writing your own paint method. The paint method is written to describe in code how the display area should look at the program's current status.

 CAUTION:

One of the most important concepts about applying the graphical features of the AWT to your programs is that every time the paint method is executed, it does not imply that any changes in the display are immediately displayed. As you will see in later chapters on multithreading, the display of changes is sometimes less important than other processes that are running in parallel to your applet.

The update and paint methods are initially implemented in the Component class of the AWT. The paint declaration in the code of the Component class is empty until you override it. The update method, by default, resets many of the settings in the Graphics instance you are using and then calls the paint method. The times you override it include occasions on which you want to change the way your displays are changed or in dealing with canvases and animation.

To include the different primitives of the Graphics class, be sure to import it into your program:

```
import java.awt.Graphics;
```

NOTE:

You can implement the update and paint methods. However, you usually don't make any calls to them. There are instances in which you want to force a call to repaint a piece of display as soon as possible. This is discussed in the section covering the repaint method in this chapter, "The repaint Method."

The GExampleApplet example applet shown in Listing 9.1 demonstrates these ideas. The output from this applet is Figure 9.1.

Listing 9.1. The GExampleApplet code listing.

```java
import java.awt.*;
import java.applet.*;

public class GExampleApplet extends Applet {

    public void paint(Graphics g)  {
        g.drawRect(10, 10, 100, 100);
    }
}
```

Figure 9.1.

The GExampleApplet when
viewed through the
AppletViewer utility.

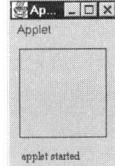

In Listing 9.1, the applet life cycle control methods (init, stop, and so on) are all left as defaults. The default paint method is overridden, and the new method includes code to draw a rectangle on the applet panel using the drawRect method included in the Graphics class. The new paint method gets called repeatedly, and the same rectangle gets drawn on the screen. Complete coverage of the graphics primitives is a major focus of this chapter.

CAUTION:

This chapter does not cover every method available in the Graphics class. If you want a description and listing of all the methods available, check the source code: SRC/JAVA/AWT/Graphics.java.

NOTE:

Note that Java's coordinate system begins with 0,0 at the top left. The bottom-right corner of a screen segment of width and height 100 would be point (100,100).

The repaint Method

Sometimes you want to demand that the Java runtime repaint a component display as soon as possible. This is done through a call to the repaint method in the Component class.

NOTE:

Remember, since almost all the visible pieces of the AWT, including applets, panels, and frames, are descendants of the Component class, when I talk about painting components, I am not just talking about buttons and scrollbars, but containers too.

There are a number of other types of calls to the repaint method. For example, you can specify exactly how long you want it to be before the component is painted again. You can also specify what portion of the component display you want to be repainted (very helpful in animations). For now, just know that a call to the repaint() method of a component makes sure that the display is updated. Simply insert a repaint() call, and the display update will be expedited by the Java interpreter executing your code.

Java Graphics Primitives

The following sections cover the multiple methods available in the Graphics class and related classes that are used to draw graphics.

The drawString Method and Fonts

The process of drawing graphical strings is very simple using the AWT. It is also very versatile. You can specify the exact size, font characteristics, and placement of the strings that you draw onto your instance of Graphics class.

The first step in drawing a string on a component is to set the font specifics that you want. This is accomplished using the Font class, which is part of the AWT package. For example, include this code line to declare an instance of the Font class representing the Courier font with an italic style and a point size of 18:

```
Font afont = new Font("Courier", Font.ITALIC, 18);
```

The first parameter sets the font that you want to use. Examples of some of the available fonts are Helvetica, Courier, and TimesRoman.

CAUTION:

Not every font is available on every system. On some systems, for example, Helvetica is not available. When the font is not available, Java reverts to a default font, which is generally Courier. It is wise to take this factor into consideration when representing strings graphically since you can easily specify TimesRoman and end up with Courier on one machine and TimesRoman on another, both running the same Java code.

The second parameter of the Font constructor describes the font constants, which define italics, bold, and so on. These constants can be Font.ITALIC, Font.BOLD, or Font.PLAIN. You can also define a font to be both bold and italic by using the sum of the two constants. To set the font to be both bold and italic, send the second parameter in as Font.BOLD + Font.ITALIC. If you want the text to be plain, use the Font.PLAIN constant as your parameter.

The third parameter sets the point size of the font in pixels.

You must set the font you have constructed to be the current font for the instance of the Graphics class that controls the display you are going to add the string to. To do this, use the setFont method of the Graphics class. The following line sets the current font of an instance of the Graphics class called g equal to the font you just declared:

```
g.setFont(afont);
```

To draw the string, you use the following line:

```
g.drawString("Leopards Aquatics", 10, 20);
```

The drawString method accepts three parameters. The first parameter is a string representing the text you want to draw, and the second and third parameters describe the x and y pixel position of the string, respectively. The following short applet demonstrates the inclusion of these statements into a complete applet that draws the string onto the applet face. The code is shown in Listing 9.2, and the resulting display is shown as Figure 9.2.

Listing 9.2. The `FirstDrawStringExample` applet code.

```java
import java.awt.*;
import java.applet.*;

public class FirstDrawStringExample extends Applet {

    private Font afont = new Font("Helvetica", Font.BOLD, 18);

    public void paint(Graphics g)  {
        g.setFont(afont);
        g.drawString("Leopards Aquatics", 10, 20);
    }
}
```

Figure 9.2.

The output from the
FirstDrawStringExample
when viewed from the
AppletViewer utility.

In the `FirstDrawStringExample`, note that an instance of the `Font` class is first declared from the AWT package that handles font business such as scaling and italicizing. Then, in the `paint` method, the font is set to be the current font for the g variable, which describes the data concerning the display area you are dealing with. Finally, the `drawString` method actually draws the string at x equals 10 pixels and y equals 10 pixels from the origin.

Table 9.1 lists some of the `Font` methods that are available.

Table 9.1. `Font` methods.

Method	Description
`String getName()`	Returns the name of the font (Helvetica, and so on).
`int getStyle()`	Returns the constant that is the style of the font.
`boolean isPlain()`	true or false depending on whether the font is `Font.PLAIN`.
`boolean isBold()`	true or false depending on whether the font is `Font.BOLD`.
`boolean isItalic()`	true or false depending on whether the font is `Font.ITALIC`.
`getFont()`	Returns an instance of the currently selected font.

Defining Colors

Just as the `Font` class implements methods and values to define the different fonts and settings, the `Color` class in the AWT package implements the ability to manage color in your programs.

There are two ways to specify a color in Java. The first way is to specify the amount of the red, green, and blue components in the color. These values range from 0 to 255 for each different component. You should probably recognize this as the RGB color scheme. Java uses a 24-bit color specification, which is called *True Color* on some platforms. To create an instance of the Color class while initially setting the color in this manner, you can utilize the Color constructor, which accepts three different integers. For example, if you want to define a color to be slightly darker than pure white, you can use the following line:

```
Color AColor = new Color (240, 240, 240);
```

In this code line, you are setting the red, green, and blue. Red is first, green is second, and blue is third.

NOTE:

There is actually a third Color constructor. It takes three float parameters that range from 0.0 to 1.0. It is basically the same as the preceding constructor, except the range per value is now 0.0 to 1.0 instead of 0 to 255. Neither method is more accurate because the method utilizing floats (from 0.0 to 1.0) simply converts those values to integers and calls this first method that takes 0 to 255.

The second way to set a color is to use one of the colors defined in the Color class itself. For example, if you want to create white, you can use the following line:

```
Color WhiteColor = new Color(Color.white);
```

Table 9.2 shows a listing of the different color constants available in the Color class.

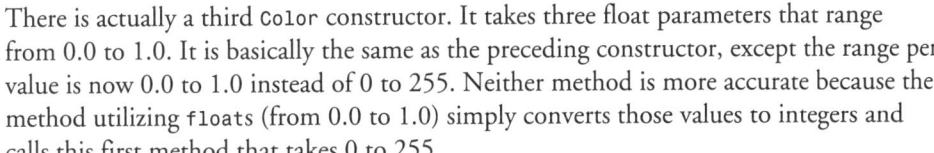

Table 9.2. The color constants available in the Color class.

Color.white
Color.lightGray
Color.darkGray
Color.gray
Color.red
Color.pink
Color.orange
Color.yellow
Color.green
Color.magenta
Color.cyan
Color.blue

Two more methods, which can prove to be very useful, are available in the Color class. One brighter method returns a brighter version of the calling color. For instance, if you want to brighten a Color called AColor, you can use the following line:

```
AColor = AColor.brighten();
```

There is also a similar method called darken along with a number of less useful methods in the Color class. For more information on these methods, check the source code in the class library. However, it isn't likely you'll need more than is described here.

Setting and Using Colors

Once you define a Color, there are a number of ways to use it.

To set the current color that you want to draw with in your instance of the Graphics class, you can use the setColor method in your paint function. This method accepts an instance of the Color class and sets the current drawing color to that color. You can imagine this to be like changing drawing-pen colors. Once you select setColor, everything you draw until you set the color again is drawn in that color. The default color is black. The following line sets the current drawing color to pink:

```
g.setColor(new Color(Color.pink));
```

Besides setting the "pen" color, you can also set the foreground and background colors for a component. These two methods are setForeground and setBackground, respectively. Call this method for a component, and the color gets set to the value of the instance of the Color class, which is sent in as the parameter. Note that these two functions set the background and foreground for the entire component, including graphics that are already drawn. If you draw some graphics in black and then set the foreground color to green, the original black drawing turns green.

The MegaColorExample explores the color capabilities of the AWT and is shown in Listing 9.3. The output is shown in Figure 9.3.

Listing 9.3. The DrawStringExample applet code.

```
import java.awt.*;
import java.applet.*;

public class DrawStringExample extends Applet {

    private Font afont = new Font("Helvetica", Font.BOLD, 18);

    public void init() {
        setBackground(Color.black);
    }

    public void paint(Graphics g) {
        g.setColor(Color.green);
        g.setFont(afont);
```

```
        g.drawString("This is krazee!", 10, 40);
    }
}
```

Figure 9.3.
The output from the
DrawStringExample applet.

In this applet, an instance of the Font class is declared and constructed. Then the init method takes care of initially setting the background color to black. The code in the paint method sets the current drawing color to be green. Then it sets the current font to be the afont variable and then draws the string on the applet panel itself.

TIP:

You can utilize the drawBytes and drawChars methods in the Graphics class. They have limited uses, but for more information, check java\src\java\awt\Graphics.java included with your JDK.

Precision String Alignment

In the preceding example applet, you had to guess where to place the string on the panel. For example, centering the string on the applet panel involves some serious measurement. But the AWT provides a class that automates and simplifies this process. This class is named FontMetrics and is incredibly useful in simplifying the process of placing graphical strings. It is highly useful in centering strings or animating strings. Table 9.3 summarizes the methods available in the named FontMetrics class.

Table 9.3. FontMetrics methods available.

Method	Description
int stringWidth(String)	Computes and returns the width of a string in pixels.
int getAscent()	Returns the number of pixels from the top of the uppercase characters to the original y.
int getDescent()	The opposite of the getAscent function.

continues

Table 9.3. continued

Method	Description
int getMaxAscent()	The maximum ascent value of all the characters in the string.
int getMaxDescent()	The maximum descent value of all the characters in the string.
int getHeight()	This returns the total height (including ascent, descent, and so on) of the font.

These methods are straightforward. To use them, you need to declare an instance of the FontMetrics class in your applet. The following code segment declares an instance of the FontMetrics class and then sets it to return information about a font called AFont:

```
FontMetrics AFontMetrics = new FontMetrics(AFont);
```

The different methods listed are all yours for the calling. To find the total height of your font using the declared AFontMetrics class, use the following line:

```
AFontMetrics.getHeight();
```

CAUTION:

Remember that the FontMetrics class is part of the AWT package, so make sure to import it into your program.

When you place lines of graphical text one after another, increment by the getHeight() function of the Font you are using. To center a string, use this.size.height() and this.size.width() to find out how wide your component screen area is. Then compute where to place your string based on this information and the width of the string in pixels that you can get using the FontMetrics class.

Drawing

So far, this chapter has covered how to draw strings, do neat things with them, and set colors. The following sections cover the graphics primitives you expect in any toolkit. The java.awt.Graphics class includes methods for drawing lines, arcs, polygons, rectangles, and so on. These methods are included in the paint method of your programs.

drawLine

drawLine is the basic graphical primitive. It takes four parameters that are two (x, y) pairs. To draw a line from (0, 10) to (50, 50) on a Graphics g, you use the following line:

```
g.drawLine(0, 10, 50, 50);
```

The first two parameters are x1 and y1, respectively, and the final two parameters are x2 and y2.

drawPolygon

The implementation of this function is just an extension of the drawLine function. There are three parameters: the first two are integer arrays and the third is the number of points, *n*, in the polygon. The first array contains the x1 through x*n*, and the second contains y1 through y*n*. The declaration for the drawPolygon method in this graphics class takes this format:

```
void drawPolygon(int x[], int y[], int numprs)  {
```

There is also a second way to draw polygons. It involves declaring an instance of the Polygon class and then adding your points to the variable one at a time. The following code segment declares an instance of the Polygon class, adds three points, and then sends the polygon to be drawn:

```
Polygon PGon = new Polygon();
PGon.add(1,2);
PGon.add(4,4);
PGon.add(30,30);
DrawPolygon(PGon);
```

Both versions work and do the same job.

drawArc

drawArc is used to draw arcs. The arc drawn is specified by a bounding rectangle. It takes six parameters: the starting x and starting y, the width and height of the bounding rectangle, and the starting and finishing degree positions of the arc. drawArc takes the format

```
drawArc(int x, int y, int WidthofRect, int HeightofRect, int StartDeg, int EndDeg)  {
```

where x and y specify the center of the arc, WidthofRect and HeightofRect specify one corner of the bounding rectangle of the arc, and the remaining two parameters specify the beginning and ending degree positions of the arc. A summary of the drawing primitives is shown in Table 9.4.

Table 9.4. The available drawing primitives.

Method	*Description*
`drawRect(int x, int y,` `int width, int height);`	This draws a rectangle. It accepts four parameters: the initial x and initial y, and the `width` and `height` of the rectangle.
`drawOval(int x, int y,` `int width, int height);`	This draws an oval whose center is (x, y), and the width and height specify the distance from the origin to the side of the bounding rectangle and the top of the bounding rectangle respectively.

`drawRoundRect(int x, int x,`
`int width, int height,`
`in arcWidth, int arcHeight);`
	This draws a rectangle with rounded corners. The parameters are the same as in the `drawRect` function except for the last two parameters. The `arcWidth` and `arcHeight` specify the bounding width and height for the curved corners.

`draw3DRect(int x,int y,`
`int width, int height,`
`boolean ThreeD);`
	This is the same as the `drawRect` method except it adds a Boolean field that specifies that the box should be raised off of the panel if it is true.

`clearRect(int x, int y,` `int width, int height)`	Draws an outlined, clear rectangle using the current background color.

Filling

Filling is as simple as it gets: for all these methods described in the "Drawing" section, replace the word "draw" with the word "fill" and you're ready to go. For example, the following code draws a filled rectangle starting at 0,0 and of width 15 and height 30:

```
g.fillRect(0, 0, 15, 30);
```

Again, to draw these same shapes filled with the current color of the graphics, simply replace the word "draw" with "fill." This also works fine with 3-D rectangles.

AdrawingExample Applet

The `AdrawingExample` example in Listing 9.4 incorporates some of these methods into an applet that draws onto its main panel. The applet has a `paint` method, which draws three different figures using the primitives discussed. There is no action, no motion, so the values stay the same in the `paint` method. When the time comes for animation later in the book, the `paint` method is the place where the work gets done. But for now, the Java runtime calls `paint` over and over, and draws the same image on the screen. The output from the applet is shown in Figure 9.4.

Listing 9.4. The `ADrawingExample` applet code.

```java
import java.awt.*;
import java.applet.*;

public class ADrawingExample extends Applet {

    public void paint(Graphics g) {

        // Draw a rectangle starting at 10, 15 with a height of 100
        // and a width of 120.
        g.drawRect(10, 15, 100, 120);

        // Draw a 3D rectangle starting at 150,15 with a height of
        // 140 and a width of 100.
        // The arc width is 15 and the arc height is 10 for the corners.
        g.drawRoundRect(150, 15, 100, 140, 15, 10);


        // Draw a filled arc which is 75% filled: going from 0
        // degrees to 270 and a bounding rectangle of 130 in
        // width and 140 in height.

        g.fillArc(280, 35, 130, 140, 10, 280);

    }
}
```

Figure 9.4.

`ADrawingExample` demonstrates the basic method to use the different drawing primitives in the AWT's `Graphics` class.

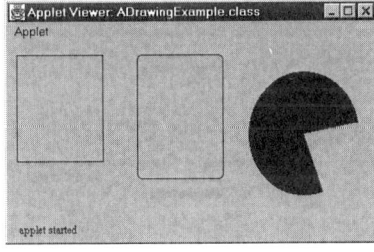

TIP:

Basically, the only tricky issue about using these methods is keeping your parameters straight. Two things can help you with this: have a reference such as this book handy to check your implementations, and print out the actual source code for the `Graphics` package and refer to it.

Displaying and Dealing with Images

Java allows different images to be imported and displayed. There are a great multitude of types of image formats in the world today, and a number of them are supported by Java.

The basic class for image storage is the `Image` class. The `Image` class is platform dependent. It is first implemented as `abstract` and then fully coded in the classes that define the platform-specific code. However, this isn't of concern to you since one of the principles of object-oriented design is that you aren't interested in how things get done, just that they do. You are guaranteed a certain specification in the `Image` and other library classes.

To declare an instance of the `Image` class use the following line:

```
Image AnImage;
```

You should notice that there is no constructor to set up an instance of the `Image` type. Instead, you go about placing pictures into the `Image` type through other methods while the construction is taken care of for you.

Getting Images

There are a couple of methods available to load images into your programs. The first method is specific to some components, and it involves using the `getImage` method and the `getDocumentBase` method to place the image into the instance of `Image`. The `getImage` function returns an instance of the `Image` class, which you then can set another instance equal to that value. The `getDocumentBase` returns the URL of the document that the applet is embedded in. You can use the `getCodeBase` function to return the position of your actual applet code if you want to place your images in the same location as your applet code.

The following line gets an image called `Spalding.gif`, which is found in the same directory as the applet class file:

```
AnImage = getImage(getDocumentBase(), "Spalding.gif");
```

This is simple enough. The first parameter is a function that defines the basis for where the image was found. It returns an instance of the `URL` class that defines an `http` address. The second, of course, is the name of the image itself.

The second method involves the direct use of the `Toolkit` class. The AWT Toolkit is used to bind with a platform-specific implementation of the toolkit. It provides different functions when using `Images`. This is a more specific manner to specify how you will get the image. To get an image using the toolkit, use the following declaration:

```
AnImage = Toolkit.getDefaultToolkit.getImage("Spalding.gif");
```

This statement accesses the default toolkit for a platform and then calls that toolkit's `getImage` function, which returns an instance of the `Image` class. This class is then placed in the `AnImage` variable. Note that the `Toolkit` is abstractly implemented in the AWT and then completely implemented in a local machine's platform-specific libraries.

NOTE:

There are a number of other implementations of the getImage method in both of these areas. For more information, check the source code in the class libraries. These implementations, however, should suit you fine for most tasks.

CAUTION:

You must use the toolkit to get images into your programs if you are creating an application. The first method is useful only with applets because Sun has incorporated the toolkit features into the applet class for simplicity.

Displaying Images

Displaying instances of the Image class after you have placed an image into them using one of the above methods is simple. You will utilize the drawImage function in the Graphic class to paint your image onto the display. The following code line tells a Graphics g to draw AnImage image you declared previously at coordinates (10,20):

```
g.drawImage(AnImage,  10, 20, this);
```

The first parameter is the image itself. The second and third parameters are integers that specify the x and y coordinates. The last one specifies an instance of ImageObserver, which sets what object receives notification of happenings during the loading and display process of the image. You learn more details about the Java Image model in the upcoming section, "The Java Model of Images." In this case, the this keyword refers to the object in which this code is contained.

The applet example ImageExample loads an image and then paints it onto the Applet panel, as shown in Listing 9.5. The output is shown in Figure 9.5.

Listing 9.5. The ImageExample applet code.

```
import java.awt.*;
import java.applet.*;

public class ImageExample extends Applet {

    private Image MyImage;

    public void init()  {
        // Load the image called Spalding.gif into the MyImage variable.
        MyImage = getImage(getDocumentBase(), "Spalding.gif");
    }
```

continues

Listing 9.5. continued

```java
public void paint(Graphics g) {
    // Paint the display with our image.
    g.drawImage(MyImage, 10, 20, this);
}
}
```

Figure 9.5.

The output from the
ImageExample applet, which
loads an image and displays it
on the applet panel.

Table 9.5 summarizes the different implementations of the drawImage method.

Table 9.5. drawImage methods available.

drawImage(Image img, int x, int y, Image Observer iob)

drawImage(Image img, int x, int y, int w, int h, ImageObserver iob)

drawImage(Image img, int x, int y, Color bgcolor, ImageObserver iob)

drawImage(Image img, int x, int y, Color bgcolor, int w, int h, ImageObserver
➥iob)

Variables	
x:	The x coordinate where the image will be placed.
y:	The y coordinate where the image will be placed.
bgcolor:	The background color onto which the image will be drawn.
w:	The allocated width for the image display.
h:	The allocated height for the image display.
iob:	An instance of the ImageObserver class (explained in the next section).

If you do not provide the exact space that your image occupies originally, it is scaled to fit. So make sure that you provide the right dimensions. Otherwise, your images will likely be distorted by the scaling. The ImageObserver in this method is notified only if the graphic is incomplete.

The Java Model of Images

The Web presents a problem when dealing with images. There is a notable amount of time that your applet needs to wait for applets to download. You don't want people browsing your pages to leave because they have to wait too long to see an image. Java is designed with this facet of networking in mind. The model of how its images are loaded is reflected in how it deals with images.

The model is based on interaction between three different pieces: the `ImageProducer`, the `ImageObserver`, and the `ImageConsumer` types. Image producers get images and then relate that image to the consumer. You don't need to worry about exactly where they are because this consumer and producer process happens out of your view for the most part. Image observers are objects that have a stake in what's going on. They can be interested in whether an image is loading or is incomplete.

For example, the `this` keyword included as a parameter in earlier declarations specified the current object to be an image observer. You commonly see an observer set to be the current object by using the `this` keyword. Using this keyword says that you want the current object to be notified if things are incomplete.

The process of handling these notifications is done through an `ImageObserver` interface included in applets and other containers. To find out exactly what has gone wrong, you access the returned flag to the interface and then compare that to the constants held in the `ImageObserver` class. This isn't really as important as it sounds, but if you are interested, check the library source code to implement it for yourself.

Some Killer Reserved Words

Here are some "killer" reserved words (powerful words) and their meanings:

`finalize`   This says that you're finished with an instance of an object and you want the runtime to free the object's resources.

`super`   A parent of a class.

`super()`   The constructor of an immediate parent of a class.

`this`   Refers to the current class.

NOTE:

The `MediaTracker` is a utility class that allows you to manage and track the loading of media components including `Images`. This class uses the concept of threading. Threading is covered in Chapter 16, "Multithreading with Java," and the class is described there.

A Final Component: Canvases

All the graphical examples so far have been drawn onto the applet panel. This has worked great, but Figure 9.6 shows what can happen if components and graphics are combined in this way on the same panel.

Figure 9.6.

The dangers of mixing components and graphics on the same panel.

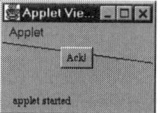

Since you don't know where exactly each of your components will end up, it is impossible to be sure that the graphics and components don't conflict when your applet appears on different machines. What is the solution? Well, Java has a component that is designed to solve this problem: the `Canvas` class.

`Canvases` are components that are designed to be drawn upon just like an artist's canvas. You can draw onto a canvas and insert it into another container or your applet display itself. The `Canvas` class has its own `paint()` method, which handles what is drawn on the canvas face just as with the `Applet` and `Frame` classes. For this reason, `Canvases` must be declared as classes separate from the class that displays them.

Here are the steps to include a `Canvas` in your applet:

1. Inside your applet file, declare another class that `extends` the `Canvas` class.
2. Declare a `public void paint(Graphics g)` method in the new class from Step 1.
3. In the `paint` void from Step 2, do whatever drawing or image displaying you want to do onto the canvas.
4. If you want to tell the `Canvas` when to refresh immediately, have your other methods in the class from Step 1 call the `repaint` method when you want to do so.
5. Declare an instance of your new class in your applet and `add` it to your applet panel.

And then you're ready to go. The `CanvasImageFiesta` applet is shown in Listing 9.6. It puts these steps into practice. It also demonstrates the process of importing and displaying images in the canvas. The resulting output is shown in Figure 9.7.

Listing 9.6. The `CanvasImageFiesta` applet code.

```
import java.awt.*;
import java.applet.*;

public class CanvasImageFiesta extends Applet  {

    public void init () {
        // Typical button delcaration here.
        Button AButton = new Button("Ack!");
```

```
        add(AButton);

        Image anImage = getImage(getDocumentBase(), "Ian.gif");

        // Declare and setup the instance of the OurCanvas class
        OurCanvas OC = new OurCanvas(anImage);

        add(OC);
    }

}

class OurCanvas extends Canvas {

    private Image AnImage;

    OurCanvas (Image InImage) {
        // We have to set the size, otherwise it is invisible.
        resize(250,200);

        // Put the image into the AnImage variable.
        AnImage = InImage;
    }

        public void paint(Graphics g)
            {
        // Draw the image on our canvas.
            g.drawImage(AnImage,5,5,this);
            }
}
```

Figure 9.7.

The output from the
CanvasImageFiesta, which
demonstrates both the use of
canvases and the importation
and display of images.

So, what's going on? Well, first you do the normal applet stuff. The init method creates a button and also an instance of the class that you created that extends the Canvas class. You also load the image and then declare an instance of the OurCanvas class.

In the second class, OurCanvas, you override the default paint method for the Canvas class and create one that draws the image that you receive in the construction of the instance. Then the image is painted on the screen.

Adding to the Order Entry System

Of course, you want to incorporate the concepts of Canvases into the Order Entry System, but to what end? First, you should complete the long-standing goal of adding a graphical logo to the system. Also, it may be nice to add some sort of graphical divider between the different sections of the applet panel. This is accomplished through the use of the Canvas class and the different methods available in the Graphics class.

Adding a Logo to the Order Entry System

To add a logo to the Order Entry System, follow the steps outlined previously in the section on Canvases. First, declare a class that is an extension of the Canvas class, as follows:

```
class LogoCanvas extends Canvas {
```

Notice that this is not a public class. In your applet file, the only class declaration that should be public is the applet class itself.

To do some setup in the new class, define a constructor for it. This constructor accepts the logo, which is loaded in the applet itself. It sets the accepted logo as the private LogoImage variable local to this class. Then the canvas is resized to fit the logo, as follows:

```
private Image LogoImage;

LogoCanvas (Image LogoInCanvas) {

    // Get the image and place it in LogoImage. .
    LogoImage = LogoInCanvas;

    // Resize the canvas to fit the Logo exactly.
    resize (425, 87);

}
```

Next, you create a paint method in the class that handles the continual updating of the display, as in the following code. The code inside the paint method draws the image onto the current graphics.

```
public void paint(Graphics g) {

    // Draw the logo on the canvas.
    g.drawImage(LogoImage,0,0,this);

}
```

Now declare an instance of this class in the original applet and call the constructor. Listing 9.7 shows the LogoCanvas class that is constructed along with an applet to display it. Figure 9.8 shows the resulting output.

Listing 9.7. The `LogoTestApplet` applet code.

```java
import java.awt.*;
import java.applet.*;
import java.net.*;

public class LogoTestApplet extends Applet  {

    // Declare our specialized canvas declared below.
    private LogoCanvas Logo;

    public void init()  {

        setLayout(new FlowLayout());

        // Declare the logo.
        Image LogoInApplet = getImage(getDocumentBase(), "OESLogo.gif");

        // Construct the new canvas. .
         Logo = new LogoCanvas(LogoInApplet);

        // Add the logo canvas to the applet face.
        add(Logo);
    }
}

class LogoCanvas extends Canvas {

    private Image LogoImage;

    LogoCanvas (Image LogoInCanvas) {

         // Get the image and place it in LogoImage. .
         LogoImage = LogoInCanvas;

         // Resize the canvas to fit the Logo exactly.
        resize (425, 87);

    }

    public void paint(Graphics g)  {

        // Draw the logo on the canvas.
        g.drawImage(LogoImage,0,0,this);

    }
}
```

Figure 9.8.

The `LogoTestApplet` when viewed from the AppletViewer utility. This applet demonstrates the use of a canvas to incorporate graphics into containers.

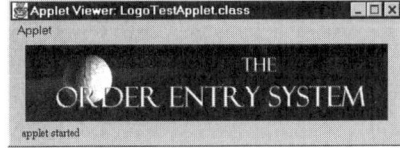

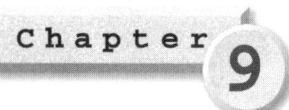

Adding Graphical Dividers to the Order Entry System

One major improvement is to better divide the applet panel so the interface is easier to use and less jumbled. Horizontal bars can be used to improve the organization. To do this, create another class that extends the `Canvas` class and have it draw a horizontal bar the width of the applet and also display a string label in the middle of the bar. Figure 9.9 shows what a bar looks like.

Figure 9.9.

A sample divider that this section will create.

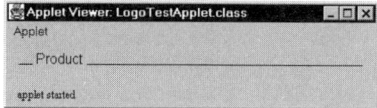

The first step in creating the divider is to create another class that displays the logo, as in the preceding section. Call the class `HorizBar`, as follows:

```
class HorizBar extends Canvas {
```

Then make a constructor that accepts two parameters—the string to display and the width of the bar—as follows:

```
    private String LineString;
    private int Width;

    HorizBar(String InString, int InWidth) {

        // Set the size of the canvas.
        resize(InWidth, 25);

        // Set the local variables equal to parameters so that
        // we can use the values in the paint method.
        Width = InWidth;
        LineString = InString;

    }
```

Then create the `paint` method, which the runtime can use to place what you want on the screen.

```
    public void paint(Graphics g)  {

        // Set the font and font metrics class.
        Font f = new Font("TimesRoman", Font.BOLD, 16);
        FontMetrics FM = getFontMetrics(f);
        g.setFont(f);

        // Draw a line from x = 0 to x = 15.
        g.drawLine(0, 20, 15, 20);

        // Draw the string.
        g.drawString(LineString, 20, 20);
```

```
        // Draw the rest of the line.
        g.drawLine(FM.stringWidth(LineString) + 25, 20, Width, 20);
    }
```

Then use it in an applet, and you're ready to go. Figure 9.10 shows this code added to the preceding `LogoTestApplet`.

Figure 9.10.

The `LogoTestApplet` with an instance of the divider class that was just added.

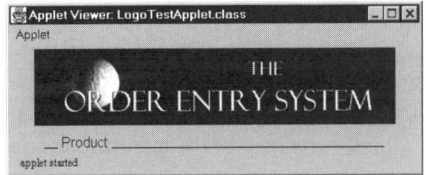

Audio in the Applet Package

There aren't any kind of sound capabilities incorporated into the Order Entry System. At the present time, the audio handling and production capabilities of Java are very limited. However, it is possible to load and play audio bytes. The only format that is currently supported is the AU format, or μ-law.

CAUTION:

These capabilities are very limited. There are no methods to manage or cut up clips. They also do not sound very good in terms of quality. For best results, you may want to use other means such as the browser's own sound production capabilities.

Audio clips are stored using variables of the type `AudioClip`. One function, `play`, is key to playing `AudioClips`.

play

The `play` method has two forms: `play(URL u)` and `play(URL u, String Filename)`. Both accept an instance of the `URL` class that specifies the location of the audio clip. The second function accepts the URL plus the file name.

NOTE:

Another method, `getAudioClip(URL u, String Filename)`, returns an instance of the `AudioClip` class. You can use this to load an audio clip one time. Then you can enter `MyAudioClip.play();` and it is played.

One final limitation of the audio in Java is that it cannot be used with the MediaTracker class discussed earlier in this chapter. Hopefully, in future releases of Java, the MediaTracker class will be extended to deal with audio. Expect further releases of Java to include more capabilities in terms of audio, graphics, and multimedia such as video.

The Order Entry System So Far

As of now, the Order Entry System is about 300 lines of code, and it would be a waste to make you suffer through reading a listing again. The changes made, however, were listed in this chapter. You have made some minor, though important, changes. First, you added two different canvas types: one holding a logo and a second, more generic, class that creates a labeled bar to better separate the panel. Figure 9.11 shows the Order Entry System user interface so far.

Figure 9.11.

The Order Entry System including modifications from this chapter.

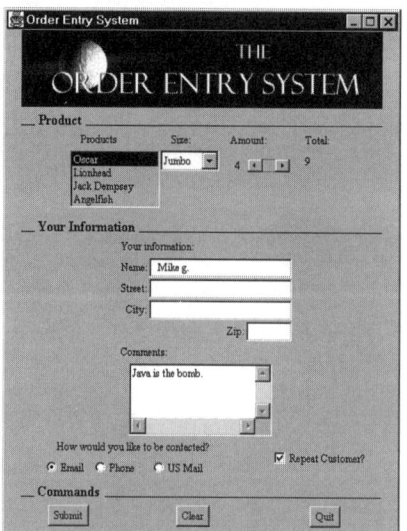

The next chapter, "The Order Entry System: Exception Handling and Browser Interaction," covers a couple of important concepts. One of these concepts is Exceptions, which are explored to see if they are useful in making the Order Entry System more robust. Also, the next chapter uses more of the applet features that allow interaction with the browser.

Chapter

10

by Michael Girdley

The Order Entry System: Exception Handling and Browser Interaction

Many languages do not have built-in capabilities to allow you to detect and deal with errors and mishaps efficiently. Luckily, Java gives you ways to handle these problems simply and effectively.

This chapter explores the process of handling exceptions and errors. In other words, you'll plan on a certain progression through your code, but you also will implement code that will cover situations when things don't go your way. One such instance of when things don't go right generates an exception called ClassNotFoundException. This, of course, is generated when the runtime looks for a class and cannot find it.

Different types of mishaps are defined in the Java libraries, each in separate classes. Each of these separate classes describes what kind of mishap occurs. You also can define your own Exception classes to customize how you are going to deal with something that goes awry in your program.

Handling exceptions and errors accomplishes several things. First, you want to minimize data loss. Also, you want to alert the user that something has gone wrong and try to specify exactly what went wrong as much as possible. You want get out of the program as cleanly as possible and minimize the effect this process may have on other applications or processes.

This chapter covers in-depth these concepts and the command structures to implement them.

This chapter also explores how you can get your applets to communicate and interact with the browser displaying them. You can instruct the browser to load and display a different URL, for example. The process of interacting with the browser also is covered in depth in this chapter.

Finally, you will finish up the Order Entry System in this chapter. You will add the capability to interact with the browser. You also will learn the ways you can get the information in the applet back to your server. A complete final listing is included at the end of this chapter.

Error and Exception Handling

Why should you use exceptions and error handling? The following code structure should look familiar to you if you have ever tried to "home-brew" some code to deal with what now are called exceptions:

```
int errcode = goGetaFile();
if (err != ALLOK) {
    // deal with things. .
} else {
    // we're cool . .
}
```

What's wrong with this? Well, a number of things. First, you have to recode the method used to deal with a certain type of mishap over and over. But suppose that you implement a function to handle this. So, for every different error type, you'll need to create a different function to handle the error. Second, you cannot always return an error code from a function. What if you want to handle errors that might result from a function that returns an integer? How would you set which value specifies an error? What if you have nested procedures or method calls? How are you going to deal with saving the data saved in higher level classes? The answer is that you can't. There must be a better way, and there is.

Error and *exception* classes, as defined in Java, enable you to safely and easily deal with situations in which you want to handle errors and abnormal occurrences. Suppose that your program calls a nonexistent method in another class, or an image cannot be loaded; these are different types of exceptions. An example of a Java error is the OutofMemoryError, which is an error resulting from a lack of necessary free memory space.

The goal of this whole process is to remove the kind of home-brewed code demonstrated earlier in this section. It should enable you to develop an easy way to identify when mishaps occur and then specify another handler function to deal with them. When an exception or error occurs, your code throws an instance of the class that defines it. It then is caught by another segment of code designed to deal with the mishap.

NOTE:

If you have any Ada or C++ programming experience, the exception-handling format discussed later in this chapter should be pretty familiar to you. Java is designed to extend and simplify exception and error handling. Ada has five exception classes, for example, whereas Java has more than three times that. C++ has only two types of exception classes. You also will notice that Java divides exceptions that normally are grouped into one category in other languages into two groups: exceptions and errors.

Both errors and exceptions are implemented in library classes that descend from the class Java.lang.Throwable. Figure 10.1 shows the inheritance path of the Exception and Error classes in the java.lang package.

Figure 10.1.

The inheritance hierarchy of the Exception and Error classes. Notice that both are descendants of the Throwable class.

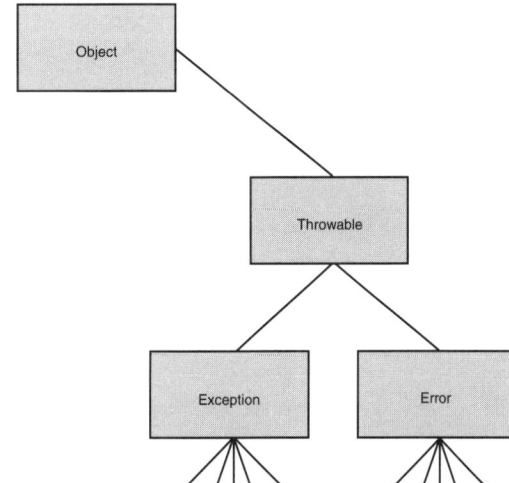

Different types of exceptions and errors are extensions of these two classes. The available Java exceptions follow:

```
ArithmeticException
ArrayIndexOutOfBoundsException
ArrayStoreException
ClassCastException
ClassNotFoundException
CloneNotSupportedException
IllegalAccessException
IllegalArgumentException
IllegalMonitorStateException
IllegalThreadStateException
IndexOutOfBoundsException
InstantiationException
InterruptedException
NegativeArraySizeException
NoSuchMethodException
NullPointerException
NumberFormatException
RuntimeException
SecurityException
StringIndexOutOfBoundsException
```

The available Java Error classes follow:

```
AbstractMethodError
ClassCircularityError
ClassFormatError
IllegalAccessError
IncompatibleClassChangeError
InstantiationError
InternalError
LinkageError
NoClassDefFoundError
NoSuchFieldError
NoSuchMethodError
OutOfMemoryError
StackOverflowError
UnknownError
UnsatisfiedLinkError
VerifyError
VirtualMachineError
```

Why the difference between exceptions and errors? The organizational difference is needed because of the ways the different types need to be handled. Errors and the classes that derive from the `Error` class result from errors inside the system, such as lack of memory or some other error beyond your control. The idea in these instances is just to keep your program from crashing hard and simply to exit cleanly or figure a way around the problem. For this reason, your programming will not have to deal with these thrown `Errors`, because they usually are implemented by other classes that make sure those kind of errors don't occur and are handled nicely (instead of, for example, locking up the machine or crashing the operating system). In other words, you don't need to worry about handling `OutofMemoryErrors`, `StackOverflowErrors` and so on; they generally already are handled for you.

You can concentrate on handling the different types of exceptions that can rear their ugly heads during your programs. Runtime exceptions normally result from your own coding mistakes. For this reason, you should plan on incorporating this process of exception handling in order to cover for your own mistakes. This makes for much more effective and robust code.

NOTE:

Error handling and exception handling are implemented by the same process. They are both thrown and caught. Situations in which you will need to handle errors are very rare. Runtime exceptions are your main concern, because they are usually your fault. A number of other exceptions are available, such as `ClassNotFoundException` or `IOException`, which you may want to use only as a means to prompt the user that something in his installation or setup of your program is wrong. If you notice when you try to load an applet that is specified by your HTML document but isn't there, a `ClassNotFoundException` is reported by Netscape.

Implementing Exception and Error Handling

What if you could just say, in an easily understood format, "Hey, I want you to try and do this stuff here and if anything goes wrong with any of the code, I want you to execute this code here to handle it." Well, that is exactly what happens in the case of handling exceptions and errors.

Four words are reserved in Java to enact the handling of `Throwable` objects. Remember that exceptions and errors are both descendants of the `Throwable` class. These four words are `try`, `catch`, `finally`, and `throw`.

Using try and catch

To implement exception handling around one specific block of code, the words try and catch are positioned in the following structure:

```
try {
    // Some code that might throw an exception. .
}
catch (SomeException EX)
{
    // Do something appropriate in response . .
}
```

So what's going on in this segment? Well, the statement says, "OK, I want you to try this code here and if anything in there throws an exception, the catch statements coming up are going to figure out what to do." If you are accessing something using the URL for that location, for example, you can use this code:

```
try {
    // Doing something with a URL . .
}
catch (MalformedURLException EX) {
    // Do something appropriate to deal with the problem . .
}
```

You also can catch multiple exceptions by using a try statement:

```
try {
    // Doing something  . .
        .
        .
        .
}
catch (MalformedURLException EX) {
    // Do something appropriate to deal with the problem . .
}
catch (Exception E) {
    // Do something appropriate to deal an exception in general . .
}
```

If some method or statement executed in the try block throws an exception, it is caught by the catch statement, which accepts the appropriate exception type and then executes the code inside its block.

Using finally

Suppose that you want some code to be executed no matter what happens in the try statement. You can use the finally clause after your try/catch block:

```
try {
    // Some code that might throw an exception . .
}
catch (SomeException SE) {
```

```
    // What to do if some exception is thrown. . .

} finally {

    // I want you to do this no matter what, if things go wrong or right.

}
```

What happens? The code in the `try` block is executed. If some exception is thrown, the `catch` statement deals with it. Whether things go right or wrong, the code in the `finally` block executes.

This code is useful, for example, if you are modifying a file on disk and you want the file to revert back to its old state without keeping any changes, regardless of what happens. The `finally` block includes the code (or a call to a method) to close the file and then copies the backup you designated as the main file.

The code also is useful if you are in the process of transmitting data across a network, for example. Even if everything goes right or something goes wrong, you want to alert the other computer that it should not be expecting any more data from you. The following code represents this process:

```
try {

    // Transmit data . .

}
catch (Error E) {
    System.out.print("Error " + E + " resulted.")
}
catch (Exception E) {
    System.out.print("Exception " + E + " resulted.");
}
finally  {
    // Tell the other computer the transmission is over . .
}
```

It is important to know that as soon as code in the `try` block generates any class descendant from `Throwable`, the execution of the code stops. If the thrown class is handled in the following `catch`, it is handled there. Otherwise, it propagates up the class line. To reiterate, when something is thrown by code in a try block, the execution of that code is halted immediately.

NOTE:

When catching exceptions or errors, when you specify one type of exception or error, that `catch` statement will catch that class along with every descendant class. For example, you might use the following code:

`catch (Throwable T) {`

This will deal with everything that throws any instance of the `Throwable` class, along with *every* descendant of the `Throwable` class (remember the `Throwable` inheritance hierarchy in Figure 10.1).

Suppose that you use this code:

```
catch (Exception E) {
```

This catches instances of the Exception class, along with every descendant of that class.

Throwing Exceptions

It is apparent that other classes and their methods throw exceptions, so you also want your own code and classes to be able to throw them. To throw an exception called EX, for example, you simply insert the following:

```
throw EX;
```

If you place this statement in a try block, you can catch the exception you just threw in the catch block following it:

```
AnException EX = new AnException();
try {

    // Something bad happens. .
    throw FX;

}
catch (AnException AnotherFX) {
    // Do something about it . .
}
```

Why would you want to do this? Suppose that you want to do something if a certain function returns a value of 0. You use that function in the try block, and then, if the value returned is 0, you throw the ZeroValueException. Then you can catch it in the catch block and deal with it accordingly.

Using Throws

Suppose that you want to have your own class or a method throw exceptions. You would define your class as the following:

```
public class ThrowSomething throws SomeException {
```

By adding the throws to the class or method definition, you alert other classes or methods that use it that they should expect the possibility of having to catch some kind of exception from your class's execution. You also can specify that you want to alert everyone else that you might want to throw more than one type of exception. To do this, simply separate multiple exception types in the declaration with commas. The following class might throw a SomeException class or an AnotherException class:

```
public class ThrowTwoSomethings throws SomeException, AnotherException {
```

NOTE:

Class declarations can get pretty heavy-duty in Java. The following is a valid declaration:

```
public class CrazeeDeclaration throws SomeException, AnException extends Applet
implements Runnable {
```

This declares a class, CrazeeDeclaration, which can throw some exception types, is an extension of the Applet class, and implements Runnable (a declaration dealing with threads, which is covered in Chapter 16, "Multithreading with Java").

TIP:

Don't set all your classes and methods to throw errors and RuntimeExceptions, or any of their descendants. All the RuntimeExceptions or any of the Error class and their descendants are handled already without your intervention. You simply don't have to worry about them.

To specify when to throw an exception, insert the throw clause inside a class that throws an exception type. The following class demonstrates this:

```
public class SomeSuckerClass throws SomeException {

    // Do some stuff . .

    // More stuff . .

    // If something went wrong . .
    If (CurrentValue == BadValue) {
        SomeException SE = new SomeException ();
        throw(SE);
    }
}
```

What happens? The code is acted on, and then if some bad thing happens that you want to throw an exception for, you create a new instance of your extension of the Exception class and then throw it. At that point, the code execution stops, the exception is thrown, and it travels up the hierarchy until it is handled. The execution does *not* come back to your code, so you should expect that when you throw an exception or an error class, you aren't coming back to execute the next line of code.

So, to sum things up, you simply alert the world that you are going to throw an exception through the throw clause. Then you create an instance of an exception and you throw it.

At times, you will want to throw your own exceptions. On these occasions, you declare your own extension of the Exception class. Notice that this was used previously when you threw an instance of AnException. The details of creating your own exception classes are covered in the next section.

Declaring Your Own Exceptions

Why do you want to declare your own instances of the Exception class? Well, there are a couple of reasons. First, if you have an exception that isn't handled adequately by any of the standard library exceptions, you can declare your own. Second, it enhances readability. But be sure not to go overboard in creating exceptions, because they easily clutter your code.

To create your own exception, simply extend the exception type or any of its descendants. Then create constructors for your class:

```
public class MyVeryOwnException extends Exception {
    // The constructor.
    MyVeryOwnException () {
    }
    MyVeryOwnException (String message) {
        super(message);
    }
}
```

NOTE:

Why the second constructor? It is typical practice for the descendants of the Throwable class to allow a message to be included in the class. To include a message when you declare an instance of a Throwable class (or one of its descendants), simply send a message as a parameter when you declare the class. The following code declares a MalFormedURLException and sets the message:

```
MalFormedURLException MFURLE = new MalFormedURLException("We're getting killed here!");
```

To retrieve the message, you can use this code:

```
AString = MFURLE.getMessage();
```

This places the message contained in the MFURLE class into the string AString.

Using Exceptions in the Order Entry System

The first place you'll use exceptions is in the UpdateValues method. You might remember that the UpdateValues method is called whenever a change is made to the User Interface values. It recomputes the new price per item, the subtotal, and the total displayed by the applet. Listing 10.1 shows the updateValues method of the Order Entry System without the exception handling you will be adding.

Listing 10.1. The `UpdateValues` void code listing.

```java
/* This void will change all of the values to match any changes
   in the input settings. First, it declares a number of variables
   local to the method.  Then, it sets a modifier variable and a
   base price variable depending on which items are selected in the
   choice box, the list, and the slider.  Then, it inserts those
   values onto the applet panel.
*/
private void updateValues() {

// The index of the selected size.
      int WhichChoice = SizeChoice.getSelectedIndex();

// The amount of items desired.
int AmountSelected = OrderAmountSlider.getValue();

// The index of the selected product.
int WhichProduct = ProductList.getSelectedIndex();

/* The initial base price and modifier.  Remember,
   the modifier is the amount the base price is multiplied
   by to get the price per item.
*/
    double CurrentBasePrice = 0.0;
    double CurrentModifier = 0.0;

/* This switch statement compares the index of the product
   list, held in WhichProduct, and sets the inital
   BasePrice accordingly.
*/
    switch (WhichProduct) {
                case 0:
                CurrentBasePrice = ProdOneBaseValue;
                break;
        case 1:
                CurrentBasePrice = ProdTwoBaseValue;
                break;
        case 2:
                CurrentBasePrice = ProdThreeBaseValue;
                break;
        case 3:
                CurrentBasePrice = ProdFourBaseValue;
                break;
           }

/* This switch statement compares the WhichChoice variable
   (which is the selected index in the sizeChoice choice
   box) to the different indexes.  And then sets the modifier
    accordingly.
*/
    switch (WhichChoice) {
                case 3:
                CurrentModifier = multiplierSmall;
                break;
        case 2:
         CurrentModifier = multiplierMedium;
         break;
```

Listing 10.1. continued

```
        case 1:
                CurrentModifier = multiplierLarge;
                break;
            case 0:
                CurrentModifier = multiplierJumbo;
                break;
        }

    // Insert the number on the slider to the applet.
    AmountLabel.setText(Integer.toString(AmountSelected)+ " ");

    // Compute the price per item and insert it onto the applet panel.
    double PricePerItem = (CurrentBasePrice*CurrentModifier);
    PricePerItemLabel.setText(Double.toString(PricePerItem)+ " ");

    // The subtotal is the number ordered times the price per item.
    double SubTotal = (CurrentBasePrice*CurrentModifier*AmountSelected);
    // Insert the subtotal onto the applet panel.
    SubTotalLabel.setText(Double.toString(SubTotal)+ " ");

    /* Since the total is the same as the subtotal
        (cause we only have one item to be ordered
        at a time), we can simply use the value in
        the subtotal.
    */
    TotalLabel.setText(SubTotalLabel.getText());
    }
```

If you examine the Order Entry System so far, you'll have a hard time finding instances that just scream *Use exception handling here!* So, you'll create one that will make for a simple example.

One thing that you might want to look for is that the AmountSelected is not 0. If it is 0, you don't really need to update the values. You can implement your own version of exception and have the updateValues method throw it to signify that the value is 0.

 NOTE:

Using exceptions in this case is a bad idea since they are completely unnecessary. You should use exceptions in much more important areas such as dealing with input and output or network connections.

The first step is to define your own Exception class. You'll simply extend the Exception class in general:

```
Exception ZeroValueException = new Exception ("Zero Value Encountered.");
```

You will place this in the `updateValues` method itself. Then you'll say that the `updateValues` method possibly will throw an instance of your new exception. This will be done by changing the class-method declaration for the `updateValues` method. The new declaration for the method follows:

```
public void updateValues throws Exception {
```

So, the next step is that if you come across a 0 value for the `AmountSelected`, you will throw the `ZeroValueException` you created before by saying this:

```
if (AmountSelected == 0) {
    throw(ZeroValueException);
}
```

This throws your exception and jumps out of the method right there before anything is computed.

Finally, you'll need to have code to handle the exception you are throwing. To do this, you'll add a `try/catch` block around the calling of the `updateValues` method in the `action` and `handleEvent` methods of the Order Entry System applet. To do this, you'll use this code:

```
try {
    updateValues();
}
catch (Exception E) {
    System.out(E.getMessage());
}
```

This simply tries the `updateValues()` method and then catches any instances of descendants of the `Exception` class that are thrown.

This (unproductive) addition to the Order Entry System is included in Listing 10.2. The code changes are shown in **bold** type.

Interacting with the Browser

It would be a waste to simply have your applets be static and encapsulated programs inside a browser. Java is designed to allow your applets to communicate with the browser and with each other.

Suppose that you want to get information in one applet and display it to another applet to be displayed. Or, you might want to tell the browser to display another Web page or load and play an audio clip. The next section tells you how to do these things.

The `AppletContext` interface is an interface designed to let applets communicate with the browser. Table 10.1 summarizes the methods available to you as part of the `AppletContext` interface.

Table 10.1. Methods available in the `AppletContext` interface.

Method	*Function*
`Applet getApplet(String name);`	Gets an applet named *name*. If it can't find it, `null` is returned.
`AudioClip getAudioClip(URL url);`	Gets an audio clip at URL *url*.
`Enumeration getApplet();`	Lists the applets available in the current context. In other words, the list of those currently displayed.
`Image getImage(URL url);`	Gets an image at URL *url*.
`public void showDocument` `(URL url, String target);`	Shows a new document in a target window or frame. This may be ignored. Accepts the target strings: `_self:show` in current frame, `parent:show` in parent frame, `top:show` in top-most frame, `blank:show` in new unnamed top-level window, and `<other>:show` in new top-level window named `<other>`.
`void showDocument(URL url);`	Tells the browser to show a document at URL *url*. Note: This may be ignored.
`void showStatus(String status);`	Sets the status string shown.

These methods are all implemented by the different browsers that can display Java applets. Notice that some of the interface methods can be ignored by the browser at their discretion. You should plan your applets accordingly. To find out how specific browsers treat the optional methods is a trial and error process. The extent to which these methods are implemented by each browser is dependent upon the manufacturer's preference.

So how do you implement these methods? Suppose that you want your applet to get an image at a specific URL. You can use this code to load an image and then store it in the `Image` class:

```
Image NetImage = getImage(url);
```

NOTE:

For more information on the URL class, see Chapter 12, "Network Programming with Java."

If you want to tell the browser to load another document contained at URL

```
http://mega.dinky.com/~girdleyj/a.html
```

you can use this code:

```
URL aURL = new URL("http://mega.dinky.com/~girdleyj/a.html");
getAppletcontext().showdocument(aurl);
```

This constructs a new instance of the URL class and then sets it. The next line then tells the browser to show that document at the URL specified.

Another version of the showDocument method is available. As summarized before, it takes this form:

```
getAppletContext().showDocument (URL aURL, String Target);
```

The URL specified tells the browser which document to load. Target tells the browser where to put it. You can tell the browser to display the document and those constants in many places (refer to Table 10.1). The most powerful of these constants are those that allow you to tell the browser to create a new frame, which can be a frame inside of a viewer or a new window itself.

Suppose that you want to tell the browser to display a document in the current frame. You can use this code:

```
getAppletContext().showDocument (aURL, "_self");
```

If you want to create a new browser window named Billy, you can use this code:

```
getAppletContext().showDocument (aURL, "Billy");
```

And it's just that easy. Figure 10.2 shows the output from the Netscape 3.0 when displaying an applet that instructs the browser to display a new window with another HTML file. In this case, the new window simply displays a junk text file.

Figure 10.2.

The output from telling the browser to open a new window using the showDocument command.

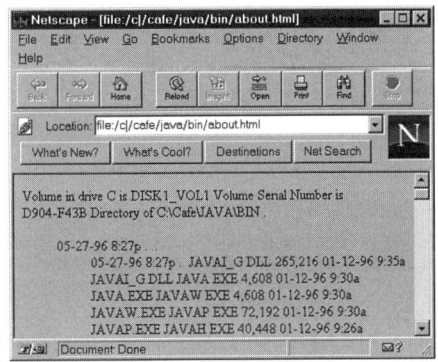

You'll use this feature to call up a new browser window that displays a help file in HTML format. You'll add this later in the chapter when you update the Order Entry System.

Why do some of the interface methods require that you first specify the `getAppletContext()` method before you can use them? Well, if you look at the actual implementation of the `Applet` class, you will notice that sometimes you can simply just use these functions from the `AppletContext` interface without specifying the interface itself, because they are declared again by the `Applet` class. To use the `showDocument` method in general, for example, you can use this code:

```
getAppletContext().showDocument(. . .);
```

If you are unable to get a method to work that you know is in the interface, you might want to try this code to call it directly instead of going through the applet itself.

Using Parameters in Applets

The `java.awt.Applet` class specifies a method called `getParameter`, which allows you to get parameters specified in the HTML document containing your applet. The parameters are referenced by name.

See Chapter 5, "Writing a Java Applet: The Order Entry System," to learn how to specify parameters for your applets.

The `getParameter` function returns a string that is the value sent in. Suppose that you have the following applet declaration:

```
<APPLET CODEBASE = "http://Madeup.com/" CODE = "YourMama.class"       WIDTH = 100
HEIGHT = 50>
<PARAM NAME = Pone value="1">
<PARAM NAME = Asd value = "Jack Dempsey">
</APPLET>
```

To retrieve the value stored in parameter `Pone`, you can use this code:

```
String InPone = getParameter ("Pone");
```

Notice that the parameter is always a string. If you want to send in values, you must convert the string to an integer. You can do this by using the `Integer` class, which is a wrapper for the integer type that provides different utility functions to deal with integers. One such method is the `ParseInt` function, which enables you to parse a string and return an integer. If you want to get the value stored in the `Pone` parameter, for example, you can use this code:

```
AnInt = Integer.parseInt(InPone);
```

This places the number in the `InPone` variable into the `AnInt` integer. Easy. This feature is useful, for example, if you are making an applet in which you want to allow users implementing it to have different choices for the colors, borders, and so on for your applet without creating a new version for each combination of choices.

Looking at the Final Listing of the Order Entry System

This chapter set a couple of goals for improving the Order Entry System with the concepts presented here. First, you'll set things so that an "about" document describing the Order Entry System appears in a new window after the Order button is clicked, as shown in Figure 10.3.

Figure 10.3.

The final appearance of the Order Entry System with separate window functions added.

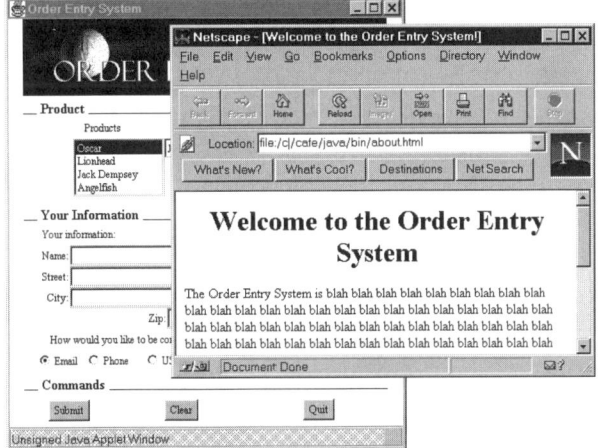

You will use the showDocument method in the AppletContext interface. The showDocument method accepts an instance of the class URL and then displays it in a target you specify. First, you'll want to create your own instance of the URL class that points to the about.html file. Use this code:

```
try {
    URL HelpURL = new URL (getDocumentBase(), "about.html");
} catch (Exception e) {
        System.out.print(e.getMessage());
    }
```

Why the try statement? Well, the constructor for the URL class might throw an exception, so you have to deal with it. If there is a problem, you need to catch the exception and deal with it appropriately.

Next, you need to tell the browser to display that document at that URL:

```
getAppletContext().showDocument(HelpURL);
```

And that's it. The new browser window loads with the about.html document displayed.

You also will want to implement the (frivolous) exception handling that was described previously in the final version.

Listing 10.2 shows the final version of the Order Entry System, with the changes made in this chapter displayed in **bold** type.

Listing 10.2. The Order Entry System Revisited.

```
import java.awt.*;
import java.applet.*;
import java.net.*;

public class OrderEntrySystem extends Applet {

    OrderEntryFrameType OESFrame;
    Button Order = new Button("Click to Order");
    Image ProductImage;

    public void init()     {
        add(Order);
    }

    public boolean handleEvent(Event InEvent) {

        // Load the logo image. .
        Image LogoInApplet = getImage(getDocumentBase(), "OESLogo.gif");

        if (InEvent.target == Order) {
          Order.disable();

            // Try to create a new URL . .
          try {
            URL HelpURL = new URL (getDocumentBase(), "about.html");
            // Show the applet in a new window. .
              getAppletContext().showDocument(HelpURL,
                      "About the Order Entry System");

        } catch (Exception e) {
          System.out.print(e.getMessage());
        }


          // Display the new window . .
          OESFrame = new OrderEntryFrameType("Order Entry System");
          OESFrame.resize(430,500);
          OESFrame.setup(LogoInApplet);
          OESFrame.show();
        }
        return super.handleEvent(InEvent);
    }
}

class OrderEntryFrameType extends Frame {

    OrderEntryFrameType (String InTitle) {

        // Call the Frame constructor . .
        super(InTitle);
```

```
    // Set the background color for the Applet frame. .
    setBackground(Color.white);

    }

WarningDialog WDialog = new WarningDialog(this,
"You have not entered a name. ");
Panel Pan = new Panel();

public void setup(Image LogoInApplet) {

    // Set the initial grid bag layout for the frame.
    GridBagLayout PrimaryLayout = new GridBagLayout();
    setLayout(PrimaryLayout);

    // Declare the constraints for the Logo.
    GridBagConstraints LogoConstraints = new GridBagConstraints();

    // Construct the new canvas. .
    LogoCanvas Logo = new LogoCanvas(LogoInApplet);

    LogoConstraints.gridwidth = GridBagConstraints.REMAINDER;

    // Set the constraints for the logoinApplet.
    PrimaryLayout.setConstraints(Logo, LogoConstraints);

    // Add the logo canvas to the applet face.
    add(Logo);

    // Declare the constraints for the Logo.
    GridBagConstraints HBarConstraints = new GridBagConstraints();

    // Construct the new canvas. .
    HorizBar ProdBar = new HorizBar("Product", 425);

    // Say that we want the logo to be the last thing on the line.
    HBarConstraints.gridwidth = GridBagConstraints.REMAINDER;

    // Set the constraints for the logoinApplet.
    PrimaryLayout.setConstraints(ProdBar, HBarConstraints);

    // Add the logo canvas to the applet face.
    add(ProdBar);

    // Declare and initialize the product panel.
    Panel ProductPanel = new Panel();

    // Set the layout for the product panel and set the constraints for
    // the components inside of the product panel.
    GridBagLayout ProductPanelLayout = new GridBagLayout();
    GridBagConstraints InProductPanelConstraints =
          new GridBagConstraints();
    ProductPanel.setLayout(ProductPanelLayout);

    // Here we will set the list panel, which will hold the
    // list choice method and insertion.
    Panel ListPanel = new Panel();
    ListPanel.setLayout(new BorderLayout());
```

Listing 10.2. continued

```
        Label ProductLabel = new Label("Products");
        ListPanel.add("North", ProductLabel);

        // Create the list, 4 items visible, no multiple
        // selections.
        ProductList = new List(4, false);

        // AddItems to the List.
        ProductList.addItem("Oscar");
        ProductList.addItem("Lionhead");
        ProductList.addItem("Jack Dempsey");
        ProductList.addItem("Angelfish");

        // Add the List to the list panel.
        ListPanel.add("Center",ProductList);

        // Add the imbedded panel to the product panel.
        InProductPanelConstraints.anchor = GridBagConstraints.NORTH;
        ProductPanelLayout.setConstraints(ListPanel,
                InProductPanelConstraints);
                ProductPanel.add(ListPanel);

        // Another panel which will be imbedded in the product panel.
        Panel SizePanel = new Panel();
        SizePanel.setLayout(new BorderLayout());


        // Add a label to the choice of sizes.
        SizePanel.add("North", new Label("Size:"));

        // Create the Choice box.
        SizeChoice = new Choice();

        // AddItems to the List.
        SizeChoice.addItem("Jumbo");
        SizeChoice.addItem("Large");
        SizeChoice.addItem("Medium");
        SizeChoice.addItem("Small");

        // Add the Choice to the Applet panel.
        SizePanel.add("Center",SizeChoice);

        // Add the imbedded panel to the product panel.
        ProductPanelLayout.setConstraints(SizePanel,
                InProductPanelConstraints);
        ProductPanel.add(SizePanel);

        // Another panel that will be imbedded in
            the product panel.
        Panel AmountPanel = new Panel();
        AmountPanel.setLayout(new BorderLayout());

        // Add a label to the slider.
        AmountPanel.add("North", new Label("Amount:"));
```

```
// Another imbedded panel that will contain
   the slider and the output label.
Panel SliderPanel = new Panel();
SliderPanel.setLayout(new FlowLayout());

// Insert the label that says how many are to be ordered
// of the item.
SliderPanel.add(AmountLabel);

// Create a vertical slider, initial value of 0,
// minimum value of 0, maximum value of 144.
OrderAmountSlider = new
     Scrollbar(Scrollbar.HORIZONTAL, 0, 0, 0, 144);

// Insert the slider to the Applet panel.
SliderPanel.add(OrderAmountSlider);

AmountPanel.add("Center", SliderPanel);

// Add the imbedded panel to the product panel.
ProductPanelLayout.setConstraints(AmountPanel,
     InProductPanelConstraints);
ProductPanel.add(AmountPanel);

// The last panel that will be imbedded in the product panel.
Panel TotalPanel = new Panel();
TotalPanel.setLayout(new BorderLayout());

// Add the subtotal label and a label saying that it is the subtotal.
TotalPanel.add("North", new Label("Total: "));
TotalPanel.add("South",TotalLabel);

ProductPanelLayout.setConstraints(TotalPanel,
     InProductPanelConstraints);
ProductPanel.add(TotalPanel);

// Add the imbedded panel to the product panel.
ProductPanelLayout.setConstraints(TotalPanel,
     InProductPanelConstraints);
ProductPanel.add(TotalPanel);

// Set the constraints for the product panel,
   which will contain product choices, size, etc.
GridBagConstraints ProductPanelConstraints = new GridBagConstraints();

// The product panel will take up the rest of the space on this line.
ProductPanelConstraints.gridwidth = GridBagConstraints.REMAINDER;

// Set the constraints for the product panel's insertion.
PrimaryLayout.setConstraints(ProductPanel, ProductPanelConstraints);

// Add the product panel to the frame.
add(ProductPanel);

// Construct the new canvas. .
HorizBar InfoBar = new HorizBar("Your Information", 425);
```

continues

Listing 10.2. continued

```
// Say that we want the logo to be the last thing on the line.
HBarConstraints.gridwidth = GridBagConstraints.REMAINDER;

// Set the constraints for the logoinApplet.
PrimaryLayout.setConstraints(InfoBar, HBarConstraints);

// Add the logo canvas to the applet face.
add(InfoBar);

// The second panel to be imbedded in the frame is the info panel.
// This panel gets the information about the user.
GridBagLayout InfoPanelLayout = new GridBagLayout();
Panel InfoPanel = new Panel();
GridBagConstraints InfoPanelConstraints = new GridBagConstraints();
InfoPanelConstraints.gridwidth = GridBagConstraints.RELATIVE;
InfoPanel.setLayout(InfoPanelLayout);

GridBagConstraints InInfoConstraints = new GridBagConstraints();
InInfoConstraints.gridwidth = GridBagConstraints.REMAINDER;
InInfoConstraints.anchor = GridBagConstraints.WEST;
Label InfoLabel = new Label("Your information: ");
InfoPanelLayout.setConstraints(InfoLabel, InInfoConstraints);
InfoPanel.add(InfoLabel);

// The name entry field area.
Panel NameFieldPanel = new Panel();
NameFieldPanel.setLayout(new BorderLayout());
NameFieldPanel.add("West",new Label("Name:"));
NameFieldPanel.add("East",NameEntryField);
InInfoConstraints.anchor = GridBagConstraints.EAST;
InfoPanelLayout.setConstraints(NameFieldPanel,
        InInfoConstraints);
InfoPanel.add(NameFieldPanel);

// The Street entry area implementation.
Panel StreetFieldPanel = new Panel();
StreetFieldPanel.setLayout(new BorderLayout());
StreetFieldPanel.add("West",new Label("Street:"));
StreetFieldPanel.add("East",StreetEntryField);
InfoPanelLayout.setConstraints(StreetFieldPanel,
        InInfoConstraints);
InfoPanel.add(StreetFieldPanel);

Panel CityFieldPanel = new Panel();
CityFieldPanel.setLayout = new BorderLayout());
CityFieldPanel.add("West",new Label("City:"));
CityFieldPanel.add("East",CityEntryField);
InfoPanelLayout.setConstraints(CityFieldPanel, InInfoConstraints);
InfoPanel.add(CityFieldPanel);

// The zip entry field implementation.
Panel ZipFieldPanel = new Panel();
ZipFieldPanel.setLayout(new BorderLayout());
ZipFieldPanel.add("West",new Label("Zip:"));
ZipFieldPanel.add("East",ZipEntryField);
InfoPanelLayout.setConstraints(ZipFieldPanel, InInfoConstraints);
InfoPanel.add(ZipFieldPanel);
```

```
PrimaryLayout.setConstraints(InfoPanel, InfoPanelConstraints);
// Add the info panel to the frame layout.
add(InfoPanel);

Panel CommentPanel = new Panel();
GridBagLayout CommentPanelLayout = new GridBagLayout();
GridBagConstraints CommentPanelConstraints =
    new GridBagConstraints();
CommentPanelConstraints.gridwidth = GridBagConstraints.REMAINDER;
CommentPanel.setLayout(CommentPanelLayout);
GridBagConstraints InCommentConstraints = new GridBagConstraints();

// The comment label.
InCommentConstraints.anchor = GridBagConstraints.WEST;
InCommentConstraints.gridwidth = GridBagConstraints.REMAINDER;
Label CommentLabel = new Label("Comments: ");
CommentPanelLayout.setConstraints(CommentLabel, InCommentConstraints);
CommentPanel.add(CommentLabel);

// Add the comment box.
InCommentConstraints.anchor = GridBagConstraints.CENTER;
InCommentConstraints.gridwidth = GridBagConstraints.REMAINDER;
CommentPanelLayout.setConstraints(CommentTextArea,
InCommentConstraints);
CommentPanel.add(CommentTextArea);

PrimaryLayout.setConstraints(CommentPanel, CommentPanelConstraints);
// Add the info panel to the frame layout.
add(CommentPanel);
// Add and create the repeat customer checkbox.
Panel ContactPanel = new Panel();
ContactPanel.setLayout(new BorderLayout());

// Add a label to the ContactMethodGroup.
ContactPanel.add("North",new
    Label("How would you like to be contacted? "));

// Declare the checkbox group, and allocate space.
CheckboxGroup ContactMethodGroup;
ContactMethodGroup = new CheckboxGroup();

// Create some checkboxes to put in the group.
Checkbox EmailBox = new Checkbox("Email",ContactMethodGroup,true);
Checkbox PhoneBox = new
    Checkbox("Phone",ContactMethodGroup,false);
Checkbox MailBox = new
    Checkbox("US Mail",ContactMethodGroup,false);

// Add the checkboxes into the applet panel.
ContactPanel.add("West",EmailBox);
ContactPanel.add("Center",PhoneBox);
ContactPanel.add("East",MailBox);

// Sets the constraints for the contact panel.
GridBagConstraints ContactPanelConstraints =
    new GridBagConstraints();
ContactPanelConstraints.gridwidth = 2;
ContactPanelConstraints.weightx = 2.0;
```

Listing 10.2. continued

```java
        PrimaryLayout.setConstraints(ContactPanel, ContactPanelConstraints);
        add(ContactPanel);

        // Insert the different checkboxes into the panel.
        GridBagConstraints CustCheckBoxConstraints =  new GridBagConstraints();
        CustCheckBoxConstraints.weightx =1.0;
        CustCheckBoxConstraints.gridwidth = GridBagConstraints.REMAINDER;
        Checkbox RepeatCustCheckBox = new Checkbox("Repeat Customer?");
        PrimaryLayout.setConstraints(RepeatCustCheckBox,
        CustCheckBoxConstraints);
        add(RepeatCustCheckBox);

        // Construct the new canvas. .
        HorizBar ButtonBar = new HorizBar("Commands", 425);

        // Set the constraints for the logoin applet.
        PrimaryLayout.setConstraints(ButtonBar, HBarConstraints);

        // Add the logo canvas to the applet face.
        add(ButtonBar);

        GridBagConstraints ButtonConstraints = new GridBagConstraints();
        ButtonConstraints.gridx = GridBagConstraints.RELATIVE;

        // Spreads the buttons out across the window.
        ButtonConstraints.weightx = 1.0;
        ButtonConstraints.weighty = 1.0;

        // Declare, set, and add the "Submit" button.
        SubmitButton = new Button("Submit");
        PrimaryLayout.setConstraints(SubmitButton, ButtonConstraints);
        add(SubmitButton);

        // Declare, set, and add the "Clear" button.
        ClearButton = new Button("Clear");
        PrimaryLayout.setConstraints(ClearButton, ButtonConstraints);
        add(ClearButton);

        // Set the constraints and insert the quit button.  This button
        // due to the REMAINDER setting will be the last on the line.
        GridBagConstraints LastButtonConstraints = new GridBagConstraints();
        LastButtonConstraints.gridwidth = GridBagConstraints.REMAINDER;
        QuitButton = new Button("Quit");
        PrimaryLayout.setConstraints(QuitButton, LastButtonConstraints);
        add(QuitButton);

        // Method that resets all of the internal values.
        resetValues();
        }

    // The subtotal and total variables.
    private double SubTotalOne = 0.0;
    private double Total = 0.0;

    // The price multipliers for each different product size.
    private double multiplierSmall = 0.5;
```

```
private double multiplierMedium = 1.0;
private double multiplierLarge = 1.5;
private double multiplierJumbo = 2.25;

// The local constant base prices.
static double ProdOneBaseValue = 1.0;
static double ProdTwoBaseValue = 1.33;
static double ProdThreeBaseValue = 1.75;
static double ProdFourBaseValue = 8.75;

// Declare all of the variables we'll use.
private Button SubmitButton;
private Button ClearButton;
private Button QuitButton;
private Checkbox RepeatCustCheckBox;

private Checkbox MailBox;
private Checkbox EmailBox;
private Checkbox PhoneBox;

private List ProductList;
private Choice SizeChoice;
private Scrollbar OrderAmountSlider;

// The labels that will be variable and change when
// the other selections are changed.
private Label SubTotalLabel = new Label("$0.0 ");
private Label TotalLabel = new Label("$0.0 ");
private Label AmountLabel = new Label("0 ");
private Label PricePerItemLabel = new Label("$0.0 ");

// The entry field for the user to enter his name.
private TextField NameEntryField = new TextField(25);
private TextField ZipEntryField = new TextField(6);
private TextField StreetEntryField = new TextField(25);
private TextField CityEntryField = new TextField(25);
// The comment entry area.
private TextArea CommentTextArea = new TextArea(4, 25);

// Our own exception . .
private Exception ZeroValueException;

private void updateValues() throws Exception {

    int WhichChoice = SizeChoice.getSelectedIndex();
    int AmountSelected = OrderAmountSlider.getValue();
    int WhichProduct = ProductList.getSelectedIndex();
    double CurrentBasePrice = 0.0;
    double CurrentModifier = 0.0;

    if (AmountSelected == 0) {
     throw(ZeroValueException);
    }

    switch (WhichProduct) {
        case 0:
            CurrentBasePrice = ProdOneBaseValue;
            break;
```

Listing 10.2. continued

```
            case 1:
                CurrentBasePrice = ProdTwoBaseValue;
                break;
            case 2:
                CurrentBasePrice = ProdThreeBaseValue;
                break;
            case 3:
                CurrentBasePrice = ProdFourBaseValue;
                break;
        }

        switch (WhichChoice) {
            case 3:
                CurrentModifier = multiplierSmall;
                break;
            case 2:
                CurrentModifier = multiplierMedium;
                break;
            case 1:
                CurrentModifier = multiplierLarge;
                break;
            case 0:
                CurrentModifier = multiplierJumbo;
                break;
        }

        AmountLabel.setText(Integer.toString(AmountSelected)+ " ");
        double PricePerItem = (CurrentBasePrice*CurrentModifier);
        PricePerItemLabel.setText(Double.toString(PricePerItem)+ " ");
        double SubTotal = (CurrentBasePrice*CurrentModifier*AmountSelected);
        SubTotalLabel.setText(Double.toString(SubTotal)+ " ");
        TotalLabel.setText(SubTotalLabel.getText());
    }

    // This method will be called when the user presses the "Clear" button and
    // also when the applet is initialized in the init() method.
    public void resetValues() {

        // Reset all of these labels to zero.
        SubTotalLabel.setText("$0.0 ");
        TotalLabel.setText("$0.0 ");
        AmountLabel.setText("0 ");
        PricePerItemLabel.setText("$0.0 ");

        // Clear all of the lists and choices.
        ProductList.select(0);
        SizeChoice.select(0);
        OrderAmountSlider.setValue(0);

        // Clear all of the text fields.
        NameEntryField.setText("");
        StreetEntryField.setText("");
        CityEntryField.setText("");
        ZipEntryField.setText("");
    }
```

```
    public boolean handleEvent(Event InEvent) {
        if (InEvent.id == Event.SCROLL_LINE_UP ||
            InEvent.id == Event.SCROLL_LINE_DOWN)  {
                try {
                    updateValues();
                } catch (Exception e) {}
        } else
        if (InEvent.target == ProductList) {
                try {
                    updateValues();
                } catch (Exception e) {}
        } else
        if (InEvent.target == ClearButton) {
                    resetValues();
        } else
        if (InEvent.target == QuitButton)  {
        // Quit the applet.
            this.dispose();
        } else
        if (InEvent.target == SubmitButton) {
         // Submit the order.
        }
        return super.handleEvent(InEvent);
    }

    public boolean action (Event InEvent, Object SomeObject) {
        if (InEvent.target == SizeChoice) {
                try {
                    updateValues();
                } catch (Exception e) {}
        return true;
        }
        else
        if (InEvent.target == NameEntryField) {
            // Is the field empty?  If so, you could add a
            // pop-up dialog box to alert the user that he
            // has not entered his name.
            WDialog.show();
            return true;
            } else
        return false;
    }

}

class WarningDialog extends Dialog {

    private Button OkButton = new Button("OK");
    private Label ALabel;

    WarningDialog(Frame HostFrame, String Message)  {
        super(HostFrame, "Warning!", false);

        ALabel = new Label(Message);
        resize(180,100);

        setLayout(new FlowLayout());
        add(ALabel);
```

Listing 10.2. continued

```
        add(OkButton);
    }

    public boolean action (Event InEvent, Object Param)  {
        if (InEvent.target == OkButton)  {
            hide();
        }
        return true;
    }
}


class LogoCanvas extends Canvas {

    private Image LogoImage;

    LogoCanvas (Image LogoInCanvas) {

        // Get the image and place it in LogoImage. .
        LogoImage = LogoInCanvas;

        // Resize the canvas to fit the Logo exactly.
        resize (425, 87);

    }

    public void paint(Graphics g)  {

        // Draw the logo on the canvas.
        g.drawImage(LogoImage,0,0,this);

    }
}


class HorizBar extends Canvas {

    private String LineString;
    private int Width;

    HorizBar(String InString, int InWidth) {

        // Set the size of the canvas.
        resize(InWidth, 25);

        // Set the local variables equal to parameters so that
        // we can use the values in the paint method.
        Width = InWidth;
        LineString = InString;

    }

    public void paint(Graphics g)  {

        // Set the font and font metrics class.
        Font f = new Font("TimesRoman", Font.BOLD, 16);
```

```
        FontMetrics FM = getFontMetrics(f);
        g.setFont(f);

        // Draw a line from x = 0 to x = 15.
        g.drawLine(0, 20, 15, 20);

        // Draw the string.
        g.drawString(LineString, 20, 20);

        // Draw the rest of the line.
        g.drawLine(FM.stringWidth(LineString) + 25, 20, Width, 20);
    }
}
```

What's Wrong with the Order Entry System?

The big problem remaining with the Order Entry System now is getting the information back to you. All the ways to do this involve opening a connection back to your server and then transferring the data in one of many ways. One of these ways involves opening an SMTP connection and then mailing the information back to you. Another means is through creating a script on your server to process the information. And finally, you can write a program that listens on a specific port waiting for you to make a connection and transfer the data. The process of constructing these and other network connections is covered in Chapter 12.

The Order Entry System has been developed to mimic the use of similar applets in the real world. To make it a good example and to include as many of Java's features as possible, however, it is not a completely realistic applet. It did give you a good feel for what Java can do and how it is done, though.

Summary

This chapter covered quite a bit of ground. First, you learned about the concepts of error and exception handling in Java. Then you learned about the implementation of these concepts into your own programs and examined many of the different Java reserved words such as `finally`, `throws`, `try`, and `catch`. You also learned how to declare your own exceptions and utilize them and how to use the `AppletContext` interface to interact with the browser displaying your applet. This skill will prove useful in your own applet programming.

You made many changes in the Order Entry System and implemented them. I also included a listing of the final version of the Order Entry System. Chapter 11, "Reading and Writing with Java," will cover the details of inputting and outputting data with Java.

Chapter

11

by Michael Girdley

Reading and Writing with Java

Reading and writing with Java is based on the concept of streams. Just as a stream of water flows in one direction, starting and ending, so does a stream of data. *Streams* are simply linear paths that connect a data producer and a consumer together to allow the *serial transmission* of data (one chunk after another). Streams can connect many different things. A stream can connect two independent processes together, for example. Or, it can connect a class to a file. It can even connect your class to a network.

NOTE:

Remember that applets can only make network or file connections back to their originating server. Streams are useful in applets only for transmitting data between the applet source and the applet itself. You will use streams in Chapter 12, "Network Programming with Java," to enable your applets to connect back to the Web server from where they came.

Streams are the most powerful means of data exchange in use today. They are perfect for Java's object-oriented nature and its multithreaded environment. Multithreading is covered in Chapter 16, "Multithreading with Java." If you aren't familiar with multithreading, you should just know for now that it is basically virtual parallel processing so that your programs can run multiple processes simultaneously.

Java uses two types of streams: input and output. These are defined abstractly in the InputStream and OutputStream classes. All the types of input and output streams descend from these two classes, which are implemented in the java.awt.io package. These two classes and their descendants are designed to help you deal with all the circumstances in which you will be implementing streams.

The `java.io` Package

The java.io package is a group of library classes that enable you to implement and use data streams in your Java programs. These classes derive from the abstract classes java.io.InputStream and java.io.OutputStream. Different subclasses of these abstract classes enable you to use different types of streams in multiple situations. FileInputStream, for example, is a subclass of the InputStream abstract class.

All classes in the java.io package generally throw IOExceptions. These exceptions deal with input and output errors. One such class that is a descendant of the IOException class is the EOFException, which is thrown when a read encounters the end of a file. You learned about exceptions in the preceding chapter. When implementing streams in your Java programs, you need to be sure to deal with these exceptions when necessary.

The Two Big Daddies

As you learned earlier, there are two major abstract classes in the java.io package from which all the stream classes descend: InputStream and OutputStream. The most important fact about these two classes is that they are all abstractly implemented. For this reason, to actually implement a stream, you will not use one of these classes, but instead will use their subclasses. InputStream and OutputStream are simply templates for the process of stream handling.

Each of these two classes is designed to cause a thread under which they are running to wait until all the input requested is available to be read or written. This comes back to the concept of multithreading. The thread in which your stream is implemented can be blocked by the read and write method until its task is done.

InputStream

The InputStream class abstractly implements a number of methods that allow for the consuming of bytes of data. These methods follow:

```
read
skip
available
close
mark
reset
```

read

The read method simply reads a byte. The InputStream class contains several read methods:

abstract int read()	Returns the next byte in the stream.
int read(byte bytearray[])	Returns an array of bytes read in from the stream. The integer returned is the number of bytes in the array.
int read(byte bytearray[], int offset, int length)	This returns the number of bytes read. The bytes read are stored in the bytearray returned, which is of size length. The offset is the offset in the bytearray where the bytes are placed.

NOTE:

As with all the methods in the io package, all these methods throw IOExceptions.

The read function returns a value of –1 to signify the end of a stream.

skip

The skip method is used to move past a number of bytes in a stream. It takes the following form:

```
long skip (long NumBytes)
```

Here, NumBytes is the number of bytes you want to skip, and the number returned is the actual number of bytes that were skipped. This number can be less than or equal to the value in NumBytes if the end of the stream is reached, for example.

available

The available function returns the amount of bytes that can be read without waiting. In other words, it returns the number of bytes that you can have right now, without your process having to wait around for more to be generated. The available function has the following declaration in the InputStream class:

```
abstract int available() throws IOException {
```

close

The close method closes the input stream after you are done with it. This method frees the resources that a stream is using and allows them to be used in other areas. This usually is included in the finally section of your try/catch block performing I/O tasks (see the preceding chapter).

mark

The mark void is implemented in only some of the stream classes. It places a marker at the current position in the stream. This marking procedure is meant to be used in situations in which you must read a little ahead to figure out what a stream contains by using some kind of general parser. Look in the library source code for the InputStream class for a better idea of how Java's designers think you would implement this kind of parser.

You can check to see whether the stream you are using allows the mark method by using the markSupported function:

```
boolean markSupported()
```

This function returns true if you can use markers; otherwise, it returns false.

The mark void accepts an integer parameter that sets the maximum number of bytes you will read before resetting back to the mark with the reset method. If you read past that number of bytes, the mark is forgotten.

reset

The `reset` void returns your read position back to the place where you just marked.

OutputStream

The `OutputStream` class abstractly defines a number of methods that enable you to produce bytes for output. These methods are `write`, `flush`, and `close`.

write

The `write` method in the `OutputStream` class does what you would expect: It places bytes into an output stream. There are three major forms of the `write` method:

`abstract void write(int b)`	Writes a byte b. It blocks your process until the byte actually is written.
`void write(byte b[])`	Writes an array of bytes. It blocks your process until the bytes actually are written.
`void write(byte b[], int off, int length)`	Writes a subarray of the byte array. `off` is the offset in the array, and the `length` is the number of bytes written. This method also blocks your process until the bytes actually are written.

Why is only one of the methods `abstract` for both the `read` and `write` methods? Well, if you look at the source of the `OutputStream` and `InputStream` classes, you'll see that the other methods that are not `abstract` simply do some manipulation and then call the original `abstract` method.

flush

The `flush` method flushes the stream. It pushes out any bytes that are buffered in the stream.

close

The `close` method closes the stream. It releases any of the resources associated with the stream.

So Many Streams in Java

The basic functions are used by the subclasses of the `InputStream` and `OutputStream` classes to allow the reading and writing of more complicated structures than bytes between a variety of sources. This variety of classes is designed to take much of the "grunt work" out of input and output for you, the programmer.

Table 11.1 lists the multiple streams available, which are described in this chapter.

Table 11.1. Java streams.

Stream Type	Types Handled	Function
BufferedInputStream	bytes	Allows the buffered input of a stream of bytes.
BufferedOutputStream	bytes	Allows the buffered output of a stream of bytes.
ByteArrayInputStream	bytes	A stream in which the source is a byte array.
ByteArrayOutputStream	bytes	A stream for which the destination is a byte array.
DataInputStream	all	Allows the input of a stream of binary data.
DataOutputStream	all	Allows the output of a stream of binary data.
FileInputStream	bytes	File-specific stream input.
FileOutputStream	bytes	File-specific stream output.
FilterInputStream	all	Parent class for implementing filtered input streams.
FilterOutputStream	all	Parent class for implementing filtered output streams.
InputStream	bytes	Generic input stream class.
LineNumberInputStream	all	Implements a stream from which you can find out what line you are on at any time.
OutputStream	bytes	Generic output stream class.
PipedInputStream	all	Allows the creation of an input pipe between one thread and a producer thread.
PipedOutputStream	all	Allows the creation of an output pipe between one thread and a consumer thread.
PrintStream	all	Allows the typical text printing of data.
PushBackInputStream	bytes	Implements an input stream with a 1-byte pushback buffer.
StringBufferInputStream	strings	Allows the buffered input of a stream of strings.

TIP:

Remember that these classes are all implemented in the `java.io` package. To implement any of them, you need to use `import java.io.*` or the specific class you will be using. It is best to import only what you need to conserve resources.

The `FileInputStream` and `FileOutputStream` Classes

The `FileInputStream` class enables you to load information from a file located in the file system. The `FileOutputStream` class does just the opposite; it writes bytes to a file in the local file system. Suppose that you want to create an input stream from a file and then load the bytes one at a time and print them. The following code shows how you can use the `FileInputStream` to accomplish this:

```java
int x;

try {
    // Declare the file input stream.
    InputStream fis = new FileInputStream("c:\isnt\it\romantic\abc.txt");

    // Read in x from the file.  If not EOF then print x out.
    while ((x = fis.read())!= -1) {
        System.out.print(x);
    }
} catch (Exception e) {
    System.out.print(e.getMessage());
}
```

NOTE:

| You do not need to open the file; it is done when the `FileInputStream` is constructed.

And there you go. There is also another function you can use with the `FileInputStream` and `FileOutputStream` classes: the `getFD` function, which returns a file descriptor of the stream.

NOTE:

The `FileInputStream` and `FileOutputStream` classes allow only the input and output of bytes.

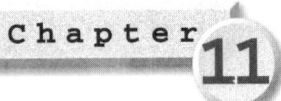
The `ByteArrayInputStream` and `ByteArrayOutputStream` Classes

These two stream types enable you to create streams to and from arrays of bytes. The following code block reads bytes from a stream and prints them to `System.out`:

```
byte b = new byte[100];

// Code to place numbers in b here . .

try {

    // Declare the new byte array input stream. .
    InputStream BAIS = new ByteArrayInputStream(b);

    while (BAIS.available > 0) {
        System.out.print(BAIS.read());
    }
} catch (Exception e) {
    System.out.print("Something went wrong sucka.");
}
```

 TIP:

You also can use `System.err` and `System.in`, in addition to `System.out`. They represent the default error, input, and output, respectively.

 CAUTION:

Using the `reset` method on the `ByteArrayInput` stream resets the read position to the beginning of the stream in all cases, no matter what you do with the `mark` method.

`FilterInputStream`, `FilterOutputStream`, and Their Children

The `FilterInputStream` and `FilterOutputStream` classes are subclasses of the `InputStream` and `OutputStream` classes, respectively. They function in the same way as their parents by making possible the existence of their children. You can implement your own filtered streams, although they will not do much good. The real difference is made by their children (this is discussed in the next section).

The `BufferedInputStream` and `BufferedOutputStream` Classes

The `BufferedInputStream` and `BufferedOutputStream` classes extend the idea of the stream to include the capability to buffer the input and output stream. In a *buffered* stream, the next chunk of read or written data first is placed into a buffer and then is made available. The next read or write, in other words, is not done to the other end of the stream but instead to a buffer in memory.

Why is using a buffered stream advantageous? Well, there is one major benefit: It reduces the overall number of reads and writes to the stream by increasing the chunks of data handled at one time. Therefore, fewer accesses and connections between the device generating the data and the consumer occur.

Two major constructors exist for each of these types:

```
BufferedInputStream(InputStream InS)
BufferedInputStream(InputStream InS, int Size)

BufferedOutputStream(OutputStream OutS)
BufferedOutputStream(OutputStream OutS, int Size)
```

In each case, the constructor takes another instance of a stream and wraps the new buffered stream around it. So, your old stream is now a buffered stream. The following code declares a buffered file output stream:

```
OutputStream FilOutStr = new FileOutputStream("/usr/bin/X11/dinky.dat");
OutputStream BufOutStr = new BufferedOutputStream(FilOutStr, 1024);
```

The second parameter in each of the cases specifies the number of bytes the buffer will contain.

NOTE:

There is also another class available that enables you to buffer an input of strings: the `StringBufferInputStream`. You also can use this class to do the same thing you do with bytes in the `BufferedInputStream` except with `Strings`.

The `PushBackInputStream` Class

The `PushBackInputStream` class implements one more method: `unread`. This method enables you to implement a 1-byte pushback buffer. In other words, it enables you to push a byte back onto the stream. It implements the new `unread` method along with the other methods available in the `InputStream` class.

The `unread` method takes one parameter: a character (or byte) that you can push back onto the stream.

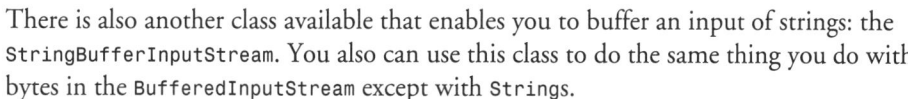

Why would you want to implement this? Suppose that you are using the first character of a stream to specify for what segment of your program this stream will be used. Each part of your program that might deal with the stream then checks the first character and, if it isn't what it is looking for, puts the character back on the stream and passes it to the next handler.

The `PrintStream` Class

Remember all those times you used the `System.out.print` statement? Well, when you did, you were using one of the methods of a class that extends the `PrintStream` class.

The `PrintStream` class enables you to easily handle the output of the normal Java language types, such as integer, strings, and so on. You use this class to output the normal `print`, `println`, and `write` methods you are accustomed to in other languages such as C++.

The `print` method of an instance of the `PrintStream` is overloaded to accept all the general Java language types. Suppose that you want to write a `long` integer. You can use this code:

```
PS.print(ALong);
```

The `println` method prints its parameter and then moves to the next line:

```
PS.println(AnInteger);
```

You also can use the `write`, `flush`, and `close` methods. The `write` method enables you to write bytes to the stream in the same format as the original abstract `OutputStream` class did.

You also can send an object to be printed. The value printed is what results from the object's `toString` function.

The `LineNumberInputStream` Class

The `LineNumberInputStream` class enables you to implement a stream that lets you know what line you currently are viewing. You can declare this stream type as a wrapper to another stream:

```
InputStream LnNoInpStr = new LineNumberInputStream(new
FileInputStream("\usr2\1997\girdley\myfile.txt"));
```

Then, at any point, you can use this code:

```
LnNoInpStr.getLineNumber();
```

This function returns an integer value of what line you are at in the file. Also available is `setLineNumber(int No)`, which enables you to specify the line number of your position. This is useful if you are looking at a file with a header and you want to start counting line numbers after it, for example.

NOTE:

Java uses two types of character types: the ASCII format and the Unicode format. The ASCII characters are a subset of the Unicode character set. The other major difference is in the byte representation of the two types. The ASCII format is stored in seven bits. The Unicode system stores characters in anywhere from 1 byte (8 bits) to 3 bytes for complete Unicode characters. In Java, all characters are stored in the Unicode format.

The `DataInputStream` and `DataOutputStream` Classes

These two classes allow you to read and write data in a binary format without having to worry about all the grunt work involved in implementing and managing that data. These two classes allow you to implement `RandomAccessFileStreams`, which is covered next. The files used by these two classes are by far the most efficient means of dealing with data in Java. You can use the methods of the two classes to read and write Java language types easily to and from a binary storage format.

The `DataOutputStream` class enables you to use a number of methods: `writeInt`, `writeChar`, and so on. There is one of these methods for each of the general Java language types. See the pattern?

The same is `true` for the `DataInputStream` class. A number of methods are available, including `readLong`, `readChar`, and so on. In both classes, you still can read and write individual bytes.

The following code loads the data in a file of integers stored in binary format and then outputs it to the standard output:

```
InputStream IS = new DataInputStream(
      new FileInputStream("/usr2/sun/yidata.dat"));
try {

    while (true) {
        System.out.print(IS.readInt());
      }
}
finally {
    IS.close();
}
```

Easy enough.

The `PipedInputStream` and `PipedOutputStream` Classes

The `PipedInputStream` and `PipedOutputStream` classes are useful for creating pipes (a feature that should be familiar to UNIX system users) that are used to connect two parallel threads (see the next chapter for more information on multithreading). To use this class, simply declare a `PipedInputStream` in one process and a `PipedOutputStream` in the other, and then connect them like this:

```
PipedInputStream InStream = new PipedInputStream();
PipedOutputStream OutStream = new PipedOutputStream(InStream);
```

Now, when one process outputs, the other process can access the data.

Dealing with Files

The `File` and `RandomAccessFile` classes enable you to perform comprehensive management and to use files and the local file system.

The `File` Class

The `File` class enables you to construct an object that contains information about an entry in the file system. Three constructors are available:

```
File(String thePath)
File(String thePath, String theFileName)
File(File dir, String Name)
```

Table 11.2 summarizes the methods available to you.

Table 11.2. File class methods.

Method	Description
public String getName()	Returns the name of the file.
public String getPath()	Returns the path of the file.
public String getAbsolutePath()	Returns the absolute path of the file.
public String getParent()	Gets the name of the parent directory.
public boolean exists()	Does the file exist?
public boolean canWrite()	Can we write to the file?
public boolean canRead()	Can we read the file?
public boolean isFile()	Does a normal file exist?
public boolean isDirectory()	Does this directory exist?
public native boolean isAbsolute();	Is the file name absolute?
public long lastModified()	Returns the last modified date. Should only be used as a comparison to a previous change.
public long length()	Returns the length of the file in bytes.

Random Access Files

The `DataInputStream` and `DataOutputStream` classes allow the implementation of random access files, which are files that you can read from and write to at any point you specify. There are two constructors for the `RandomAccessFile` class:

```
RandomAccessFile(String FileName, String FileMode)
RandomAccessFile(File theFile, String FileMode)
```

The first parameter in each of these constructors specifies the file with which you are dealing. The second parameter is r, w, or rw, which sets the mode of the file to be read, write, or read-write, respectively.

Table 11.3 summarizes some of the methods available in the `RandomAccessFile` class.

Table 11.3. `RandomAccessFile` class methods.

Description	Method
`public final FileDescriptor getFD()`	Returns the opaque file descriptor object.
`public final void readFully(byte b[], int off, int len)`	Reads the remaining bytes in a file.
`public int skipBytes(int n)`	Skips a number of bytes in a file.
`public native long getFilePointer() throws IOException;`	Returns the current location of the file pointer.
`public native void seek(long pos) throws IOException;`	Sets the file pointer to the specified absolute position.
`public native long length()throws IOException;`	Returns the length of the file.
`public native void close() throws IOException;`	Closes the file.

The normal `read` and `write` methods also are implemented.

The following code block opens a file for reading and then prints a character at byte position 1000 in the file:

```
RandomAccessFile RAF = new RandomAccessFile("HalBialeck.dat", "r");
RAF.seek(1000);
System.out.print(RAF.read());
```

Summary

This chapter covered the java.io package. As you saw, there are two "Big Daddies" in this package. You learned about each of the standard methods available in each of those classes. Next, you saw how the library classes that descend from those two major classes function to allow easy implementation of different stream types in Java. You learned about the special details of operating on files.

Chapter 12, "Network Programming with Java," will cover the techniques of creating applets to utilize network resources. Chapter 12 will make a strong use of the information in this chapter to implement streams across network connections.

Part

III

Advanced Java Applets

Chapter

12

by Keith Orpen

Network Programming with Java

Because you're reading this book, you probably don't need to be told what the Internet is. On the other hand, it's easy to use the World Wide Web and various high-level features of the Internet and never think about the amazing kinds of hardware and protocol standards that are humming away efficiently behind the scenes. You could fill a library with all the books and papers that have been written about how the Internet works, but luckily you don't have to. Java programs typically access network resources at a very high level of abstraction, and the gory details are largely hidden from view.

The `java.net` package contains the classes that make network programming so easy in Java. These classes are described in Chapter 3, "An Introduction to Java Classes," and in the Java API. The examples in this chapter make heavy use of them.

The Protocol Zoo

The Internet started out around 1969 as a kind of science fair project by the U.S. military, and it was known as the ARPANET. That network no longer exists, but various protocols that were invented for it are still in use. These protocols allow a collection of physical networks to link up over gateways and become a sort of internetwork, or Internet. These physical networks generally are Ethernet LANs, dial-up lines, and so on. The *Internet* is a logical network cobbled together out of various physical networks that cooperate so they appear to the user as one large network.

This vague definition leaves undefined the word *cooperate*, which is where things get slightly complicated. The various protocols that implement this cooperation have acronymic titles such as IP (*Internet Protocol*), TCP (*Transfer Control Protocol*), UDP (*User Datagram Protocol*), ICMP (*Internet Control Message Protocol*), ARP (*Address Resolution Protocol*), and so on. You certainly can tell it's a defense department project!

As a user of the Internet, you need only a basic understanding of what IP, TCP, and UDP can do for you, as well as a nodding acquaintance with DNS domain names. The other low-level protocols are of interest mainly to network administrators, hackers, and generally anybody with just too much time on their hands.

IP

The Internet is the Frankenstein monster of *packet-switching* networks. Packet switching means that data is sent down a wire (or other medium) in little packets (or datagrams) with a destination address and control fields slapped on the front. It's sort of like the postal system; you have to address your letters correctly. You've probably seen IP addresses hanging around on the Internet, looking like `123.45.67.89` or something similar (this is called *dotted quad notation*). These addresses are 32-bit numbers that identify a particular network device on the Internet (your Ethernet card, for example), via a mapping known as *Address Resolution Protocol* (ARP). The *Internet Protocol*

(IP) defines the basics of how datagrams are addressed and routed, as well as who receives or forwards them.

Whatever you might think of the post office, it at least tries to get your letter delivered reliably. The IP protocol makes no such guarantee. Nor can it; the underlying hardware is intentionally made to be occasionally unreliable in the interests of speed and economy of design. Packets can be dropped (intentionally!) without notice; they may arrive out of sequence or with their data garbled.

Techno-geeks sum this up by saying that IP lives on the *network layer*. In a conceptual tower of ISO networking layers, this is the second floor; it assumes only that there is a way of sending packets down the wire to a specific destination. It's up to the higher layers to provide as little or as much error control and recovery as necessary.

UDP

The next level up from the network layer is called the *transport layer*. This layer defines end-to-end communications in two flavors: UDP and TCP. An endpoint for communication is defined by a *socket*, which is the conjunction of an IP address and a port number. A *port number* is a positive integer that identifies a logical "port" on your machine. These ports are not physical entities; they simply distinguish data arriving over a single physical connection so that it can be delivered to any of hundreds of different "sockets" owned by the various applications on the machine. This provides for a virtually limitless number of end-to-end connections through a single network interface.

The *User Datagram Protocol* (UDP) lets you send datagrams of your own to another host and port number. Essentially, you are just using IP, but with the addition of port numbers and with the various details of IP headers and such hidden from view. Just as with IP, there is no guarantee of delivery, error detection, or sequencing of datagrams.

If you want to use UDP from Java, the `java.net.DatagramSocket` and `java.net.DatagramPacket` classes are what you need. Examples of their use follow.

TCP

The *Transfer Control Protocol* (TCP) slaps a reliable and sequenced connection on top of the unreliable, unsequenced functionality of IP. This is why you often will see the whole setup referred to as *TCP/IP*. A *TCP socket* is again the conjunction of an IP address with a port number. The data you send over a TCP socket is divvied up into datagrams and stamped with sequence numbers and error-detection codes. At the receiving end, the packets are checked for errors and then lined up in sequence order. *Protocol* Packets are resent as necessary, so that the whole stream of bytes arrives intact at the receiving end. It's kind of like registered mail.

Because of the reliable and sequenced nature of TCP sockets, they often are called *stream sockets*; you can read and write data in continuous streams of bytes without worrying about packets, headers,

and so on. Because streams figure so prominently in the `java.io` classes, it's logical to suppose that TCP sockets are a natural in Java—and they are! Stream socket functionality in Java is provided by the classes `java.net.ServerSocket` and `java.net.Socket`.

DNS

Not really a protocol, but more like an entire subsystem of the Internet, the Domain Name Service (DNS) makes it easier on the carbon unit peripherals (humans!) when it comes to remembering IP addresses. DNS is a collection of programs and protocols that allow a central authority to assign symbolic names to Internet hosts based on a hierarchy of domains and subdomains. It's a huge, distributed database of nicknames—one for every Internet host registered in a domain. Suppose that you work at Widgets Galore Company, and your machine has the nickname `wallaby`. Your DNS name will look like this:

`wallaby.WidgetsGalore.com`

The `.com` ending signifies a commercial institution. Reading from right to left, you move from the general to the specific in your DNS hierarchy: not just any commercial interest, but one called `WidgetsGalore`. Not any machine at Widgets Galore, but the one known as `wallaby`. The leftmost word is always the local host name for the machine in question. The remaining words specify the domain of that machine. There may be other machines in the world named `wallaby`, but not in your domain.

The name servers and resolver libraries on the various hosts in your domain know how to answer queries about wallaby; they return the actual IP address of your machine—a 32-bit number. From the user's point of view, this all happens more or less automatically, which lets us poor humans forget about memorizing 32-bit IP addresses and get on with memorizing important stuff, like 20-bit phone numbers.

In Java, IP addresses are encapsulated in the class `java.net.InetAddress`, whether they are given as symbolic DNS names or 32-bit numbers in dotted quad form.

World Wide Web

For many people, the World Wide Web *is* the Internet. It certainly is the most painless and fun way to be a virtual tourist, zooming around looking at pictures of people you've never met and places you'd like to visit. It's also full of ways to search for information on any topic whatsoever. Most importantly for Java enthusiasts, the WWW is the natural habitat for Java applets.

Applets are embedded in Web pages using the `APPLET` tag. When you tell your Web browser to load a certain Web page, it opens a socket connection to a Web server specified in the URL of the page. (A URL is a *Uniform Resource Locator*—the address of a resource on the Web. For a general discussion of URLs, see `java.net.URL` in Chapter 3.) The Web server then writes the contents of the page over the socket connection. Your browser decodes the contents and then displays them according to their type. If your browser understands applets, it reads the APPLET tag to figure out what additional data it must request from the Web server. This data consists of the Java class files defining your applet, which your browser then must load and execute. A Java-compatible Web browser knows how to be a Java virtual machine.

The language of the Web is HyperText Transfer Protocol (HTTP). The browser sends HTTP requests, such as GET and POST, to the server, and the server responds with an HTTP header and body. The header defines (among other things) the content type and content encoding of the body. There are many standard types and encodings, which are known as MIME types. The MIME type for standard Web pages is text/html, which also is known as HyperText Markup Language (HTML). I'm not going to talk much about HTML because you know all about that anyway.

Java allows for flexible interaction with Web servers, including the GET and POST methods of HTTP. But the Web is more than hypertext alone; a URL can specify any one of a number of different protocols to be used for fetching a resource. These include FTP, Gopher, NNTP (Usenet news), and so on. Better yet, you can teach Java about these or any protocol because the way in which java.net.URL objects interpret their contents is fully extensible, via the classes java.net.URLStreamHandler and java.net.ContentHandler (and other related classes).

Sockets in Java

To open a socket in Java, you specify an IP address and a port number. IP addresses in Java are represented by the class java.net.InetAddress, which doesn't care whether you want to specify the dotted quad or the DNS name of a host. You can get an InetAddress for the fictional machine wallaby.WidgetsGalore.com, for example, by using the static method getByName():

```
InetAddress wally = InetAddress.getByName("wallaby.WidgetsGalore.com");
```

On the other hand, you could give the string in dotted quad form:

```
InetAddress wally = InetAddress.getByName("123.45.67.89");
```

It really doesn't matter. To get the address of the local host (the machine you're running on), you can pass the null reference to getByName(), or you can use InetAddress.getLocalHost(). These methods throw an UnknownHostException if (you guessed it!) the host is not known to DNS. An InetAddress object has a constant value; you can't change it, so just throw it away when you're done with it.

An InetAddress alone does not make a socket. You must have a port number. In a typically asymmetric client/server application, only the server side needs to worry about which port number it uses, because only the server side needs to be found at a well-known socket location. So, you can specify a port number or use the magic port number 0, which means, give me any available port. If you ask for a port that is already in use, you trigger an exception. Users generally should avoid using ports 1 through 1024 because these are reserved for system-based services.

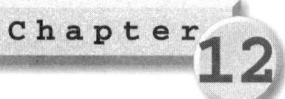

Stream Socket Classes

The handiest sockets for use in Java are TCP stream sockets. For this reason, they receive prime consideration in Java's naming scheme, and they simply are called java.net.Socket. A Socket's whole *raison d'etre* is to be connected to another Socket, so think about how this happens. In order to get a connection happening between two machines, one of them has to ask first, or initiate the connection. This machine is playing the role of client, and the one who answers is a server (these distinctions are a bit arbitrary—after the connection is established, it is symmetrical).

ServerSocket

If the client asks for a connection, somebody had better be listening on the server end. This somebody is a java.net.ServerSocket—an object that creates a passive socket on your local host and then sits and listens to a specific port. Listing 12.1 is a fragment containing a very minimal server class, which accepts connections and then does nothing with them. The main() method calls the handle_connection() method to do any actual work with the socket.

Listing 12.1. A minimal server.

```
public class SillyServer
{
  // A bare-bones example: exception handling omitted!

  public static void main( String args[] )
  {
    ServerSocket serv;
    serv = new ServerSocket( 8081 );
    while ( true )  {
      Socket s;
      s = serv.accept();            // Wait for a connection
      handle_connection( s );       // Got one, now do something!
      s.close();
    }
  }
}
```

This code fragment just listens forever on port number 8081 until a connection is requested and then calls the method handle_connection() to deal with the new connection (the name handle_connection() is arbitrary here; it serves to describe a place to put your application-specific code). The accept() method blocks forever until a connection is received, at which point it returns a new Socket object representing the connection; you should close the Socket when you're done with it. After accepting a connection, the server socket returns to its listening state, and you can accept() further connections on the same ServerSocket as often as you want.

The infinite looping behavior in this server program is typical. After all, you want servers to hang around and service any number of requests. In case another request for a connection arrives before you have a chance to accept it, it is kept waiting in a queue of pending connections. You can specify the length of this queue by an optional second argument to the ServerSocket constructor. It typically defaults to five. When the queue is full of unserviced connections, further connections are refused. In practice, though, handling requests in a single thread is not a good idea unless each connection can be handled very quickly. Most real-life server programs should start a new thread for each connection accepted.

A connected Socket always knows the address and port of the remote socket it's connected to; these are made available by the Socket methods getInetAddress() and getPort(). This allows your server to reject certain connections out of hand; just close the Socket if you don't like the client's address.

Socket

On the client's end, you need to ask the server for a connection. This is done with a java.net.Socket object, which you construct yourself, as shown in Listing 12.2.

Listing 12.2. A minimal client.

```
import java.io.*;
import java.net.*;
public class SillyClient
{
  Socket sock;
  DataInputStream in;
  DataOutputStream out;

  public SillyClient( String server, int port ) throws IOException
  {
    // Create a socket connected to the server:
    sock = new Socket( server, port );

    // Okay, now attach some streams to it.
    in = new DataInputStream( sock.getInputStream() );
    out = new DataOutputStream( sock.getOutputStream() );
  }
}
```

Notice how the client needs to know the exact port number of the server's socket as well as the IP address. You can specify the address as a String or as an InetAddress instance. If the Socket constructor succeeds (throws no exception), you're connected! Also, you never specify which local port is to be used. For the client end, it simply doesn't matter beforehand which port you are using. After connecting, you can find out the local port number by calling getLocalPort().

These are supposed to be stream sockets, so there had better be a way to get a stream attached to them. The methods getInputStream() and getOutputStream() do just that. They return an object of class InputStream or OutputStream, which allows you to read or write using the given socket.

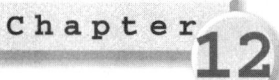
A socket can have a stream of either type or both attached to it; sockets provide a two-way flow of information. When you're done with the stream, it's good programming practice to close() it before you close the associated socket. If you use a form of BufferedOutputStream, you might want to explicitly flush() it on occasion; it certainly never hurts to do so.

For security reasons, applets usually are allowed to connect only to sockets that live at the same IP address as their own class files. This prevents various antisocial behaviors, but it also puts a real crimp in what you can do from a typical Web browser environment. An applet can find out the InetAddress of its home machine by examining its getCodeBase() URL. But keep your applets portable—don't hard code the IP address!

These restrictions don't apply to stand-alone programs (unless your SecurityManager is quite paranoid).

A Basic Client/Server Applet

You'll now do a simple client/server transaction. The server will be a stand-alone program, listening on a specific port on the machine wallaby.WidgetsGalore.com, and the client will be an applet. The client calls up the server, and the server prints a short sales report back to the client. Then the transaction is complete. For this, you just need to flesh out the SillyServer class used earlier—call it SimpleServer, as shown in Listing 12.3.

Listing 12.3. A simple server program.

```
import java.io.*;
import java.net.*;
public class SimpleServer
{
  static final int DEFAULT_PORT      = 8081;

  static void handle_connection( Socket s ) throws IOException
  {
    PrintStream out = new PrintStream(s.getOutputStream());
    DataInputStream in = new DataInputStream(new FileInputStream( "sales.txt" ));
    String line;
    System.err.println( "Connection from " + s.getInetAddress() );
    while ( (line = in.readLine()) != null )
      out.println( line );
    in.close();
    out.close();
  }

  public static void main( String args[] )
  {
    int port;
    ServerSocket serv;

    if (args.length == 1)
      port = new Integer(args[0]).intValue();
    else
      port = DEFAULT_PORT;
```

```
    try  {
      serv = new ServerSocket( port );
    } catch ( IOException e ) {
      System.err.println( "I/O exception: " + e );
      return;
    }

    System.err.println( "listening on port " + port );

    while ( true )  {
      Socket s = null;
      try  {
        s = serv.accept();              // Wait for a connection
        handle_connection( s );         // Got one, now do something!
      } catch ( IOException e ) {
        System.err.println( "I/O exception: " + e );
      } finally  {
        if (s!=null) try { s.close(); } catch (IOException e) {}
      }
    }
  }
}
```

Notice that the server program still does everything sequentially in a single thread. You can get away with this only because the entire transaction lasts just a fraction of a second.

The corresponding applet, SimpleClient, has a button named load, which you click to open a socket and copy the data to a TextArea. Listing 12.4 shows the important parts of the applet code.

Listing 12.4. A simple client applet.

```
public class SimpleClient extends Applet
{
  String server;
  int port;
  Label title = new Label( "A Simple Client Applet", Label.CENTER );
  TextArea text = new TextArea();
  Button load = new Button( "Load Sales Report" );

  public void init()
  {
    // Initialize the applet ...
  }

  void loadSales()
  {
    Socket s = null;

    try  {
      s = new Socket( server, port );
      DataInputStream in = new DataInputStream(s.getInputStream());
      String line;
      while ( ( line = in.readLine() ) != null )
        text.appendText( line + "\n" );
```

Listing 12.4. continued

```
      in.close();
    } catch (IOException e)  {
      showStatus( "I/O Exception: " + e );
    } finally  {
      if (s!=null) try { s.close(); } catch (IOException e) {}
    }
  }

  public boolean action(Event e, Object o)
{
    if ( e.target == load )  {
      loadSales();
      return true;
    }
    return false;
  }
}
```

Now, on the server end, you must provide a file sales.txt, with any text you want in it. After the client-side user clicks the Load Sales Report button, the contents of that file are transferred over the socket and printed in the TextArea. Because applets often are disallowed from opening local files, this is a useful alternative.

In a more complicated application, you need to define a protocol for client/server interaction over the stream socket. The basics of how you connect and use the socket always remain the same, however. It is worth pointing out that for large client/server and distributed applications, packages are available to ease the task. One such package is called *Remote Method Invocation* (RMI), which provides a transparent way to call on the methods of a remote Java object. Later, I'll discuss another approach that is used in ChatApplet.java.

Datagram Sockets

Stream sockets provide a reliable connection to a fixed destination socket, but you pay for this convenience. A slight overhead is involved in checking for errors and correctly sequencing the packets. Moreover, for some applications, using stream sockets for every transmission would be prohibitively complex. Consider the example of a chat applet, which would be a member of a network of similar applets. These applets are to send messages typed by the user to all the members of the network. Using stream sockets, this requires each applet to open a socket for every other applet in the network, so in a network of N machines, there will be roughly N × N sockets open, occupying just as many ports. This is quite wasteful and, in any case, the nature of a chat network is discrete; messages are dispatched in small quantities of text. For this purpose, datagrams are ideal. A datagram or UDP socket occupies one port but can send datagrams to any remote UDP socket. The datagram is sent immediately, and the sending thread does not block waiting for its delivery, regardless of whether anyone actually receives the packet. Short of using some kind of IP multicasting or broadcasting protocol, this is the most efficient way to reach a large number of peers with discrete update-type information.

Although user datagrams are not checked for data errors, you can choose to implement your own checksums. You also might want to have a mechanism for verifying that a datagram has arrived.

DatagramSocket

The `java.net.DatagramSocket` class represents a UDP socket on the local host. You can create it on a specific port:

```
DatagramSocket ds = new DatagramSocket( 9876 );
```

or on any available port:

```
DatagramSocket ds = new DatagramSocket();
```

After the socket is created, you can send and receive datagram packets using the `send()` and the `receive()` methods. The packets themselves are represented by `java.net.DatagramPacket` objects, which you can construct from an array of bytes and addressing information. The `send()` method requires the `DatagramPacket` to be fully constructed; it must be filled in with a correct data buffer, data length, remote `InetAddress`, and remote port. The `receive()` method requires only a data buffer and a maximum length to receive. The `receive()` method blocks until a datagram arrives and then fills in the buffer of the specified datagram. The actual length of the data received then is available via `getLength()`. For example, you can receive string data like this:

```
DatagramSocket sock = new DatagramSocket();
byte b[] = new byte[1000];
DatagramPacket p = new DatagramPacket( b, 1000 );
sock.receive( p );        // wait for a packet
byte data[] = p.getData();
int len = p.getLength();
String s = new String( data, 0, 0, len );
```

Similarly, data to be sent is constructed from an array of bytes. Suppose that you want to send a string. You can use this code:

```
String message;
InetAddress remoteaddr;
int remoteport;
DatagramSocket sock = new DatagramSocket();

// Set the message, remoteaddr and remoteport ...

byte b[] = new byte[ message.length() ];
message.getBytes( 0, m.length(), b, 0 );
DatagramPacket p = new DatagramPacket(b, m.length(), remoteaddr, remoteport);
try {
  sock.send( p );
} catch (IOException e)  {
  // Uh-oh! Do something.
}
```

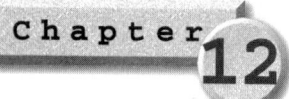

A Basic Datagram Application

This section looks at a very basic use of datagrams: the two-way chat program DatagramChat.java, as shown in Figure 12.1. The user is expected to enter the remote host name and port number, so this program is not really very user-friendly. However, this does avoid the complication of having a central hookup server, which otherwise would be necessary in order to let the chat windows find each other's sockets.

Figure 12.1.

A datagram chat applet.

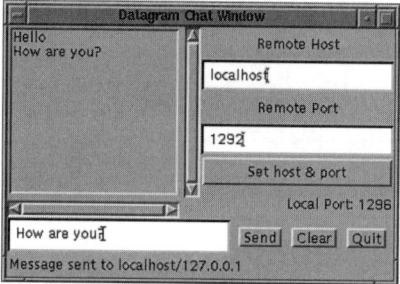

After the user types a message in the input TextField and then clicks Send, the message is sent in a DatagramPacket, along with a leading byte with the value PRINT or ECHO (in this case, PRINT). Listing 12.5 shows the code that the DatagramChat class uses to send a message datagram.

Listing 12.5. Sending a datagram in class DatagramChat.

```java
void sendMessage()
{
  if ( remoteaddr==null )  {
    status.setText( "You must specify a remote host and port!" );
    return;
  }

  String m = input.getText().trim();
  if (m.length() < 1) return;

  byte b[] = new byte[ m.length()+1 ];
  b[0] = PRINT;
  m.getBytes( 0, m.length(), b, 1 );
  DatagramPacket p = new DatagramPacket(b, m.length()+1, remoteaddr, remoteport);

  try  {
    sock.send( p );
    status.setText( "Message sent to " + remoteaddr );
  } catch (IOException e)  {
    status.setText( "Message send failed: " + e.getMessage() );
  }
}
```

The same window must be able to receive messages from the remote peer. To accomplish this, it implements the Runnable interface and has its run() method execute in a separate Thread. All the run() method does is wait for messages and then respond—an infinite loop. The response to a message is to print it in a TextArea, and (if it is marked PRINT) send back the same message, now marked ECHO. Messages marked ECHO also are printed to the TextArea, but they are not returned to the sender. This means that the chat window supports remote echoing; if you don't see the message in the TextArea, chances are the remote user doesn't see it either. Listing 12.6 shows the run() method of the DatagramChat class.

Listing 12.6. The run() method of DatagramChat.

```
public void run()
{
  byte b[] = new byte[MTU];

  while ( sock != null ) {
    try {
      DatagramPacket p = new DatagramPacket( b, MTU );
      sock.receive( p );

      byte data[] = p.getData();
      int len = p.getLength();
      byte op = data[0];
      String s = new String( data, 0, 1, len-1 );
      print( s );

      if ( op==PRINT ) {
        // Echo the packet back to the sender
        data[0] = ECHO;
        DatagramPacket q  = new DatagramPacket(data, len, p.getAddress(),
        ➥p.getPort());
        sock.send(q);
      }
    } catch (IOException e) {}
  }
}
```

The troublesome thing about this program is that it is hard to run as an applet (it is provided as DatagramChatApplet.java). The Web browser usually will not permit you to receive datagrams in an applet (although my applet viewer lets me do this if I load the applet locally). Of course, it's possible to run this as a stand-alone application (java DatagramChat), but that defeats much of the purpose of having applets at all.

For this reason, chat applets in Java will have to use a stream socket connection to a server program running on their *home server*—the Web server where the applet's class files reside. This star-like configuration loads down the server and eats up several port numbers. Not only that—it requires a carefully designed protocol to make sure that client and server can accomplish essentially asynchronous tasks in a sequential conversation and still recover from unexpected conditions. Worse, it makes the response time unacceptably slow if chat groups of a few dozen applets or more exist. Nevertheless, any applet that wants to communicate with other applets using sockets has to live with these restrictions. The next section discusses one way to achieve this.

A Chat Applet

The program ChatApplet.java on the book's accompanying CD-ROM is a more realistic attempt at a chat applet (see Figure 12.2). It uses a stream socket to talk to a central server program (ChatServer.java), located on the same machine as the applet's code. The server program coordinates connections to several clients, grouping them into chat pools (different channels or *rooms*). The trans package provides a uniform way for client and server to communicate requests and commands to each other. The server's port number defaults to 8081, but any port number can be given as the single command-line argument. The applet itself is just a panel containing a ChatWindow, in which you can set the server name, port number, and initial screen name by parameters in the APPLET tag (server, port, and name). It won't be necessary to specify the server, because the applet figures out its home server by using the getCodeBase() method (don't forget to have the server running, though). The ChatApplet class contains a single instance of class ChatWindow, which does all the work. The ChatWindow class can also run as a stand-alone program.

Figure 12.2.

The ChatApplet.java applet.

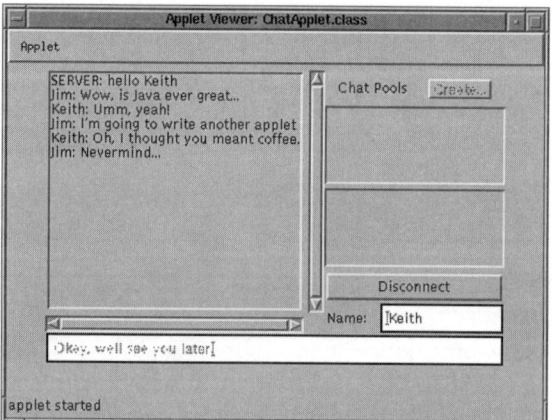

The server program has most of the smarts about which chat pools are defined and who is in them. The client applets just act as a user interface to the server, which updates the pools at will. Ideally, the smarts would be distributed somewhat more democratically in a web of interconnected applets, but due to security restrictions (discussed earlier), you are forced into the star configuration. This limits the usefulness of the applet, because large numbers of clients will bring the server to a crawl, and because the system is not fault-tolerant.

A detailed discussion of the mechanics of these programs is really beyond the scope of this chapter, but this section will go over the basic idea of how the client/server transactions are performed.

The `trans` Package

The `trans` package used by `ChatApplet.java` and `ChatServer.java` provides an artificial kind of remote procedure call functionality. Transactions are sent back and forth over a stream socket in a semi-asynchronous way. The transactions are instances of a subclass of the abstract class `Transaction`. The socket is encapsulated in an object of type `TChannel`. This is a smart channel for initiating and responding to transactions. Either side can be the client (or initiator) of a transaction (depending only on the transaction type itself), so there is no essential asymmetry built in.

Each `Transaction` object exists only to be converted to and from its *properties*, which are pairs of name/value strings written in a `TProps` object, which is essentially a jazzed-up `Hashtable` with better `read` and `write` methods than the `java.util.Properties` class has. The exact class of the transaction determines its type, so the inheritance mechanism is used here basically as a way to discriminate among the different types of transactions while treating them on an equal footing as objects characterized by their properties. The properties are accessed via the `getProperty()` and `setProperty()` methods. On creation, the constructor sets the properties to reflect the transaction parameters. The transaction is sent by passing it to the `initiate()` method of an opened `TChannel` object. The `ChatServer`, for example, greets the client and asks for its screen name by initiating a transaction of class `Hello`, as Listing 12.7 shows.

Listing 12.7. How the `ChatServer` says *hello*.

```
class ClientManager extends TChannel
{
  // ...
}

class HandleClient extends Thread
{
  ClientManager cm;

  // ...

  try {
    Hello h = new Hello();   // a Hello object has no initial props
    cm.initiate(h);          // start the transaction
    cm.name = h.name;        // this gets the result: a screen name
    // ...
  } catch ( IOException e ) {}
}
```

Initiating a transaction means that the following items are written to the stream socket:

○ An opcode byte (indicating REQ (request) or ACK (acknowledge)
○ A serial number (this serves to match replies to previous requests)
○ The name of the transaction class (here, it is Hello)
○ The properties of the transaction (a TProps object, written out)

The best way to write primitive Java types over a stream socket is to use a DataOutputStream attached to the socket (see Chapter 3 for a full discussion of data I/O). The opcode is written using writeByte(), the serial number with writeInt(), and the various strings with writeUTF(). The receiving socket then can read the data using a DataInputStream, in a parallel fashion.

The most important methods in a Transaction class are its build() and decode() methods. The build() method is run on the receiving end, and it accepts a single TProps object as an argument. These properties are the ones that were written on the socket at the initiating end, and the build() method's job is to take some action based on the values of these properties. The build() method can use setProperty() to set some return properties as well (on entry to build(), the receiver-side transaction's properties are guaranteed to be empty).

When the build() method finishes, the result properties are written back (even if they remain empty), with an opcode of ACK (acknowledge). It then is the job of the decode() method to make sense of these return properties on the initiating end. The result of a Hello transaction is a screen name, for example. This means that the build() and the decode() method each take half the responsibility for the encoding and decoding, whereas the constructor need not do anything at all. Listing 12.8 shows the complete code of the Hello class (here, ChatTransaction extends Transaction).

Listing 12.8. The Hello Transaction class.

```
import java.net.*;
import trans.TProps;

// A Hello transaction requests that the client identify itself.

public class Hello extends ChatTransaction
{
  static String NAME = "name";

  String name;

  public Hello() {}

  protected void build( TProps p )
  {
    setProperty( NAME, getWindow().screenname );
  }

  protected void decode()
  {
```

```
    name = getProperty( NAME );
  }
}
```

Even though the constructor is empty here, you still must declare it, if only to make it public. The `trans` package requires that all `Transactions` be public classes with a public constructor that takes no arguments (a *null constructor*). This is because the receiving `TChannel` actually instantiates a new transaction of the correct type by using the class descriptor's `newInstance()` method:

```
// This code instantiates a Transaction of class named in the String tClass:

try {
    Class c = Class.forName( tClass );
    t = (Transaction)c.newInstance();
} catch (Exception ex) {
    throw new TransactionException();
}
```

Transactions appear synchronous to the initiating thread; the `initiate()` method does not return until the transaction's return properties have been read and decoded. The same `TChannel` can act as both initiator and receiver simultaneously, however, and each received transaction has its `build()` method executed in a separate thread. If this `build()` method decides to `initiate()` another transaction back to the sender, you have a subtransaction, and that's okay, too. In this way, entire conversations of transactions and subtransactions can be carried out more or less transparently. The instigating thread doesn't see any of the subtransactions, because it is blocked, waiting on the outcome of the entire process. This multithreading requires that some care be taken in determining which methods should be synchronized and which should not, in order to avoid deadlock.

The downside of the approach is that there currently is no way to provide a time-out period for transactions to complete. Also, in the event of an error, there is no defined way to restore the `TChannel` to a sane state. It also would be nice to have a form of `initiate()` that returns immediately, executing the transaction in another thread and optionally notifying the caller by executing an agreed-upon method call when the transaction is completed (this is best done by defining an interface—for example, `TransactionObserver`). Performing these improvements would be fairly straightforward (after reading about multithreaded programs), so consider it an exercise!

The WWW in Java

The main reason behind the phenomenal rise of Java is its potential to become the *lingua franca* of interactive applications on the Internet. The exponential growth of the World Wide Web (WWW) has started a drive to redistribute the burden of computation, which has until now rested almost completely on the Web server. The CGI scripts so common today require no cleverness on the client end, but this simplicity comes at a price. The variety and semantics of CGI interaction are limited by the HTML form syntax and the strictures of HTTP, and a single server is forced to think on behalf of a potentially limitless number of clients. Java, on the other hand, is a real programming language that loads once and executes at the client end. This makes an enormous difference in terms of efficiency, both from the client's point of view (faster execution) and from the point of view of the network (lower bandwidth). So, although Java will soon be powering telephones and stereos, it is on the Web that Java finds its first natural home.

In this section, you'll see how Java programs can interact with Web servers and also with existing CGI programs. Java can convert URLs (Web addresses) into usable program objects. On a lower level, Java can read the raw contents of a URL. Java applets can also request certain actions of their host browser, such as displaying a status line or loading a new document.

The URL Class

A *URL* refers to a specific resource on the Web: an HTML file, image, animation, or whatever the case may be. URLs look like this:

```
http://www.WidgetsGalore.com/~MrWidget/sales.html
```

URLs specify a protocol (`http`), a server (`www.WidgetsGalore.com`), and a path to the resource in question. In Java, URLs are encapsulated in a constant object of class `java.net.URL`, which is described in Chapter 3.

An applet can use a URL to load a new browser page, as shown in this code:

```
class MyApplet extends Applet
{
  // Other stuff ...

  public void showNewPage( URL u )
  {
    getAppletContext().showDocument( u );
  }
}
```

If you use framesets in your document, there is also an optional second argument to specify the target frame or window.

Java URL objects have a `getContent()` method for converting the contents of the URL into a Java object, assuming that such a conversion is defined. A URL can reference an image, and then `getContent()` returns an `Object` whose runtime class is some subclass of `Image`, for example. The content type of most Web pages is `text/html`, which has no defined conversion. You can use the URL object to open an `InputStream` to read the contents of the URL, however:

```
URL url = new URL("http://www.WidgetsGalore.com/~MrWidget/home.html");
DataInputStream in = new DataInputStream(url.openStream());
String line;
while ( ( line = in.readLine() ) != null )
  System.out.println( line );
in.close();
```

When it is defined, the getContent() conversion is performed by a ContentHandler object. The following sections tell you how to define custom ContentHandlers for your own types of objects.

The URLConnection Class

The URL class may get a lot of credit, but the URLConnection class really does most of the work. A URLConnection object manages an interaction with a Web server at a given URL. When you call on a URL's getContent() method, the URL object creates a URLConnection to do the dirty work. You can retrieve the URLConnection associated with a URL by calling the openConnection() method of the URL. This can give you access to the values of the HTTP header fields, which tell you such things as the last modification date. It lets you specify details of the interaction, such as retrieval conditional on the last modification time (use setIfModifiedSince() or set the If-Modified-Since header field using setRequestProperty()).

A URLConnection object remains unconnected until its connect() method is called, which happens when some operation such as getContent() requires that a connection be made. Before it is connected, you are free to modify the fields that control the transaction. After it is connected, this is an error. URLConnections that use the HTTP protocol can perform the HTTP GET and POST methods because they are smart enough to wait for you to access their I/O streams before connecting to the Web server and issuing a GET or a POST request; basically, the POST method is used only if you actually write some output. You'll see how to do this soon.

The built-in functionality of URLConnections is centered on the HTTP protocol, but a URL object can use any protocol name that has an associated URLStreamHandler. A URLStreamHandler object must implement the abstract method openConnection(), which returns a URLConnection object given a URL. The URL knows where to get the stream handler for a given protocol by consulting the URLStreamHandlerFactory. You can define your own protocols by writing a class implementing the URLStreamHandlerFactory interface and then setting it to be the stream-handler factory using the static method URL.setStreamHandlerFactory(). In practice, though, you're almost always better off using HTTP and defining new content handlers corresponding to custom MIME types. The exception is if you're trying to write a reusable set of classes to perform FTP or some other such protocol that already exists.

CAUTION

Don't assume that your Java implementation supports a protocol type just because it is common; my implementation doesn't understand ftp or news (moreover, the file protocol completely ignores the server field and loads a local file regardless). This isn't all that surprising; for example, a URLStreamHandler for the news protocol would have to produce a URLConnection object that knows how to talk to a news server and serve up a new Java object corresponding to each news URL. This functionality is too specific to be part of a standard API.

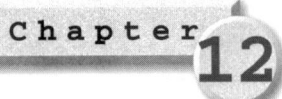

MIME Types and Content Handlers

How does a resource sitting on a Web server get converted into a usable Java object? First, when the Web server returns the contents of the corresponding URL, it includes header fields indicating the MIME type and encoding of the content to follow. For a GIF image, the MIME type is identified by the string `image/gif`. For HTML, it is `text/html`. When a URL or URLConnection performs its `getContent()` method to create a new object from a URL, it needs to find a content handler for whatever MIME type the server returns. The `java.net` package automatically parses the MIME type from the appropriate HTTP header field and then passes it to a `ContentHandlerFactory`, which returns the required handler or `null` (or throws a runtime exception). If you want to know the MIME type explicitly, the `getContentType()` method is available in the class `URLConnection`.

A content handler is an object of class `java.net.ContentHandler`, with a method `getContent()`, which takes a `URLConnection` and returns an `Object`. A different content-handler class exists for each recognized MIME type, because they each must do different things with the data from the URL.

The correspondence between MIME types and `ContentHandler`s is established by the `ContentHandlerFactory`. A Java program has one `ContentHandlerFactory`: an object implementing the interface `java.net.ContentHandlerFactory`, which has been installed as the `ContentHandlerFactory`, as shown in this code:

```
URLConnection.setContentHandlerFactory( chf );
```

The `ContentHandlerFactory` interface specifies one method; the `createContentHandler()` method accepts a MIME type name string and returns a `ContentHandler` object for that MIME type, or `null` if one is not known. You never call on a `ContentHandler` or `ContentHandlerFactory` directly; they are there to be used by the higher level classes `URL` and `URLConnection`, and to be subclassed by programmers who want to add new MIME-type capabilities to Java.

Now look at a functioning but simple example. Consider a Java class called `Colleague`:

```
class Colleague
{
  String name;
  String phone;
  String fax;
  Date birthday;
  Date nextMeeting;
}
```

To prepare for loading `Colleague` objects from a URL using HTTP, you perform the following steps:

- ○ Define a new MIME type to the HTTP server.
- ○ Implement a `ContentHandler` class for the type.
- ○ Install a custom `ContentHandlerFactory` that understands the new type.

Defining a New MIME Type

You can call the new MIME type anything, as long as it doesn't mess up other MIME types on the same server. Call it application/java-Colleague to avoid trouble. To tell the Web server about the new MIME type, you have to add a local configuration directive. For NCSA httpd, one of the most common servers, you put the following line in an .htaccess file in the same directories as your Colleague URLs:

```
AddType application/java-Colleague .coll
```

The server then recognizes any URLs with the .coll file name extension as belonging to the MIME type application/java-Colleague and reports them as such. This won't work if your site disallows per-directory access configuration for httpd. Talk to your system administrator if you're not sure; she may prefer to define the new type for you in a global configuration file. Also, other servers provide this functionality in different ways.

Writing a Custom ContentHandler

Listing 12.9 shows a very simple ContentHandler for the class Colleague.

Listing 12.9. A Custom ContentHandler class.

```
class ColleagueHandler extends ContentHandler
{
  // Read from the URL and create a Colleague:

  public Object getContent( URLConnection c ) throws IOException
  {
    DataInputStream in = new DataInputStream( c.getInputStream() );
    Colleague coll = new Colleague();
    String s;

    coll.name = in.readLine();
    coll.phone = in.readLine();
    coll.fax = in.readLine();
    try {
      coll.birthday = new Date( in.readLine() );
      coll.nextMeeting = new Date( in.readLine() );
    } catch (Exception e)  {
      throw new IOException( e.getMessage() );
    }
    return coll;
  }
}
```

This class knows how to read from a URLConnection and construct a new Colleague object. It defines the format; there are five lines in a .coll file, representing the name, phone, fax, birthday, and next meeting date of that given colleague. For a real application, you should use tagged fields (for example, Birthday: Jun 5 1972). This makes it easier to define new versions of your format without invalidating old URLs.

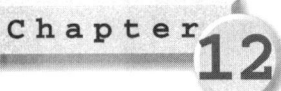

Using a Custom `ContentHandlerFactory`

Writing a content handler factory class is easy, but it's a good idea to make it flexible (because you only get to install it once!). You might want to make a class like the one shown in Listing 12.10, which lets your program add new MIME types at will.

Listing 12.10. A custom `ContentHandlerFactory`.

```java
class MyContentHandlerFactory implements ContentHandlerFactory
{
  Hashtable handlers = new Hashtable();

  void addMimeType( String mimetype, ContentHandler handler )
  {
    handlers.put( mimetype, handler );
  }

  public ContentHandler createContentHandler( String mimetype )
  {
    return (ContentHandler)handlers.get( mimetype );
  }
}
```

This class is flexible, because other classes from the same package can add new `ContentHandlers` on-the-fly by calling `addMimeType()`. Listing 12.11 shows a little demo program which does this (`ContentHandlerDemo.java`).

Listing 12.11. `ContentHandlerDemo.java`: using a custom `ContentHandler`.

```java
public class ContentHandlerDemo
{
  public static void main(String args[])
  {
    if ( args.length != 1 )  {
      System.err.println( "please give a URL argument!" );
      System.exit(1);
    }

    MyContentHandlerFactory chf = new MyContentHandlerFactory();
    ColleagueHandler collHandler = new ColleagueHandler();
    chf.addMimeType( "application/java-Colleague", collHandler );
    URLConnection.setContentHandlerFactory( chf );

    try  {
      URL url = new URL( args[0] );
      Colleague coll = (Colleague)url.getContent();
      System.out.println("Loaded colleague:");
      System.out.println("name = " + coll.name);
      System.out.println("phone = " + coll.phone);
      System.out.println("fax = " + coll.fax);
      System.out.println("birthday = " + coll.birthday);
      System.out.println("next meeting = " + coll.nextMeeting);
```

```
    } catch ( Exception e )  {
      System.err.println( "Exception: " + e ) ;
      System.exit(1);
    }
  }
}
```

To use this, define a colleague in a file. `Fred.coll`, for example, could contain this text:

```
Fred Fredrickson
800-8001
805-8123
Jan 12 1970
Jul 26 1996 3:15 PM
```

Then, by giving the URL to `Fred.coll`, the `ContentHandlerDemo` program should be able to load the information from the server, as this example shows (using the UNIX command prompt as an example):

```
wallaby$ java ContentHandlerDemo http://www.WidgetsGalore.com/~MrWidget/colleagues/
➥Fred.coll
Loaded colleague:
name = Fred Fredrickson
phone = 800-8001
fax = 805-8123
birthday = Mon Jan 12 00:00:00 PST 1970
next meeting = Fri Jul 26 15:15:00 PDT 1996
```

If you can't get this working, make sure that your file is in a location where your Web server expects to find it. Also make sure that you have defined a new MIME type to the server and provided the correct URL on the command line.

TIP

If an HTTP error occurs, the server returns an error screen of type `text/html`. Be warned that there is no predefined `ContentHandler` for this type, so you might want to detect this by explicitly examining the content type of the `URLConnection` object (if you don't, the `java.net` package throws a rather nondescriptive runtime exception (`ClassNotFoundException`) of its own.

The GET method

The GET method is the usual HTTP method for retrieving a URL, so you actually are using it every time you follow a hypertext link that isn't a Submit button on an HTML form. Some URLs expect to be fed additional information, however, which is appended onto the URL after a question mark. This so-called query information is useful for passing argument values to executable

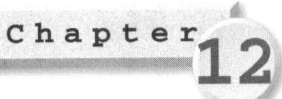

CGI scripts, such as WWW pages interfacing to databases or search engines. The query information is a sequence of attribute names and values, as this code shows:

```
http://www.myserver.edu/searchquery.cgi?text=My+Favorite+Foods&name=Fred
```

This query information encodes the name/value pairs `"text=My Favorite Foods"` and `"name=Fred"`. Any CGI application that expects to receive query information must be able to decode this information. The encoding is a standard one, in which space characters are mapped to + and any troublesome characters (control codes, +, %, and so on) are mapped to `%xx`, where *xx* is the hexadecimal value of the character. Separating name/value pairs by ampersands (&) is the usual thing to do when there is more than one pair.

To interact with such a CGI program, you can use the `java.net.URLEncoder` class to encode the URL. Somewhat surprisingly, the `URLEncoder` class maps & and = to their hexadecimal code equivalents, so if you want to use the syntax described in the preceding paragraph, you need to encode each value separately and concatenate the results with ampersands and equal signs yourself. The CGI program must retrieve the information from the environment variable `QUERY_STRING` and reverse the encoding process described earlier. Look at some established CGI scripts if you're not sure how this works.

To use the information returned by the CGI script, you can read an `InputStream` furnished by `URL.openStream()` or `URLConnection.getInputStream()`. Alternatively, you can furnish a content handler for the MIME type of the object returned and just do a `getContent()` on the encoded URL. To avoid extensibility problems, you might not want to provide content handlers for common MIME types such as `text/html` (unless you are writing a Web browser in Java!).

The POST Method

The `POST` method is the method used when submitting an HTML form. Generally, it enables you to write to a `URLConnection` so that whatever you write is fed to the referenced object (usually a CGI program) on its standard input stream. Because of the way HTTP transactions work, you should write and close the output stream before you read the input or do anything else that would cause the `URLConnection` to connect. The server can require that the content length of the input be specified along with the request, and this can be done only before connecting. This also lets the `URLConnection` object realize what you're up to and then specify the `POST` method rather than `GET`.

Listing 12.12 shows a simple example of how to use the `POST` method to interface with a CGI program. The `PostMethodDemo` applet posts the contents of a `TextArea` to a little CGI program called `wordcount.cgi` and then shows the result. You have to call this applet by its full URL, because it uses its code base to construct a URL to the CGI program, which should be in the same directory. Depending on your server configuration, you might not be allowed to execute CGI programs in user directories. Then you should move `wordcount.cgi` to your `cgi-bin` directory on the Web server and modify the applet source to supply the correct URL.

Listing 12.12. `PostMethodDemo.java`: using the POST method.

```java
import java.io.*;
import java.net.*;
import java.awt.*;
import java.applet.Applet;

public class PostMethodDemo extends Applet
{
  Label title = new Label( "An Applet using the POST method", Label.CENTER );
  TextArea text = new TextArea();
  Button load = new Button( "Post!" );

  public void init()
  {
    // Initialize the applet
    setLayout( new BorderLayout() ); add( "North", title );
    add( "Center", text );
    Panel p = new Panel();
    p.add( load );
    add( "South", p );
    validate();
  }

  void postText()
  {
    try {
      String s;
      URL u = new URL( getCodeBase(), "wordcount.cgi" );
      URLConnection c = u.openConnection();
      PrintStream out = new PrintStream(c.getOutputStream());
      out.print( text.getText().trim() );
      out.close();
      DataInputStream in = new DataInputStream(c.getInputStream());
      text.setText("");
      while ( ( s = in.readLine() ) != null )
        text.appendText( s + "\n" );
      in.close();
    } catch (IOException e) {
      text.appendText( "Exception: " + e + "\n" ); return;
    }
  }

  public boolean action(Event e, Object o)
  {
    if ( e.target == load ) {
      postText();
      return true;
    }
    return false;
  }
}
```

The CGI program `wordcount.cgi` is just a simple Perl script that counts words and lines. You should make sure that it has world execute permissions and that it finds your local Perl compiler correctly (try running it by hand!). Notice that the first thing it prints is a header line indicating

the content type, `text/plain`, followed by a blank line. The blank line is mandatory, and it is not part of the content. It separates the head information from the content body:

```perl
#!/usr/bin/perl

$words = 0;
$lines = 0;

print "Content-type: text/plain\n\n";

while (<>)  {
  $lines++;
  $words += s/\S+//g;
}

print "You entered $words words on $lines lines.\n";
```

Using the POST method doesn't prevent you from also passing query information along with the URL if you choose, just as with the GET method (of course, this depends on the CGI program being smart enough to look for the query string).

Summary

In this chapter, you've explored the various networking capabilities of Java. Several levels of functionality are available: the entire gamut from plain sockets (both TCP and UDP), to manipulating URLs and URL connections on the Web, right up to fetching Java objects from URLs by using content handlers. Though applets are hobbled in their connectivity by security restrictions, there is still quite a bit that can be done. Stand-alone programs can avoid the problem entirely, and new Java environments are being developed that should make the security interface more user-configurable.

Java complements and enhances existing CGI programs, which are still appropriate for a number of database lookup tasks. Java is also ideal for writing stand-alone server programs to service socket requests, and could even serve as a CGI language itself.

In Chapter 13, "General Purpose Classes," you'll learn about the utility classes provided in Java. These general-purpose classes provide some of the handiest data structures that every programmer needs. It's important to understand what they can do so that you can use them to save time and trouble in solving your own programming problems.

Chapter 13

by Michael Girdley and Richard Lesh

General Purpose Classes

In this chapter, you will learn about the `java.util` package of classes in the Java class library. These classes implement many of those features or functions usually left for the programmer or someone else to implement. In programming experiences, I regularly find myself saying: "It would be so much easier if there were a built-in object that would do *some common but complicated task.*" The `java.util` package is a well-designed and effective attempt to satisfy many of these specialized needs.

In many languages you will find yourself implementing a stack or a hash table class and all of the corresponding methods. Java has an already built-in stack type, which will enable you to quickly and efficiently include your own stack data structures in your Java programs. This frees you to deal with more important design and implementation issues. These classes are also useful in a variety of other ways and are the fundamental building blocks of the more complicated data structures used in other Java packages and in your own applications.

What's in This Chapter

This chapter covers

- ○ Each of the features of the utilities package
- ○ The implementation of each of the different classes in the package

NOTE:

Unless otherwise noted, all of the interfaces and classes discussed in this chapter extend the `java.lang.Object` class.

Table 13.1 shows the classes that are part of the utilities package that will be discussed.

Table 13.1. Utilities package classes.

Class	Description
BitSet	Implements a collection of binary values
Date	Date and time data storage and use
Dictionary	Used to store a collection of key and value pairs
Hashtable	Used to store a hash table
Observable	Used to store observable data
Properties	Storage and use of a properties list that can be saved
Random	Used to generate a pseudo-random number
Stack	A class to store and implement a stack
StringTokenizer	Used to tokenize a string
Vector	Used to store a vector data type

NOTE:

You may not be familiar with some of these data types. The `Dictionary` class is used to implement a dictionary in your program. A hash table is a storage data type whose speed in searching is much greater than that of other data structures because it stores data items based on a key derived from some given formula. A stack, of course, functions as if you were stacking data items on the floor one upon the other in a single stack. As a consequence, the only two manipulations you can make to the stack are to remove the top item or to place another on top. The `Vector` class implements an interesting data structure that has the capability to begin with a limited capacity and then change in size to accommodate the data items you insert into it. It can be descibed as a "growable array."

Linked Lists, Queues, Search Trees, and Other Dynamic Data Structures

One would expect that the `Vector` class, as described previously, would eliminate the necessity for creating your own data structures. But there may be times when you might want to conserve space to the maximum or access your data in a specialized way. In these cases, there is a technique to implement such data structures in Java.

As you learned before, Java has no pointers. Since dynamically linked lists and queues are implemented using pointers, is it then impossible to create these two data structures in Java? Not quite. Just as with many other tasks in Java, you need to do a little "funky stepping" to get it right, because the implementation of lists, queues, and other dynamic data structures is not intuitive.

To define your own dynamic data structures, you will want to make use of the fact that references to *objects* in Java are already dynamic. This is demonstrated and necessitated by the practices Java utilizes, such as interfaces and abstract implementations.

If you are accustomed to implementing dynamically linked lists or queues in C++, the format you will use to create your own version of these structures should seem very familiar to you. For example, the following creates a `Node` class for the list that contains a string:

```
class Node {
    String Name;
    Node Prev;
    Node Next;
}
```

This would be a *doubly linked list*, which has links backward and forward to other nodes containing strings. You could just as easily convert this type to link objects in just about any way to exhibit just about any behavior you want: queues, stacks (remember, there is already a `Stack` object in the class library), doubly linked lists, circular lists, binary search trees, and the list goes on.

To implement such a list, you could create a `DoubleList` class that would contain one such `Node` object and links strung out from there. You can use the keyword `null` to represent an empty object. Here is an example of the `DoubleList` declaration:

```
class DoubleList {
    // Declare the listhead to be of the Node type we created above.
    // Also, set it to be an empty object.
    Node ListHead = null;
.
.
.
}
```

Next you create methods to act upon the list, such as `InsertNode` or `ClearMyListJerk`—whatever you want.

You would also probably want to create a constructor method for the `Node` class that would accept parameters to set the previous and next nodes at construction time; or you could create a method such as `SetNext` or `SetNextToNull`. Either way would work just fine.

NOTE:

Out of all this you get a surprise bonus: No worry about freeing space allocated to create nodes because the Java Garbage Collection processes take care of all that for you. Just create *objects* when you need them, and then let Java take care of it.

Using the Utilities Package

The utilities package has two interfaces that can be used in classes of your own design: `Enumeration` and `Observer`. An interface is a set of methods that must be written for any class that claims to *implement* the interface. This provides a way to consistently use all classes that implement the interface. The following list summarizes the `Enumeration` and `Observer` interfaces:

`Enumeration`	Interface for classes that can enumerate a vector
`Observer`	Interface for classes that can observe observable objects

The `Enumeration` interface is used for classes that can retrieve data from a list, element by element. For example, there is an `Enumeration` class in the utilities package that implements the `Enumeration` interface for use in conjunction with the `Vector` class. This frees you from hard-core traversal of the different classes of data structures.

The `Observer` interface is useful in designing classes that can watch for changes that occur in other classes.

CAUTION:

Some of the examples in this chapter are not applets, but applications. Many of these data structures are best exhibited by just plain text input and output. Removing the baggage that would have come along with applets allowed the examples to be simplified so that the topic being demonstrated would be clearer.

When you are applying any code segments from this chapter in your own applets, remember that some of the examples here are not true applets and you need to deal with the differences inherent between them.

Enumeration

This interface specifies a set of methods used to enumerate—that is, iterate through—a list. An object that implements this interface may be used to iterate through a list only once because the Enumeration object is consumed through its use.

For example, an Enumeration object can be used to print all the elements of a Vector object, v, as follows:

```
for (Enumeration e=v.elements();e.hasMoreElements();)
    System.out.print(e.nextElement()+" ");
```

The Enumeration interface specifies only two methods: hasMoreElements() and nextElement(). The hasMoreElements() method must return True if there are elements remaining in the enumeration. The nextElement() method must return an object representing the next element within the object that is being enumerated. The details of how the Enumeration interface is implemented and how the data is represented internally are left up to the implementation of the specific class.

Observer

This interface, if implemented by a class, allows an object of the class to observe other objects of the class Observable. The Observer is notified whenever the Observable object that it is watching has been changed.

The interface only specifies one method, update(Observable, Object). This method is called by the observed object to notify the Observer of changes. A reference to the observed object is passed along with any additional object that the observed object wishes to pass to the Observer. The first argument enables the Observer to operate on the observed object, while the second argument is used to pass information from the observed to the Observer.

Classes

The utilities package supplies ten different classes that provide a wide variety of functionality. Although these classes don't generally have much in common, they all provide support for the most common data structures used by programmers. The techniques described next will enable you to create your own specialized classes to supplement those missing.

The classes supplied in the java.util package, however limited, do provide a great advantage over previous languages. The main advantage is that these classes simplify some things and eliminate a lot of the garbage that you were stuck with in the past, in terms of freeing memory and doing mundane programming tasks.

However, there are a number of limitations. For example, you have to "dance a little bit" to implement some of the more complicated data structures. Also, if you want speed, there are much faster languages to choose from. Java provides a combination of power and simplicity while sacrificing speed. However, don't worry that your programs will be slugs. Although Java is not nearly as efficient as C++ and C, it still beats Visual Basic in terms of size and speed.

BitSet

This class implements a data type that represents a collection of bits. The collection will grow dynamically as more bits are required. It is useful for representing a set of True/False values. Specific bits are identified using non-negative integers. The first bit is bit 0.

This class is most useful for storing a group of related True/False values, such as user responses to Yes/No questions. For example, if the applet had a number of radio buttons, you could slap those values into an instance of the BitSet class.

It is also useful in terms of bitmapping your own graphics. You can create bitsets that can represent a pixel at a time (of course, it would be much easier to use the Graphics class instead).

Individual bits in the set are turned on or off with the set() and clear() methods, respectively. Individual bits are queried with the get() method. These methods all take the specific bit number as their only argument. The basic Boolean operations AND, OR, and XOR can be performed on two BitSets using the and(), or(), and xor() methods. Because these methods modify one of the BitSets, one generally will use the clone() method to create a duplicate of one, and then AND, OR, or XOR the clone with the second BitSet. The result of the operation then will end up in the cloned BitSet. The BitSet1 program in Listing 13.1 illustrates the basic BitSet operations.

Listing 13.1. BitSet1.java—BitSet sample program.

```
import java.io.DataInputStream;
import java.util.BitSet;

class BitSet1 {
    public static void main(String args[])
```

```
        throws java.io.IOException
    {
        DataInputStream dis=new DataInputStream(System.in);
        String bitstring;
        BitSet set1,set2,set3;
        set1=new BitSet();
        set2=new BitSet();

        // Get the first bit sequence and store it
        System.out.println("Bit sequence #1:");
        bitstring=dis.readLine();
        for (short i=0;i<bitstring.length();i++){
            if (bitstring.charAt(i)=='1')
                set1.set(i);
            else
                set1.clear(i);
        }
        // Get the second bit sequence and store it
        System.out.println("Bit sequence #2:");
        bitstring=dis.readLine();
        for (short i=0;i<bitstring.length();i++){
            if (bitstring.charAt(i)=='1')
                set2.set(i);
            else
                set2.clear(i);
        }
        System.out.println("BitSet #1: "+set1);
        System.out.println("BitSet #2: "+set2);

        // Test the AND operation
        set3=(BitSet)set1.clone();
        set3.and(set2);
        System.out.println("set1 AND set2: "+set3);

        // Test the OR operation
        set3=(BitSet)set1.clone();
        set3.or(set2);
        System.out.println("set1 OR set2: "+set3);

        // Test the XOR operation
        set3=(BitSet)set1.clone();
        set3.xor(set2);
        System.out.println("set1 XOR set2: "+set3);
    }
}
```

The output from this program looks like this:

```
Bit sequence #1:
1010
Bit sequence #2:
1100
BitSet #1: {0, 2}
BitSet #2: {0, 1}
set1 AND set2: {0}
set1 OR set2: {0, 1, 2}
set1 XOR set2: {1, 2}
```

Table 13.2 summarizes all the various methods available in the `BitSet` class.

Table 13.2. The `BitSet` interface.

	Constructors
`BitSet()`	Constructs an empty `BitSet`
`BitSet(int)`	Constructs an empty `BitSet` of a given size
	Methods
`and(BitSet)`	Logically ANDs the object's bit set with another `BitSet`
`clear(int)`	Clears a specific bit
`clone()`	Creates a clone of the `BitSet` object
`equals(Object)`	Compares this object against another `BitSet` object
`get(int)`	Returns the value of a specific bit
`hashCode()`	Returns the hash code
`or(BitSet)`	Logically ORs the object's bit set with another `BitSet`
`set(int)`	Sets a specific bit
`size()`	Returns the size of the set
`toString()`	Converts bit values to a string representation
`xor(BitSet)`	Logically XORs the object's bit set with another `BitSet`

In addition to extending the `java.lang.Object` class, `BitSet` implements the `java.lang.Cloneable` interface. This, of course, allows instances of the object to be cloned to create another instance of the class.

Date

You will regularly run into instances in which you will need to access and manipulate dates and times in your applets on the Web. For example, you might want an applet to display the current time or date during its execution. Or, if you are programming a game, you can use the system clock to get your elapsed time right.

The `Date` class is used to represent dates and times in a platform-independent fashion. For example, the current date or a specific date can be printed as shown in Listing 13.2.

Listing 13.2. Date1.java—Date sample program.

```
import java.util.Date;

public class Date1{
    public static void main (String args[]){
```

```
        Date today=new Date();
        System.out.println("Today is "+today.toLocaleString()+
            " ("+today.toGMTString()+")");

        Date birthday=new Date(89,10,14,8,30,00);
        System.out.println("My birthday is"+
            birthday.toString()+" ("+birthday.toGMTString()+")");

        Date anniversary=new Date("Jun 21, 1986");
        System.out.println("My anniversary is "+
            anniversary+" ("+anniversary.toGMTString()+")");
    }
}
```

The output from this program looks like this:

```
Today is 01/21/96 19:55:17 (22 Jan 1996 01:55:17 GMT)
My birthday is Thu Nov 14 08:30:00  1989 (14 Nov 1989 14:30:00 GMT)
My anniversary is Sat Jun 21 00:00:00  1989 (21 Jun 1986 05:00:00 GMT)
```

The default constructor is used when the current date and time are needed. A specific date and time can be used to initialize a `Date` object using the constructors that take three, five, and six integers. These constructors allow the date and time to be specified using YMD, YMDHM, or YMDHMS. Any parts of the time not specified by the three- and five-integer constructors will be set to zero.

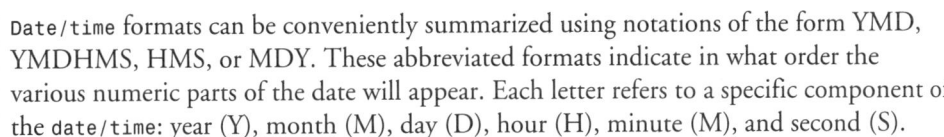

NOTE:

`Date/time` formats can be conveniently summarized using notations of the form YMD, YMDHMS, HMS, or MDY. These abbreviated formats indicate in what order the various numeric parts of the date will appear. Each letter refers to a specific component of the `date/time`: year (Y), month (M), day (D), hour (H), minute (M), and second (S). Whether the letter M refers to month or minute depends on the context.

Alternately, a `Date` object can be constructed using a single string that represents a date and time using a variety of different syntax. One of the most important is the international standard date syntax of the form, "Sun, 14 Aug 1995 9:00:00 GMT." Continental U.S. time zone abbreviations are understood, but time zone offsets should be considered for general use; for example, "Sun, 14 Aug 1995 9:00:00 GMT+0600" (six hours west of the Greenwich meridian). The local time zone to the computer executing the code is assumed if none is supplied.

NOTE:

The `Date` class intends to store date and time information in UTC (Coordinated Universal Time). However, it does not necessarily achieve this goal. UTC is a time standard based on an atomic clock. Time specifications using UTC are considered equal to GMT

(Greenwich Mean Time). The implementation of the Date class is limited by the time set by the underlying operating system. Because modern operating systems typically assume that a day is always 86,400 seconds, the extra leap seconds, which are needed about once a year to accurately reflect UTC, usually are not added.

The date can be converted to a text representation using the methods toString(), toGMTString(), and toLocaleString(), which convert the date and time to the standard UNIX, GMT, or local time formats, respectively. The toLocaleString function is very useful since you do not have to determine what your system's date format is. This may not sound like much, but it is just another piece of the very complicated puzzle that Sun has put together to allow your applets and applications to flow seamlessly into the system on which they are running.

When a date is being converted to a string by an automatic coercion, the toString() method will be used. The resulting string returned by the toString function follows UNIX time and date standards.

The Date class also has methods for setting and querying the date and time component values once the Date object is constructed. The individual parts of the date (month, date, year) and time (hours, minutes, seconds) are always specified in local time. When referring to the various parts of the date and time, the first letter of each part typically is used in an abbreviation. For example, YMDHMS would indicate that all six parts (year, month, date, hour, minute, second) are present. Each of these parts of the date and time have a specific range of acceptable values, as illustrated in Table 13.3.

Table 13.3. Date component ranges.

Year	Year minus 1900
Month	0-11 (January=0)
Date	1-31
Day	0-6 (Sunday=0)
Hour	0-23
Minute	0-59
Second	0-59

The date and time also can be specified using a single integer UTC value that represents the number of milliseconds that have elapsed since a specific starting date (which might vary from system to system). For UNIX systems this date is January 1, 1970. The program Date2 in Listing 13.3 shows how this single value corresponds to the normal YMDHMS representation.

Listing 13.3. Date2.java—Date sample program.

```java
import java.util.Date;

public class Date2{
    public static void main (String args[]){
        Date beginning=new Date(0);
        Date anniversary=new Date("Jun 21, 1986");
        Date today=new Date();

        System.out.println(beginning+"="+beginning.getTime());
        System.out.println(anniversary+"="+anniversary.getTime());
        System.out.println(today+"="+today.getTime());
    }
}
```

The output from this program looks like this:

```
Wed Dec 31 18:00:00  1969=0
Sat Jun 21 00:00:00  1986=519714000000
Sun Jan 21 19:55:17  1996=822275717000
```

Dates can be compared to each other by using this UTC value or by using the methods `after()`, `before()`, or `equals()`.

CAUTION:

Don't try to launch space shuttles or coordinate nuclear attacks based on your operating system's local time as reflected by Java. Although the API is intended to reflect UTC it doesn't do so exactly. This inexact behavior is inherited from the time system of the underlying OS. The vast majority of all modern operating systems assume that 1 day = 3600 seconds × 24 hours, and as such, they reflect time to the accuracy that UTC does.

Under the UTC, about once a year there is an extra second, called a "leap second," added to account for the wobble of the earth. Most computer clocks are not accurate enough to reflect this distinction.

Between UTC and standard OS time (UT/GMT), there is this subtle difference; one is based on an atomic clock and the other is based on astronomical observations, which for all practical purposes is an invisibly fine hair to split.

For more information, Sun suggests you visit the U.S. Naval Observatory site, particularly the Directorate of Time at `http://tycho.usno.navy.mil` and their definitions of different systems of time at `http://tycho.usno.navy.mil/systime.html`.

Table 13.4 summarizes everything available in the Date class.

Table 13.4. The Date interface.

Constructors	
Date()	Constructs a date using today's date and time
Date(long)	Constructs a date using a single UTC value
Date(int, int, int)	Constructs a date using YMD
Date(int, int, int, int, int)	Constructs a date using YMDHM
Date(int, int, int, int, int, int)	Constructs a date using YMDHMS
Date(string)	Constructs a date from a string
Static Methods	
UTC(int, int, int, int, int, int)	Calculates a UTC value from YMDHMS
parse(string)	Returns the single UTC value of a date in text format
Methods	
after(Date)	True if the date is later than the specified date
before(Date)	True if the date is earlier than the specified date
equals(Object)	True if the date and the specified date are equal
getDate()	Returns the day of the month
getDay()	Returns the day of the week
getHours()	Returns the hour
getMinutes()	Returns the minute
getMonth()	Returns the month
getSeconds()	Returns the second
getTime()	Returns the time as a single UTC value
getTimezoneOffset()	Returns the time zone offset, in minutes, for this locale
getYear()	Returns the year after 1900
hashCode()	Computes a hash code for the date
setDate(int)	Sets the date
setHours(int)	Sets the hours
setMinutes(int)	Sets the minutes
setMonth(int)	Sets the month

setSeconds(int)	Sets the seconds
setTime(long)	Sets the time using a single UTC value
setYear(int)	Sets the year
toGMTString()	Converts a date to text using Internet GMT conventions
toLocaleString()	Converts a date to text using locale conventions
toString()	Converts a date to text using UNIX ctime() conventions

One of the most helpful methods available in the Date class is the parse method. This void takes an instance of the String type and then parses that string. The result of that parse is then placed in the calling instance of the class. If you had a date called ADate, you could set its value to be the date in the SomeString class with the code line:

```
ADate.parse(SomeString);
```

You will also find the before and after functions useful. They enable you to send in another instance of the Date class and then compare that date to the value in the calling instance. The sample applet in Listing 13.4 demonstrates the use of the Date class in your own applet.

Listing 13.4. Using the Date class.

```
import java.awt.*;
import java.util.*;

public class MichaelSimpleClock extends java.applet.Applet {

    Date TheDate = new Date();
    Button DateButton = new Button(
        "                    Click me!                    ");

    public void init()  {
        add(DateButton);
    }

    public boolean handleEvent(Event e) {
        if (e.target == DateButton) {
            DateButton.setLabel(TheDate.toString());
        }
        return true;
    }

}
```

Figure 13.1 is a screenshot of the MichaelSimpleClock applet. Note that the clock in the applet is wrong: it is not actually 8:00 am. There is no way I would write that early in the morning.

Figure 13.1.

The `MichaelSimpleClock`
applet.

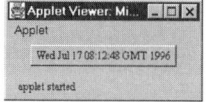

What about a real-time clock that updates as the clock changes? To accomplish this small feat, you need to include in the applet a loop that has each iteration reconstructing the internal `Date` instance. Then, regularly `repaint` that value inside the applet's `paint` method. You'll also need to include *threading* to prevent locking up your system during the applet's execution. *Threading* will not be covered until a later chapter, so a real-time clock was not included in this section.

Random

Essential to the programming of games and many other program types is the capability to generate random numbers. Java includes the capability to generate random numbers efficiently and effectively.

The `Random` class implements a pseudo-random number data type used to generate a stream of seemingly random numbers. To create a sequence of different pseudo-random values each time the application is run, create the `Random` object as follows:

```
Random r=new Random();
```

This will seed the random generator with the current time. On the other hand, consider the following statement:

```
Random r=new Random(326);    // Pick any value
```

This will seed the random generator with the same value each time, resulting in the same sequence of pseudo-random numbers each time the application is run. The generator can be reseeded at any time using the `setSeed()` method.

TIP:

Want to get really random numbers? Well, you can't. But a common practice to simulate actual random numbers in computer programs is to seed the random number generator with some variant of the current time or date. If, for example, you wanted to seed a random number generator with the sum of the current seconds, minutes, and hours, you could say:

```
int OurSeed = ADate.getSeconds() + ADate.getHours() + ADate.getMinutes();
Random = new Random(OurSeed);
```

This should suffice for most tasks.

Pseudo-random numbers can be generated by using one of these functions: `nextInt()`, `nextLong()`, `nextFloat()`, `nextDouble()`, or `nextGaussian()`. The first four functions return *integers*, *longs*, and

so on. (For more information on the Gaussian distribution, see the next Note.) For example, the program Random1 in Listing 13.5 will print out five pseudo-random uniformly distributed values using these functions.

Listing 13.5. Random1.java—Random sample program.

```java
import java.lang.Math;
import java.util.Date;
import java.util.Random;

class Random1 {
    public static void main(String args[])
        throws java.io.IOException
    {
        int count=6;
        Random randGen=new Random();

        System.out.println("Uniform Random Integers");
        for (int i=0;i<count;i++)
        System.out.print(randGen.nextInt()+" ");
        System.out.println("\n");

        System.out.println("Uniform Random Floats");
        for (int i=0;i<count;i++)
        System.out.print(randGen.nextFloat()+" ");
        System.out.println("\n");

        System.out.println("Gaussian Random Floats");
        for (int i=0;i<count;i++)
            System.out.print(randGen.nextGaussian()+" ");
        System.out.println("\n");

        System.out.println("Uniform Random Integers [1,6]");
        for (int i=0;i<count;i++)
            System.out.print((Math.abs(randGen.nextInt())%6+1)+" ");
        System.out.println("\n");
        }
}
```

The output from the preceding program looks like this:

```
Uniform Random Integers
1704667569 -1431446235 1024613888 438489989 710330974 -1689521238

Uniform Random Floats
0.689189 0.0579988 0.0933537 0.748228 0.400992 0.222109

Gaussian Random Floats
-0.201843 -0.0111578 1.63927 0.205938 -0.365471 0.626304

Uniform Random Integers [1,6]
4 6 1 6 3 2
```

If you need to generate uniformly distributed random integers within a specific range, the output from nextInt(), nextLong(), or nextDouble() can be scaled to match the required range. A simpler approach is to take the remainder of the result of nextInt() divided by the number of different values plus the first value of the range. For example, if the values 10 to 20 are needed one can use the formula nextInt()%21+10. Unfortunately, although this method is much simpler than scaling the output of nextInt(), it only is guaranteed to work on truly random values. Because the pseudo-random generator might have various undesired correlations, the modulus operator might not provide acceptable results—one might get all odd numbers, for example. In other words, don't plan on simulating the detonation of your new H-bomb in Java because you might find yourself a couple of miles too close.

NOTE:

Uniformly distributed random numbers are generated using a modified linear congruential method with a 48-bit seed. Uniformly distributed random numbers within a given range will all appear with the same frequency. This class can also generate random numbers from a Gaussian or Normal distribution. The Gaussian frequency distribution curve is also referred to as a bell curve. For information on this, see Donald Knuth, *The Art of Computer Programming*, Volume 2, Section 3.2.1.

Table 13.5 summarizes the complete interface of the Random class.

Table 13.5. The Random interface.

Constructors	
Random()	Creates a new random number generator
Random(long)	Creates a new random number generator using a seed
Methods	
nextDouble()	Returns a pseudo-random uniformly distributed Double
nextFloat()	Returns a pseudo-random uniformly distributed Float
nextGaussian()	Returns a pseudo-random Gaussian distributed Double
nextInt()	Returns a pseudo-random uniformly distributed Int
nextLong()	Returns a pseudo-random uniformly distributed Long
setSeed(long)	Sets the seed of the pseudo-random number generator

Refer also to Random().

The following applet, shown in Listing 13.6, demonstrates a bit of what you can do with Random.

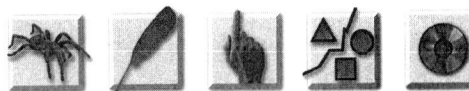

Listing 13.6. Using the Random Class.

```java
import java.awt.*;
import java.util.*;

public class TheWanderer extends java.applet.Applet {

        int xpos = 100;
        int ypos = 100;

    // Our current date.
    Date D = new Date();

        // The movement button
        Button theButton = new Button("Click Me");

        // Our random number generator.
        Random R;

        public void init() {
                add(theButton);
                setBackground(Color.white);

        // Our random number generator seeded with the current seconds.
        int seed = D.getSeconds();
                R = new Random(seed);
        }

        public boolean handleEvent (Event e) {
                if (e.target == theButton) {
                        // Move our thing.
                        xpos = xpos + (Math.abs(R.nextInt())%10-7);
                        ypos = ypos + (Math.abs(R.nextInt())%10-7);

        // repaint the sucker.
                        repaint();
        }
                return super.handleEvent(e);
    }

    public void paint(Graphics g) {
                g.setColor(Color.black);
                g.fillOval(xpos,ypos, 50, 50);
    }
}
```

Figure 13.2 shows TheWanderer applet during its execution.

Figure 13.2.

TheWanderer applet.

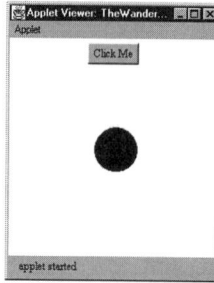

StringTokenizer

This section will describe the function of the `StringTokenizer` class, which also could have been appropriately grouped with other classes in Chapter 11, "Reading and Writing with Java," since it is so vital to the input and output functions demonstrated in that chapter. This class enables you to parse a string into a number of smaller strings called *tokens*. This class works specifically for what is called "delimited text," which means that each individual substring of the string is separated by a delimiter. The delimiter can be anything ranging from a "*" to "YabaDaba". You simply specify what you want the class to look for when tokenizing the string.

This class is included here because it has uses that would prove helpful in everything from a spreadsheet applet to an arcade game applet.

The delimiter set can be specified when the `StringTokenizer` object is created, or it can be specified on a per-token basis. The default delimiter set is the set of *whitespace* characters. The class would then find all of the separate words in a string and tokenize them. For example, the `StringTokenizer1` code in Listing 13.7 prints out each word of the string on a separate line.

Listing 13.7. `StringTokenizer1.java`—`StringTokenizer` sample program.

```java
import java.io.DataInputStream;
import java.util.StringTokenizer;

class StringTokenizer1 {
    public static void main(String args[])
        throws java.io.IOException
    {
        DataInputStream dis=new DataInputStream(System.in);

        System.out.println("Enter a sentence: ");
        String s=dis.readLine();
        StringTokenizer st=new StringTokenizer(s);
        while (st.hasMoreTokens())
            System.out.println(st.nextToken());
    }
}
```

Here is the output from this listing:

```
Enter a sentence:
Four score and seven
Four
score
and
seven
```

Pure excitement. The method countTokens() returns the number of tokens remaining in the string using the current delimiter set—that is, the number of times nextToken() can be called before generating an exception. This is an efficient method because it does not actually construct the substrings that nextToken() must generate.

In addition to extending the java.lang.object class, the StringTokenizer class implements the java.util.Enumeration interface.

Table 13.6 summarizes the methods of the StringTokenizer class.

Table 13.6. The StringTokenizer interface.

Constructors	
StringTokenizer (string)	Constructs a StringTokenizer given a string using whitespace as delimiters
StringTokenizer (string, string)	Constructs a StringTokenizer given a string and a delimiter set
StringTokenizer (string, string, boolean)	Constructs a StringTokenizer given a string and a delimiter set
Methods	
countTokens()	Returns the number of tokens remaining in the string
hasMoreTokens()	Returns True if more tokens exist
nextToken()	Returns the next token of the string
nextToken(string)	Returns the next token, given a new delimiter set
hasMoreTokens()	Returns True if more elements exist in the enumeration
nextElement()	Returns the next element of the enumeration using the current delimiter set

Vector

As was stated before, Java doesn't include dynamically linked list, queue, or other data structures of that type. Instead, the designers of Java envisioned the Vector class, which would be able to handle occasions when you need dynamic storage of objects. Of course, there are positive and negative consequences of this decision by the designers at Sun. On the positive side, it contributes to the simplicity of the language. The major negative point is that, at face value, it severely limits programmers from utilizing more sophisticated programs.

In any case, the Vector class implements a dynamically allocated list of objects. It attempts to optimize storage by increasing the storage capacity of the list when needed by increments larger than just one object. Typically with this mechanism, there is some excess capacity in the list. When this capacity is exhausted, the list is reallocated to add another block of objects at the end of the list. Setting the capacity of the Vector object to the needed size before inserting a large number of objects will reduce the need for incremental reallocation. Because of this mechanism, it is important to remember that the capacity (the available elements in the Vector object) and the size (the number of elements currently stored in the Vector object) usually are not the same.

For example, say a Vector with capacityIncrement equal to three has been created. As objects are added to the Vector, new space is allocated in chunks of three objects. After five elements have been added, there still will be room for one more element without the need for any additional memory allocation.

After the sixth element has been added, there is no more excess capacity. When the seventh element is added, a new allocation will be made that adds three additional elements, giving a total capacity of nine. After the seventh element is added, there will be two remaining unused elements.

The initial storage capacity and the capacity increment both can be specified in the constructor. Even though the capacity is automatically increased as needed, the ensureCapacity() method can be used to increase the capacity to a specific minimum number of elements, whereas trimToSize() can be used to reduce the capacity to the minimum needed to store the current elements. New elements can be added to the Vector using the addElement() and insertElementAt() methods. The elements passed to be stored in the Vector must be derived from type Object. Elements can be changed using the setElementAt() method. Removal of elements is accomplished with the removeElement(), removeElementAt(), and removeAllElements() methods. Elements can be accessed directly using the elementAt(), firstElement(), and lastElement() methods, whereas elements can be located using the indexOf() and lastIndexOf() methods. Information about the size and the capacity of the Vector are returned by the size() and capacity() methods respectively. The setSize() method can be used to directly change the size of the Vector.

For example, the Vector1 code in Listing 13.8 creates a Vector of integers by adding new elements to the end. Then, using a variety of techniques, it prints the Vector.

Listing 13.8. Vector1.java—Vector sample program.

```
import java.lang.Integer;
import java.util.Enumeration;
import java.util.Vector;

class Vector1 {
```

```
public static void main(String args[]){
    Vector v=new Vector(10,10);
    for (int i=0;i<20;i++)
        v.addElement(new Integer(i));

    System.out.println("Vector in original order using an Enumeration");
    for (Enumeration e=v.elements();e.hasMoreElements();)
        System.out.print(e.nextElement()+" ");
    System.out.println();

    System.out.println("Vector in original order using elementAt");
    for (int i=0;i<v.size();i++)
        System.out.print(v.elementAt(i)+" ");
    System.out.println();

    // Print out the original vector
    System.out.println("\nVector in reverse order using elementAt");
    for (int i=v.size()-1;i>=0;i++)
        System.out.print(v.elementAt(i)+" ");
    System.out.println();

    // Print out the original vector
    System.out.println("\nVector as a String");
    System.out.println(v.toString());
    }
}
```

The output from this program looks like this:

```
Vector in original order using an Enumeration
0 1 2 3 4 5 6 7 8 9 10 11 12 13 14 15 16 17 18 19
Vector in original order using elementAt
0 1 2 3 4 5 6 7 8 9 10 11 12 13 14 15 16 17 18 19

Vector in reverse order using elementAt
19 18 17 16 15 14 13 12 11 10 9 8 7 6 5 4 3 2 1 0

Vector as a String
[0, 1, 2, 3, 4, 5, 6, 7, 8, 9, 10, 11, 12, 13, 14, 15, 16, 17, 18, 19]
```

NOTE:

The expression new Integer() was used to create integer objects to store because the fundamental types, such as int, are not objects in Java. This technique is used many times throughout this chapter.

Notice the use of the Enumeration object as one way to access the elements of a Vector. Look at the following lines:

```
for (Enumeration e=v.elements();e.hasMoreElements();)
    System.out.print(e.nextElement()+" ");
```

One can see that an Enumeration object, which represents all of the elements in the Vector, is created and returned by the Vector method elements(). With this Enumeration object, the loop can check to see if there are more elements to process using the Enumeration method hasMoreElements(), and the loop can get the next element in the Vector using the Enumeration method nextElement().

The Vector2 program in Listing 13.9 illustrates some of the vector-accessing techniques. It first generates a vector of random integers; then allows the user to search for a specific value. The locations of the first and last occurrences of the value are printed by the program using the indexOf() and lastIndexOf() methods.

Listing 13.9. Vector2.java—Vector sample program.

```java
import java.io.DataInputStream;
import java.lang.Integer;
import java.lang.Math;
import java.util.Enumeration;
import java.util.Random;
import java.util.Vector;

class Vector2 {
    public static void main(String args[])
        throws java.io.IOException
    {
        int numElements;
        DataInputStream dis=new DataInputStream(System.in);
        Vector v=new Vector(10,10);
        Random randGen=new Random();

        System.out.println("How many random elements? ");
        numElements=Integer.valueOf(dis.readLine()).intValue();
        for (int i=0;i<numElements;i++)
            v.addElement(new Integer(Math.abs(
                randGen.nextInt())%numElements));

        System.out.println(v.toString());

        Integer searchValue;
        System.out.println("Find which value? ");
        searchValue=Integer.valueOf(dis.readLine());
        System.out.println("First occurrence is element "+
            v.indexOf(searchValue));
        System.out.println("Last occurrence is element "+
            v.lastIndexOf(searchValue));
    }
}
```

The output from this program looks like this:

```
How many random elements?
10
[0, 2, 8, 4, 9, 7, 8, 6, 3, 2]

Find which value?
```

```
8
First occurrence is element 2
Last occurrence is element 6
```

In addition to extending the `java.lang.Object` class, the `Vector` class implements the `java.lang.Cloneable` interface. Table 13.7 summarizes the methods of the `Vector` class.

Table 13.7. The `Vector` interface.

Variables	
capacityIncrement	Size of the incremental allocations, in elements
elementCount	Number of elements in `Vector`
elementData	Buffer where the elements are stored
Constructors	
Vector()	Constructs an empty vector
Vector(int)	Constructs an empty vector with the specified storage capacity
Vector(int, int)	Constructs an empty vector with the specified storage capacity and `capacityIncrement`
Methods	
addElement(Object)	Adds the specified object at the end of the `Vector`
capacity()	Returns the capacity of the `Vector`
clone()	Creates a clone of the `Vector`
contains(Object)	True if the specified object is in the `Vector`
copyInto(Object[])	Copies the elements of this vector into an array
elementAt(int)	Returns the element at the specified index
elements()	Returns an `Enumeration` of the elements
ensureCapacity(int)	Ensures that the `Vector` has the specified capacity
firstElement()	Returns the first element of the `Vector`
indexOf(Object)	Returns the index of the first occurrence of the specified object within the `Vector`
indexOf(Object, int)	Returns the index of the specified object within the `Vector` starting the search at the index specified and proceeding toward the end of the `Vector`
insertElementAt(Object, int)	Inserts an object at the index specified
isEmpty()	True if the `Vector` is empty

continues

Table 13.7. continued

	Methods
`lastElement()`	Returns the last element of the `Vector`
`lastIndexOf(Object)`	Returns the index of the last occurrence of the specified object within the `Vector`
`lastIndexOf(Object, int)`	Returns the index of the specified object within the `Vector` starting the search at the index specified and proceeding toward the beginning of the `Vector`
`removeAllElements()`	Removes all elements of the `Vector`
`removeElement(Object)`	Removes the specified object from the `Vector`
`removeElementAt(int)`	Removes the element with the specified index
`setElementAt(Object, int)`	Stores the object at the specified index in the `Vector`
`setSize(int)`	Sets the size of the `Vector`
`size()`	Returns the number of elements in the `Vector`
`toString()`	Converts the `Vector` to a string
`trimToSize()`	Trims the `Vector`'s capacity down to the specified size

Refer also to `Vector`, `Hashtable`.

Stack

The `Stack` data structure is key to many programming efforts, ranging from building compilers to solving mazes. The `Stack` class in the Java library implements a *Last In, First Out* (LIFO) stack of objects. Even though they are based on (extends) the `Vector` class, `Stack`s are typically not accessed in a direct fashion. Instead, values are pushed onto and popped off of the top of the "stack." The net effect is that values that were most recently pushed are the first ones to be popped.

 NOTE:

While the `Stack` class implements a LIFO removal strategy, the *queue* data structure discussed early in the chapter is based on a *First In, First Out* (FIFO) strategy.

The `Stack1` code in Listing 13.10 pushes strings onto the stack, and then retrieves them. The strings will end up being printed in reverse order from which they were stored.

Listing 13.10. Stack1.java—Stack sample program.

```java
import java.io.DataInputStream;
import java.util.Stack;
import java.util.StringTokenizer;

class Stack1 {
    public static void main(String args[])
        throws java.io.IOException
    {
        DataInputStream dis=new DataInputStream(System.in);

        System.out.println("Enter a sentence: ");
        String s=dis.readLine();
        StringTokenizer st=new StringTokenizer(s);
        Stack stack=new Stack();
        while (st.hasMoreTokens())
            stack.push(st.nextToken());
        while (!stack.empty())
            System.out.print((String)stack.pop()+" ");
        System.out.println();
    }
}
```

The output from this program looks like this:

```
Enter a sentence:
The quick brown fox jumps over the lazy dog
dog lazy the over jumps fox brown quick The
```

Even though Stack objects normally are not accessed in a direct fashion, it is possible to search the Stack for a specific value using the search() method. It accepts an object to find and returns the distance from the top of the Stack where the object was found. It will return −1 if the object is not found.

The method peek() will return the top object on the Stack without actually removing it from the Stack. The peek() method will throw an EmptyStackException if the Stack has no items.

Table 13.8 summarizes the complete interface of the Stack class.

Table 13.8. The Stack interface.

Constructors	
Stack()	Constructs an empty Stack
Methods	
empty()	True if the Stack is empty
peek()	Returns the top object on the Stack
pop()	Pops an element off the Stack
push(Object)	Pushes an element onto the Stack
search(Object)	Finds an object on the Stack

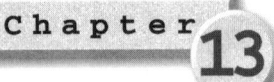

Dictionary

This class is an abstract class that is used as a base for the Hashtable class. It implements a data structure that allows a collection of key and value pairs to be stored. Any type of object can be used for the keys or the values. Typically, the keys are used to find a particular corresponding value.

Because this class is an abstract class that cannot be used directly, the code examples presented cannot actually be run. They are presented only to illustrate the purpose and use of the methods declared by this class. The following code would, hypothetically, be used to create a Dictionary with these values illustrated:

```
Dictionary products = new Dictionary();
products.put(new Integer(342), "Widget");
products.put(new Integer(124), "Gadget");
products.put(new Integer(754), "FooBar");
```

The put() method is used to insert a key and value pair into the Dictionary. The two arguments both must be derived from the class Object. The key is the first argument and the value is the second.

A value can be retrieved using the get() method and a specific key to be found. It returns the null value if the specified key is not found. For example:

```
String name = products.get(new Integer(124));
if (name != null) {
    System.out.println("Product name for code 124 is " + name);
}
```

Although an individual object can be retrieved with the get() method, sometimes it is necessary to access all of the keys or all of the values. There are two methods, keys() and elements(), that will return Enumerations that can be used to access the keys and the values, respectively.

Table 13.9 summarizes the complete interface of the Dictionary class.

Table 13.9. The Dictionary interface.

Constructors	
Dictionary()	Constructs an empty Dictionary
Methods	
elements()	Returns an Enumeration of the values
get(Object)	Returns the object associated with the specified key
isEmpty()	True if the Dictionary has no elements
keys()	Returns an Enumeration of the keys
put(Object, Object)	Stores the specified key and value pair in the Dictionary
remove(Object)	Removes an element from the Dictionary by its key
size()	Returns the number of elements stored

Refer also to Enumeration, Hashtable, Properties.

Hashtable

The Hashtable data structure is very useful when dealing with the search for and manipulation of data. You would want to use this class if you will be storing a large amount of data in memory and then searching it. The time needed to complete a search of a hash table is decidedly less than in the Vector class. Of course, for small amounts of data, it won't make much difference whether you use a hash table or a linear data structure, since the overhead time will be much greater than any search time would be. See the next Note for more information on search times in the different classes.

Hash table organization is based upon keys, which are computed based upon the data being stored. For example, if you were going to insert a number of words into a hash table, you could base your key upon the first letter of the word. When you came back to search for a word later on, you could then compute the key for the item being sought. By using this key, search time is drastically reduced because the items are stored based upon the value of their respective key.

The Hashtable class implements a hash table storage mechanism for storing key and value pairs. Hash tables are designed to quickly locate and retrieve information stored by using a key. Keys and values may be of any object type, but the key object's class must implement the hashCode() and equals() methods.

NOTE:

Big "O" notation is used to measure the "worst case scenario" time requirements in terms of searching while using different data structures. Linear searching, such as that used in the Vector class, is *O(n)*, whereas hash table searching is *O(log n)*. This basically means that over a large number of objects, you'll be saving a large amount of time when searching, since the *log* of a number is always less than the number itself. For times when you will be doing a large amount of searching through data, a hash table will likely be much more efficient.

The sample Hashtable1 in Listing 13.11 creates a Hashtable object and stores 10 key and value pairs using the put() method. It then uses the get() method to return the value corresponding to a key entered by the user.

Listing 13.11. Hashtable1.java—Hashtable sample program.

```
import java.io.DataInputStream;
import java.lang.Integer;
import java.lang.Math;
```

continues

Listing 13.11. continued

```java
import java.util.Random;
import java.util.Hashtable;

class Hashtable1 {
    public static void main(String args[])
        throws java.io.IOException
    {
        DataInputStream dis=new DataInputStream(System.in);
        int numElements=10;
        String keys[]={"Red","Green","Blue","Cyan","Magenta",
            "Yellow","Black","Orange","Purple","White"};
        Hashtable ht;
        Random randGen=new Random();

        ht=new Hashtable(numElements*2);
        for (int i=0;i<numElements;i++)
            ht.put(keys[i],new Integer(Math.abs(
                randGen.nextInt())%numElements));

        System.out.println(ht.toString());

        String keyValue;
        System.out.println("Which key to find? ");
        keyValue=dis.readLine();
        Integer value=(Integer)ht.get(keyValue);
        if (value!=null) System.out.println(keyValue+" = "+value);
    }
}
```

The output from this program looks like this:

```
{Cyan=4, White=0, Magenta=4, Red=5, Black=3,
➥Green=8, Purple=3, Orange=4, Yellow=2, _Blue=6}
Which key to find?
Red
Red = 5
```

In addition to the get() method, the contains() and containsKey() methods can be used to search for a particular value or key, respectively. Both return True or False depending on whether the search was successful. The contains() method must perform an exhaustive search of the table and is not as efficient as the containsKey() method, which can take advantage of the hash table's storage mechanism to find the key quickly.

Because hash tables need to allocate storage for more data than actually is stored, a measurement called the *load factor* indicates the number of used storage spaces as a fraction of the total available storage spaces. It is expressed as a value between 0 and 100 percent. Typically, the load factor should not be higher than about 50 percent for efficient retrieval of data from a hash table. When specifying the load factor in a program, use a fractional value in the range 0.0 to 1.0 to represent load factors in the range 0 to 100 percent.

Hash tables can be constructed in three different ways: by specifying the desired initial capacity and load factor, by specifying only the initial capacity, or by specifying neither. If the load factor is not specified, the Hashtable will be rehashed into a larger table when it is full—otherwise it is rehashed when it exceeds the load factor. The constructors will throw an IllegalArgumentException if the initial capacity is less than or equal to zero, or if the load factor is less than or equal to zero.

The clone() method can be used to create a copy (clone) of the Hashtable. However, it creates a shallow copy of the Hashtable, which means that the keys and values themselves are not clones. This local method overrides the inherited clone() method.

CAUTION:

The clone() method is a relatively expensive operation to perform in terms of memory utilization and execution time. Because the new Hashtable still refers directly to the objects (keys and values) stored in the old table, caution should be used to avoid making changes that will disrupt the original Hashtable.

The Hashtable class extends the java.util.Dictionary class and implements the java.lang.Cloneable interface. Table 13.10 summarizes the methods of the Hashtable class.

Table 13.10. The Hashtable interface.

Constructors	
Hashtable()	Constructs an empty Hashtable
Hashtable(int)	Constructs an empty Hashtable with the specified capacity
Hashtable(int, float)	Constructs an empty Hashtable given capacity and load factor
Methods	
clear()	Deletes all elements from the Hashtable
clone()	Creates a clone of the Hashtable
contains(Object)	True if the specified object is an element of the Hashtable
containsKey(Object)	True if the Hashtable contains the specified key
elements()	Returns an Enumeration of the Hashtable's values
get(Object)	Returns the object associated with the specified key
isEmpty()	True if the Hashtable has no elements
keys()	Returns an Enumeration of the keys
put(Object, Object)	Stores the specified key and value pair in the Hashtable
rehash()	Rehashes the contents of the table into a bigger table

continues

Table 13.10. continued

	Methods
remove(Object)	Removes an element from the Hashtable by its key
size()	Returns the number of elements stored
toString()	Converts the contents to a very long string

Refer also to hashCode, equals.

Properties

The Properties class is what enables end-users to customize their Java program. For example, you can easily store values such as foreground colors, background colors, and font defaults, and then have those values available to be reloaded. This would be most useful for Java applications, but you can also implement them for applets. If you have an applet that is regularly used by multiple users, you could keep a properties file on your server for each different user, which would be accessed each time that user loaded the applet.

The Properties class is a Hashtable, which can be repeatedly stored and restored from a stream. It is used to implement persistent properties. It also allows for an unlimited level of nesting, by searching a default property list if the required property is not found. The fact that this class is an extension of the Hashtable class means that all methods available in the Hashtable class are also available in the Properties class.

The sample program Properties1 in Listing 13.12 creates two properties lists. One will be the default property list and the other will be the user-defined property list. When the user property list is created, the default Properties object is passed. When the user property list is searched, if the key value is not found, the default Properties list will be searched.

Listing 13.12. Properties1.java—Properties sample program.

```java
import java.io.Data7InputStream;
import java.lang.Integer;
import java.util.Properties;

class Properties1 {
    public static void main(String args[])
        throws java.io.IOException
    {
        int numElements=4;
        String defaultNames[]={"Red","Green","Blue","Purple"};
        int defaultValues[]={1,2,3,4};
        String userNames[]={"Red","Yellow","Orange","Blue"};
        int userValues[]={100,200,300,400};
        DataInputStream dis=new DataInputStream(System.in);
        Properties defaultProps=new Properties();
```

```
    Properties userProps=new Properties(defaultProps);

    for (int i=0;i<numElements;i++){
        defaultProps.put(defaultNames[i],
            Integer.toString(defaultValues[i]));
        userProps.put(userNames[i],
            Integer.toString(userValues[i]));
    }
    System.out.println("Default Properties");
    defaultProps.list(System.out);
    System.out.println("\nUser Defined Properties");
    userProps.list(System.out);

    String keyValue;
    System.out.println("\nWhich property to find? ");
    keyValue=dis.readLine();
    System.out.println("Property '"+keyValue+"' is '"+
        userProps.getProperty(keyValue)+"'");
    }
}
```

Notice that the `getProperties()` method is used instead of the inherited `get()` method. The `get()` method only searches the current `Properties` object. The `getProperties()` method must be used in order to have the default `Properties` list searched. An alternative form of the `getProperties()` method has a second argument, which is that a default `Properties` list is to be searched instead of the default specified when the `Properties` object was created.

The `propertyNames()` method can be used to return an `Enumeration`, which can be used to index through all of the property names. This `Enumeration` includes the property names from the default `Properties` list. Likewise, the `list()` method, which prints the `Properties` list to the standard output, will list all of the properties of the current `Properties` object and those in the default `Properties` object.

`Properties` objects can be written to and read from a stream using the `save()` and `load()` methods, respectively. In addition to the output or input stream, the save method has an additional string argument that will be written at the beginning of the stream as a header comment.

Table 13.11 summarizes the methods of the `Properties` class.

Table 13.11. The `Properties` interface.

Variables	
defaults	Default `Properties` list to search
Constructors	
Properties()	Constructs an empty property list
Properties(Properties)	Constructs an empty property list with specified default

continues

Table 13.11. continued

Methods	
getProperty(string)	Returns a property given the key
getProperty(string, string)	Returns a property given the specified key and default
list(PrintStream)	Lists the properties to a stream for debugging
load(InputStream)	Reads the properties from an InputStream
propertyNames()	Returns an Enumeration of all of the keys
save(OutputStream, string)	Writes the properties to an OutputStream

Observable

This class acts as a base class for objects that you wish to have observed by other objects that implement the Observer interface. An Observable object can notify its Observers whenever the Observable object is modified using the notifyObservers() method. This method accomplishes the notification by invoking the update() method of all of its Observers, optionally passing a data object that is passed to notifyObservers. Observable objects may have any number of Observers.

Table 13.12 summarizes the complete interface of the Observable class.

Table 13.12. The Observable interface.

Constructors	
Observable()	
Methods	
addObserver(Observer)	Adds an Observer to the observer list
clearChanged()	Clears an observable change
countObservers()	Returns the number of Observers
deleteObserver(Observer)	Deletes an Observer from the observer list
deleteObservers()	Deletes all Observers from the observer list
hasChanged()	True if an observable change occurred
notifyObservers()	Notifies all Observers if an observable change occurred
notifyObservers(Object)	Notifies all Observers of a specific observable change
setChanged()	Sets a flag to indicate that an observable change occurred

Refer also to Observer.

Summary

This chapter described the classes that make up the Java utilities package. This package provides complete implementations of the basic data structures and some of the most useful data types (other than the fundamental numeric types) needed by programmers. Many of the data types and data structures that you will develop using Java will be based on the classes found in the utilities package. For smaller applets, many of these classes will not be necessary. However, as your applets increase in complexity, you will find these classes to be very useful. In any case, this chapter has been a good starting point for understanding the utility of these important Java classes and for understanding how to use them effectively.

Chapter

14

by Thomas L. Fredell

Extending Java

- The Runtime and Process Classes
- Extending Java Using Native Methods
- Applets and Security Restrictions

By any measure, Java provides a deep set of standard tools that can be used to create terrific applets. Various Java packages described in the preceding chapters provide excellent access to network, file input/output, window manipulation, and numerous desirable functions.

Naturally, Java doesn't provide a completely comprehensive set of tools; it's currently impossible to do so in a cross-platform manner, given the diversity of platforms and operating systems as well as the rapid pace of technological innovation and change. Sometimes it's necessary to compensate for a deficiency in Java by extending it.

NOTE:

Sun appears to have some interest in the development of a Java-based operating system. In a Java operating system, every aspect of the OS could be exposed as an integral java class.

Two basic means of extending the Java environment are provided with the Java development kit: the Runtime and Process classes, and native methods. The Runtime and Process classes can be used to call external non-Java programs. Native methods can be used to directly integrate methods implemented in C or C++ with standard Java methods. Each mechanism has certain advantages. For very simple tasks, it is easier to implement a separate executable than a class with native methods. However, it's more difficult to pass parameters to separate executables, and parameters are less integrated with the Java runtime execution environment than native methods. Subsequent sections of this chapter examine the use of separate executables and classes with native methods.

The Runtime and Process Classes

One of the simplest means of integrating Java with non-Java systems involves the creation of one or more command-line driven executables that use the non-Java components directly. The Runtime and Process classes in the java.lang package provide methods that allow a Java application to execute and monitor non-Java processes.

The Java application communicates with the executable by creating a command array and calling Runtime.exec(). The executable can communicate a simple integer back using its return code. If more complex communication is required, the Java application can read from the process standard output and write to the process standard input.

Typical use of the Runtime and Process objects involves setting up the command or command/argument array to execute, executing the command, retrieving the input and output streams of the spawned process, and monitoring the process status.

The disadvantage to using command-line driven executables is that the executables are not very tightly integrated with the Java application. Parameter passing is complex, and the interface certainly doesn't resemble the clean clarity of a set of defined Java classes. However, for simple cases, it is probably simpler to define separate executables than classes with C-based native methods.

Executing External Programs Using `Runtime`

The `Runtime` class exposes several versions of an `exec()` method that may be used to execute non-Java processes. The simplest version takes one argument—a string containing the system command to execute. Other versions include arrays of arguments to pass to the system command. The `exec()` method returns a Java `Process` object that can be used to monitor the spawned process.

NOTE:

Because the `Runtime` class can be used to execute non-Java applications, the `Runtime.exec()` method isn't available from Java applets. Applets can't be allowed to execute non-Java processes because the processes aren't forced to obey Java security restrictions.

The `Runtime` class can't be used to instantiate a `Runtime` object. Instead, the `Runtime` class includes a static method, `getRuntime()`, that returns a pre-existing `Runtime` object. You can call the `exec()` method from that object.

Monitoring Executed Applications Using `Process`

The `Runtime.exec()` method returns a `Process` object. `Process` objects can be used to control and monitor the execution of spawned processes. The `getErrorStream()`, `getInputStream()`, and `getOutputStream()` methods of the `Process` object can be used to get the stderr, stdout, and stdin streams of the spawned process. The user might wait for the natural termination of the process using the `waitFor()` method, or can force termination using the `destroy()` method. The exit code of the process after termination can be retrieved using the `exitValue()` method.

The following code demonstrates the use of the `Runtime` object to spawn a `Process` whose output and exit value are monitored by a Java application:

```
Process proc = Runtime.getRuntime().exec(ANonJava.exe@);
InputStream in = proc.getInputStream();
byte buff[] = new byte[1024];
int cbRead;

try {
    while ((cbRead = in.read(buff)) != -1) {
        // Use the output of the process...
    }
} catch (IOException e) {
    // Insert code to handle exceptions that occur
    // when reading the process output
}
```

```
// No more output was available from the process, so...

// Ensure that the process completes
try {
    proc.waitFor();
} catch (InterruptedException) {
    // Handle exception that could occur when waiting
    // for a spawned process to terminate
}

// Then examine the process exit code
if (proc.exitValue() == 1) {
    // Use the exit value...
}
```

TIP:

When you retrieve a handle to the output stream of a spawned process with the `Process.getInputStream()` method, it isn't possible to use the `available()` method on the returned `InputStream` object. A reasonable workaround is to use the `read(byte[])` method of the `InputStream`, which returns -1 when the end of the stream is reached.

If you're developing executables that pass information back to Java classes using standard output, you should probably adopt an easily parsable output format. This enables your java class to split up and coerce the data from your executable as necessary.

A Practical Example: DAOCmd

The DAOCmd project, available on the source code CD-ROM, includes a java class that calls a non-Java executable that returns the results of a database query. The parameters are passed from the java class to the non-Java executable by means of the command line, and the results of the database query are written to standard output by the executable. The java class reads the results and, in the example, simply echoes the results to the standard output of the Java environment.

The TestDAO class does all of the work on the Java side; the main() method creates the command line for the executable, runs the executable, and reads and echoes the results. The implementation of the main() method follows:

```
public static void main(String args[]) {
    Runtime rt = Runtime.getRuntime();
    Process proc;

    // Create the command array to pass to the executable
    String cmd[] = new String[args.length+1];
    cmd[0] = "DAOCmd";

    // Prepare the command array for the executable
```

```
for (int iArg = 0; iArg < args.length; iArg++) {
    // All arguments are quoted to ensure that
    // arguments are passed correctly to the
    // spawned process
    cmd[iArg+1] = "\"" + args[iArg] + "\"";
}

// Attempt to loop and retrieve all of the output
// from the spawned process
try {
    proc = rt.exec(cmd);
    DataInputStream in = new DataInputStream(proc.getInputStream());
    String strLine;
    boolean tContinue = true;
    byte buf[] = new byte[256];
    int cbRead;

    while ((cbRead = in.read(buf)) != -1) {
        // Simply echo the output from the spawned process
        // to the Java application's stdout
        System.out.print(new String(buf, 0, 0, cbRead));
    }

    // Wait for the spawned process to terminate
    proc.waitFor();
} catch (Exception e) {
    System.out.println(e);
}
}
```

The first step is to create the command array for the executable. The first element of the command array is the constant DAOCmd, which is the name of the executable. The remaining arguments are from the command line that was used to run the java class. Each argument is quoted to ensure that it is interpreted by the executable as a string (if an argument to the java class was one or more words enclosed in quotes—the Java interpreter strips off the quotes but maintains the string with embedded white space as a single string within the argument array passed to main()).

Next, the executable is executed using the Runtime.exec() method. The standard output stream of the executable is retrieved from the Process object returned by exec(). The Java method loops to retrieve the output of the Process using the read() method. When no more data is available to read, the loop terminates, at which point the java class waits for the process to terminate using the waitFor() method. After the process has terminated, the java class can retrieve the process exit code using the Process.exitValue() method, and act accordingly.

Extending Java Using Native Methods

One of the best aspects of Java is its platform independence. Any applet that you write basically performs in exactly the same manner, regardless of the platform or operating system of the host computer. Thanks to Java's broad support for everything from GUI windowing in the `java.awt` classes to networking support in the `java.net` class, most tasks can be accomplished directly within Java.

CAUTION:

Even though Java is platform independent, there are some platform-specific bugs. For example, in the Windows 95 AWT implementation, windows shown modally do not actually behave modally. The status of bugs in Sun's Java interpreter is available at `http://www.javasoft.com`.

Because Java is platform independent, however, it doesn't support all of the features of its host computer or operating system. The Win32 API supported by Microsoft Windows NT and Windows 95 includes, among many other useful features, a set of functions for establishing network connections with the modem, using Remote Access Services (RAS). Programmatically establishing a remote connection to a network can be very useful to support, for example, automatic registration of a commercial Java-based application.

Another reason to use native methods is the multitude of libraries that provide C interfaces to various systems. Many APIs are currently supplied as a set of statically linked library files with associated C header files and possibly some dynamically linked libraries. Unfortunately, very few APIs are currently supplied with Java wrapper classes.

There are basically two means of accessing non-Java libraries; the first, the use of separate processes, has been discussed earlier in this chapter. The disadvantage of using a separate process is its loose integration with the Java environment. Parameter passing is very limited, and communication between Java and the separate process and runtime may be impossible, or simply too tedious. The second means of accessing non-Java libraries is through the use of *native methods*.

Native methods are methods defined within Java classes using the `native` keyword. Within the `java` class, they have no implementation specified—only the name of the method, access specification, parameters, and return value.

Basic Mechanics of Creating Native Methods

When creating a native method, you must first define it in a `java` class using the `native` keyword. For example, to define a public native method returning an integer called `fastStringScan(String str, String strToFind)` in a class named `StringUtils`, you would use the following code:

```
class StringUtils {
    public native int fastStringScan(String str, String strToFind);
    ...
}
```

NOTE:

Literally any Java method, with the exception of object constructors, can be implemented as a native method. If you need to call some function implemented as a native method during the creation of your object, you can create a private native method that performs the initialization and call the method when the constructor executes.

Obviously, the implementation of the native method must reside somewhere. It is typically part of a dynamically-linked library; on the Microsoft Windows 95 or Windows NT platform it is in a DLL.

Java provides tools to generate wrappers for native code implementations in C. The wrappers generated by Java provide a fairly easy-to-use interface between native method implementations and the Java runtime environment. The use of wrappers is not optional; the Java interpreter expects to find functions with specific names determined from the native method definition. Implement the following steps to create native code wrappers:

1. Compile the `java` class that contains the native method declaration.

   This is done by running `javac MyClass.java` from the command prompt.

2. Create a header file that declares the structure representing the `java` class.

   The Java JDK provides a utility, `javah`, that does this for you. Typing `javah MyClass` from the command line generates a `MyClass.h` file containing the structure of the class (as used by native methods) and native method function prototypes.

3. Create a stub file that contains function wrappers that call the native functions you implement.

   Using `javah -stubs MyClass` generates a file called `MyClass.c` that contains function stubs. A section later in this chapter, "The Stubs File," provides more information about the stubs file.

4. Develop the implementation of the native methods.

The header file created in step 2 contains the structure definitions and function prototypes that you need to implement your native methods. You must implement each function listed in the header file.

CAUTION:

Be very careful if you add another member to your class! Make sure to recompile the `java` class with the native method declarations, and make sure that you rerun the `javah` utility and recompile your DLL. Failing to recompile or rerun can lead to some very frustrating—but not straightforward—problems! You may set a class member, but continue to see it as null because the offsets calculated by the compiler no longer match up with the `java` class declaration.

It's definitely worthwhile to modify your `makefile` to include a dependency step that updates the native method header file.

The Stubs File

The following are the contents of the `StringUtils.c` stub file generated from the previously mentioned `StringUtils` class.

```
/* DO NOT EDIT THIS FILE - it is machine generated */
#include <StubPreamble.h>

/* Stubs for class StringUtils */
/* SYMBOL: "StringUtils/fastStringScan(Ljava/lang/String;
➡Ljava/lang/String;)I", Java_StringUtils_fastStringScan_stub */
__declspec(dllexport) stack_item *Java_StringUtils
➡fastStringScan_stub(stack_item *_P_,struct execenv *_EE_) {
    extern long StringUtils_fastStringScan(void *,void *,void *);
    P_[0].i = StringUtils_fastStringScan(_P_[0].p,((_P_[1].p)),((_P_[2].p)));
    return _P_ + 1;
}
```

The Stubs file contains function stubs that Java expects when it attempts to call a function with a dynamic link library that implements a native method. The included `StubPreamble.h` file contains all of the type and structure definitions required by Java stub functions. Notice that all of the stub functions are exported using the `_declspec(dllexport)` directive. They are the entry points to the DLL that contains the native methods; the functions that you write do not need to be exported.

The stub functions basically repackage the arguments from a Java interpreter function call into single parameters with specific types. The internal prototype, in this case `extern long StringUtils_fastStringScan(void *,void *,void *)`, uses void pointers for all of the arguments. However, the function that you implement has specific parameter types. The function declarations for the functions that you implement are contained within the `StringUtils.h` header file. The `fastStringScan()` function is defined within that file as `extern long StringUtils_fastStringScan(struct HStringUtils *,struct Hjava_lang_String *,struct Hjava_lang_String *)`.

The Header File

The following are the contents of the `StringUtils.h` header file generated by `javah` from the previously mentioned `StringUtils` class.

```
/* DO NOT EDIT THIS FILE - it is machine generated */
#include <native.h>
/* Header for class StringUtils */

#ifndef _Included_StringUtils
#define _Included_StringUtils
```

```
typedef struct ClassStringUtils {
    char PAD;      /* ANSI C requires structures to have a least one member */
} ClassStringUtils;
HandleTo(StringUtils);

#ifdef __cplusplus
extern "C" {
#endif
struct Hjava_lang_String;
extern long StringUtils_fastStringScan(struct HStringUtils *,
➡struct Hjava_lang_String *,struct Hjava_lang_String *);
#ifdef __cplusplus
}
#endif
#endif
```

The header file contains all of the function prototypes that you need to implement, as well as all of the includes that you need to call useful Java functions. Peeking through the Java API files included automatically in the header file is a worthwhile exercise. Several include files are nested within the native.h header. Without additional documentation, it's very difficult to determine the purpose of many of the structures and functions in some of the included files; but the native.h header file can occasionally shed light on problems that you may encounter during compilation.

If you are implementing the native methods in C++, you must be sure to wrap the inclusion of the StringUtils.h header file in an extern "C" block, as the following example demonstrates:

```
/**
 * StringUtilsImpl.cpp
 *
 * Contains implementation of native methods.
 */

extern "C" {
#include <StringUtils.h>
}
```

The StringUtils class is represented as a C structure in the header file. Accessing object instance variables involves using members of the ClassStringUtils structure; further descriptions are listed in the following sections.

Calling Java from Native Methods

It is frequently necessary to call Java methods from within native methods. In order to do so, it is essential to understand method signatures, and to know how to dispatch Java method calls. The following sections describe method signatures and method call dispatching in detail.

It is also frequently important to be able to create Java objects from within native methods. This is particularly important, for example, when returning a Java object, such as a String, from a native method.

Identifying Methods: Method Signatures

Within a class, each method is distinguished from other methods by the method's name and signature. The name is simply the name of the method. The signature is a string that describes the method parameters and the method return value. This allows Java to perform function overloading by enabling the interpreter to dynamically look up and dispatch functions that have the same name but have different arguments or return types.

Method signatures consist of a set of method parameter type descriptions enclosed within parentheses and followed by a return type description. Primitive types are designated differently from object types; object types are prefixed with an "L", include the fully distinguished name of the `object` class delimited by "/" rather than ".", and are terminated with a ";".

Given a Java method `repeatSubString()`, defined as `String repeatSubString(int begOffset, int endOffset, int repeatCount, String string)`, the method signature would be `"(IIILjava/lang/String;)Ljava/lang/String;"`. If an array is passed, the type of the array element should be prefixed by a `"["` in the method signature. The method signature for `int findString(String stringToFind, String[] strings)` would be `"(Ljava/lang/String;[Ljava/lang/String;)I"`.

The signature prefixes or characters are defined within the `signature.h` header file. The most frequently used signature characters follow:

```
[ - Array
B - Byte
C - Char
L - Beginning of Class name
; - End of Class name
F - Float
D - Double
I - Integer
J - Long
S - Short
V - Void
Z - Boolean
```

Calling Java Object Methods from Native Methods

You will frequently want to make a Java object perform some action from a native method. To do so, you call a method on the object. To call a method on an object from a native method, you use the `execute_java_dynamic_method()` function.

The full definition of the function from `interpreter.h` follows:

```
long execute_java_dynamic_method(ExecEnv *,
                      HObject *obj,
                      char *method_name,
                      char *signature,
                      ...);
```

The first argument is the execution environment, or ExecEnv. You should generally use the EE() function, which returns the current execution environment. The execution environment has little or no documentation provided with the JDK 1.0 release; you can glean some of its uses by examining the execenv structure in interpreter.h and associated macros. The second argument is an object instance that provides the method you want to call. The third argument is the method name, sans signature. It is the raw name of the method without access specifiers, parameters, return types, etc. For a method defined as public int foo(String str), the method name would simply be foo. The fourth argument is the signature of the method, as described in the previous section.

The remaining arguments are the object or primitive datatype parameters required by the method. The arguments must correspond to the types defined in the method signature.

Notice that the execute_java_dynamic_method() returns a long. Your code should cast the long appropriately, given the return type defined in the method signature.

The execute_java_dynamic_method() function enables you to call methods on an object instance, but it doesn't enable you to call static methods defined for a class. Calling static methods requires the use of the execute_java_static_method() function, defined as follows in interpreter.h:

```
long execute_java_static_method(ExecEnv *,
                                ClassClass *cb,
                                char *method_name,
                                char *signature,
                                ...);
```

The arguments of execute_java_static_method() are almost identical to the arguments for execute_java_dynamic_method(). The only difference is the second argument, which is a pointer to a Class object rather than a Java object instance. The Java interpreter creates a Class object for every loaded class. The ClassClass structure is defined in the oobj.h header file.

You can use the FindClass() function to get a Class object with a class name; it's defined in interpreter.h as:

```
ClassClass *FindClass(struct execenv *ee, char *name, bool_t resolve);
```

To find the java.lang.System class object, you use the following function call:

```
ClassClass *System = FindClass(EE(), "java/lang/System", FALSE)
```

Accessing Java Object Instance Variables from Native Methods

One of the most common reasons to access object instance variables from native methods is to set instance variables for the object that contains the native method that you implement. Using the following definition for a NonJavaFile class:

```
public class NonJavaFile {
    public native void getFileAttributes(String strFile);
    public String strAttr1;
```

```
    public int iAttr2;
    public boolean bAttr3;
}
```

The native method implementation for getFileAttributes() would no doubt require the ability to set the various Attribute variables of the NonJavaFile instance. The native method shell, generated using javah as described previously, includes a parameter that is not visible in the Java getFileAttributes() method declaration. The additional parameter is the pointer to the handle of the object instance that was used to call the native method. Use the unhand() function to acquire the C structure that contains the Java object instance variables.

Using the NonJavaFile example, the implementation of getFileAttributes() might look like:

```
void NonJavaFile_getFileAttributes(struct HNonJavaFile *me,
                                   struct Hjava_lang_String *strFile)
{
    ClassNonJavaFile *NonJavaFile = (ClassNonJavaFile*)unhand(me);

    // Use the strFile argument to perform some action(s)
    ...

    // Modify some of the Java object instance variables (or, in other
    // words, members of the ClassNonJavaFile structure)
    char achAttr[] = "Some File Attribute";
    NonJavaFile->strAttr1 = makeJavaString(achAttr, sizeof(achAttr));
    NonJavaFile->iAttr2 = 100;
    NonJavaFile->bAttr3 = TRUE;
}
```

Creating Java Objects in Native Methods

The Java API function execute_java_constructor() is the key to creating Java objects from native methods. Its arguments include the name of the class to create, the desired constructor signature, and the arguments (which must, of course, correspond to the constructor signature) to the constructor. If the constructor executes successfully, it returns a pointer to a new Java object. If failure occurs, the function returns NULL, and an exception is raised.

The full prototype for the execute_java_constructor() function, as defined in interpreter.h, follows:

```
execute_java_constructor(ExecEnv *,
                         char *classname,
                         ClassClass *cb,
                         char *signature, ...);
```

If you already have a Class object for the class instance that you want to create, you can pass it in as the cb argument and pass NULL for the classname. This is somewhat faster than the alternative, which is to pass the classname and omit the Class object (pass NULL for cb), because the Java interpreter must find the Class object based on the class name.

The Java `String` class is a special case; the process of creating `String`s is simplified by the `makeJavaString()` function prototyped in the `javaString.h` header file. The full function prototype follows:

```
Hjava_lang_String *makeJavaString(char *, int);
```

The function returns a new `String` object given a C character pointer and the length of the string.

Writing Well-Behaved Native Code

All of the classes provided with the Java Development Kit fully use Java's standard security, error handling, and synchronization mechanisms. Native methods aren't forced to conform to any of the aforementioned standards. Deliberate effort is required on the behalf of native method implementer to use them.

The following sections describe the standard mechanisms, as well as means of conforming to their requirements.

Error Handling in Native Methods

Java's error handling mechanism is centered around the use of exceptions. Literally any method called on any Java object may throw one or more types of exceptions. Exceptions are used to indicate that an anomalous situation occurred during the execution of method code. The members of the Exception object describe the type of exception that occurred.

Java enforces the explicit capturing or throwing of exceptions. If your Java code calls a method that indicates in its definition that it throws one or more exceptions, your calling code must either catch the exceptions, or explicitly indicate that it throws the exceptions. Use of exceptions within Java code is further described in Chapter 10, "The Order Entry System: Exception Handling and Browser Interaction."

Native methods should, when appropriate, throw Java exceptions. They should also declare the Java exceptions that can be thrown by Java class methods executed by the Java code, giving the Java compiler information that it needs to enforce Java's rules for exception capturing.

Handling Exceptions Thrown by Java Code

Within Java code, the handling of exceptions is automatic. Frames with exception handlers can be established to catch exceptions. Native methods must use the following Java API function to detect exceptions thrown by Java methods:

```
exceptionOccurred(ee)
```

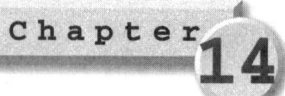
The `exceptionOccurred()` function returns true if a Java exception has been raised. To handle the exception, you can retrieve additional information about it using the `exc` member of the exception union within the `execenv` structure. The `exc` member contains a pointer to the Java exception object.

Typical native code that calls a Java method, then checks for and handles Java exceptions, might look like the following:

```
// Call some Java method
long lResult = execute_java_dynamic_method(EE(), theObj, "someMethod",
    "()V");
if (exceptionOccurred(EE())
{
    // Check if the exception that occurred is a dao.DaoException
    // in this example (NOTE: the dao.DaoException is mentioned in
    // the DAOLayer example)
    JHandle *exception = EE()->exc;
    ClassClass *DaoExceptionClass = FindClass(EE(), "dao/DaoException", TRUE);
    if (is_instance_of(exception, DaoExceptionClass, EE()))
    {
        // The exception is a dao.DaoException, so I can include
        // code to handle the exception
        EXCEPTION HANDLING CODE GOES HERE...

        // After I have handled the exception, I clear it so that
        // it isn't propagated back to the Java interpreter
        exceptionClear(EE());
    }
}
```

This is the rough functional equivalent of the following Java code:

```
try {
    theObj.someMethod();
} catch (dao.DaoException e) {
    EXCEPTION HANDLING CODE GOES HERE...
}
```

The native code is much more involved than the Java code. That's one of the disadvantages of using native methods. Java code doesn't have to worry about explicitly testing the type of the exception that is generated—the Java interpreter matches the exception with the corresponding `catch` clause, if an appropriate `catch` clause exists. After the code in the `catch` clause executes, the Java interpreter handles clearing the exception and resetting the Java execution environment.

The native code clears the Java exception explicitly using `exceptionClear()`. The `exceptionClear()` function is implemented as a macro in `interpreter.h`; its only parameter is a pointer to an `execenv` structure. The `exceptionClear()` macro is used to clear the current exception. It should be used if you catch and handle an exception in your native method code. Use it with caution; you will want to propagate (throw) some exceptions back to the code that called your native method.

If an exception occurs, the type of the exception is tested using the `is_instance_of()` function, which returns `true` if an object is an instance of a specific class. The definition of `is_instance_of`, from `interpreter.h`, follows:

```
bool_t is_instance_of(JHandle * h, ClassClass *dcb, ExecEnv *ee);
```

The first argument is the Java object you want to test, the second is the class object that you want to check the object against, and the third is a pointer to an execenv structure. The `is_instance_of` function returns `true` if the object is an instance of the class or a subclass of the class.

Throwing Exceptions

Throwing exceptions from native methods is very straightforward. The only Java API function that is required is `SignalError()`. The prototype for `SignalError()` follows:

```
void SignalError(struct execenv *, char *, char *);
```

The first argument is a pointer to an execenv structure. You can use the `EE()` function to pass the active execenv structure to `SignalError()`. The second argument is a null-terminated C string indicating the fully distinguished name of the exception that you're throwing. As usual, the periods separating the packages in which the class is defined should be replaced with the forward slash (/). The third argument is a null-terminated string that describes details of the exception; you can pass null if you don't want to specify additional information.

You can learn more about Java exceptions in Chapter 10. The DAOLayer native methods example, described later in this chapter, also demonstrates throwing exceptions from native methods.

Security in Native Methods

As previously indicated, Java native methods aren't subject to the same security restrictions as pure Java methods. That's not to say that they are completely exempt; for example, if you attempted to open a file using the `java.io` classes from a native method, the open call would fail with a `SecurityException` if the Java application doesn't have sufficient security privileges.

However, a native method could circumvent that security by using non-Java input-output mechanisms. If the native method uses standard C library functions for file input and output, it would be allowed to do so irrespective of the security restrictions of the current Java execution environment.

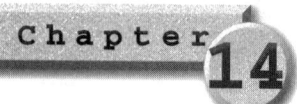

Consequently, to write truly well-behaved native methods, it is necessary to explicitly check the active security restrictions. As a matter of fact, this is precisely the behavior of implementations in the Java standard library. The following excerpt, from `File.java` in the `java.io` package, illustrates a security check:

```
/**
 * Deletes the specified file. Returns true
 * if the file could be deleted.
 */
public boolean delete() {
    SecurityManager security = System.getSecurityManager();
    if (security != null) {
        security.checkDelete(path);
    }
    return delete0();
}
```

Obviously, the security check is performed here within a Java wrapper method that calls a native method, `delete0()`, that actually performs the file deletion. If you need to perform a simple, single-step security check, using the wrapper method may suffice.

If you have a native method that performs several different types of actions that might each be subject to different security restrictions, it may be more convenient for you to include the security checks within the body of the native method. The following code illustrates one means of performing those types of security checks:

```
ClassClass *System = FindClass(EE(), "java/lang/System", TRUE);
Hobject *phSecMgr = (Hobject*)execute_java_static_method(EE(), System,
    "getSecurityManager", "()Ljava/lang/SecurityManager;");

if (NULL != phSecMgr)
{
    // Perform security check - for this example, check the ability
    // to delete a file in the local file system
    execute_java_dynamic_method(EE(), phSecMgr,
        "checkDelete", "(Ljava/lang/String;)V", phFile);
    if (exceptionOccurred())
    {
        // Perform some action…
    }
}
```

NOTE:

The default `SecurityManager` that comes with the Java development kit throws a `SecurityException` on every check that is performed.

Using Java's Synchronization/Wait-Notification Mechanisms

The architecture of Java was defined with the goal of directly supporting multithreading. Consequently, thread creation, notification, and synchronization mechanisms are provided within Java. Because every class is a sub-class of `java.lang.Object`, every class supports the `wait()` and `notify()` synchronization functions. Entire methods can be protected automatically by Java if they are defined with the `synchronized` keyword. The `java.lang.Thread` classes contain a synchronized static `nextThreadNum()` method; the `synchronized` keyword assures that the function may be called by only one Java object at a time.

Native Method Wait/Notify

To wait on a Java object you must call the object's `wait()` method. Doing so is straightforward, as the following code snippet illustrates:

```
execute_java_dynamic_method(EE(), theObject, "wait", "()V");
```

To notify a Java object you must call the object's `notify()` or `notifyAll()` method. The following code illustrates a call to the `notify()` method:

```
execute_java_dynamic_method(EE(), theObject, "notify", "()V");
```

Using `wait()` and `notify()` with Java objects is very useful when, for example, your native method consumes objects from a queue filled by a separate Java thread.

You should note that `wait`s may be interrupted, in which case an `InterruptedException` is thrown by the `wait` method. Consequently you may want to check for a Java exception after executing the `wait`, as shown in the following snippet:

```
// Wait for the object to be notify()ed
execute_java_dynamic_method(EE(), theObject, "wait", "()V");

// Check for the occurrence of an InterruptedException
if (exceptionOccurred(EE()))
{
    // Handle the exception - check for Interrupted, or other...
}
```

If you don't check for the `InterruptedException`, you may erroneously execute code that assumes that a waited object was notified. This isn't an issue within pure Java code because exceptions are enforced by the Java interpreter.

An Interface to Microsoft Data Access Objects (DAO)

One of the most useful and easy-to-use commercial APIs is the Microsoft DAO object model for Windows 95 and Windows NT. The DAO objects provide a simple, powerful abstraction that wraps ODBC-compliant database systems. DAO objects are directly exposed as a set of COM and OLE automation classes; the Microsoft Visual C++ development environment includes the DAO C++ API, which provides a simple mechanism to use the DAO OLE classes. The DAO classes are used to access databases and tables in the previously mentioned DAOCmd project.

NOTE:

Microsoft recently released an open beta of their Visual J++ Java development environment, available at `http://www.microsoft.com/VisualJ`. The Visual J++ environment, which runs on Windows 95 and Windows NT, incorporates support for the COM object model and allows the developer to instantiate and use OLE objects directly within Java, as well as create COM/OLE objects using Java. Because of the built-in COM support, Visual J++ applications can call DAO objects directly.

Microsoft Visual C++ also provides some DAO wrapper classes within the Microsoft Foundation Classes. The DAO wrappers handle some of the details of the creation and destruction of DAO objects for you. Because of their ease of use, they are a compelling choice as a set of classes to integrate with Java. The DAOLayer project, included with source code on the CD-ROM provided with this book, demonstrates fairly simple integration of Java classes with Microsoft MFC DAO C++ classes.

DAOLayer is designed to illustrate the integration of Java with Microsoft MFC DAO C++ classes using native methods. The DAOLayer project consists of several C/C++ header files and source files, as well as two Java classes that provide class definitions. You can get information about the DAO objects from the on-line help provided with the Microsoft Visual C++ compiler package.

Design Issues: Mapping C++ Objects to Java Objects

The Microsoft MFC DAO classes are already divided into discrete functional units. Consequently, defining a mapping from C++ to equivalent Java classes is straightforward. Wrapping a C API is slightly more complex due to the fact that there aren't necessarily any inherent objects within a C API. Your options when mapping a C API are basically to either create objects with methods that provide an interface to several logically related C functions, or to simply create a class that exposes static methods that wrap the C functions.

The DAOLayer project wraps the MFC `CDaoDatabase` class and the `CDaoRecordset` class. The Java classes `dao.Database` and `dao.Recordset` wrap the `CDaoDatabase` class and the `CDaoRecordset` class respectively. Only a few of the C++ member functions are exposed within the Java wrapper classes; `dao.Database` provides open and close methods, and `dao.Recordset` provides open, close, navigation, and field value retrieval functions. An implementation that was more full would provide additional functionality, such as write access, to field values in a `Recordset`.

Defining the **Database** Java Wrapper Object

The `dao.Database` class is a wrapper for the MFC `CDaoDatabase` class. It provides the ability to open databases that may be used to retrieve recordsets using the `Recordset` object.

The `dao.Database` object is, in some respects, the most important class in the DAOLayer `dao` package. It contains Java code to load the library containing the native methods that implement the `dao.Database` functionality. The excerpt that loads the DAOLayer dynamic link library follows:

```
static {
    System.loadLibrary("DAOLayer");
}
```

The `dao.Database` object also contains two very important static native methods, `initDAO()` and `termDAO()`. The MFC DAO library must be initialized using explicit calls to `AfxDaoInit()` and `AfxDaoTerm()` functions when it is used within a dynamic link library; the native methods `initDAO()` and `termDAO()` wrap those functions respectively. It's the responsibility of the Java code that uses the `dao.*` package to call `dao.Database.initDAO()` before using any classes in the package, and call `dao.Database.termDAO()` when finished.

The following section describing the `Recordset` object includes more details about wrapping C++ classes with Java objects.

Defining the **Recordset** Java Wrapper Object

The DAO `Recordset` object provides the ability to access a set of records from a DAO database. The MFC DAO `CDaoRecordset` class has numerous member functions that can be used to retrieve a set of records using an SQL statement, navigate through the records, and retrieve and update field values in records. For the sake of simplicity, the implementation of the `Recordset` provides only a few of the functions from the C++ class. It should be fairly simple for you to extend the class to add more functionality.

The definition of the `dao.Recordset` object follows:

```
package dao;

public class Recordset {
    public native void open(String strSQL) throws DaoException;
    public native void close() throws DaoException;
```

```
public native boolean isEOF() throws DaoException;
public native void moveFirst() throws DaoException;
public native void moveNext() throws DaoException;
public native String getFieldValue(String strField) throws DaoException;

protected dao.Database db;
protected int pRec; // Pointer to CDaoRecordset instance
protected native void allocRecObject();
protected native void deleteRecObject();

public Recordset(dao.Database db) {
    this.db = db;
    allocRecObject();
}

protected void finalize() throws Throwable {
    super.finalize();
    deleteRecObject();
}
}
```

Each of the public methods defined in the dao.Recordset class corresponds to a member function in the C++ class. Literally the only difference is that the names of the methods are prefixed with a lowercase letter, in accordance to standard Java method capitalization conventions, as opposed to uppercase, as per the C++ class member definitions. The effects of the functions correspond to the equivalently named C++ member functions. Most of the native methods are simple dispatching functions that call C++ functions.

At this point you may be wondering how the native methods call C++ functions. The private instance variable pRec is used to store a pointer to a CDaoRecordset object. The native method casts the pRec from an integer (which is a C long) back to a CDaoRecordset pointer, then calls the desired CDaoRecordset member function. The implementation of the moveNext() native method follows:

```
void dao_Recordset_moveNext(struct Hdao_Recordset* me)
{
    try {
        getRecPtr(me)->MoveNext();
    } catch (CDaoException* pe) {
        throwTranslatedDaoException(pe);
        pe->Delete();
    }
}
```

NOTE:

Notice that the name of the native method, dao_Recordset_moveNext(), includes the name of the package as a prefix. If the Recordset class were defined in a web.db.dao package, the Recordset_moveNext() method would have the prefix web_db_dao_.

The `getRecPtr()` function is a useful utility function that returns a pointer to a `CDaoRecordset` object, given a handle to a Java `Recordset` object. It is implemented as follows:

```
CDaoRecordset* getRecPtr(struct Hdao_Recordset* daoRec)
{
    return ((CDaoRecordset*)
        ((struct Classdao_Recordset*)unhand(daoRec)->pRec));
}
```

The complementary set function, `setRecPtr()`, includes the assertion that a Java `int` member variable, which is defined in the Java C structure as a `long`, is the same length in bytes as a `CDaoRecordset` pointer. The function is implemented as

```
void setRecPtr(struct Hdao_Recordset* daoRec, CDaoRecordset* pRec)
{
    ASSERT(sizeof(long) == sizeof(CDaoRecordset*));
    ((struct Classdao_Recordset*)unhand(daoRec))->pRec = (long)pRec;
}
```

The `get` and `set` functions are used as simple convenience functions that obviate the need to maintain complicated sequences of casts and calls to the `unhand()` function.

As previously indicated, the `java` class includes a member that is used to store a pointer to a `CDaoRecordset` instance. One of the issues in mapping Java classes to C++ classes is the lifetime of the objects. You'll notice a call to a protected `allocRecObject()` function in the constructor of `dao.Recordset`. That function is used to create a `CDaoRecordset` instance and connect it to `pRec`. The class finalizer includes a call to the matching `delete` function, `deleteRecObject()`, that deletes the C++ object when the lifetime of the Java object ends.

Passing C++ Exceptions to Java

In the implementation of the `Recordset.moveNext()` method, you may notice that the call to the C++ `CDaoRecordset::MoveNext()` member function is contained within a C++ `try/catch` block. The `MoveNext()` function may raise a C++ exception of type `CDaoException`. To maintain the semantics of the class, from the Java perspective, with regards to the exception behavior, the C++ exception is converted to a Java exception by the `throwTranslatedDaoException()` function. The `throwTranslatedDaoException()` function is implemented as follows:

```
void throwTranslatedDaoException(CDaoException* pe)
{
    CString strErr;
    CDaoErrorInfo *pErr = pe->m_pErrorInfo;

    strErr.GetBuffer(512);
    strErr.Format("%s (%ld) - %s", pErr->m_strSource, pErr->m_lErrorCode,
        pErr->m_strDescription);
    SignalError(EE(), "dao/DaoException", (char*)(LPCSTR)strErr);
}
```

The function takes a pointer to a CDaoException object. When an exception occurs, a pointer to the exception is acquired in the catch block that brackets the call to CDaoRecordset::MoveNext(). Using the convenient MFC CString class, the function creates a readable string that represents the CDaoException that occurred. After the string is created, an exception is raised using the SignalError() Java API function.

For the throwTranslatedDaoException() function, a dao.DaoException is thrown. The Java dao.DaoException class, defined in DaoException.java, is a straightforward subclass of the java.lang.Exception class.

After the Java exception is thrown, the C++ exception is deleted. For the CDaoException class, the CDaoException::Delete() member function must be called. Other C++ exceptions may be deleted by the standard C++ delete operator. The Java interpreter doesn't detect the occurrence of the Java exception until the native method returns, at which point the Java exception object is available to the Java code that called the native method.

Applets and Security Restrictions

Most Web browsers severely restrict the security for executing applets. Consequently, most applets can't be extended using either the separate process method with Runtime.exec(), or native methods implemented in C or C++.

This is obviously a fairly severe restriction. It's possible to use some type of client-server applet to access functionality unavailable through Java, or to perform remote procedure calls using RMI (described in the following section). To implement a client-server applet without using RMI, you need to create an applet that uses, for example, sockets to communicate with a Java server application that uses the external process or calls native methods. This avoids the applet security restrictions because the server does the work, not the applet. However, those mechanisms are only useful when integrating with systems that don't need to run on the host machine.

For example, if you want to develop an applet that uses GUI functionality unavailable through the java.awt package, you may want to use native methods. In that situation, a call to a Java object on a server won't suffice.

To remedy this situation, there has been some talk of signed applets or applets with associated certificates. Applets would only be allowed to run if they had an associated certificate trusted by the browser loading the applet. If certificates are implemented, then a future browser may allow applets with native methods to run, assuming that the user of the browser trusts the presenter of the certificate for the applet.

Java Remote Method Invocation

Java Remote Method Invocation (RMI) provides a simple mechanism for converting standard Java classes into client/server classes. Java RMI is essentially an integrated remote procedure call mechanism that allows method calls to a local object to be forwarded transparently to a server object. To use RMI, you define an implementation class and an interface class; the interface class uses some RMI magic to package parameters and transfer them to a remote object, an instance of the implementation class.

RMI could be used to provide a simple workaround to applet native method security restrictions. Instead of implementing some arbitrary and complex client/server applet, you could create two versions of the class that uses native methods. The interface class would simply provide function stubs that, due to the fact that they're implemented in Java, would be callable by a Java applet. The implementation class, running on the remote object server, would use native method implementations.

Java RMI is currently in Beta. If you want to find out more about RMI, and download a Beta version, check out Sun's Java Web site at `http://www.javasoft.com`.

Summary

Java has a great set of standard packages that provide much of the functionality required by Java applets or applications. However, there are occasionally tasks that require the use of non-Java objects. For example, an interface to a non-Java database may require some intermediary between a Java application and the non-Java database engine or API.

Within Java, there are two basic options. The simplest option may be to create a command-line driven executable that returns information to Java using its standard output. The previously mentioned DAOCmd project illustrates this means of integration. The problem with that type of integration is that it's weakly integrated with the Java runtime environment; dynamically passing parameters or exception information between Java and the running non-Java process is difficult or impossible.

The second option is to create a class with native methods. Native methods provide a very powerful means of extending the Java environment with non-Java code. This chapter's examples and the DAOLayer project illustrate that it is possible to tie well-behaved native methods seamlessly into the Java environment.

Chapter

15

by Michael Girdley and George Reese

Developing Database Applications and Applets with the JDBC

- Why the Java Database Connectivity (JDBC) Specification?

- Storing Data for the Web

- Providing Access to Data

- The JDBC API

- Simple Database Access Using the JDBC Interfaces

- Result Sets and the Meta-data Interfaces

- Other JDBC Functionality

- Building a JDBC Implementation

- Extending JDBC

- Designing a Database Application

Perhaps the most exciting and powerful use of computers involve heavy duty storage of data and organized access to that data. For example, business users have long benefited from the ability to centrally store data for many different users to access. By connecting the millions of once-isolated home computers on a common network, the Internet has empowered developers to bring the advantages of client/server computing into the home. Until Java, such Web applications have primarily used CGI for connecting to databases.

For a few years now, the business solution to client/server development has been rapid application development tools such as Borland Delphi, Sybase PowerBuilder, and Microsoft Visual Basic. These applications provide both rapid GUI development through the use of drag-and-drop screen painting as well as a library of tools for accessing data housed in relational databases. Unfortunately, these applications are not well suited to Internet development, where platform independence, security, and distribution are all imperative.

A major strength of rapid application development products is their database connectivity. Ideally, you would have wanted the Order Entry System to access a real database and function off of that data. For example, the applet could report to a customer whether a certain item was available when the order was sent in. Or, even better, the applet could check and feature only those items that were in stock. But, as you saw, the Order Entry System by the time you finished with it was already becoming unwieldy. This chapter will provide you with the basis to include these database access and manipulation features into your own applets. I will also create a number of coded examples that will demonstrate these features and techniques that you can apply to your own Web programming.

NOTE:

This chapter focuses on the mechanics of how Java can interact with databases, not on explaining many concepts key to database use. For that reason, some concepts of databases I refer to in this chapter may seem like gibberish if you are not familiar with databases. If you want to implement a database, a number of good resources such as books and documents on the Web will help you. The information in this chapter will then show you how to create Java programs that will interact with your database. The Java Database Connectivity (JDBC) standard is very similar to Microsoft's Open Database Connectivity (ODBC) standard, which can be a starting point for your introduction to databases.

Why the Java Database Connectivity (JDBC) Specification?

The Java specification, as well as the original release of the Java Developer's Kit (JDK), made no provisions for Java database access. To create access to a database, a programmer had to create an intermediary program between the database manager and the Java program that would access the data. To force a multitude of programmers all to write code that does essentially the same thing is truly a waste. Of course, each different programmer would do it his/her own way and suddenly you'd have a large mess on your hands. It is entirely inefficient not to have a standardized access format between Java code and database management systems.

Another reason that a standardized database interface proves necessary stems from security issues. By making a standard JDBC specification, database manufacturers can produce interfaces for their database, regardless of the internal storage format, so that the standardized interface could work with any Java program. This is a large bonus: Any Java program that implements database features can manipulate and access any database that has a JDBC-compliant interface. Also, the standardized classes and interfaces of the database interface classes can join the ranks of "trusted" classes that Web browsers can then safely use. Of course, home-brewed database interfaces would not be trusted or put into wide use and applets would not be able to use databases at all.

For these reasons, some kind of standardized database capability is necessary. In March 1996, Sun Microsystems, Inc. addressed this need with the draft release of the Java Database Connectivity specification, JDBC. As of this writing, the JDBC specification is still in a request-for-comments phase and is scheduled to be available soon in a full release. This chapter addresses the problem of database access in Java and demonstrates how to write code that conforms to and enhances the JDBC interface.

A hidden plus of the JDBC standard is that implementing database features in a Java program should make it easy to use that same implementation on another database. Of course, standardizing all of these functions comes at a price. It is less efficient to include the JDBC interface as another layer between your program and the database itself, but you should be accustomed to the tradeoff between standardization and simplicity and efficiency.

Currently, a number of database system developers have committed to developing JDBC-specification-compliant interfaces for their database systems. As of July 1996, database system producers ranging from Borland to tiny companies have stated their intent to develop JDBC interfaces immediately. As always, the latest information on Java database developments can be found at Java's home page:

```
http://java.sun.com/
```

Storing Data for the Web

Simple applets rarely need to perform database access. They are generally executed as on-off programs without the need to save any state information across executions. As Java developers move their work out of the realm of the simple applet, they will find the need to access some sort of data store. A popular yet simple example is the ubiquitous page counter. Of course, a page counter is simply an applet or CGI script that keeps track of how many times a particular page has been hit and displays that number on the page (see Figure 15.1).

Figure 15.1.

A Web page running a
counter applet.

At the other extreme in complexity are the search engines with which you can perform keyword searches to find the most trivially related pages of information existing on the Internet. No matter how complex the application, the basic data management needs are the same. Many users need to gain access to the same piece of information and require an application built in such a way that it can access and/or modify centrally stored data. The developer must then take the following steps to provide users with access to data:

○ Select and install a database management system (DBMS)

○ Build data processing logic

○ Build a user interface

Providing Access to Data

Whether Java or some other language is used to build these pieces, the DBMS used will have a direct impact on the implementation. A detailed discussion of database management systems is well beyond the scope of this book. When you choose among the various technologies, however, keep your needs (and your wallet) in mind and resist the dazzle of technology. Three basic data storage technologies that serve various needs follow:

○ Object-oriented database (OODBMS)

○ Relational database (RDBMS)

○ Object-relational database (OORDBMS)

With the advent of the high multimedia content data storage needs of the Internet, developers have been more open to the idea of using object databases. In addition to being better suited to the unusual demands of storing multimedia data, object databases also help provide a true object paradigm from data store to client application.

What does this mean to you? You'll be concerned with a couple of issues, the first of which are the time and storage space requirements necessary for each different type of database manager. If you're trying to store a large amount of customer orders, for example, you should choose the appropriate database management system, such as a simple relational database. Or, if you're going heavy into multimedia, you'll want to use an object-based database manager.

The second issue is how the choice will affect how easily you can access the database. As you probably know, accessing a pure object database with any front-end tool is a challenge. Because the JDBC specification revolves around ANSI SQL-2 compliance and few object databases have SQL support, accessing an object database through Java will prove to be doubly challenging.

For developers not faced with the need to store complex data, any traditional relational databases should do exactly what you need. The grand trick to programming in Java with a relational database, or doing any object programming against a relational database, is mapping between the dynamic realm of objects and the static realm of pure data.

Paving the road between these two seemingly disparate technologies are the object-relational databases. For developers with complex data modeling needs, an object-relational database can provide the object modeling power of an object database while maintaining the ease of data access afforded by traditional relational systems.

The JDBC API

To provide a common base API for accessing data, Sun Microsystems, Inc., with support from a number of independent software vendors, developed JDBC. JDBC defines a number of Java interfaces to enable developers to access data independent of the actual database product being used to store the data. In theory, an application written against the basic JDBC API using only SQL-2 can function against any database technology that supports SQL-2. Of course, the key words are "in theory." The idea is that the interaction between your Java program and any database is standardized through the JDBC specification standard.

Database Requirements

You may store data in a wide variety of formats using various technologies. In addition to the three major modern database management systems, you will want to consider other systems, such as hierarchical databases and file systems. Any low-level API trying to find some common ground between all of these systems would be unsuccessful. JDBC mandates no specific requirements on the underlying DBMS, however. In other words, the JDBC doesn't care what's going on underneath the interface as long as it meets the ANSI SQL-2 standards. Rather than dictating what sort of DBMS an application must have to support JDBC, the specification places all of its requirements on the JDBC implementation.

Each platform and database-specific implementation of the JDBC by a software developer will provide a standardized environment in which your Java programs can operate. The JDBC specification primarily mandates that a JDBC implementation supports at least ANSI SQL-2 Entry Level. Because most common relational database systems and object-relational database systems support SQL-2, this requirement provides a reasonable baseline from which software developers can build Java database access. In addition, because SQL-2 is required only at the JDBC implementation level, that implementation can provide its own SQL-2 wrapper around non-SQL data stores.

The most important thing for you to remember when developing in Java is that your applications and applets are limited to accessing databases that support the ANSI SQL-2 standard. These databases naturally follow this standard or have had a specialized JDBC-compliant interface written for them.

The JDBC Interfaces

The JDBC defines eight interfaces that must be implemented to be JDBC-compliant:

- ○ java.sql.Driver
- ○ java.sql.Connection
- ○ java.sql.Statement
- ○ java.sql.PreparedStatement
- ○ java.sql.CallableStatement
- ○ java.sql.ResultSet
- ○ java.sql.ResultSetMetaData
- ○ java.sql.DatabaseMetaData

Figure 15.2 shows these interfaces and how they interact in the full JDBC object model.

The central object around which the whole concept revolves is the java.sql.DriverManager object. This object is responsible for keeping track of the various JDBC implementations that may exist for an application. If, for example, a system were aware of Sybase and Oracle JDBC implementations, the DriverManager would be responsible for tracking those implementations. Any time an application desires to connect to a database, it asks the DriverManager to give it a database connection using a database URL through the DriverManager.getConnection() method. Based on this URL, the DriverManager searches for a Driver implementation that accepts the URL. It then gets a Connection implementation from that Driver and returns it to the application.

Figure 15.2.
The JDBC object model.

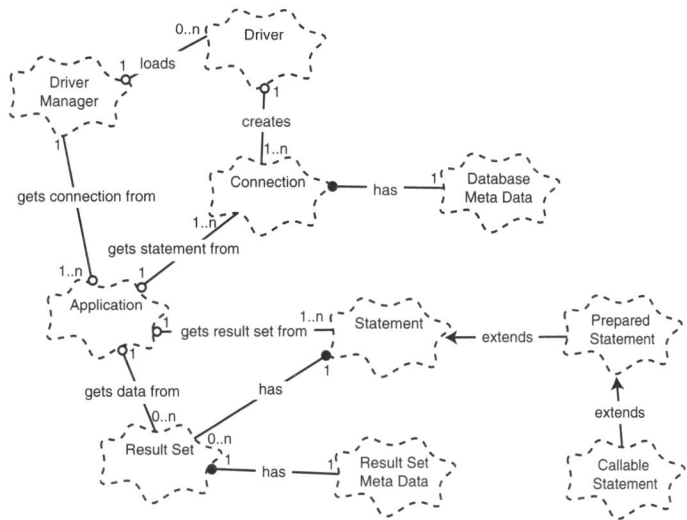

NOTE:

What is a database URL? To enable an application to specify the database to which it wants to connect, JDBC uses the Internet standard Universal Resource Locator (URL) system. A JDBC URL consists of the following pieces: `jdbc:<subprotocol>:<subname>`. As with URLs you have seen all over the Internet, the first element is the resource protocol—in this case, a JDBC data source. The subprotocol is specific to the JDBC implementation. In many cases, it likely will be the DBMS name and version; for example, syb10 might indicate Sybase System 10. The subname element is any information specific to the DBMS that tells it where it needs to connect. For mSQL, the JDBC URL is in the format of `jdbc:msql://hostname:port/database`. JDBC itself does not much care what a database URL looks like. The important thing is simply that a desired JDBC implementation can recognize the URL and get the information it needs to connect to a database from that URL.

The `DriverManager` is the only instantiated class provided by JDBC other than exception objects and a few specialized subclasses of `java.util.Date`. Additional calls made by an application are written against the JDBC interfaces that are implemented for specific DBMSs.

java.sql.Driver

A `Driver` is essentially a `Connection` factory. The `DriverManager` uses the `Driver` to determine whether it, the `DriverManager`, can handle a given URL. If it can handle the URL, it should create a connection object and return it to the `DriverManager`. Because an application only indirectly references a `Driver` through the `DriverManager`, applications are rarely concerned with this class.

java.sql.Connection

A `Connection` is a single database session. As such, it stores state information about the database session it manages and provides the application with `Statement`, `PreparedStatement`, or `CallableStatement` objects to make calls during the session.

java.sql.Statement

A `Statement` is an unbound SQL call to the database. It is generally a simple UPDATE, DELETE, IN-SERT, or SELECT for which no columns need to bind to Java data. It provides methods for making such calls and returns to the application the results of any SELECT statements, or the number of rows affected by an UPDATE, DELETE, or INSERT.

`Statement` has the subclass `PreparedStatement`, which is in turn subclassed by `CallableStatement`. A `PreparedStatement` is a precompiled database call that requires binding parameters. An example of a `PreparedStatement` might be a stored procedure call that has no OUT or INOUT parameters. For stored procedures with OUT or INOUT parameters, an application should use the `CallableStatement` interface.

java.sql.ResultSet

A SELECT query returns data to an application by implementing this interface. Specifically, the `ResultSet` object enables an application to retrieve sequential rows of data returned from a previous SELECT call. It provides a multitude of methods that enable you to retrieve a given row as any data type to which it makes sense to convert it. For example, if you have a date stored in the database as a datetime, you can retrieve it through the `getString()` method to use it as a string.

The Meta-data Interfaces

Meta-data is data about data. Specifically, it is a set of data that gives you information about the database and data retrieved from the database. Java provides two meta-data interfaces: `java.sql.ResultSetMetaData` and `java.sql.DatabaseMetaData`. The `ResultSetMetaData` provides a means for getting information about a particular `ResultSet`. For example, among other things, it provides information on the number of columns in the result set, the name of a column, and its type. The `DatabaseMetaData` interface, on the other hand, gives the application information on the database in general, such as what levels of support it has, its name, version, and other features.

Simple Database Access Using the JDBC Interfaces

An application for which database independence is paramount, in other words, one in which you want to write a program that can use different databases using a JDBC interface, should be written to the JDBC specification without using database-specific calls and without making use of SQL that is not part of the ANSI SQL-2 standard. In such code, no reference should be made to a specific implementation of JDBC. Writing a simple database application using only JDBC calls involves the following steps:

1. Ask the `DriverManager` for a `Connection` implementation.
2. Ask the `Connection` for a `Statement` or subclass of `Statement` to execute your SQL.
3. For subclasses of `Statement`, bind any parameters to be passed to the prepared statement.
4. Execute the `Statement`.
5. For queries, process the `ResultSet` returned from the query. Do this for each result set (if you have multiple result sets) until none are left.
6. For other statements, check the return value for the number of rows affected.
7. Close the `Statement`.
8. Process any number of such statements and then close the connection.

The Counter Applet Example

The counter applet discussed earlier in this chapter provides a simple example of JDBC programming. Using the JDBC interfaces, this applet connects to a database, determines how many times the page on which it appears has been hit, updates the page to reflect the new hit, and displays the number of hits. To use this example, you need a database engine to run your database and a JDBC driver to access that database engine. If you do not have a database engine, download mSQL and JDBC, which are both free for noncommercial use. Links to mSQL and the JDBC class may be found through

```
http://www.imaginary.com/Java/.
```

In addition, you need to create a table called t_counter with the fields counter_file (CHAR(100), PRIMARY KEY) and counter_num (INT, NOT NULL). The following mSQL script creates the table:

```
DROP TABLE t_counter\p\g

CREATE TABLE t_counter(

        counter_file    CHAR(100)    PRIMARY KEY,

        counter_num     INT          NOT NULL
)\p\g
```

The applet consists of two classes, Counter and Database. The Counter class is the subclass of applet that provides the user interface to the applet. It contains two instance variables: count, which is the number this applet is supposed to display, the number of page hits, and database, which is an instance of the Database class that provides wrappers for the JDBC access needed by the applet.

Counter does not define any new methods; rather, it simply overrides the java.applet.Applet.init() and java.applet.Applet.paint() methods. The init() method is used to create a Database instance and find out from it what the page hit count is for display. The paint() method displays the page hit count.

This interesting JDBC-related work is all encapsulated inside the Database class. This class has a single instance variable, connection, which is an instance of a JDBC Connection implementation. The connection variable is initialized in the Database class constructor:

```
public Database(String url, String user, String pass)
 throws java.sql.SQLException  {

    connection = DriverManager.getConnection(url, user, pass);

}
```

By getting an instantiated Connection object, the applet is ready to access whatever database it needs.

TIP:

As of the printing of this book, the java.sql package has not been incorporated into Java browsers such as Netscape. Due to a security feature of such browsers, which prevents the loading of classes in the java.* namespace, the applet examples in this chapter will not work properly. So how do I know they work at all? To get an applet using the java.sql classes to work, simply rename your java.sql packages to something else and recompile them. That moves them from the java.* namespace so that such browsers can load them. This problem does not affect stand-alone applications and it will not apply once the JDBC specification is finalized and java.sql classes are incorporated into the browser releases.

The applet uses the getCount() method to calculate how many page hits this particular access to the Web page represents. That seemingly benign query actually represents several steps:

1. Create a Statement object.

2. Formulate and execute the SELECT query.

3. Process the result.

4. Increment the hit count.

5. Format and execute an UPDATE or INSERT statement.

6. Close the Statement and Connection objects.

The Statement is created through the JDBC call:

```
java.sql.Statement statement = connection.createStatement();
```

You want the number of hits for this page from the t_counter table:

```
sql = "SELECT counter_num FROM t_counter " +

    "WHERE counter_file = '" + page + "'";

result_set = statement.executeQuery(sql);
```

The result_set variable now holds the results of the query. For queries that return multiple rows, an application loops through the next() method in the result set until no more rows exist. This query should only return one row with one column, unless the page has never been hit. If the page has never been hit, the query will not find any rows and the count variable should be set to 0:

```
if( !result_set.next() ) count = 0;
```

Otherwise, you need to retrieve that row into the count variable as an integer:

```
else count = result_set.getInt(1);
```

After incrementing the count to reflect this new hit, close out the Statement object and get a new one to prepare for the UPDATE:

```
count++;

statement.close();

statement = connection.create Statement();
```

If this is the first time the page is being hit, the applet needs to INSERT a new row into the database. Otherwise, it should UPDATE the existing row:

```
if( count == 1 ) {
    sql = "INSERT INTO t_counter " +

            "(counter_file, counter_num) " +

            "VALUES ('" + file + "', " + count + ")";
}

else {
    sql = "UPDATE t_counter " +

            "SET counter_num = " + count + " " +

            "WHERE counter_file = '" + file + "'";
}

statement.executeUpdate(sql);
```

The method then cleans up and returns the hit count.

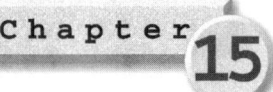

Listing 15.1 puts the whole applet together.

Listing 15.1. The Counter applet.

```
import java.sql.Connection;
import java.sql.DriverManager;
import java.sql.ResultSet;
import java.sql.Statement;
import java.awt.Graphics;

public class Counter extends java.applet.Applet {

    Database db;

    String count;

    public void init() {

        String driver = getParameter("driver");

        String url = getParameter("url");
        String user = getParameter("user");

        String pass = getParameter("password");
        String page = getParameter("page");

        try {

            Class.forName(driver).newInstance();

            db = new Database(url, user, pass);

            count = db.getCount(page);

        }
    catch( java.sql.SQLException e ) {

            e.printStackTrace();
            count = "Database exception";

        }
    catch( Exception e ) {

            e.printStackTrace();

            count = "Unable to load driver";

        }

    }


    public void paint(Graphics g) {

        g.setFont(new java.awt.Font(getParameter("font"),
```

```
                                              java.awt.Font.BOLD, 14));

        g.drawString(count, 5, 15);

}

}


class Database {

    private Connection connection;

    public Database(String url, String user, String pass)
 throws java.sql.SQLException {

    connection = DriverManager.getConnection(url, user, pass);

    }


public String getCount(String page) {

        int count = 0;


        try {
            java.sql.Statement statement =
                connection.createStatement();

            java.sql.ResultSet result_set;

                String sql;

          sql = "SELECT counter_num FROM t_counter " +
                              "WHERE counter_file = '" +
               page + "'";

          result_set = statement.executeQuery(sql);

           if( !result_set.next() ) count = 0;

                           else count = result_set.getInt(1);


           count++;

          statement.close();


          statement = connection.createStatement();

          if( count == 1 ) {
```

continues

Listing 15.1. continued

```
                        sql = "INSERT INTO t_counter " +
                              "(counter_file, counter_num) " +
                              "VALUES ('" + page + "',." +count+ ")";

            } else {

                        sql = "UPDATE t_counter " +
                              "SET counter_num = " + count + " " +
                              "WHERE counter_file = '" + page + "'";

            }

            statement.executeUpdate(sql);
                  statement.close();
                  connection.close();

        }
    catch( java.sql.SQLException e ) {

            e.printStackTrace();

        }

    return ("" + count);

    }

}
```

NOTE:

How are drivers registered with the DriverManager? In the previous example, it was done by specifically loading the driver passed into the program through the driver parameter. A JDBC-compliant driver must notify the DriverManager of its existence when it is instantiated. The preferred method of listing multiple JDBC drivers for the DriverManager is through the jdbc.drivers property.

Result Sets and the Meta-data Interfaces

In simple applications such as the counter applet, there is no need to perform any tricks with the results from a query—the data is simply retrieved sequentially and processed. More commonly, however, an application will need to process the data in a more complex fashion. For example, a set of classes might want to deal with data on a more abstract level than the Database class from the counter example. Instead, such classes might not know exactly what data is being retrieved. They can query the meta-data interfaces to process intelligently such data that they would otherwise not know. Listing 15.2 shows a generic database view class that is populated with database objects based on a result set.

Listing 15.2. A generic database view class.

```java
import java.sql.ResultSet;
import java.sql.ResultSetMetaData;
import java.util.Hashtable;
import java.util.Vector;


public class View {

    private Vector objects;
    public void populate(ResultSet result_set, String cl) {

        ResultSetMetaData meta_data;

        int i, maxi;


        try {

            objects = new Vector();

            meta_data = result_set.getMetaData();

            maxi = meta_data.getColumnCount();

            while( result_set.next() ) {

                Hashtable row = new Hashtable();
                DataObject obj;
                for(i=1; i<=maxi; i++) {

                    String key;

                    Object value;

                    int t;

                        key = meta_data.getColumnLabel(i);

                    t = meta_data.getColumnType(i);
```

continues

Listing 15.2. continued

```
                    value = result_set.getObject(i, t);
                                    row.put(key, value);
            }

                obj = (DataObject)Class.forName(cl);
                                obj.restore(row);

                    objects.addElement(obj);

        }

        }
    catch ( java.sql.SQLException e ) {

            e.printStackTrace();

            objects = new Vector();

            return;

        }

    }

}
```

In the View class, reference is made to a DataObject class that implements a restore(java.util.Hashtable) method not listed.

Because many applications will use this generic class, the class knows nothing about the queries it is executing. Instead, it takes any random result set and assumes that each row corresponds to an instance of the class named by the second parameter to populate().

To get the information it needs for performing the data retrievals, the populate() method first obtains the meta-data object for this result set. This method is specifically interested in knowing how many columns, as well as the names of the columns, are in the result set.

To store the columns in a Hashtable object that the DataObject object can use for restoring itself, all data must be in the form of objects. Thus, for each column in the result set, the DataObject finds its data type from the meta-data and retrieves the column as an object. The final step is to store it in the Hashtable.

Other JDBC Functionality

The JDBC provides functionality beyond the commonly used methods already discussed in terms of the following features:

○ Transaction management
○ Cursor support

○ Stored procedure support

○ Multiple result set processing

Transaction Management

JDBC implementations should default automatically to committing transactions unless the application otherwise requests that transactions require an explicit commitment. An application may toggle the automatic commit of the JDBC implementation it is using through the `Connection.setAutoCommit()` method. An example follows:

```
connection.setAutoCommit(false);
```

Of course, by not setting the `AutoCommit` attribute or by setting it to true, the JDBC implementation will make certain that the DBMS commits after each statement you send to the database. When set to false, however, the JDBC implementation requires specific commits from the application before a transaction is committed to the database. A series of statements executed as a single transaction would look like this:

```java
public void add_comment(String comment) {

    try {

        Statement s;

        ResultSet r;

        int comment_id;

        connection.setAutoCommit(false);

        s = connection.createStatement();

        r = s.executeQuery("SELECT next_id " +
                "FROM t_id " +
                    "WHERE id_name = 'comment_id'");

        if( !r.next() ) {

            throw new SQLException("No comment id exists " +
                                            "in t_id table.");

        }

        comment_id = r.getInt(1) + 1;

            s.close();
```

```
                          s = connection.createStatement();

            s.executeUpdate("UPDATE t_id " +

                "SET comment_id = "
                + comment_id + " " +

                        "WHERE next_id = 'comment_id'");

            s.close();

            s = connection.createStatement();


            s.executeUpdate("INSERT INTO t_comment " +
                                        "(comment_id, comment_text) " +

                "VALUES(" + comment_id + ", '" +

                comment + "')");
            connection.commit();

        }
    catch( SQLException e ) {

            e.printStackTrace();

            try {
            connection.rollback();

            } catch( SQLException e2 )  System.exit(-1);

        }

    }
}
```

This method adds a comment to a comment table for some applications. To insert the new comment, the method needs to generate a new comment_id and then update the table for generating IDs so that the next one will be one greater than this one. Once the program has an ID for this comment, it then inserts the comment into the database and commits the entire transaction. If an error occurs at any time, the entire transaction is rolled back.

JDBC currently has no support for a two-phase commit. Applications written against distributed databases require extra support to allow for a two-phase commit.

Cursor Support

JDBC provides limited cursor support. It enables an application to associate a cursor with a result set through the ResultSet.getCursorName() method. The application can then use the cursor name to perform positioned UPDATE or DELETE statements.

Stored Procedures

Stored procedures are precompiled SQL statements stored in the database that enable faster execution of SQL. JDBC supports stored procedures through the CallableStatement class. In the counter applet, you could have used a stored procedure to update the page hit count in the following way:

```
CallableStatement s = connection.prepareCall(
          "{call sp_upd_hit_count[?, ?]}");

s.setStringParameter(1, "file");

s.setIntParameter(2, count);

s.executeUpdate();
```

Multiple Result Sets

In some cases, especially with stored procedures, an application can find a statement by returning multiple result sets. JDBC handles this through the method Statement.getMoreResults(). Although result sets are left to be processed, this method returns true. The application can then obtain the next ResultSet object by calling Statement.getResultSet(). Processing multiple result sets simply involves looping through as long as Statement.getMoreResults() returns a value of true.

Building a JDBC Implementation

Building a JDBC implementation requires a lot more in-depth knowledge of both your DBMS and the JDBC specification than does simply coding to it. Most people will never encounter the need to roll their own implementation because database vendors logically want to make them available for their product. Understanding the inner workings of JDBC can help advance your application programming, however.

JDBC is a low-level interface that provides direct SQL-level access to the database. Most business applications and class libraries abstract from that SQL-level access to provide such features as object persistence and business-aware database access. A narrow example of such an abstraction is the Database class from the counter example.

The ideal object method of accomplishing these goals is to reuse existing JDBC implementations for the DBMS in question and to add custom interfaces on top of those implementations. If the DBMS is an oddball DBMS, or perhaps if you are concerned about the available implementations that exist, writing one from scratch makes sense.

Implementing the Interfaces

The first concern of any JDBC implementation is how it will talk to the database. Figure 15.3 illustrates the architecture of three possible JDBC implementations. Depending on the design goals in question, one of these methods will suit any JDBC implementation:

○ A native C library

○ A socket interface

○ Extending a vendor JDBC implementation

Figure 15.3.

Possible JDBC implementa-
tion architectures.

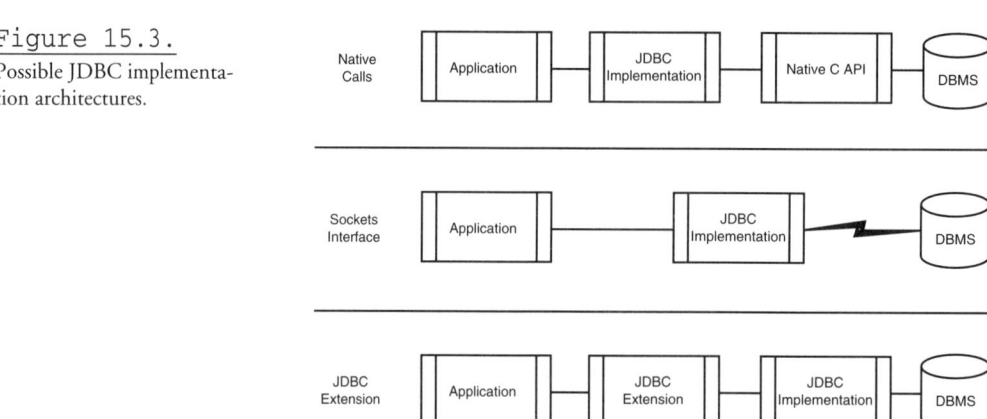

Of course, extending a vendor JDBC implementation is not really the same as building a JDBC implementation. Because a key to any object-oriented project is reusing code instead of building from scratch it is listed here.

With all three architectures, the application is apparently isolated from the actual communication mechanism. In truth, however, the native C library method places severe restrictions on any application using a JDBC implementation built on top of it. Because it uses native calls, it is naturally not portable across operating systems. In addition, due to virtual machine restrictions on most browsers, native calls are either severely limited or fully restricted.

To use one of these mechanisms for database communication, you need to construct the four basic interfaces: `java.sql.Driver`, `java.sql.Connection`, `java.sql.Statement`, and `java.sql.ResultSet`. These interfaces will provide minimum functionality so that you can test against simple queries and updates. Once these interfaces are functional, the implementation needs the meta-data interfaces as well as the `Statement` subclasses to be complete and JDBC-compliant.

Extending JDBC

Nothing requires an application to use the JDBC interface to access a database. In fact, before JDBC, developers programmed to Java classes written specifically to go against several major

database engines. JDBC isolates the database access behind a single interface. This isolation provided developers with the ability to write database access in Java without having to know which database engine their application is actually hitting. With a single prevalent database API, finding people with experience programming against it proves much simpler than finding people to program against a proprietary API. JDBC is, however, a low-level specification that requires developers to write both SQL code as well as Java code.

Both examples in this chapter demonstrate two different ways in which you can extend JDBC. In the counter applet, a database class was created as a wrapper around the JDBC implementation. The applet itself was divided into a representational portion, the Counter class, and a functional portion, the Database class. If you make changes to the visual representation, such as making the hit count appear through an odometer graphic, you won't have to make changes to the functional logic because it is isolated in a separate class. In fact, if the applet were more complex, requiring multiple developers, all the SQL would still be isolated in a class specifically interested in the functional behavior of the application. This reduces the number of people who need to write SQL code.

The View class example was a more abstract way of extending JDBC. The View class assumes that rows in result sets translate into business objects. In an application using this class, View objects are created to make JDBC calls and populate the applications with meaningful objects.

Another manner in which you can extend JDBC is to take advantage of database-specific features. Although it is prudent to question the need to make use of any proprietary features of a given DBMS, it is equally important that you do not ignore the extra power a specific DBMS gives you. It is, after all, very rare that an application actually needs to switch database engines.

Designing a Database Application

Knowing the JDBC API and coding cute applets is naturally just the start to database programming in Java. To harness the advantages of Java, application designers need to be able to address the design issues Java raises. The entire Java paradigm empowers developers to write database applications and applets using architectures that before were either very complex or simply not supported by other tools. Two such buzzwords that have been flying around the client/server world for a while are distributed objects and three-tier client/server.

Security Issues

Before going off the edge and into the deep end, Java does put some restrictions on applets for security reasons that can appear to be particularly limiting to the database developer. The following two particular applet restrictions affect database programmers:

○ Limited access to native libraries
○ Limited network access

The native call limitation affects programmers who need to use some sort of C- or operating system-level library to design an applet. This is especially troublesome to applet writers who take advantage of a database-specific feature not supported outside of native calls.

To veteran client/server developers, however, the most troubling idea is likely that your Web server must be on the same machine to which your applet connects for database access. Specifically, most Java virtual machines restrict applets from connecting to any machine except the host that served the applet. The applet cannot connect directly to any local or third-machine databases. As limiting as this particular restriction seems, a three-tier architecture provides a liberating solution.

Constructing a Three-tier Application

Two-tier applications tend to push a lot of processing onto the client machines. This architecture poses several problems:

○ Client-side resource requirements balloon with the extra processing needs. It is not uncommon to find business applications requiring Pentiums with 32M of RAM.

○ User interface and business processing tend to get rolled together, especially with the rapid application development tools on the market. With the user interface so closely tied to business processing, changes to one end up having a direct impact on the other, making maintenance a headache.

○ With all this redundant processing occurring on many client machines rather than in a central location, new applications are forced to reinvent the wheel when dealing with the same business processing.

With the guaranteed execution environment of the Java virtual machine and an easy-to-use Internet socket interface, Java is actually well suited to implementing three-tier systems. A three-tier application is one in which a third application layer exists between the client and server layers of traditional two-tier client/server development. This middle layer has a wide variety of uses depending on the application.

In the three-tier architecture, the middle layer separates business processing from the visual representation of data. This layer, called the application server, is responsible for knowing how to find and manipulate business data. The client evolves into a much leaner application, responsible only for retrieving information from the application server and displaying it on the screen.

In addition to removing a huge processing burden from client machines, this application server can be used to consolidate enterprise-wide business rules.

Where business rules had to be rewritten for each two-tier application thrust on the desktop, application servers process business rules in a single place for multiple applications to use. When the business rules change, a change to the application server takes care of that change for all the applications being run by the business.

Of specific interest to Java developers is the ability to hide any knowledge of the database server from the client. Because Internet clients view the applet or application as interfacing with a single application server, you can use that application server to determine such issues as where the data really exists. Additionally, this back-end independence enables applications to scale much easier across CPUs. Figure 15.4 shows a three-tier architecture.

Figure 15.4.

A three-tier Java applet or application.

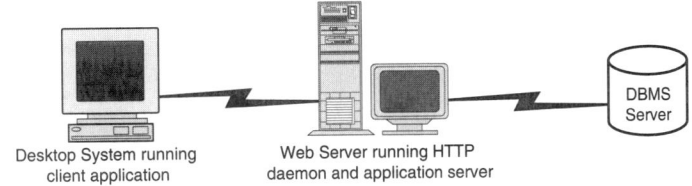

Desktop System running
client application

Web Server running HTTP
daemon and application server

DBMS
Server

A Three-tier Bug Tracking System

The application server forms the core of a three-tier architecture. In it, the business rules are defined and processed. Implementing the counter using a three-tier architecture would naturally be overkill. Instead, the ideal application for a three-tier design is one in which some manipulation of data occurs or where the data can be viewed in multiple fashions (or even better, by multiple applications). The first step in building an application server would thus be to identify the data processing needs of the application.

Implementing a Three-tier Application with Java

Figure 15.5 shows a bug tracking application implemented as a three-tier Java application.

The only processing done on the client is the painting of GUI widgets and user data entry. On the other end, the database server runs on a machine otherwise inaccessible to the client applet. The application server bridges this gap by finding desired data, mapping it from its relational state into objects, and performing operations on those objects.

With any three-tier architecture, the greatest programming challenge is getting the three layers to communicate with one another. JDBC or some similar set of database access classes should handle the application server-to-database server communication in a manner transparent to the application developer. The client-to-application server solution is still left wanting.

The two best methods for providing such communication in Java are Java sockets or distributed objects.

Figure 15.5.

A bug tracking system using a
three-tier architecture.

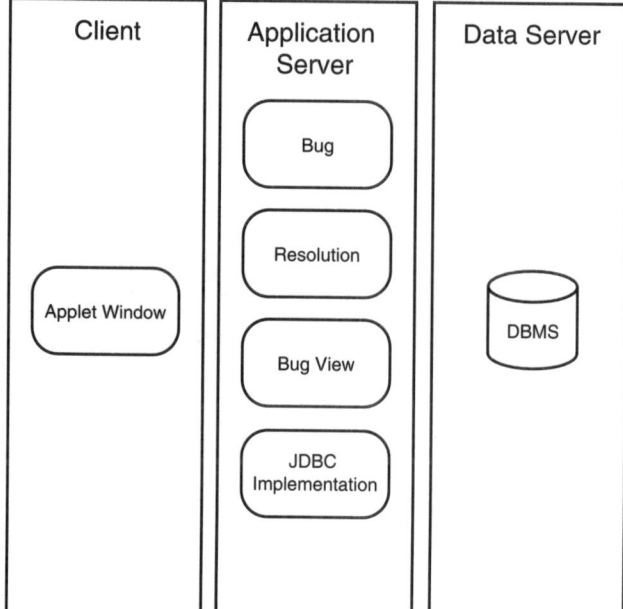

Compared to sockets from other languages, Java sockets are quite simple to use. Sockets, however, force the developer to make esoteric decisions about exactly what is being communicated between client and application server because method calls and object passing are better handled by the distributed objects solution. A socket solution generally best fits an application when the scope of communication is limited and well-defined. The bug tracking system would be best implemented in this manner.

Distributed objects provide the more elegant solution. From the developer's point of view, the application server objects appear to be part of the same application as the client, just residing on a central server and available to other applications simultaneously. The developer handles communication simply through method calls.

Summary

Although the original Java release did not address the issue of database access, the JDBC specification attempts to address this issue by defining a set of interfaces that can give applications access to data independent of the DBMS being used to store that data. Though this back-end independence can be very liberating, it is important to balance it with the advantages of the DBMS being used.

Many books cover only the subjects of database application design and programming. This chapter does not attempt to delve into those matters; instead, it focuses on the application of Java to database programming.

Programmers interested in using Java to write database applications should become familiar with the general subject matter.

In spite of the vastness of the subject matter, this chapter should whet your appetite for database programming and prepare you at least enough to write simple applets and applications. Much of the Java experience you already have translates into many of the issues specific to Java database programming. For example, applets written to use a database must work around the strict security limitations of Java virtual machines. Using the basics of a three-tier architecture can help an applet get around this limitation while giving it greater functionality. It is, however, important not to overdesign a simple applet just for the sake of doing a three-tier design.

Chapter 16

Multithreading with Java

by Brian Gloyer

What Is a Thread?

A thread executes a series of instructions. Every line of code that is executed is done so by a thread. Some threads can run for the entire life of the applet, while others are alive for only a few milliseconds. A thread also creates a new thread or kills an existing one. Threads run in methods or constructors. The methods and constructors themselves are lifeless. The threads go into the methods and follow their instructions. Methods and constructors reside in the computer's memory. Figure 16.1 shows threads, constructors, and methods in a typical applet.

<u>Figure 16.1.</u>
Two threads running through three classes.

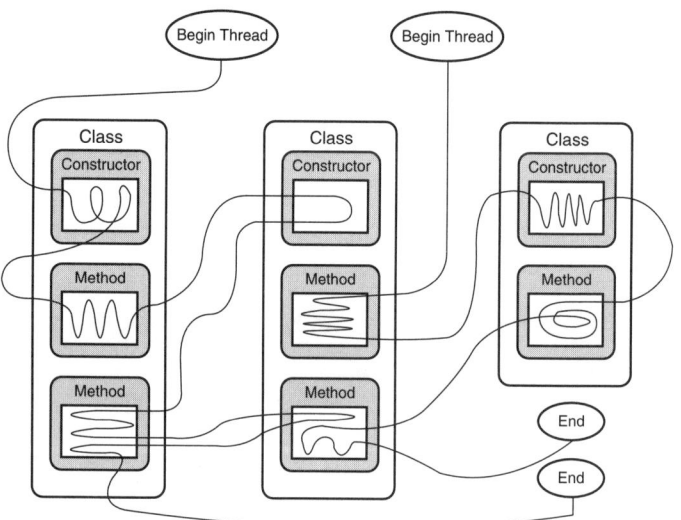

The applet methods start(), paint(), and so on are all called by underlying threads. These threads are created by the Web browser. When there is a mouse click or a repaint() has been called, the underlying thread calls the appropriate thread in the applet. While the threads are running in the applet methods, they cannot do anything else. If the applet holds these threads too long, it locks up the browser. If an applet needs to do something that will take some time in one of its methods, it should start a new thread. Some specific uses for threads are listed below:

○ Long initiations.   Threads are used in applets that may take a while to initialize. The applet may need to do something like wait for an image to be loaded. A thread is used so that the system thread can handle other events.

○ Repetitive or timed tasks.   Threads are used to do tasks that happen repetitively. A common example of this is found in animations. Every few milliseconds a new frame is shown. A thread displays a frame, sleeps for a while, and then repeats the process.

○ Asynchronous events.   Threads are used to handle events. An example of this is a mouse click. If the user clicks the mouse, a new thread is created to render a new frame in an image.

○ Multiple tasks.   Threads are used to do more than one thing at once. One thread controls an animation, while another does a computation.

The Thread Class

The class `java.lang.Thread` is used to create and control threads. To create a thread, a new instance of this class must be created. However, the thread does not start running right away. `Thread.start()` must be called to actually make the thread run. When `Thread.start()` is called, the thread begins executing in the `run()` method of the target class. A new `Thread` class always starts running the `public void run()` method of a class. There are two ways to create a thread:

○ Extend the `Thread` class.   With this technique the new class inherits from the class `Thread`. The thread can start running in the class's `run` method.

○ Implement the `Runnable` interface.   This technique is probably more common than extending the `Thread` class. It is not necessary to define a new class to run the thread. If a thread is to start running in the applet, it must use the `Runnable` interface. The applet cannot inherit from both the `Thread` and `Applet` classes. An applet with the `Runnable` interface must have a `run()` method for the thread to start.

There isn't much difference between the two approaches. Both extending the `Thread` class and implementing the `Runnable` interface have the same functionality. The interface approach must be used if the thread is to actually start in the `applet` class. But if the thread is going to be running in its own class, it may be more convenient to extend the `Thread` class. Examples of both approaches are in this chapter.

The `Thread` class has seven constructors. All of them create a new thread. The thread does not start running until `Thread.start()` is called. When `Thread.start()` is called, the new thread starts running in the `run()` method of an object. The constructors are the following:

```
Thread()
Thread(Runnable)
Thread(ThreadGroup)
Thread(String)
Thread(ThreadGroup,String)
Thread(Runnable,String)
Thread(ThreadGroup,Runnable,String)
```

The constructors can use three possible parameters:

○ `String`   The name of the new thread is the parameter `String`. A thread can get its name by calling `Thread.getName()`.

○ `ThreadGroup`   The new thread will belong to the group specified by the parameter `ThreadGroup`. A `ThreadGroup` can be used to organize a thread.

○ `Runnable`   The `Runnable` parameter is an object that has implemented the `Runnable` interface. The thread will start executing in the `run()` method of the `Runnable` parameter when `Thread.start()` has been called.

There are many methods in the Thread class. Some of them, such as destroy(), don't seem to have been implemented yet, and may never be. Some of the methods that control the thread execution are the following:

○ start() This method starts the thread. It starts executing in the run() method of its Runnable target that was set when the constructor was called. This method can be called only once.

○ suspend() This method suspends the execution of the thread. It remains suspended until resume() is called.

○ resume() This method resumes the execution of a suspended thread. It has no effect on a thread that is not suspended.

○ stop() This method stops and kills a running thread. Currently, the thread does not stop unless it is running. If it is suspended, it does not die until it starts running again. However, this may be fixed someday.

○ sleep(int *m*)/sleep(int *m*,int *n*) The thread sleeps for *m* milliseconds, plus *n* nanoseconds.

Simple Thread Examples

Listing 16.1 shows how to start, stop, suspend, and resume threads. It uses the Runnable interface. Threads like this are useful for things like controlling animation sequences or repeatedly playing audio samples. This example uses a thread that counts and prints a string every second. The thread starts when the applet is initialized. It continues to run until the user leaves the page. If the user returns to the page (and all is well), the thread continues from where it left off. This allows applets to retain their states while the user is away.

Listing 16.1. Thread examples.

```
import java.lang.Thread;
import java.applet.Applet;

public class InfiniteThreadExample extends Applet implements Runnable
{
  Thread myThread;

  public void init()
    {
      System.out.println("in init() -- starting thread.");
      myThread= new Thread(this);
      myThread.start();
    }

  public void start()
    {
      System.out.println("in start() -- resuming thread.");
```

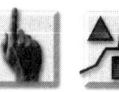

```
         myThread.resume();
      }

   public void stop()
      {
         System.out.println("in stop() -- suspending thread.");
         myThread.suspend();
      }

   public void destroy()
      {
         System.out.println("in destroy() -- stoping thread.");
         myThread.resume();
         myThread.stop();
      }

   public void run()
      {
         int i=0;
         for(;;)
           {
              i++;
              System.out.println("At " + i + " and counting!");
              try {myThread.sleep(1000);}
              catch (InterruptedException e ) {}
           }
      }
}
```

SimpleThreadExample Output

The output of InfiniteThreadExample is shown here. The applet ran for nine seconds until it was stopped.

```
in init() -- starting thread.
At 1 and counting!
in start() -- resuming thread.
At 2 and counting!
At 3 and counting!
At 4 and counting!
At 5 and counting!
At 6 and counting!
At 7 and counting!
At 8 and counting!
At 9 and counting!
in stop() -- suspending thread.
in destroy() -- stoping thread.
```

The applet has only five methods:

○ public void init()   The thread is initialized and is started in this method. In this example, the constructor Thread takes the argument this. When the Thread.start() method is called, the thread looks for a public void run() method in the this object.

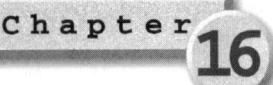

○ `public void start()`   When this method is called by the system, the thread resumes execution. If the thread is already running, this method has no effect.

○ `public void stop()`   This method suspends the thread.

○ `public void destroy()`   This method stops the thread. `Thread.stop()` stops and kills the thread. However, it only kills a thread that is running, so `Thread.resume()` is called beforehand.

○ `public void run()`   This is where the thread actually starts running. This example has an infinite loop that prints a string and then sleeps for a second. Long running threads should sleep every once in a while to give other threads a chance to run. If not, the system may not even get a chance to paint the applet.

When Are the Methods in `InfiniteThreadExample` Called?

Unfortunately, its not always possible to know exactly when or if the methods are called. It can vary from browser to browser, or even by how the user has the browser configured. Netscape 3.0 calls `init()` and then calls `start()` the first time the applet is loaded. If the user leaves the page with the applet, `stop()` is called. Returning to the applet calls `start()`, but it is possible that `init()` may be the first called. It depends on whether or not the applet is still residing in memory. If it is, then only `start()` is called; otherwise, both `init()` and `start()` are called again.

The method `destroy()` is called before the applet is removed from memory. All threads should be destroyed at this time so that its resources can be used by other applets. The browsers can only handle so many threads. If the user visits too many applets that don't clean up after themselves, the browser may crash. Generally, threads should be suspended when the user leaves the page and killed when the applet is destroyed. It is possible to leave threads running while the user is visiting other pages, but the user may not appreciate it.

Listing 16.2 shows how to use threads to handle events. When an event that existing threads shouldn't take the time to handle happens in the applet, a new thread is spawned to handle that event. After the event is handled, the new thread quietly dies. Listing 16.2 uses threads to handle mouse clicks. Each thread draws a blue target, as you can see in Figure 16.2. Methods such as `mouseDown()` or `mouseUp()` are called by threads external to the applet. While the thread is running in the applet, no other mouse movements are detected. Keeping the external thread may not just affect the applet, but possibly the whole browser. Generally, these methods should be returned as soon as possible. If it is necessary to do a long computation or wait for something else, a new thread should be started. By starting a new thread, the external thread can return almost immediately.

Listing 16.2. Handling an event with threads.

```
import java.applet.Applet;
import java.awt.*;
```

```java
public class FiniteThreadExample extends Applet
{
  Image offImage;        /* off screen image     */
  Graphics offGraphics;  /* Graphics for offImage */

  public void init()
    {
      offImage=createImage(400,300);
      offGraphics=offImage.getGraphics();
    }

  public void paint(Graphics g)
    {
      g.drawImage(offImage,0,0,null);
    }

  public void update(Graphics g)
    {
      paint(g);
    }

  public boolean mouseDown(Event e, int x, int y)
    {
      new DrawTarget(this,x,y,offGraphics);
      return true;
    }
}

class DrawTarget extends Thread
{
  int xPos,yPos;         /* position of the target */
  Applet myMaster;       /* who to repaint         */
  Graphics offGraphics;  /* Graphics to draw on    */

  public DrawTarget(Applet a, int x, int y, Graphics g)
    {
      xPos=x; yPos=y;
      myMaster=a;
      offGraphics=g;
      start();
    }

  public void run()
    {
      int i;  /* i is direction the circles are moving */
      int r;  /* r is the radius of the current circle */

      offGraphics.setColor(Color.white);
      offGraphics.setXORMode(Color.blue);
      for(r=0,i=10;i>-20;i-=20)        /* i=(10,-10)                */
        for(r+=i;(r<90)&&(r>0);r+=i) /* r=(10,20...80,80,70...10) */
          {
            offGraphics.fillOval(xPos-r,yPos-r,2*r,2*r);
            myMaster.repaint();
            try {sleep(200);}
            catch (InterruptedException e) {}
          }
    }
}
```

The class `FiniteThreadExample` is used to paint the applet, to catch the mouse clicks, but not to start the threads. The applet uses a class that extends the `Thread` class to start new threads. The class `FiniteThreadExample` has four methods shown below that sets up things, handles the painting, and catches the mouse clicks:

○ `public void init()`   This method creates an image and gets a `Graphics` context for that image.

○ `public void paint(Graphics)`   This method paints the Image `offImage` on the screen.

○ `public void update(Graphics)`   This method isn't really necessary. It overrides `update(Graphics)` in `java.awt.Component`, and is used to reduce flickering.

○ `public boolean mouseDown(Event, int, int)`   This method is called when there is a mouse click in the applet. It creates a new instance of the class `DrawTarget`. `DrawTarget` is defined in the next class.

`DrawTarget` is where the threads are created to draw the targets. `DrawTarget` inherits properties from `java.lang.Thread` and has a single constructor and method, which are listed below:

○ `public DrawTarget(Applet a, int x, int y, Graphics g)`   The constructor copies the parameters to instance variables and starts the thread. `Applet` is needed so the `run` method can tell the applet to repaint. The integers x and y are the coordinates of target. `Graphics` is the graphics context on which the targets are drawn. The thread is started by simply calling `start()`.

○ `public void run()`   This method is where the thread starts and draws the targets. It is called sometime after `start()` is called in the constructor. The method first sets `offGraphics` to XOR-Mode. In this mode, if something is drawn on something previously drawn, it reverts back to its original color. Next, the thread enters the nested `for` loops. Each iteration draws a circle, asks the applet to repaint, and sleeps for 200ms. The radius of the circle is varied from 10 to 80, and then from 80 back to 10. The thread dies on its own after it exits the loops, so there is no need to call `stop()`.

Figure 16.2.
The applet in Listing 16.2
draws targets.

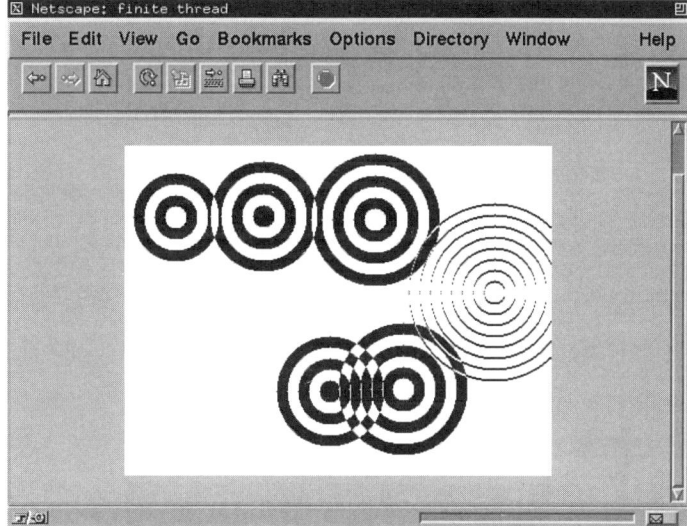

Problems with Multithreading

Listing 16.3 shows how data can be corrupted in a multithreaded environment. If more than one
thread manipulates shared variables or objects at the same time, corruption may result. Instance
variables are shared between threads. If one is modified by a thread, the change affects the other
threads. Method variables are unique for each threads. Each Thread has its own copy. Listing 16.3
uses 2 classes, ProblemThreadExample and CorruptedDataExample. The class ProblemThreadExample
extends the Applet class. It has two methods, which are listed after Listing 16.3.

Listing 16.3. How to get corrupted data.

```
import java.lang.*;
import java.applet.Applet;

public class ProblemThreadExample extends Applet
{
  CorruptedDataExample CDE;

  public void start()
    {
      int i;

      CDE=new CorruptedDataExample();
      for(i=0;i<20;i++)  /* start 20 threads */
        new Thread(CDE,new String("booThread"+i)).start();
    }

  public void stop()
```

continues

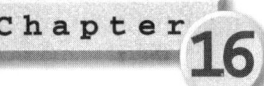
Listing 16.3. continued

```
      {
        CDE.stopThreads();
      }
  }
}

class CorruptedDataExample extends Object implements Runnable
{
  int num=0;   /* num will be corrupted  */

  public void run()
    {
      int i=0;
      for(;;)
        {
          for(i=0;i<1000;i++)
            {
              num=num+10;
              num=num-10;
            }

          try {Thread.sleep(10000);}
          catch (InterruptedException e ) {}
          System.out.println(Thread.currentThread().getName()+
                    " sees the number: " + num);
        }
    }

  void stopThreads()
    {
      Thread tArray[];
      int numThreads;

      numThreads=Thread.activeCount();
      tArray=new Thread[numThreads];
      Thread.enumerate(tArray);
      for(int i=0;i<numThreads;i++)
      if(tArray[i].getName().startsWith("booThread"))
        tArray[i].stop();
    }
}
```

○ `public void start()`   This method gets a new instance of the `CorruptedDataExample` class and starts 20 threads. Each thread has an individual name that is from `"booThread0"` to `"booThread19"`. The threads start running in `CorruptedDataExample`'s run method.

○ `public void stop()`   This method calls `stopThreads()` in `CorruptedDataExample`. The class `CorruptedDataExample` does not guard against corruption of its instance variable `num`. The class has two methods, which are as follows:

○ `public void run()`   This method has an infinite loop that shows how data can be corrupted by multiple threads. Twenty threads are executed in this loop at the same time. The loop does the following:

Adds 10 then -10 to num 1000 times

Sleeps

Prints a string that contains num

The first step is the cause of the corruption. It serves no purpose other than illustrating how data is corrupted.

○ `void stopThreads()`   All of the `booThreads` are stopped in this method. A list of threads is fetched. All of the threads that have names that begin with `booThread` are stopped.

The following is the `ProblemThreadExample` output:

```
booThread0 sees the number: 0
booThread1 sees the number: 0
booThread2 sees the number: 0
booThread3 sees the number: 0
booThread4 sees the number: 10
booThread6 sees the number: 10
booThread7 sees the number: 10
booThread8 sees the number: 10
booThread9 sees the number: 10
booThread10 sees the number: 0
booThread11 sees the number: 0
booThread12 sees the number: 0
booThread13 sees the number: 0
booThread5 sees the number: 0
booThread14 sees the number: 0
booThread15 sees the number: 0
booThread16 sees the number: 0
booThread17 sees the number: 0
booThread18 sees the number: 0
booThread19 sees the number: 0
booThread0 sees the number: 0
booThread1 sees the number: 0
booThread3 sees the number: 0
booThread4 sees the number: 0
booThread6 sees the number: 0
booThread8 sees the number: 0
booThread9 sees the number: 0
booThread2 sees the number: 0
booThread7 sees the number: 0
booThread10 sees the number: 10
booThread11 sees the number: 0
booThread12 sees the number: -10
booThread13 sees the number: -10
booThread5 sees the number: -10
booThread14 sees the number: -10
booThread16 sees the number: -10
booThread17 sees the number: -10
booThread18 sees the number: -10
booThread19 sees the number: -10
```

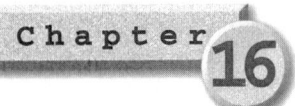

What Goes Wrong?

The first step in the infinite loop would have no ill effect in a single-threaded environment. It simply adds and then subtracts 10 to a variable with the net result being no change. However, in a multithreaded environment, the operations can interfere with each other. You can see one scenario in the following steps in which two threads try to add 10 at the same time.

Step	Thread A	Thread B	num
1.	Atmp→num		0
2.	Atmp→Atmp+10		0
3.		Btmp→num	0
4.		Btmp→Btmp+10	0
5.		num→Btmp	10
.	.	.	.
.	.	.	.
.	.	.	.
10.	num→Atmp		10

Two num=num+10; operations have been executed, but the value of num has only increased by 10. The problem here is that Thread A was interrupted in the middle of its operation before it could save its results. Threads A and B have added 10 to the same number.

This type of problem is somewhat rare, but should not be ignored. In the previous example, 10 is added and subtracted 1000 times in 20 threads, and the problem still did not occur that often. The bad thing about these types of bugs is that they can be extremely difficult to find. Imagine that num is the index of an array. The problem may not show up until long after num has been corrupted. Generally, these bugs are not reproducible, so they are hard to catch. In some ways the problem is amplified in Java because Java is expected to run on so many platforms. On some systems, num=num+10 may be an atomic operation (cannot be interrupted). In this case, everything works fine. A developer may create an applet on such a system thinking that everything is fine, but it may not work when someone from a different system views the applet. Data corruption can also be more common with other data types. Integer operations are simple compared to many others. Arrays or other data structures can take much longer to process so it is much more likely to be corrupted.

Thread Names and Current Threads

In Listing 16.3, the threads are given names. They are named booThread0 through booThread19 when they are created by the constructor Thread(Runnable,String). The names can be used to identify the threads. The thread names are printed along with num in the run() method of

CorruptedDataExample. The `Thread` method `current.Thread()` is called to get a reference to the currently running thread.

The names are also used to stop the threads. A reference is needed for each thread so that `stop()` can be called to kill it. `Thread.enumerate(Thread[])` gets a reference to every thread in this group. Some of these threads are the `booThreads`, but they may be others. The other threads should not be killed. Before each thread is killed it is checked to see if its name starts with `booThread`.

Java's synchronized

A way to prevent data from being corrupted by multiple threads is to prevent the interruption of *critical regions*. Critical regions are places like `num=num+10` above, where only one thread should be running at once. Java's `synchronized` can be used to ensure that only one thread is in a critical region at once. When the thread enters a synchronized code block, it tries to get a lock on that region. While the thread is in the critical region, no other thread can enter the critical region. If a thread tries to enter and the code is already locked, the thread has to wait for the other thread to leave the critical region. Listing 16.3 can be fixed by synchronizing the access to `num`. The `run()` method in `CorruptedDataExample` can be modified to the following:

```
public void run()
  {
    int i=0;
    int tmp;        /*new*/
    for(;;)
      {
        for(i=0;i<1000;i++)
          {
              synchronized (this)  /*new*/
              {
                num=num+10;
                num=num-10;
              }
          }

        try {Thread.sleep(10000);}
        catch (InterruptedException e ) {}
        synchronized (this)                    /*new*/
        {tmp=num;}                             /*new*/
        System.out.println(Thread.currentThread().getName()+
                " sees the number: " + tmp); /*new*/
      }
  }
```

The following lines make up a protected critical region:

```
        synchronized (this)
    {
      num=num+10;
      num=num-10;
    }
```

synchronized (this) ensures that only one thread can be in the following code block. The argument this tells the thread to use the lock for this this object.

The variable num is also referenced when the string is printed. The new code is as follows:

```
synchronized (this)                               /*new*/
{tmp=num;}                                        /*new*/
System.out.println(currentThread().getName()+
        " sees the number: " + tmp);      /*new*/
```

A critical region is used to copy num to temporary storage. The string is then printed using the temporary storage. It would have been possible to synchronize the print line directly, but it would cut performance because the print line does many other things that have nothing to do with referencing num. All the threads waiting to enter the critical region will needlessly wait longer while the print line is executed. Generally, the synchronized blocks should be as small as possible while still protecting the critical region.

You may also think that the other variables in the run method, i and tmp, also need to be synchronized, but it's not necessary. Both i and tmp are method variables so each running thread has its own private copy. There are 20 i's and tmp's but there is only one num.

Synchronizing Threads

Listing 16.4 can be seen in Figure 16.3. This example shows how synchronized can be used to control critical regions. There are two synchronized methods: drawRoundTarget() and drawSquareTarget(). If a thread is in a synchronized method, no other thread can be in any synchronized method that uses the same lock. This example draws only one square or circle at a time. The seven methods of the SynchronizedThreadExample applet are shown after Listing 16.4.

Listing 16.4. Using synchronized.

```
import java.applet.Applet;
import java.awt.*;

public class SynchronizedThreadExample extends Applet
implements Runnable
{
  Image offImage;        /* off screen image      */
  Graphics offGraphics;  /* Graphics for offImage */
  Thread Thr1, Thr2;     /* threads               */

  public void start()
    {
      offImage=createImage(400,300);
      offGraphics=offImage.getGraphics();
      offGraphics.setColor(Color.white);
      offGraphics.setXORMode(Color.blue);
```

```
      Thr1=new Thread(this);   Thr1.start();
      Thr2=new Thread(this);   Thr2.start();
   }

public void stop()
   {
      Thr1.stop();
      Thr2.stop();
   }

public void paint(Graphics g)
   {
      g.drawImage(offImage,0,0,null);
   }

public void update(Graphics g)
   {
      paint(g);
   }

public void run()
   {
      for(;;)
         {
            drawRoundTarget();
            drawSquareTarget();
         }
   }

synchronized void drawRoundTarget()
   {
      for(int r=0,i=10;i>-20;i-=20)   /* i=(10,-10)                     */
         for(r+=i;(r<90)&&(r>0);r+=i) /* r=(10,20...80,80,70...10) */
            {
               offGraphics.fillOval(200-r,150-r,2*r,2*r);
               repaint();
               try {Thread.currentThread().sleep(200);}
               catch (InterruptedException e) {}
            }
   }

synchronized void drawSquareTarget()
   {
      int i,r;
      for(r=0,i=10;i>-20;i-=20)        /* i=(10,-10)                     */
         for(r+=i;(r<90)&&(r>0);r+=i) /* r=(10,20...80,80,70...10) */
            {
               offGraphics.fillRect (200-r,150-r,2*r,2*r);
               repaint();
               try {Thread.currentThread().sleep(250);}
               catch (InterruptedException e) {}
            }
   }
}
```

Figure 16.3.

Listing 16.4 draws a square.

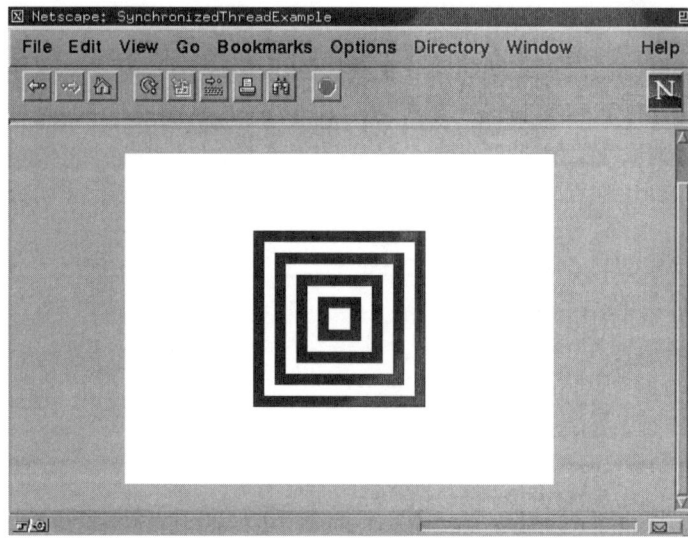

The methods of the `SynchronizedThreadExample` applet are as follows:

- ○ `public void start()/stop()`   The threads are started and stopped in these methods.
- ○ `public void paint/update(Graphics)`   These methods paint the applet.
- ○ `public void run()`   Both threads start executing in this method. It is an infinite loop that draws round and then square targets.
- ○ `synchronized void drawRoundTarget()`   This method is synchronized. Only one thread can be inside drawing circles.
- ○ `synchronized void drawSquareTarget()`   This method is like `drawRoundTarget`, but draws squares instead of circles.

Multiple Locks

What if two locks are needed?

The current applet only allows one target to be drawn at a time, be it round or square. Suppose that you want the applet to draw a round and a square target at the same time; you would need two locks for two independent critical regions. The problem is that each object has only one lock.

Creating separate classes for drawRoundTarget() and drawSquareTarget() could solve the problem, but it may not be convenient. A better way is to create new objects, and to use their locks to control the methods. This is done by modifying Listing 16.4 as follows:

```
           .              .
           .              .
           .              .
Object RoundSync,SquareSync;                 /*new*/

public void start()
  {
           .              .
           .              .
           .              .
    RoundSync=new Object();                  /*new*/
    SquareSync=new Object();                 /*new*/
    Thr1=new Thread(this);   Thr1.start();
    Thr2=new Thread(this);   Thr2.start();
  }

void drawRoundTarget()
  {
    synchronized (RoundSync)                 /*new*/
      {
        for(int r=0,i=10;i>-20;i-=20)
           .              .
           .              .
           .              .
      }
  }

  void drawSquareTarget()
  {
    synchronized (SquareSync)                /*new*/
      {
        for(r=0,i=10;i>-20;i-=20)
           .              .
           .              .
           .              .
      }
  }
}
```

Two new Objects are created: RoundSync and SquareSync. The Objects don't actually do anything themselves, but their locks are used when drawing the targets. The instances of Object are obtained in the start method. synchronized (RoundSync) is put in front of the for loops in the drawRoundTarget() method and drawSquareTarget() is modified similarly. When a thread tries to execute the body of the target drawing methods, it first has to get a lock. drawRoundTarget() gets a lock from the object RoundSync and drawSquareTarget() gets a lock from SquareSync(). After these modifications have been made, the drawRoundTarget() and drawSquareTargets() methods do not block each other. The applet draws round and square targets at the same time. But it is not able to draw two round targets or two square targets at the same time. Figure 16.4 shows the results of the modifications.

Figure 16.4.

A square and round target being drawn at the same time.

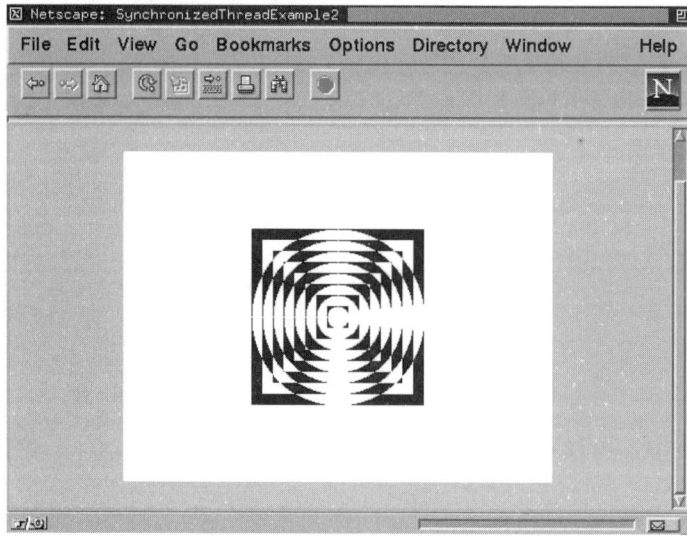

The Dining Philosophers Problem

The Dining Philosophers problem is a classic concurrent programming problem. In the problem, a philosopher only does two things, think and eat. A philosopher thinks for a while, and then gets hungry. Then it eats until it gets full, and then starts thinking again. Each philosopher is so involved in its own thinking or eating that it's oblivious to anything else. The problem has five philosophers that are sitting at a table. Between neighboring philosophers there is a single chop stick. A philosopher must have both the stick on its right and the stick on its left in order for it to eat. Obviously, no two neighboring philosophers can be eating at the same time. The philosophers cannot disturb each other. If a philosopher wants to start eating and its neighbor has one of the sticks, the philosopher must wait until the stick becomes available. To solve the problem, an algorithm must be designed to let all of the philosophers eat.

A simple algorithm for the philosophers could be:

Think
Get right chopstick
Get left chopstick
Eat
Drop left chopstick
Drop right chopstick
Repeat

There is one very serious problem with this algorithm. Suppose that each philosopher picks up the right chopstick at the same time. When they try to get the left stick, it won't be there. The neighbor to the left has it. All of the philosophers starve to death with a chopstick in one hand and food on the table. This is known as a deadlock.

Deadlocks

Deadlocks are always a danger in multithreaded environments. A deadlock has occurred because

- ○ Each thread needed exclusive use of the chopsticks.
- ○ One thread is not allowed to take a chopstick from its neighbor.
- ○ Each thread is waiting while holding a chopstick that another thread is waiting for.

All deadlocks in any problem have the same reasons for deadlocking. Instead of waiting for chopsticks, they are waiting for some other resource or resources. If only one of the conditions can be broken, a deadlock will not occur.

The first condition is usually hard to break. In the previous algorithm this could done by allowing philosophers to share a chopstick, but that isn't really possible. Sometimes threads need exclusive use of a resource. Things like the instance of a class or a socket may require that only one thread may use it at once.

The second condition can sometimes be used to avoid deadlocks. If a philosopher was allowed to take a chopstick from its neighbor, there would not be a deadlock. However, if the philosophers keep taking sticks from each other, they may never get a chance to take a bite. Some problems can be solved by allowing resource stealing. It depends on the resource and the problem.

If the deadlock cannot be avoided with the other conditions, it should be avoided by breaking the third condition. The philosophers can avoid a deadlock if there is a special chopstick that they aren't allowed to hold while they are waiting for the second chopstick. They are allowed to eat with the special stick, but they can't just hold it. An algorithm should not be too strict, otherwise the resources may be underused. For example, an algorithm could be made that only allows one philosopher to eat at once. Obviously, there would be no deadlocks, but a philosopher may have to wait longer before it can eat.

A Solution to the Dining Philosophers Problem

There are many solutions to the Dining Philosophers problem. One solution follows.

One of the chopsticks is marked as gold, while the rest are wood. No philosopher is allowed to hold the gold stick without eating. This prevents the philosophers from deadlocking. The philosophers picks up one chopstick then the other. If the gold stick is picked up first, it is put down and the other stick is picked up. It is possible that in the time between putting down the gold chopstick and picking up the other chopstick, all the other philosophers will have eaten and moved the gold chopstick all the way around the table, so when the philosopher picks up the other chopstick, it too is the gold chopstick. If this happens, the philosopher starts over. The solution is as follows:

Think
Pick up right chopstick
If right chopstick is gold
Drop right chopstick
Pick up left chopstick
If left chopstick is gold
      Start over
Pick up right chopstick
Else
Pick up left chopstick
Eat
Switch chopsticks in hands
Drop right chopstick
Drop left chopstick
Repeat

The chopsticks are switched when the philosopher puts down the chopsticks. This allows the philosophers equal chances to eat. Otherwise, the philosopher to the left of the gold chopstick would be disadvantaged.

The philosophers may interfere with each other when they try to pick up a chopstick. A critical region is used to ensure that one philosopher can pick up or put down a chopstick. If one philosopher is picking up or putting down a stick, its neighbor is not allowed to touch the stick. What if a philosopher enters the critical section to get a chopstick, but the chopstick is not there? The philosopher must wait until the stick returns. This is done by a special wait in the critical section. The philosopher releases its lock and waits in the critical section. This allows the other philosopher to enter the critical section to return the chopstick. After the chopstick is returned, the waiting philosopher is woken up. After awakening, the philosopher reacquires the lock and continues executing. At any one time there can be only one philosopher running in the critical section, but it is OK if another philosopher is also sleeping in the critical section.

Java's wait() and notify()

Java has three wait() and two notify() methods that aid in synchronizing threads. The wait() methods cause the thread to pause in the critical region. While paused, the thread releases its lock. It must get the lock again before it starts executing again. The notify() methods wake up threads that have called wait(). Calling notify() when no wait() has been called has no effect. The methods shown below are in the Object class and can only be called in a synchronized block or method.

○ public final void wait()　This method causes the thread to wait forever until a notify() or notifyAll() is called. The thread releases its lock on the critical regions so that other threads may enter.

○ `public final void wait(long m)` This method causes the thread to wait m milliseconds for a `notify()` or `notifyAll()` to be called. After the time is expired, the thread tries to resume execution. However, it must first reobtain the lock for the critical region. Another thread may have entered the critical section while the thread was waiting.

○ `public final void wait(long m, int n)` This method is similar to the previous one except that it waits for m milliseconds plus n nanoseconds.

○ `public final void notify()` This method wakes up a thread that has previously called `wait()`. The thread that was waiting has to get the lock before it can resume execution. It has to wait until the current thread leaves the critical region. Only one thread that has called `wait()` is woken up. It is not guaranteed that the first thread that called `wait()` is the first one woken up.

○ `public final void notifyAll()` This method wakes up all the threads that have called `wait()`. Each waiting thread has to get the lock for the critical region before it resumes. There can still be only one thread running in the critical section at once.

Dining Philosophers Example

The Dining Philosophers applet uses four classes: the ones shown in Listings 16.5, 16.6, 16.7, and 16.8. The first class, `DiningPhilosophers`, extends the `Applet` class. The structure of this class is similar to the first example. `Philosopher` threads are created when the applet is initialized. They are suspended if the user leaves the page and resumed if the user returns. However, unlike the first example, no threads are created in this class. The Dining Philosophers example can be seen in Figure 16.5.

Figure 16.5.
The Dining Philosophers example.

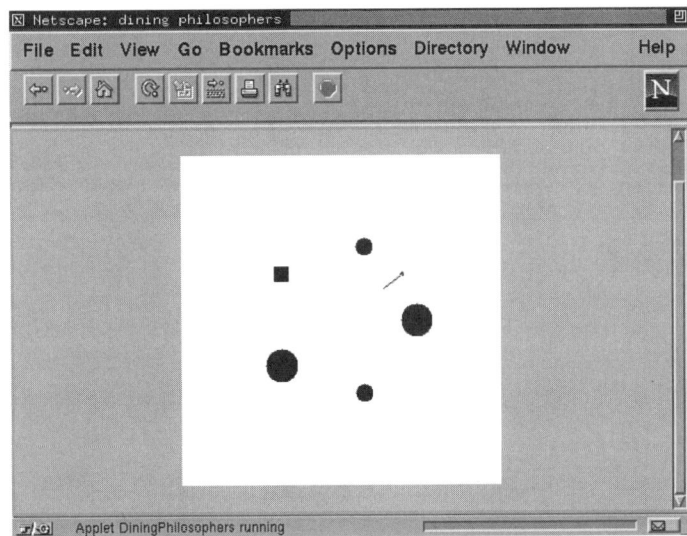

Listing 16.5. The class DiningPhilosophers.

```java
public class DiningPhilosophers extends Applet
{
  final int numPhils=5;

  Image offImage;         /* off screen image      */
  Graphics offGraphics;   /* Graphics for offImage */
  Philosopher Phil[] = new Philosopher[numPhils];
  Chopstick Stick[] = new Chopstick[numPhils];
  ScenePainter painter;

  public void init()
    {
      int i;

      offImage=createImage(400,300);
      offGraphics=offImage.getGraphics();
      painter=new ScenePainter(offGraphics,this,numPhils);

      for(i=0;i<numPhils;i++)
        Stick[i]=new Chopstick (i==0 ? Chopstick.gold :
                                       Chopstick.wood,
                                painter,i);
      for(i=0;i<numPhils;i++)
        Phil[i]= new Philosopher(Stick[i],Stick[(i+1)%numPhils],
                                 painter,i);
    }

  public void start()
    {
      int i;
      for(i=0;i<numPhils;i++)
        Phil[i].resume();
    }

  public void stop()
    {
      int i;
      for(i=0;i<numPhils;i++)
        Phil[i].suspend();
    }

  public void destroy()
    {
      int i;
      for(i=0;i<numPhils;i++)
        {
          Phil[i].resume();
          Phil[i].stop();
        }
    }

  public void paint(Graphics g)
    {
      g.drawImage(offImage,0,0,null);
    }
```

```
  public void update(Graphics Dijkstra)
    {
      paint(Dijkstra);
    }
}
```

The class `DiningPhilosophers` has six methods and is similar to the `InfiniteThreadExample`.

○ `public void init()`   This method initializes the applet. It creates five instances of the classes `Chopstick` and `Philosopher`. One of the `Chopstick` classes is created as a gold chopstick, the rest are wood. Each `Philosopher` can reach two `Chopsticks`. On the right is `Chopstick i`, and on the left is `Chopstick i+1 mod 5`.

○ `public void start()`   This method resumes philosopher execution.

○ `public void stop()`   This method suspends philosopher execution.

○ `public void destroy()`   This method kills the philosophers.

○ `public void paint()/update()`   These two methods paint the state of the philosophers.

Each philosopher at the table is its own thread. The thread is created in the class `Philosopher` by extending `Thread`. The methods in the class control the philosopher's life of thinking and eating. Initially, the philosopher is thinking. After some time, the philosopher picks up the two chopsticks next to it and starts eating. It calls methods in the `Chopstick` class (see Listing 16.7) to get the chopsticks. The philosopher also paints its state by calling methods in the `ScenePainter` class (see Listing 16.8).

Listing 16.6. The class `Philosopher`.

```
class Philosopher extends Thread
{
  final int ThinkTime=5000, EatTime=3000;
  Chopstick rightStick,leftStick;
  ScenePainter painter;
  int rightHand,leftHand;
  int myNum;

  public Philosopher(Chopstick right, Chopstick left,
                     ScenePainter p, int n)
    {
      painter=p;
      myNum=n;
      rightStick=right;
      leftStick=left;
      start();
    }

  public void run()
    {
      for(;;)
```

continues

Listing 16.6. continued

```
        {
          think();
          PickUpSticks();
          eat();
          PutDownSticks();
        }
    }

  void think()
    {
      painter.drawThink(myNum);
      try {sleep((int)(ThinkTime*Math.random()));}
      catch (InterruptedException e) {}
      painter.drawThink(myNum);
    }

  void PickUpSticks()
    {
      for(boolean gotem=false;!gotem;)
        {
          painter.drawFirstGrab(myNum);
          rightHand=rightStick.grabStick();

          painter.drawSecondGrab(myNum);
          if(rightHand==Chopstick.gold)
            {
              painter.drawGoldGrab(myNum);

              rightStick.dropStick(rightHand);
              leftHand=leftStick.grabStick();
              if(leftHand==Chopstick.gold)
                {
                  leftStick.dropStick(leftHand);
                  continue;  /* gold stick went around table */
                }
              rightHand=rightStick.grabStick();
              painter.drawGoldGrab(myNum);
            }
          else leftHand=leftStick.grabStick();

          painter.drawSecondGrab(myNum);
          painter.drawFirstGrab(myNum);
          gotem=true;
        }
    }

  void eat()
    {
      painter.drawEat(myNum);
      try {sleep((int)(EatTime*Math.random()));}
      catch (InterruptedException e) {}
      painter.drawEat(myNum);
    }

  void PutDownSticks()
    {/* swap sticks and put them down */
```

```
        rightStick.dropStick(leftHand);
        leftStick.dropStick(rightHand);
    }
}
```

The class `Philosopher` is used to start the threads for the Dining Philosophers applet. The class has the following five methods:

- ○ `public void run()`   This method defines the philosophers actions. Each philosopher thinks, waits to pick up its chopsticks, eats, returns the chopsticks, and repeats the cycle.
- ○ `void think()`   This method is where the philosopher thinks. The thinking image is drawn and the philosopher sleeps for a random amount of time.
- ○ `void PickUpSticks()`   In this method, the philosopher picks up the chopsticks in a way that is fair and avoids deadlocks.
- ○ `void eat()`   This method is where the philosopher eats. The eating image is drawn and the philosopher sleeps for a random amount of time.
- ○ `void PutDownSticks()`   In this method, the philosopher returns the sticks. The chopsticks are switched when they are put down so that the gold stick is not always in the same place.

All of the synchronization is done in the `Chopstick` class. There is one instance of this class for each chopstick on the table. The class is used by the philosophers when they want to pick up or return a chopstick. The three states of the chopstick are represented by the variable `stickHolder`: `noStick` means the chopstick is gone, `wood` means this is the wooden stick, and `gold` means this is the golden stick. `stickHolder` is an instance variable. More than one philosopher may be trying to get/drop it at once, so there is a danger of data corruption. The methods of this class are synchronized to ensure that `stickHolder` does not get corrupted (see Listing 16.7).

Listing 16.7. The class `Chopstick`.

```
class Chopstick extends Object
{
  final static int noStick=0;
  final static int wood=1;
  final static int gold=2;
  ScenePainter painter;
  int stickHolder;
  int myNum;

  public Chopstick(int stick, ScenePainter p, int n)
    {
      painter=p;
      myNum=n;
      dropStick(stick);
    }
```

continues

Listing 16.7. continued

```
synchronized int grabStick()
  {
    int Thuy;

    if(stickHolder==noStick)
      try {wait();} catch (InterruptedException e) {}
    painter.drawStick(myNum,stickHolder);
    Thuy=stickHolder;
    stickHolder=noStick;
    return Thuy;
  }

synchronized void dropStick(int stick)
  {
    stickHolder=stick;
    painter.drawStick(myNum,stickHolder);
    notify();
  }
}
```

The class Chopstick is used to synchronize the threads in the Dining Philosophers applet. The class has the following two methods:

○ synchronized int grabStick() Philosophers (threads) will come into this method when they attempt to get a stick. If the stick is there, the method gives the stick to the philosopher. If the stick has already been taken by its neighbor, the philosopher waits for the stick to be returned.

○ synchronized void dropStick() The philosophers use this method to return the sticks. If the other philosopher is waiting for this chopstick, it is woken.

The class ScenePainter is used by the philosophers to paint their state. If a philosopher starts eating, puts down a stick, or does anything else, it calls methods in this class. The states of philosophers (for example, eating or waiting for a stick) are represented by different shapes. When a philosopher starts thinking, it calls drawThink(myNum) to draw the philosopher in its thinking state. Then, when it is done thinking, it calls drawThink(myNum) again to erase the philosopher. All of the methods in this class are called in pairs. The first call draws a state and the second erases it.

Listing 16.8. The class ScenePainter.

```
class ScenePainter extends Object
{
  int sX1[], sY1[], sX2[], sY2[], pX[], pY[];
  final int xOffset=150, yOffset=150, Tscale=70;
  final int rg=2, rEating=15, rThinking=8, rFirst=7;
  final int rSecond=3, rGold=5;
  Graphics G;
  Component C;
```

```
public ScenePainter(Graphics g, Component c, int numPhils)
  {
    int i;
    pX  = new int[numPhils]; pY  = new int[numPhils];
    sX1 = new int[numPhils]; sY1 = new int[numPhils];
    sX2 = new int[numPhils]; sY2 = new int[numPhils];
    double arc=Math.PI/numPhils;

    G=g; C=c;

    for(i=0;i<numPhils;i++)
      {
        pX[i]= (int)(xOffset+   Tscale*Math.cos(i*2*arc));
        pY[i]= (int)(yOffset+   Tscale*Math.sin(i*2*arc));
        sX1[i]=(int)(xOffset+   Tscale*Math.cos(i*2*arc+arc));
        sY1[i]=(int)(yOffset+   Tscale*Math.sin(i*2*arc+arc));
        sX2[i]=(int)(xOffset+.7*Tscale*Math.cos(i*2*arc+arc));
        sY2[i]=(int)(yOffset+.7*Tscale*Math. sin(i*2*arc+arc));
      }
    G.setColor(Color.white);
    G.setXORMode(Color.blue);
  }

void drawStick(int num, int stick)
  {
    G.drawLine(sX1[num],sY1[num],sX2[num],sY2[num]);
    if(stick==Chopstick.gold)
      G.fillOval(sX1[num]-rg,sY1[num]-rg,rg+rg,rg+rg);
    C.repaint();
  }

void drawEat(int num)
  {
    fillCircle(num,rEating);
  }

void drawThink(int num)
  {
    fillCircle(num,rThinking);
  }

void drawFirstGrab(int num)
  {
    fillSquare(num,rFirst);
  }
```

The class ScenePainter is used to draw the state of all the philosophers in the Dining Philosophers applet.

○ public ScenePainter(Graphics, Component, int) The constructor for this class
  calculates the position of each philosopher and chopstick.

○ void drawStick(num, stick) This method draws/erases the chopstick specified by num.
  A stick is represented by drawing a line between the two philosophers that may use it. If
  stick is the gold chopstick, a small circle is added to the end of the chopstick.

○ void drawEat(num)   This method draws/erases the philosopher specified by num in its eating state. A large circle represents the eating state.

○ void drawThink(num)   This method draws/erases a small circle that represents a philosopher in its thinking state.

○ void drawFirstGrab(num)   This method draws/erases a small square. The method is called when the philosopher tries to grab the first stick.

○ void drawSecondGrab(num)   This method erases/draws a smaller square inside the square drawn by drawFirstGrab(num). The method is called after the philosopher already has one chopstick and is trying to grab the second. A philosopher in this state is represented by a small hollow square.

○ void drawGoldGrab(num)   This method is called if the first stick the philosopher picked up is the gold stick. It is only called after both drawFirstGrab(num) and drawSecondGrab(num) have been called. A philosopher in this state is represented by a small hollow square with a tiny circle in the middle.

Summary

Threads are the life in an applet. Some threads are created by the system, but others are started in the applet. Threads can be started to remove some of the burden from a system thread, or to start its own line of execution.

This chapter contained several applets that started threads. The examples showed specific uses of threads that can be expanded to general use. Most threading problems can be solved by using slight variations of the first two examples. These examples have threads that do not communicate with other threads. If threads need to communicate with each other, care must be taken to avoid data corruption. The third example shows data corruption and the steps that must be taken to avoid it. The forth example shows how two threads can be synchronized so that they can do things in the right order. The final example, the Dining Philosophers, shows many of the subtle problems in a multithreaded environment. If threads in an applet compete for common resources, a deadlock can occur unless care is taken to avoid it. The examples in this chapter are just that, examples. The reader is encouraged to experiment with them, tweak some of the parameters, add more threads, but most of all, have fun.

Chapter

by Jim Morey

Advanced Graphics: Multimedia

Introduction: The Information Age

There is no doubt that we are in the information age. Right now, people are reading books, newspapers, magazines, journals, listening to radios, and watching TV. Information is flowing like a million rivers spreading their spider web tributaries across the world. Information is a profitable commodity with large corollary industries. There are many different distribution paths for information. An example is a book, which is directly bought (and read). A more complex distribution path is the use of advertisers to support TV and radio stations' programs (the information). Stations attempt to draw in the most viewers possible so that advertisers have a large pool of viewers' time to buy.

One of the newest distribution paths for information is the Internet. Information is put on the Internet to be read. Since there is such an abundance of information on the net, the information needs to be very impressive for people to want to read it. Advertisers may wish to embed their advertisements in Internet information with a high readership, just as they target radio and TV stations that have high viewerships. But regardless of whether information providers seek to sell time to advertisers with their information, they are still likely to make their information as impressive as possible to the readers.

The best way to create impressive presentations is to understand the medium. For instance, an example of misuse of a medium is a TV show that scrolls by the text of a Shakespearean play. This is unsuccessful because it is not using the benefits of the TV medium—moving picture and sound. For the text of a Shakespearean play, this interface is much worse than a book as a medium because the TV scroll does not account for the reader's speed, a reader cannot refer back to earlier passages to check forgotten characters or internal references, and such. Thus most viewers prefer to watch a mindless sitcom on TV—which more effectively uses the TV medium's potential benefits—than read a Shakespearean play on TV, even though the play has considerably more quality content than the sitcom.

The Internet Medium

What is the Internet as a medium about? As with TV, information on the Internet can be displayed by pictures and sound. However, on the Internet, viewers have more freedom in what they view, they can interact with the information they view, and they can interact with other viewers. The Internet can use most forms of media (visual, auditory, textual, and so forth).

However, the Internet does have two serious drawbacks: bandwidth limitations and accessibility. Radio shows and songs can be heard over the Internet (with RealAudio http://www.realaudio.com), but the bandwidth problems reduce the sound quality. Similarly, TV has bandwidth problems that reduce picture quality. Books on the other hand can be comfortably downloaded but the interface is not as physically convenient as a hand-held novel. Even for interactive computer games and educational tools, CDs are better because all of the information is local. It is therefore much

quicker than the Internet—again, a bandwidth problem. On the other hand, CDs are static, so there is no real interaction with the information. Accessibility is another problem as there are still many individuals and companies who lack Internet access. Once accessed, the information is not always portable.

The best use of the Internet as a medium is one that maximizes its potential benefits and minimizes the problems like bandwidth limitations and accessibility. The Internet is therefore the best medium for numerous uses, including the following:

○ Information that changes frequently

○ Information with a high degree of specificity

○ Inexpensive worldwide distribution of information

○ User interaction with the information

Information Format

How can the information be displayed effectively? This question brings up the focus of this chapter. Computers are very good at manipulating and massaging data. It is important to give the computer the information in a format such that the computer can play with it and output the data in many ways. For instance, text of many Web pages can be configured by viewers. They can change the font, font size, and page size and search for key words. If, instead of using primitive text, the text is scanned in from a page in a book (maybe in the format of a bitmap), then viewers can do very little with the information. The format of the information is thus of vital importance, and choosing a format that is appropriate needs to be stressed.

When designing a format for graphics, you can learn from the flexibility shown in the text format, as in the previous example. Finally, you arrive at a strategy for making impressive graphics. Right now, there are many pages that use `ImageloopItem` written by James Gosling at Sun Systems or its descendants like the Animator. `ImageloopItem` takes a series of GIFs and flips through them, making a short animation. The Java mascot Duke is a classic example. Duke waves every once in a while—it is very impressively done. The animation consists of ten images that are 55x68 pixels. In total, it consists of approximately 20K of data and 3K of class files. I contrast this example with my program `Rotator`, which uses a very different technology. `Rotator` uses more primitive data and constructs the images from the data. The example I use has 1K of data and 16K of class files.

Rotator

All the previous discussion leads to `Rotator`. `Rotator` is a utility that displays rotating 3-D shapes. The shapes are composed of colored polygons that fit together snugly. The output (the picture) is shown on a `Canvas` whose size is determined at runtime. The main method of achieving a 3D effect with the shape is to keep the picture rotating continuously, but perspective, shading, and hidden face removal also help achieve this effect. There is a simple interface that allows the user to move the shape around. The original intent of the utility was to make geometrical objects accessible, but this utility can also be used to make 3-D logos spin, bounce, and move in fascinating patterns. Much of the appeal of these 3-D logos compared with many of the standard 3-D logos is that they are interactive, and they have infinite variety, as opposed to a fixed collection of frames.

Rotator is an extension of Canvas, which is a "component." This means Rotator inherits a large number of methods that relate to input from the keyboard and mouse, and graphics (these methods can be found in the API User's Guide). Rotator is thus in the same family as Label, Button, List, TextComponent and such, which means that it is simple to place Rotator within a complex applet like a data entry form or the game in Chapter 18, "Serious Play: Game Applets."

For instance, Listing 17.1 is a section of code that adds Rotator to a panel.

Listing 17.1. Excerpt from SimpleApplet.

```
Rotator rotator= new Rotator(this,solid,W,H);
new Thread(rotator).start();
rotator.background = new Color(255,200,200);
add(rotator);
show();
```

This code comes from SimpleApplet.java. Rotator has its own thread, making the continuous rotating independent and easy.

The classes that Rotator uses are Solid (which later gets extended to NCSolid—non-convex solid) and Omatrix. The Solid class holds all the information about the shape: faces, colors, position, and how to draw the shape. The Omatrix class holds all the information about orientations of shapes: how the shape sits in space. With these general class descriptions in mind, take a look at the code for Rotator in Listing 17.2.

Listing 17.2. Rotator.

```
import java.io.*;
import java.applet.*;
import java.awt.*;
import java.net.*;
import java.lang.*;
import Solid;
import Omatrix;

/*------------------------------------------------------------------*/
public class Rotator extends Canvas implements Runnable {
  public Color background;
```

```
private int W,H,delay,oldx,oldy;
private double angle,angle0=0,bounce=0;
private boolean keep_going;

private Solid solid;
private Omatrix tmp,tmp2,tmp3,M0;
private Image im;
private Graphics offscreen;
```

The only public variable is `background`; all the other variables can only be accessed by `Rotator`'s methods. The purpose of the variables will become clear later, as they are used.

Listing 17.3 shows the constructor (there is only one for now).

Listing 17.3. Constructor for `Rotator`.

```
/* - - - - - - - - - - - - - - - - - - - - - - - - - - - - - */
Rotator(Applet applet,Solid solid_,int width,int height) {
  solid = solid_;
  W = width;
  H = height;
  M0 = new Omatrix();
  tmp = new Omatrix();
  tmp2 = new Omatrix();
  tmp3 = new Omatrix();
  angle0 = 0;
  delay = 100;

  resize(W,H);
  im = applet.createImage(W,H);

  background = Color.lightGray;
  setBackground(background);
  offscreen = im.getGraphics();
}
```

Now, look at two major aspects of the above code. First, the reference `solid` is set to match the reference passed in `solid_` since `solid_`'s scope is only the constructor; these references are now equivalent. The reference refers to the object that knows everything about the shape to be drawn. Similarly, `W` and `H` are set to the values passed in. Then four orientation matrices (`Omatrix`) are instantiated. `M0` stands for the initial orientation, and all `tmp`s signify temporary matrices that are used to do calculations.

Second, regarding the display, the `Canvas` is resized to the desired width and height, creating an image, `im`, that is used for double buffering. This means that instead of drawing directly to the screen, you can create an image that you can take your time drawing and then when you are finished drawing, you can throw the whole image to the screen. This stops the distracting flicker that some programs have. The image is basically a block of memory for which the object, `offscreen`, can manipulate with the graphics methods like `fillRect`, `setColor`, `drawPoly` and so forth.

The Subtleties of Update and Paint

Since this is the graphics chapter, I had better start drawing things! The three essential methods in a Canvas are paint, update, and repaint. The first information to know about these methods is how they fit in the hierarchy. Paint and update are methods called by the parent. The parent calls the Canvas' paint method when the Canvas is initialized. Also, if part or all of the Canvas gets covered by another window, the parent can call the paint command to fix its appearance. If the Canvas is static, this is the only method required. If the Canvas changes, as in the case of animation, then the Canvas calls the 'repaint,' which notifies the parent that it should update the Canvas; the parent then calls the Canvas' update method.

Often it is easier to redraw the whole picture than to change only what needs to be changed. The following strategy achieves this:

```
public void update(Graphics g) {
  paint(g);
}
```

Unfortunately, this solution introduces a flicker problem. The paint method starts by clearing the Canvas, and then numerous commands draw the picture. There can be a noticeable time lag between the execution of the first and last commands in the drawing sequence, which is distracting.

The way to solve this problem is by reversing the roles of update and paint: have paint call update. As well, you may add a double buffer. The update is likely called more frequently than the paint, so it makes sense for it to be the dominant method of the two.

Listing 17.4 shows Rotator's paint and update methods.

Listing 17.4. Rotator's paint and update methods.

```
../* - - - - - - - - - - - - - - - - - - - - - - - - - - */
  public void paint(Graphics g) {
    update(g);
  }
  public void update(Graphics g) {
    offscreen.setColor(background);
    offscreen.fillRect(0, 0, W, H);

    solid.Draw(offscreen,(int)(W/2),(int)(H/2),bounce);

    g.drawImage(im, 0, 0, null);
  }
```

This simple update draws a filled rectangle to offscreen (which effectively clears anything that is on the off screen) and then draws the solid. The offscreen image, im, is then drawn to g. This g is a graphics context like offscreen, but it is beyond the scope of this class; it must be supplied by the parent.

In the update method of Rotator, there is little that can change except the variable bounce. Another value that may change—although it is not readily apparent—is the orientation matrix of the shape that is encapsulated in the object, solid. In the run method of Rotator, repaint is called. The update then draws the picture using the current bounce and shape orientation values. If they have changed since the last update, the current picture may be drastically different from the previous picture.

Rotator on the Run

The run method of Rotator is conceptually simple, as shown in Listing 17.5. It updates the height and the orientation of the shape and then redraws the shape. It then loops until it is told to stop.

Listing 17.5. Run method for Rotator.

```
/* - - - - - - - - - - - - - - - - - - - - - - - - */
public void run(){
   keep_going = true;
   angle=0;
   while(keep_going){
     /* .. modify bounce and solid.orient .. */

     angle += 0.1;
     tmp3.Rotation(1,2,angle);
     tmp2.Rotation(1,0,angle*Math.sqrt(2)/2);
     tmp.Rotation(0,2,angle*Math.PI/4);
     solid.orient = tmp3.Times(tmp2.Times(tmp.Times(M0)));

     bounce = Math.abs(Math.cos(0.5*(angle+angle0)))*2-1;
     repaint();
     try {Thread.sleep(delay);} catch (InterruptedException e){}
   }
 }
```

Referring to the loop in the above code, solid.orient (the shape's orientation) is a function of angle, with M0 as the initial value. Bounce (the shape's height), however, is a function of angle, with angle0 as its initial value. The values of solid.orient exhibit interesting behavior: theoretically, the orientation never repeats. The Rotation and Times methods are discussed later in the chapter.

After the request to update via the repaint command, the run thread sleeps for a while to give up the CPU for other threads. This process continues as long as keep_going is true.

A simple and logical interface is essential to any interactive application. Now look at a simple interface for Rotator that gives the user control of the shape's orientation, rather than leaving the shape to tumble in accordance with the convoluted function. The interface design is this: the tumbling stops when users press a mouse button. They may then drag the mouse to rotate the shape in chosen directions at will. Letting go of the mouse button returns the shape to its tumbling.

The first step in designing this interface is to stop the run thread when a mouse button is pressed, as shown in Listing 17.6.

Listing 17.6. `Rotator: mouseDown` routine.

```
/* - - - - - - - - - - - - - - - - - - - - - - - - - - - */
public boolean mouseDown(java.awt.Event evt, int x, int y) {
  keep_going = false;
  try {Thread.sleep(delay*2);} catch (InterruptedException e){}
  M0 = solid.orient;
  angle0 += angle;
  angle = 0;
  oldx = x;
  oldy = y;

  return true;
}
```

The first line ensures that the run process eventually finishes. The sleep command waits to make sure this is so. The current value of the shape's orientation is saved, as it becomes the new initial value. When the tumbling resumes, it thus resumes from the current orientation. The variables `oldx` and `oldy` record the position where the mouse has been pressed; this is used to determine how much the mouse moves during a `mouseDrag`. The "return true" tells the `Rotator`'s parent that the `mouseDown` event has been handled, so there is no need for another thread or process to handle the `mouseDown` event.

The responsibility of returning the shape to the tumbling shape falls on the `mouseUp` method, as shown in Listing 17.7. But all it has to do is start a new run thread.

Listing 17.7. `Rotator: mouseUp` routine.

```
/* - - - - - - - - - - - - - - - - - - - - - - - - - - - */
public boolean mouseUp(java.awt.Event evt, int x, int y) {
  new Thread(this).start();
  return true;
}
```

The `mouseUp` event starts the shape tumbling again by starting the `this` thread, that is, starting the run method of this object (`Rotator`).

Finally, you arrive at the sensitive part of this interface. The `mouseDrag` method allows the user to manipulate the shape. You use the difference between the old and new mouse position to calculate how you want the shape moved.

Listing 17.8. `Rotator: mouseDrag` routine.

```
/* - - - - - - - - - - - - - - - - - - - - - - - - */
public boolean mouseDrag(java.awt.Event evt, int x, int y) {
  tmp2.Rotation(0,2,(x - oldx) * Math.PI/ solid.W);
  tmp.Rotation(1,2,(oldy - y) * Math.PI/ solid.H);
  M0 = tmp.Times(tmp2.Times(M0));
  solid.orient = M0;
  oldx = x;
  oldy = y;

  repaint();
  return true;
}
```

The first line of this method causes the shape to rotate in the XZ–plane by an angle that relates to the drag motion in the x direction, the angle being equal to (x–oldx)*constant. Similarly, the second line rotates in the YZ–plane. This case differs from the previous one by a minus sign; this is because the origin is in the upper left corner, and traveling down the screen corresponds to an increase in the y value. Since M0 always refers to the current orientation during `mouseDrag`, when the `mouseUp` is called the shape begins tumbling again starting with the current orientation.

Although this finishes the brief discussion of this interface, the next chapter looks more deeply into good interfaces.

Omatrix and Solid Classes

In the following section, there are some difficult mathematical concepts, so rather than going through every detail, a general picture of what is happening is presented. For those who like more details, you may check the CD and go over the code that is there. Part of the appeal of object-oriented code is that the programmer doesn't need to understand all of the code to effectively use it. For this reason, big projects benefit from using object-oriented programming languages.

Omatrix

The basis of the `Omatrix` method used by `Rotator` is that shapes are defined in terms of points, in the form (x, y, z). For a simple visualization of this form, imagine x as a horizontal axis across the width of the screen, y as a vertical axis along the length or height of the screen, and z as an axis along a direction perpendicular to the screen, with one end pointing in toward the screen and the other end pointing out toward the user. Call this the standard orientation.

The class Omatrix describes an orientation. The way it does this is it replaces the standard x–y–z axes with new axes. These new axes are 3 vectors; call them x'–y'–z'. You store x'–y'–z' as the columns of a matrix. For x'–y'–z' to make sense as an orientation, these vectors must each have a unit length, and must also be perpendicular to each other—like the standard orientation (1,0,0)–(0,1,0)–(0,0,1).

In Listing 17.9, you have the initial code for the Omatrix class. It mainly concerns itself with the 3-by-3 matrix. When an Omatrix is constructed, it is set to the standard axis.

Listing 17.9. First section of the Omatrix class.

```
public class Omatrix{
  public double[][] M;
  private int row,col,k,l;

  Omatrix(){
    M = new double[3][3];

    Assign(1,0,0,0,1,0,0,0,1);
  }

  /* - - - - - - - - - - - - - - - */
  public void Assign(double a, double b, double c,
                     double d, double e, double f,
                     double g, double h, double i ){
    M[0][0] = a;
    M[1][0] = b;
    M[2][0] = c;
    M[0][1] = d;
    M[1][1] = e;
    M[2][1] = f;
    M[0][2] = g;
    M[1][2] = h;
    M[2][2] = i;
  }
```

This matrix, M, is the data part of the class. The other variables declared are row, col, k, and l. These dummy variables are used often. In general, it is safer to have dummy variables declared in the methods that require them, but this setup works here because no two methods are called at the same time.

In the Omatrix constructor, the space for M is allocated, and the method Assign sets the initial value of M equal to the standard orientation. The following two methods are the major tools used by Rotator to change the orientation: Rotation and Times.

Rotation

The method `Rotation` replaces the matrix, M. It is replaced with a matrix that represents an orientation different from the standard orientation by a rotation in one of the coordinate planes by "angle" (in radians). Here, `i` and `j` are the numbers of the axes that get changed. For instance, 0 and 1 represent that the change occurs in the first and second columns—the x and y axis. `Rotation(0,1,0.5)` sets the orientation, M, to the following:

Orientation Matrix

$$
\begin{bmatrix}
\cos(0.5) & \sin(0.5) & 0 \\
-\sin(0.5) & \cos(0.5) & 0 \\
0 & 0 & 1
\end{bmatrix}
$$

Figures 17.1 and 17.2 show the result.

Figure 17.1.

The same shapes viewed with the standard basis.

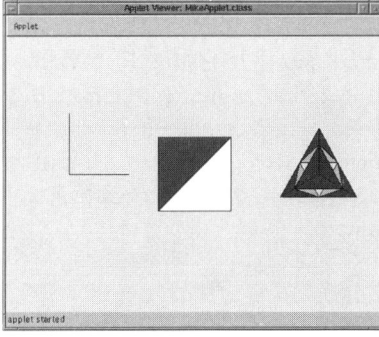

Figure 17.2.

The same shapes after a rotation of half a radian.

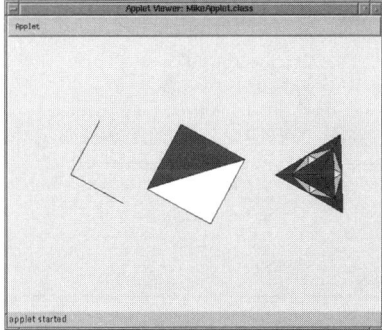

Listing 17.10 shows how "rotation" works.

Listing 17.10. Rotation method in Omatrix.

```
/* - - - - - - - - - - - - - - - */
  public void Rotation (int i, int j, double angle) {
    Assign(1,0,0,0,1,0,0,0,1);

    M[i][i] = Math.cos(angle);
    M[j][j] = M[i][i];
    M[i][j] = Math.sin(angle);
    M[j][i] = -M[i][j];
  }
```

Times

The next method, shown in Listing 17.11, allows you to make changes in the orientation relative to any given orientation. In matrix notation, this operation is multiplication or Times. Unlike the method Rotation, Times returns a new orientation object rather than changing M. This turns out to be convenient, as seen in Rotator. Notice that every instance Times is called, a new Omatrix object is created. Happily, however, garbage collection is automatic, so the old Omatrix objects are cleared away.

Listing 17.11. Times method of Omatrix.

```
/* - - - - - - - - - - - - - - - - */
  public Omatrix Times(Omatrix N){
    Omatrix temp = new Omatrix();
    for (row=0; row < 3; row++) {
      for (col=0; col <3; col++) {
        temp.M[row][col] = 0.0;
        for (k=0; k < 3; k++) {
          temp.M[row][col] += M[row][k] * N.M[k][col];
        }
      }
    }

    return temp;
  }
```

In Figure 17.3, you can see the result of two rotations composed by using Times. Combining the methods Rotation and Times together allows you to make any orientation. This completes the explanation of the Omatrix methods used by Rotator. However, there are several more methods to Omatrix, some of which are quite interesting. They are used in the next chapter.

Figure 17.3.

An orientation constructed by combining two simple rotations.

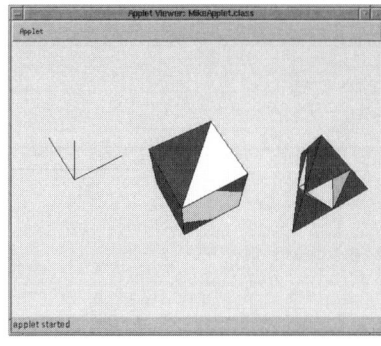

Solid

Next is an explanation about the Solid class. This class holds all of the shape's information. In general, the shapes are made up of faces; these faces are all flat. The faces are polygons that have only one side, or plane, that is visible. All the faces put together form the outside of a convex shape. In other words, the polygons are all joined along their sides to form one shape, for which there is a perspective that only sees the planes that face upwards. The upward-facing planes vary with the shape's orientation. This description of a shape is very narrow; it will be extended when NCSolid is described, but for now, these restrictions help draw the shape without a sorting routine, and without redrawing the same areas of the picture.

The method CalcScrPts (calculate screen coordinates) is a routine that takes the orientation of the shape in space and computes all the screen coordinates. First, it computes the points relative to the new basis, then it projects each of the points to the screen. This means that you can draw a wire frame diagram of the shape by connecting all the appropriate screen coordinates. This is a bad idea, however, since the back and front of the object often become hard to identify.

Instead, the Draw method uses faceUp to decide which faces it draws. The faceUp method returns a true if the face is pointing upwards; this is where the one-sidedness of the face is important. The faces have a top that you want drawn, and a bottom that you don't want drawn (as you never see the bottoms). Since the shape is convex, all the hidden faces return a false value for faceUp, and therefore don't need to be drawn. Thus all of the hidden face removal is taken care of. The getColour method then computes the shading, and the polygons are drawn with DrawPoly.

Since this Draw method is fairly specific, there is another Draw method that is more general but slower. This Draw method is part of the class NCSolid in Listing 17.12, which extends Solid.

Listing 17.12. The class `NCSolid`.

```java
import java.io.*;
import java.awt.*;
import Solid;

public class NCSolid extends Solid{
  private int order[],min;

  NCSolid (InputStream is, int wid, int heig, int ncolour_)
    throws IOException{
    super(is, wid, heig, ncolour_);
    order = new int[nface];
  }

  /* - - - - - - - - - - - - - - - */
  public void Draw(Graphics offscreen,int x0,int y0,double z){
    CalcScrPts((double)x0,(double)y0,z);

    /* .. put in a list all the faces that are point up.. */
    i=0;
    for (f=0;f<nface;f++)
      if (faceUp(f)) {
        order[i] = f;
        i++;
      }

    /* .. find the face farthest away and draw it 'i' times .. */
    for (j=0;j<i;j++){
      min = j;
      for (k=j+1;k<i;k++)
        if (rotPts[order[k]+nface][2]<rotPts[order[min]+nface][2]) min =k;

      if (min !=j) {
        f = order[min];
        order[min] = order[j];
      } else f = order[j];

      for (k=1;k<faces[f][0]+1;k++)
        DrawPoly(offscreen,faces[f][k],getColour(f,k));
    }
  }
}
```

The following line is a check to see which one of the faces is closer to the screen:

```java
if (rotPts[order[k]+nface][2]<rotPts[order[min]+nface][2]) min =k;
```

This line is used to sort the faces into an order that delineates farthest to closest.

Here are some examples of Rotator being used. Figure 17.4 uses Solid. Figure 17.5 uses NCSolid.

Figure 17.4.
A sample of SimpleApplet
(cubeR.html).

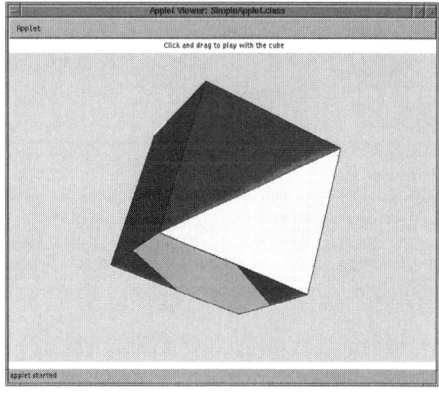

Figure 17.5.
A sample of SimpleApplet2
(tetraR.html).

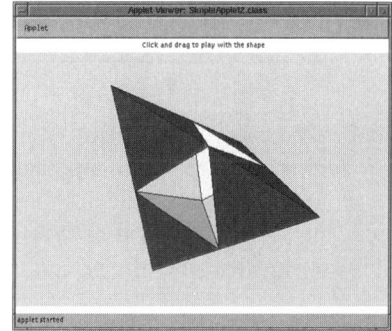

Summary: The Bottom Line Is Bandwidth

How economical has the bandwidth been so far? Table 17.1 shows the data for the cube.

Table 17.1. The breakdown of data needed to be transferred with
SimpleApplet.

Data	Size
SimpleApplet.class	1885 bytes
Rotator.class	3010 bytes
Solid.class	6274 bytes
Omatrix.class	4385 bytes
cube.dat	947 bytes
Total	16501 bytes = 16.5K

Table 17.2 shows the data for the tetrahedron with the center missing (the second image).

Table 17.2. The breakdown of data needed to be transferred with SimpleApplet2.

Data	Size
SimpleApplet2.class	1889 bytes
Rotator.class	3010 bytes
Solid.class	6274 bytes
NCSolid.class	1197 bytes
Omatrix.class	4385 bytes
tetra.dat	1451 bytes
Total	18206 bytes = 18.2K

Since the bandwidth has been used sparingly so far (under 20K), go ahead and make Rotator more interesting by adding a background image, and call it ImageRotator (see Listing 17.13). Following the NCSolid example of sub-classing, add more data into the constructor, and replace the Draw routine. Just as the Solid is supplied to Rotator from Rotator's parent, the Image for Rotator's background is also supplied from the parent.

Listing 17.13. The class ImageRotator.

```
/*--------------------------------------------------------------------*/
public class ImageRotator extends Rotator implements Runnable {
  Image gif;
  int gifx,gify;

  /* -  -  -  -  -  -  -  -  -  -  -  -  -  -  -  -  -  -  -  - */
  ImageRotator(Applet applet,Solid solid_,Image gif_,int width,int height) {
    super(applet,solid_,width,height);
    gif = gif_;
  }

  /* -  -  -  -  -  -  -  -  -  -  -  -  -  -  -  -  -  -  -  - */
  public void update(Graphics g) {
    offscreen.setColor(background);
    offscreen.fillRect(0, 0, W, H);
    gifx = (int)((W - gif.getWidth(null))/2);
    gify = (int)(((H - gif.getHeight(null))/2)*(1-bounce));
    offscreen.drawImage(gif,gifx, gify, null);

    solid.Draw(offscreen,(int)(W/2),(int)(H/2),bounce);

    g.drawImage(im, 0, 0, null);
  }
}
```

The image that can be passed follows the general description of an Image. In the example of SimpleApplet3 in Listing 17.14, you will pass in an Image that is created from a GIF.

Listing 17.14. SimpleApplet3's inclusion of Rotator.

```
URL here = this.getDocumentBase();
...
     Image gif = getImage(new URL(here,image));
     add(new Label(title,Label.CENTER));
     ImageRotator rotator= new ImageRotator(this,solid,gif,W,H);
...
```

Figure 17.6 shows the program's output.

Figure 17.6.

A sample of SimpleApplet3
(tetraRB.html).

Table 17.3 shows how much information is sent over the Net.

Table 17.3. The breakdown of data needed to be transferred with SimpleApplet3.

Data	Size
SimpleApplet3.class	2025 bytes
Rotator.class	3010 bytes
ImageRotator.class	1265 bytes
Solid.class	6274 bytes
NCSolid.class	1197 bytes
Omatrix.class	4385 bytes
tetra.dat	1451 bytes
something.gif	92375 bytes
Total	111982 bytes = 112.0K

Even in this small example that uses only one GIF, the GIF is a large portion of what has been sent. Notice as well, the pictures are no longer scaleable: when the size of the Canvas is changed, the shape is scaled, but the GIF has a fixed resolution. This takes away some of the flexibility. Instead of using the GIF, the graphics primitives can be used to create the background Image. This, no doubt, uses less information than needs to be sent, but the information is in a format that allows the computer to manipulate it. Thus the image also comes alive and dances and the viewer doesn't have to wait for everything to download.

So the real goal of graphics programming is to find the happy medium for bandwidth, flexibility, and really cool graphics. This must be solved by carefully choosing the format of the graphics information and pushing the format to its limit. Reflect on the 92K GIF and think of all the wonderful Java code and data that can be downloaded in the same time.

Chapter

18

by Jim Morey

Serious Play: Game Applets

"What's your game?" Maybe that should be, "What's your definition of a game?" Games play an important role in our society. But what are games?

There are common components to all games: a goal, rules, and a world (or a framework) in which the game is played. The goal of a game drives the players to perform or to achieve. In chess, the goal is to capture the opponent's King. The rules, in a way, are impediments to achieving goals instantly. Often, the rules make the game fair so that anyone playing the game has the same chance at winning. In tic-tac-toe, for example, one rule is that players must alternate turns; otherwise, one player easily would dominate the game and win. The world in which games are played provides a place where both the goal and the rules make sense; it is the ground on which the struggle for the goal can be enacted. As the rules always require, to succeed at the game, players must remain in that world. The world of Monopoly, for example, is a microcosm of the business world, and the players' goal is to achieve financial domination. Players must travel around this world searching for business prospects, acquiring properties, and becoming wealthy. They are given the neighborhoods, currency, and power to achieve that goal. Sometimes these components (goal, rules, world) are difficult to identify, but in varying forms, they always exist. For every game, when players know the rules, understand the world, and want the goal, they can build strategies they can use to play each game.

The ability to build strategies is important for every aspect of life, so this chapter takes the viewpoint that games are a testing ground for life skills. Consider the game of chess as a testing ground for strategy, concentration, and sequencing; the game of poker focuses on the skills of computing probability, managing stress, and judging other players' reactions and behaviors. This viewpoint gives you a common starting point.

What makes a good game? Good games have innumerable qualities to them, as diverse as people's varying talents, and just as impossible to list with any accuracy or completeness. Qualities that make a game good engage players on the following levels:

Achievement—challenge/improvement
Adrenaline—risk/chance/excitement
Relations—social/wit/interplay
Senses—sensual/auditory/tactile
Creativity—imagination/allusion/aesthetic

A game that is rich with these attributes can be a good game only if this richness is balanced with approachability. Players then can experience the game's richness because it is accessible. This chapter examines some examples of games and their various attributes.

Computer Games

How do these ideas about the concept of games relate to computers? The first step is to examine the medium. Computers are good at manipulating and massaging information, but they have very little tactile input and diminished human interaction. A good computer game must take all this

into account. In Solitaire, for example, there is no human interaction, and shuffling and redealing are time consuming. Solitaire therefore is a good example of an ideal game to be computerized. Although the tactile handling of the cards is lost, most people prefer the efficiency of computer shuffling and redealing.

Instead of computerizing an existing game, many games have been designed especially for computers. Descent, a fully 3-D battle game, makes wonderful use of the computer medium. Specifically, the game uses the computer's capability to manipulate 3-D information. Any other medium would have great difficulty creating the world of Descent. A problem with Descent, however, is that it has a complex interface. This detracts from its popularity.

The game Lemmings, on the other hand, makes innovative use of the computer medium with an approachable interface. The concepts in Lemmings break new ground with interface and game design. Players guide a group of lemmings through a maze-like world by assigning a series of jobs to individual lemmings who aide the others in completing the maze. Most other contemporary computer game designs focus on manipulating only one object for success, whereas Lemmings' focus is on a group's success, possibly at the expense of a few individuals. The innovation in the interface is the player's ability to control multiple individuals within one group.

Net Games

Now that home computers have the capacity to use the Internet, there are many innovative possibilities for games. An existing board game that would greatly benefit from a networked computer is Diplomacy, which reenacts the First World War. The players role-play the leaders of important European countries. Because there is no element of chance to the game, players must conspire with other leaders to achieve their individual goals of European domination. Unfortunately, while playing the board game, the players often are aware of who is talking to whom. This greatly affects the trust factor in agreements. Imagine the game now with the assistance of the net's anonymity. Conspiracy and backroom politics are handled with secrecy. Much like the Solitaire example, this game shows how a game can be enhanced by a new medium.

A good example of existing net games is multiuser dungeons (MUDs). These let multiple people interact in one game world. Because these games are mainly text based, they appeal to individuals' imaginations, much like radio programs did before the advent of television. Unfortunately, even though the text in the game can be very appealing for imaginative purposes, the text—as an interface to move around and interact with the world—also detracts from the game because it is complex and cumbersome for beginners to use.

Interface Design

Looking at games now as a designer/programmer, the key concept is the way in which players interact with the world: the interface. A difficult interface makes a game less approachable and also can diminish the fun of play, especially if a lot of the difficulty of the game lies in the interface and not in the content of the game.

A good interface is intuitive and responsive. A good way to test whether an interface is intuitive is to have some noncomputer people play the game with minimal prior instruction, and then see whether they can figure it out. One thing that helps people figure things out is to ensure that the game is responsive to input.

Just as you saw games as a training ground for life skills, a good way to look at computer-game design is as a training ground for interface-design skills. Computers are information tools; the easier it is to use the tool to process the information into a more desirable form, the better the tool is. In the creation of a game, the programmer is free to design innovative interfaces without having the burden of conventional or real-world problems. Considering the richness of games, a revolution in interface design probably will spring from a game interface.

The Game of CopyCat

 The CD-ROM included with this book contains an example of a game I developed that has a good interface. The game is called CopyCat, and it, too, has a goal, rules, and a world. The goal of the game is to copy a picture created by several patterned faces of a cube or some other shape. The one rule is that players can slide or roll the shape around only in specific ways. Here, the interface plays a central role, because the complexity of the game springs from the way players must manipulate the shape. The world consists of the picture to be copied, a blank frame where the copy of the picture will be, a shape with the patterned faces with which to make the copy, some regions where the shape can be rolled, and a duplicate shape used for reference.

Looking At Objects and Data Flow

To start off, you will look at the overall workings of the program. The crucial step in programming a game is to be able to identify the objects that are needed; it is about pattern recognition and being able to break down the program into objects by searching for commonalties. Finding the essence of the program often takes a bit of work and usually requires abstract thinking. The pieces I broke the CopyCat game into follow:

```
CopyCat
PlayArea
Board
BoardBox
GroupGraph
TFSolid
```

Pieces also include your old friends from the preceding chapter:

```
Rotator
Solid
Omatrix
```

CopyCat is the applet, and it is the foreman of the program; it gets all the other objects going and then checks on them when needed. PlayArea is a Canvas where the important actions are performed. Most of your interest will be focused on this class. Board is a class that holds all the important information about the Board—the picture to be replicated. BoardBox is the Canvas that displays the desired picture. The GroupGraph holds the geometrical information about the shape/solid. TFSolid stands for Top-Face-Solid, which is a subclass of Solid with special importance to the top face of the solid or shape.

Figure 18.1 shows an overview of how those pieces fit together (after everything is instantiated by CopyCat). I suggest that you play the game before reading the rest of this chapter.

Figure 18.1.
The flow of CopyCat.

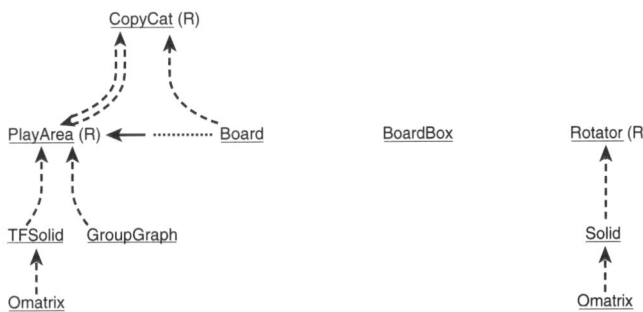

The symbol (R) stands for runnable
An arrow shows the direction of information

Three runnable objects are in this program: CopyCat, PlayArea, and Rotator. You already saw what Rotator does, so now take a look at the other two objects. This system actually is event driven, with the threads sleeping most of the time. You can think of CopyCat as a lazy foreman who snoozes at his desk and only wakes up when PlayArea tells him that there has been some event that may be interesting—something has changed. He deals with the event and promptly goes back to sleep. Similarly, PlayArea works on this event-driven idea, except he is more like a fast food cashier because he gets a lot of events: mouse down, mouse up, and mouse drag. He receives all his events through the event handler. The separate thread in PlayArea runs animations during the play; these are used to place the top face of the shape on the game Board. I will go into detail about how this all works, but for now, get a feel for the data flow.

Notice that Rotator and BoardBox are separate from the rest of the program. Rotator is used to display a duplicate of the shape for reference. BoardBox is responsible for displaying the goal—the picture to be copied. Both BoardBox and Rotator are there only to provide static information about the game; the shape doesn't change midway through the game and neither does the goal. So after they are instantiated, they have no contact with the rest of the program. Figure 18.2 shows the visible components of CopyCat: PlayArea, Rotator, and BoardBox.

Figure 18.2.

The visible components of CopyCat: PlayArea, Rotator, and BoardBox.

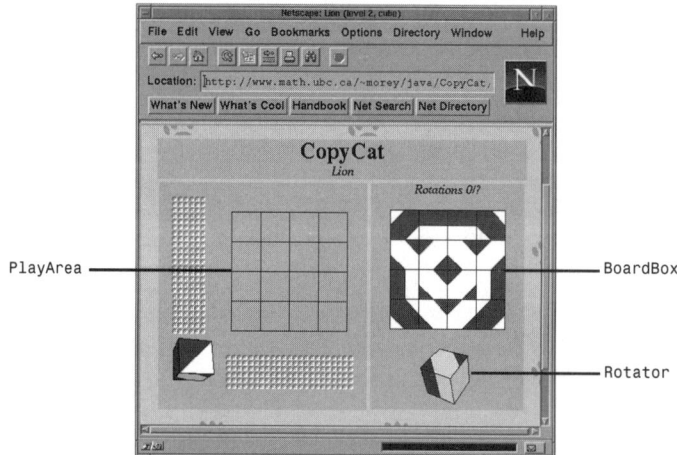

Coordinating CopyCat and PlayArea

Now look at how CopyCat and PlayArea communicate. It is a simple interaction. CopyCat wants to sleep until PlayArea has changedThings. Both CopyCat and PlayArea use Board. Board stores the current state of the Board; PlayArea changes the current state of the Board every time a top face of the shape is placed. Then CopyCat simply checks to see whether the Board is finished by seeing whether Board.finished is true. In CopyCat's run method, shown in Listing 18.1, the line PlayArea.thingsChange(); is really a question: "Have things changed?" The answer to the question is always yes, but that is because PlayArea waits for the answer to be yes before it responds to the request. After CopyCat waits for things to change, it checks to see whether something important has changed. If the number of rotations has changed from what it was before, it updates rotations and displays it to the screen by RecordScore. If the player has completed the pattern, it displays the appropriate Finished message and plays a little tune.

Listing 18.1. The run method from CopyCat.

```
/* - - - - - - - - - - - - - - - - - - - - - - - - - - - - - - - */
public void run(){
  rotations=0;
  while(true){
    /* .. wait for things to change .. */
```

```
        PlayArea.thingsChange();

        if (rotations != PlayArea.rotations){
          rotations = PlayArea.rotations;
          RecordScore(rotations);
        }
        if (Board.finished && !finished){
          finished = true;
          subtitle.setBackground(new Color(255,150,150));
          if (level1)
            subtitle.title=(String) "Finished ("+rotations+"/"+Board.minRot+")";
          else
            subtitle.title=(String) "Finished ("+rotations+"/?)";
          purrr.play();
          subtitle.centre();
subtitle.repaint();
        }
      }
    }
```

thingsChange works like a door at a high-school dance, where the organizers want the same number of girls and boys to enter. The organizers ensure this by only accepting a girl, then a boy, then a girl, and so on. So if the last person let in was a boy, the next boy to come in must wait for a girl to enter. Keeping this analogy in mind, take a look at the code. Suppose that when the variable nochange equals false, it indicates "a girl was the last person let in." When nochange is true, it indicates "a boy was the last person let in." The question thingsChange is like the boy, and changedThings is like the girl. When CopyCat calls PlayArea.thingsChange();, it checks whether the last person admitted was a boy (nochange is true); if so, then it waits/sleeps. If, while CopyCat is sleeping, someone wakes the boy, he checks to see whether a girl has gone through. Eventually, a girl will go through and the boy will be let in. After going in, the nochange variable must be set to false, which shows that the last person through was a boy. Just in case a girl was waiting to come in, this variable wakes up everyone. As it turns out, the counterpart changedThings is exactly the same (see Listing 18.2).

Listing 18.2. The run method from PlayArea.java.

```
/* - - - - - - - - - - - - - - - - - - - - - - - - - */
public synchronized void thingsChange() {
  while (nochange == true)
    try{ wait(); } catch (InterruptedException e){}
  nochange = true;
  notifyAll();
}

/* - - - - - - - - - - - - - - - - - - - - - - - - - */
public synchronized void changedThings() {
  while (nochange == false)
    try{ wait(); } catch (InterruptedException e){}
  nochange = false;
  notifyAll();
}
```

Dealing with Events

How does `PlayArea` deal with its events? Now that you've finished with the interaction between `PlayArea` and `CopyCat`, you start to see that `PlayArea` is the component that does the real work.

First, you must identify all the events `PlayArea` knows how to deal with. As in `Rotator`, mentioned in the preceding chapter, the events dealt with are mouse down, mouse drag, and mouse up. `Rotator`'s methods are much simpler than these, so I encourage you to revisit that chapter if this next section gets a bit too convoluted; a reasonable understanding of `Rotator`'s event handling will be very helpful. It is important to understand the overall goal for the interface so that you can use it as a torch to light your way through some complicated code.

The goal is to have a responsive control to move the shape. The mouse down event is interpreted as an attempt to grab the object. The `mouseDown` will be successful if the pointer is relatively close to the shape; otherwise, nothing happens. If the shape is under the control of the mouse, the `mouseDrag` makes sense. This `mouseDrag` method is fairly intuitive. Dragging the shape simply slides the shape to where the mouse points. The tricky part occurs when the mouse drags the shape over an *oriented rough surface*. These rough surfaces make the shape roll in a particular direction. The rolling behaves like a ratchet. During a roll, the shape locks into the desired set positions and doesn't allow the user to go back to the previous locked position. The desired position usually has one of the faces pointing upright; this is referred to as the *top face*. The mouse up event is interpreted as letting go of the shape. The only tricky part to `mouseUp` is that if the shape is let go in a place on the `Board` where the top face will fit, the `mouseUp` method calls up a small animation that shows how the top face is placed on the `Board`. If this interface outline is a little fuzzy, I suggest that you play the game and pay close attention to the interface.

Now you can break down each of the three methods that handle the interface. The next section starts with the easiest: `mouseDown`.

mouseDown

In the `mouseDown` method, the fast-food cashier handles the event as long as an animation isn't running and if the pointer is close enough to the shape. As you will see later, all events are ignored if an animation is running. If the mouse down event is handled, to indicate to the player that the shape now is being held, the shape is raised; the `height` of the shape becomes slightly bigger. Also, the `onSolid` flag is set to `true`. This tells `mouseDrag` that the shape is within the control of the mouse (see Listing 18.3).

Listing 18.3. The method `mouseDown` from `PlayArea`.

```
../* - - - - - - - - - - - - - - - - - - - - - - - - - - - - - - */
  public boolean mouseDown(java.awt.Event evt, int x, int y) {
    /* .. pick up the solid .. */
    if (!animation_running){
      if (Math.abs(x-solid.cenx)<solid.W && Math.abs(y-solid.ceny)<solid.H){
        onSolid = true;
```

```
        height = 0.2;
        return true;
      }
   }
   return false;
}
```

mouseDrag

Unfortunately, all the handling of events isn't so simple. The next event handler for `PlayArea` is `mouseDrag`, shown in Listing 18.4. If not for the rolling part, the interface would be easy. On the other hand, the rolling is the most important part of the interface and the program.

The drag has several behaviors or modes: TRANSLATE, IN_A, and IN_B. The mode used depends on whether the mouse is over one of the rough surfaces. The TRANSLATE mode is the default mode. Being in this mode means that the object will only slide, because it is not on a rough surface. The orientation of the shape will stay fixed. Being in the IN_A and IN_B modes means that the mouse is over one of the rough surfaces. Dragging the shape over either of the rough surfaces might make the shape roll over. There are two different modes because, depending on which of the two regions the mouse is over, the shape rolls in different directions.

Because this method is very long, I'll explain it in small pieces at a time. Listing 18.4 shows the method, along with commentary inserted between sections of code. I'll leave the mathematical explanations to you, because a discussion of this would bog down an already convoluted method.

Listing 18.4. The method `mouseDrag` from `PlayArea`.

```
/* - - - - - - - - - - - - - - - - - - - - - - - - - - - */
  public boolean mouseDrag(java.awt.Event evt, int x, int y) {
    /* .. move the around the solid -- maybe roll it .. */
    if (onSolid && !animation_running){
      solid.cenx = x;
      solid.ceny = y;
```

First, to perform the drag, the player must be holding the shape: `onSolid` must be `true`. The other condition is that the animations aren't running, so the variable `animation_running` is `false`. The next two lines center the shape to where the mouse now is pointing.

```
    /* .. find the newMode--TRANSLATE, IN_A, or IN_B
         this is used to find out whether the mode has changed .. */
    newMode = TRANSLATE;
    for (int i=0;i<2;i++){
      int chX = (int)((solid.cenx-region[i][0])*vec[i][0]+
          (solid.ceny-region[i][1])*vec[i][1]);
      int chY = (int)((solid.cenx-region[i][0])*vec[i][1]-
          (solid.ceny-region[i][1])*vec[i][0]);
```

```
    if (chX>=0 && chX<region[i][2] &&
        chY>=0 && chY<region[i][3]) newMode = i;
}
```

This segment of code figures out which region of `PlayArea` the mouse is on. `TRANSLATE`, `IN_A`, and `IN_B` are `public` `static` `final` variables or constants; they are used to make values of the mode easy to identify. The only purpose is to compute the `newMode`.

```
...
    if (mode == TRANSLATE) {
        if (mode != newMode) {
            mode = newMode;
            start_roll = true;
        }
```

The `TRANSLATE` mode is the easiest mode, because the shape already follows the mouse's pointer. The only thing it must do is prepare the shape for a roll if the `newMode` is different from `TRANSLATE`. The Boolean variable, `start_roll`, is used as a flag to run some code later. Actually, a better way to handle starting a roll is to construct a method called `startRoll`. The code that computes the `newMode` probably should be its own method, too.

```
    }else {
        /* .. mode = IN_A or IN_B .. */
        if (mode != newMode) {
            /* .. not in roll region anymore .. */
            mode = TRANSLATE;
            if (ang < sign(angle)*angle/2) {
                group.pos = oldPos;
                if (ang>SMALL_ANG) sounds[THUD].play();
            }else {
                sounds[THUD].play();
                rotations++;
                changedThings();
            }
            solid.orient = group.element[group.pos];
```

This section deals with being on a rough surface. If the `newMode` is different from the old mode (this means that the mouse is off the rough surface it was on), you must ensure that the shape is in one of the standard positions and not partially rotated. This is one of the underlying properties of the modes; a given mode assumes that the shape has a certain orientation. If the shape is not in one of the fixed positions, you take it to the closest fixed position. This is determined by how close `ang` is to `angle`, where `ang` is the current angle of rotation of the shape relative to the last fixed position, and `angle` is the amount of rotation needed to get from the last fixed position to the new fixed position. So the question really is, *Is* `ang` *closer to zero or to* `angle`? If it falls back to the old position, it will only make a `THUD` noise if the fall was big enough—that is, `ang` exceeded `SMALL_ANG`. Otherwise, the shape falls to the new position, the number of `rotations` is incremented, and `CopyCat` is informed of the change.

```
    } else {
        /* .. in roll region .. */
        ang = (vec[mode][0]*(x-lastPt[0]) + vec[mode][1]*(y-lastPt[1]))*
            ROLL_VALUE/solid.W;
```

```
        if (ang<0) {
          ang = 0;
          lastPt[0] = x;
          lastPt[1] = y;
        }
        if (ang>Math.abs(angle)) { /* .. finished one rotation .. */
          rotations++;
          changedThings();
          sounds[THUD].play();
          solid.orient = group.element[group.pos];
          start_roll = true;
        } else {
          tmp.Rotation(1,2,sign(angle)*ang);
          solid.orient = mid.Times(tmp.Times
          ➥(mid.Transpose().Times(group.element[oldPos])));
        }
      }
    }
```

Here, the mode has not changed; the shape is still on a rough surface. The variable ang represents the angle at which the shape will be rotated toward the new position. It depends on how far away the mouse position is from the start of the roll, lastPt, in a certain direction. The interface works like a ratchet; when putting in a bolt, the ratchet is free to turn counterclockwise and the bolt is not turned, but the ratchet locks into the last position it passed when it is turned clockwise, and then the bolt can be turned. Taking this analogy back to the interface, the shape rolls freely when you move the mouse in one direction, analogous to the counterclockwise ratchet. Moving the mouse in the other direction locks the rolling mechanism of the shape, like the locked clockwise-turning ratchet. Here, if ang turns out to be negative, the shape does not rotate; with a positive ang, however, the shape does rotate. After ang reaches angle (the angle of the next position), you must increment the number of rotations, inform CopyCat of the change, make the THUD noise, and start a new roll. Otherwise, you must calculate the orientation of the shape in the intermediate position between the old fixed position and the new fixed position.

```
if (start_roll){
        oldPos = group.pos;
        group.pos = group.arrows[group.pos][mode];
        angle = mid.FindTran(solid.orient,group.element[group.pos]);
        lastPt[0] = x;
        lastPt[1] = y;
        start_roll = false;
    }
```

Here, you finally have the code for how to start a new roll. The old fixed position, oldPos, is saved and the new position, group.pos, is figured out. The angle to the new position is calculated, and the matrix mid is computed to help figure out the intermediate positions. Finally, the lastPt is recorded so that it can be used for the calculation of ang.

```
repaint();
      return true;
    }
    return false;
  }
```

All the changes then are thrown to the screen with repaint. return true; tells the event handler that the mouseDrag has been handled. It turns out that the only real things you affected in this whole method are the orientation and position of the shape. It is a good idea to keep the event handlers as simple as possible, because these method are called very often. Even though the code looks long, because there are really only three methods in this method, it is fairly fast. Figures 18.3 and 18.4 demonstrate two drags.

Figure 18.3.

A drag in the TRANSLATE mode.

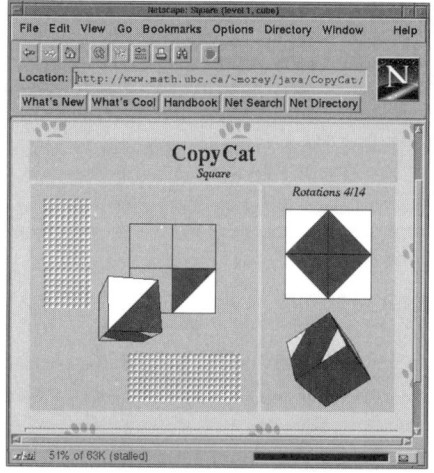

Figure 18.4.

A drag in the IN_B mode.

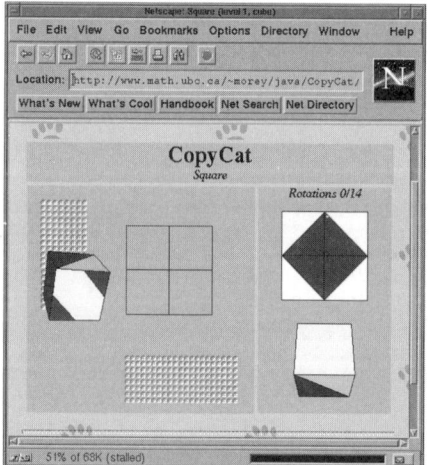

mouseUp

The mouseUp method associates releasing the mouse button with letting the shape go. If the shape is let go close enough to a place where it fits on the Board, the top face of the shape is placed on the Board. Otherwise, the shape is placed by changing the height variable. One other case also must be handled; if the player drops the shape outside of PlayArea, it brings the shape back to the initial position. Of course, not taking care of that case would mean that the player would never be able to retrieve the shape, which would really slow down the game.

```
/* -  -  -  -  -  -  -  -  -  -  -  -  -  -  -  -  -  -  -  -  -  -  -  - */
  public boolean mouseUp(java.awt.Event evt, int x, int y) {
    /* .. place the pattern down .. */
    if (onSolid && !animation_running){
      /* .. See if it's close enough to a location that is the same type .. */
      onSolid = false;
      height = -0.05;
      if (Board.ClosestFace(x,y,CLOSE_ENOUGH))
        if (group.blank[Board.face[Board.closestface]]==group.blank[group.pos]){
          solid.cenx = Board.vertex[Board.closestface][0];
          solid.ceny = Board.vertex[Board.closestface][1];
          Board.faceTry[Board.closestface] = group.smallestFace[group.pos];
          Board.finished = (Board.nvert == Board.NumCorrect());
          changedThings();
          if (level1) solid.ExplodePrep(group.tilt);
          else solid.StampPrep(group.tilt);
          new Thread(this).start();
        }
      if (x<0 || x>W || y<0 || y>H) {
        goToStart(false);
        repaint();
      }
      return true;
    }
    return false;
  }
```

If the shape is placed on the Board, there is some bookkeeping to take care of: centering the shape over the Board where the top face will be placed, updating the Board and notifying CopyCat of the change, and starting the animation of placing the top face on the player's copy of the picture. The animations are either an explosion (level 1), where the top face lands on the Board (this takes about 10 frames); or a 20-frame animation (level 2), where the shape flips and stamps the Board, leaving a mirror image imprint of the top face. See Figures 18.5 and 18.6.

Figure 18.5.
Dropping the shape in a
location not desired.

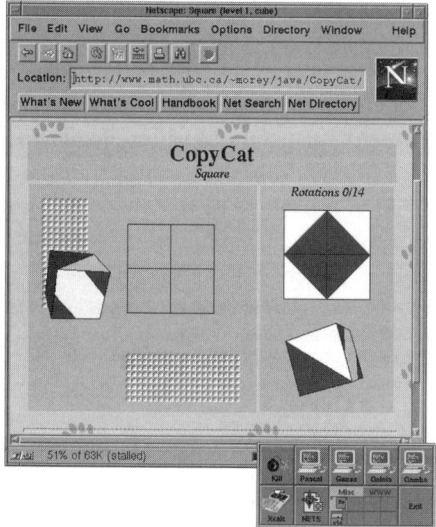

Figure 18.6.
Dropping the shape in a place
it fits on the board—the top
face drops to the board and
the other faces blow away.

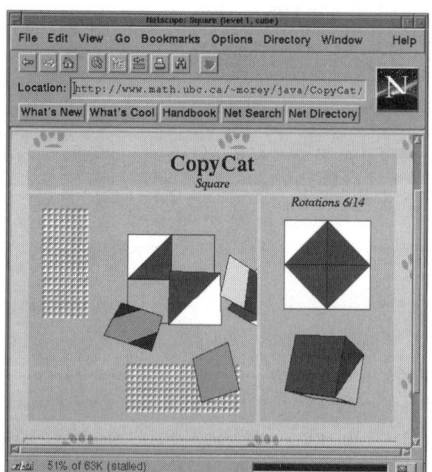

Interface and Communication

Computer games take on many different forms, so it is difficult to come up with useful programming tips and examples that would apply to all games. I have two principles that I follow in game design. One is to delegate the responsibilities of managing the game world to simpler objects that communicate with one other. Another is to search for a responsive, intuitive interface—some natural way that players can communicate their will to the game's world. With these ideas for designing an effective interface and an efficient internal representation of the game world, a good game concept can be turned into a good game. Without these designing ideas, however, this same concept easily could turn into one of the many "cr-applets" on the net.

I have illustrated these ideas with the game CopyCat. I broke down CopyCat into its functional parts, which communicate with each other to present and manage the game's world. In general, decomposing a game into usable objects can be very tricky. Deciding where to draw the lines between objects depends on not only the specific original intended uses of the objects, but also on possible future uses. Developing an eye for pattern recognition, along with learning good data structures, will help you develop this skill of decomposition. For beginning game programmers to learn this skill, it is good practice to constantly revise and redesign the internal workings of games to try to push the flexibility of their games. The flexibility of a game is a good measure of how well the internal workings of the game were thought out.

Also, CopyCat has a responsive intuitive interface. The essence of CopyCat's interface is that for every action the player makes in the game, there is a response so that the player knows the computer understood the attempted action. Every time the player "picks up the shape," for example, it raises slightly; the shape lowers when the player lets go of it. The control of the rolling allows for many intermediate positions. Generically, this is like a conversation between the player and the game. The player says, "blah blah blah," and the game has some response. The game may merely nod so that the player can continue talking, knowing that the last statement was understood; or, the game may do something more noticeable, depending on what the player has said. In designing the interface, the programmer is designing a limited language that the player uses to interact or converse with the game. The simpler or more familiar the language, the easier it is for the player to play the game. In CopyCat, the interface is relatively easy because it draws on people's experiences with the physical world: rolling and sliding shapes, ratchets, ink stamps, puzzles, and probably a lot more. This physicality, along with the drag-and-drop idea, makes the interface/language familiar to a lot of people.

With these principles, a sprinkle of the ideas from Chapter 12, "Network Programming with Java," some laser pistols or swords, and a lot of sleepless nights, you could be the creator of the greatest net game to ever be caught in the Web.

Summary

The Web has changed not only the way we view information, but also the way we interact with it. Web games can help us acquire the new life-skills of this information age.

The Java language provides simple but powerful tools for designing professional interfaces. The CopyCat applet shows the ease of dealing with the mouse events to communicate complex messages to the world of the game. Now it is up to you to tame the event handlers and catch some sockets and do some serious playing around.

Chapter 19

by Kathryn A. Jones

Security Issues

If you have been reading the trade magazines or browsing the Java sites on the Internet, you have probably heard a lot of the buzz about security in Java. Rightfully so, as the failure to provide adequate security to protect the systems that download Java applets guarantees Java's demise. Realistically, any Internet application that downloads and runs foreign executables, and dynamically links in classes at runtime that have been created by unknown programmers, can be as dangerous as it is powerful. While these features afford you the ability to seamlessly run code from anywhere on the Web, there is no guarantee that this code is not defective. Any programmer can intentionally or unintentionally produce code that can damage your system. There is no way you can predict that the code you plan to execute is faulty. Even the code provided by reputable organizations should not be completely trusted.

You might have already read that many bugs have been discovered in Java's security system. While it is true that many bugs have been found in Java, they are primarily related to the functionality of Java and not to its security. A few important security holes have been discovered at the time of this writing, and they are either fixed in the JDK 1.01 and Netscape Navigator 2.01, or are in the process of being fixed.

These bugs should not scare you away from using Java. Java has gone through beta testing. Sun Microsystems has distributed its JDK for free to anyone who wants it, and Sun has therefore reaped the rewards of the expeditious discovery of bugs and holes in its software by a huge user base that has exposed the product to high levels of scrutiny. With each new beta release, the Java team repaired new bugs. By the time Java 1.1 is released for general availability, it should have repaired the most serious holes in its security model. Inevitably, hackers will find ways to get around Java's security, as they do with many systems, but it is in the best interest of the Java team to be committed to providing constant security updates to its product as usage by the Java community evolves.

`http://www.io.org/~mentor/J___Notes.html`

TIP:

As you work with Java, be sure to keep an eye out for articles and announcements in magazines and on the Web about bugs and patches. One sight to add a bookmark for is Digital Espresso, a useful source of newly reported Java bugs. You can find it at the following address:

`http://www.io.org/~mentor/J___Notes.html`

Java's security structure is actually quite promising and is better than anything else out there today with similar power. It is a multilayered security system. This means that Java's security system is implemented in separate steps at each layer of the Java environment that code travels through before it is actually executed on your machine. Such depth of security is important because the Java programming environment is divided into layers. It is conceivable that any Java tool in the environment can be rewritten to circumvent the Java security structure. Although the security specifications implemented at the language and compiler layers allow you to create code with confidence that it is reasonably secure, they do not guarantee the security of Java code run from the Internet that is created and compiled by unknown programmers. There is nothing stopping a programmer from building a new compiler that allows code with security violations to compile cleanly and therefore destroy your system if you run it. Therefore, the other layers of the Java environment must be able to subject compiled bytecode from foreign sources to extreme levels of scrutiny.

Java's runtime environment that you install on your own system trusts no executable, no class, no instruction, or no parameter. It provides several additional layers of security that interrogate code before it is executed. This chapter examines all of Java's layers of security in detail, as well as the bugs that currently exist in August, 1996.

The Java Language

The first place that security is implemented in Java is, appropriately, in its language. The Java language provides security through its class libraries. Chapter 11, "Reading and Writing with Java," and Chapter 12, "Network Programming with Java," cover the security features of two of the class libraries: Java.io and Java.net. To summarize, Java.net provides the interfaces to handle the various network protocols (FTP, HTTP, Telnet, and so on). This package guards against tampering at the network interface level. The networking package can be configured at different levels of security to

○ Disallow all network accesses.
○ Allow network accesses to only the sources from which the code was imported.
○ Allow network accesses only outside the firewall if the code came from outside.
○ Allow unlimited network accesses.

Java.io provides many classes that have already been extensively tested, so it is recommended that you use these abstract classes in your code. Using Java.io classes to receive and send data to different input and output devices ensures that such activities are performed in the most secure manner. This holds true for all of Java's built-in packages. They have all been tested and should be used to ensure that your code does not violate any rules.

The Java language also adds security by providing access restrictions for encapsulation of classes, methods, and variables. Any class not declared public, for instance, is inaccessible by foreign classes. Any class declared protected is accessible only by its objects and subclasses. Any class declared private limits access to objects instantiated from it.

The Java language also eliminates pointer arithmetic and prevents you from explicitly controlling pointers in any manner. Instead, the compiler assigns symbolic references to methods, and the interpreter automatically assumes the responsibility of managing memory allocation and deallocation. As you have learned, pointers and pointer arithmetic used in other C-type programs are a leading source of bugs that crash systems.

Moreover, you can use the Java language to create your own security manager. The Java runtime environment has its own security manager that is constantly active at runtime. This security manager is an object that authorizes all operations before they are executed. The security manager throws a `SecurityException` if it rejects an operation. Otherwise, it passes the operation and allows it to run.

The `Java.lang` package provides an abstract security manager class that you can subclass to create your own security manager. The class provides methods that inspect classloaders on the execution stack.

Note that you cannot install a new security manager in an applet. Applets are subject to the security manager of the application in which they are running (your browser or Java AppletViewer).

The Java Compiler

The Java compiler not only checks that your syntax is correct in your source code that was created in the Java language, but it ensures that the code doesn't violate the language's safety rules. The compiler ensures that you have not made any errors, such as casting objects that are incompatible or using incorrect parameters.

As discussed in Chapter 2, "Getting Started," the Java Compiler works similarly to compilers in C-type languages in that it takes intelligible source code and converts it to code for a machine to interpret. The difference is that the machine that the Java compiler compiles for is the Java Virtual Machine, and the code is not native machine code for your CPU, it is bytecode for the JVM. Additionally, the Java compiler does not convert references to numbers and does not create a memory layout for the program at compile time. Although performance takes a hit since references in Java must be looked up in an object index at runtime instead of referring to exact memory addresses with the code, these changes were made for security reasons.

The compiler enforces sizes for bytecode commands and symbolic address references it creates. Each bytecode command consists of an *opcode* and an *operand*. The opcode is the command that the interpreter recognizes. The operand is the data needed by the opcode. Opcodes are executed sequentially and stored in 8-bit numbers. Operands vary in length, but are divided into bytes. Each opcode has a 32-bit symbolic address reference, or handle. The interpreter is able to locate pieces of code in memory using the opcodes assigned by the compiler. It is important that these sizes remain constant for portability, and the compiler ensures that they are.

The Java Interpreter

The Java interpreter performs many functions, some of which are performed solely for the purpose of the security of the system, and others that are performed as a part of the execution of the Java application, but require that security is enforced at each step.

One function that the interpreter performs for the purpose of security is laying out the memory map at runtime. This is unlike C and C++, in which the memory map is laid out by the compiler. The interpreter's allocation of memory in a Java application might vary depending on the user's hardware and software platform. This prevents a hacker from predicting where a class exists in memory, and then directly manipulating it.

Because memory is allocated by the runtime interpreter, Java has the luxury of eliminating the use of pointers in the language that explicitly addresses memory space. This prevents an innocent programmer from accidentally placing the wrong memory address in the code for a method, which would result in crashing your system. The compiled code references memory with handles that are resolved to exact memory addresses at runtime by the Java interpreter. You are unable to forge pointers to memory in Java, because the memory layout and object index do not exist until runtime and are controlled entirely by the Java interpreter.

Without pointers to locate a method, for example, the Java interpreter's memory layout is used to locate the method during runtime. When a method is called for the first time in a program, the interpreter refers to an object index of symbolic references, created by the compiler, that it checks against the memory layout it has created and finds where it placed the method in memory when the class was loaded. Subsequent calls to this method do not require such a lookup because the index contains the proper memory address.

Such symbolic references solve the fragile superclass security problem, which occurs in programs created in C and C++ when a superclass has been updated, possibly changing the memory layout. If a subclass tries to call a method from the updated superclass, its placement might be different in memory, and the program jumps to an obscure area of memory, inadvertently jeopardizing the system. In Java, the subclass calls methods symbolically from the superclass, and the interpreter locates the method using its memory layout and object index. Therefore, the correct method is called from the correct area of memory every time.

In addition to the security inherent in its runtime memory layout and object index referencing, the interpreter enforces security in three layers: the *class loader, bytecode verifier,* and *runtime system.* The class loader brings in the Java file, plus any classes referenced or inherited by the classes in the code. The bytecode verifier ensures that the code adheres to Java standards and doesn't violate the integrity of your system. The runtime system executes the code on your hardware.

The Class Loader

The class loader is responsible for loading classes that are called while a Java program is executing and laying them out in memory in such a way that they are not able to interfere with each other without explicit measures set forth in the language. It loads both local classes and foreign classes that have been determined clean by the bytecode verifier.

You can think of the execution environment of a Java application as a set of classes that are partitioned into separate namespaces. The class loader provides a layer of security by placing incoming classes in their own namespaces. Classes do not interfere with classes in other namespaces, or partitions, without explicit calls to their symbolic references and the permission of the target class to be accessed by the foreign classes (the target class must not have declared any access restrictions).

The class loader assigns one namespace for all of the classes that come from the local file system (built-in Java classes), and a separate namespace for the each source of imported classes. This protects local classes from foreign classes. When a class references another class, it first searches the local system's namespace, then the namespace of the referencing class. Foreign classes have no way of simulating a local class. Likewise, built-in classes cannot interfere with imported namespaces without referencing their classes explicitly. Foreign classes are similarly partitioned from each other because they are each assigned their own namespaces.

The Bytecode Verifier

The Java Interpreter passes all incoming code to a bytecode verifier. The responsibility of the bytecode verifier is to subject every piece of code that the interpreter passes it to a rigorous series of integrity tests. It performs a variety of tests that run from simple verification that the format of a line of code fragment is consistent with the language specification, to passing each line of code through a theorem prover to trap the following types of problems:

- Forged pointers
- Access restriction violations (private, public, or protected)
- Mismatching of object types
- Operand stack overflows and underflows
- Incorrect bytecode parameters
- Illegal data conversion

After code has been approved by the bytecode verifier, you can be reasonably sure that the language does not violate your system with harmful instructions that fit any of these conditions. To maintain system performance, after code passes the verifier tests and is approved it will not be checked again. This enables the interpreter to reliably execute the code at full speed without stopping to check its integrity.

The Java class loader and bytecode verifier make no assumptions about the primary source of the bytecode stream. The code may have come from the local system, or it may have come from a system in another country. The bytecode verifier is the last line of defense against errant code. Java requires that imported code passes the verifier's tests before it is executed by any means on the system.

The Execution of Code

Once the code has been loaded, laid out in memory, and verified, it is executed a piece at a time by the interpreter. The interpreter can execute bytecodes that have been coded for the Java Virtual Machine specification directly. It also provides a just-in-time compiler that compiles intermediate bytecode to native machine code at runtime for cases that you are willing to sacrifice portability to allow the bytecode to run at full speed. Security can be implemented at runtime by coding traps and exception handlers into your program.

Java Virtual Machine

At this point in the book, you might be curious as to how the Java Virtual Machine actually works. A grasp of the fine points of the JVM gives you a greater understanding of the security structure of Java. This section unravels the mystery of the JVM.

The JVM is intended to provide a set of specifications that the Java language, compiler, and interpreter adhere to in order to ensure secure, portable programs and runtime environments. The JVM provides a strict set of rules that can be used by a developer to create an original implementation of an interpreter that runs Java code on any machine it is installed on. These rules require that the runtime interpreter include all of the following pieces:

- A set of *bytecode instructions* similar to that of a CPU, which contains opcodes and operands, and their values and alignments
- A set of *registers* that tracks the state of the program at a given time
- A *Java stack*, which stores information about the states of methods in stack frames
- A *garbage collection heap*, which stores memory that is to be allocated to objects
- *Memory areas for storage,* which store constants and methods

The Bytecode Instruction Set

When Java code is compiled, it is converted to bytecode, which is similar to the assembly language created by C and C++ compilers. Each instruction in the bytecode contains an opcode followed by an *operand*. The following list contains examples of opcodes and their descriptions:

- `iload` loads an integer
- `aload` loads a pointer
- `ior` logically or two integer

Opcodes are represented by 8-bit numbers. Operands vary in length. They are aligned to eight bits, and therefore, operands larger than eight bits are divided into multiple bytes. The reason

Java uses such small memory spaces is to maintain compactness of memory. The Java team felt that compact code was worth the performance hit on the CPU while locating each instruction, a hit that results from the inability of the interpreter to judge exactly where each instruction is due to the varying lengths of instructions. This decision reclaims lost performance as compact bytecode travels across networks more quickly than code found in other programming languages that contains unused memory space left free as a result of larger, fixed instruction lengths. Of course, code with fixed instruction lengths runs more quickly on the CPU because the interpreter can jump through instructions, anticipating their lengths and exact locations.

The instruction set provides specifications for opcode and operand syntax and values, and identifier values. It also includes instructions for invoking methods.

Opcode recognizes the primitive data types described in Chapter 1, " An Overview of Java." In addition, it recognizes the symbolic object reference, which is a type of 32-bit length. The Java compiler manages these types. It assigns bytecodes that are appropriate for each type and each method.

The JVM Register Set

The JVM contains four 32-bit registers that store information about the current state of the system. These registers are updated after the execution of each bytecode.

- ○ `pc` The counter that keeps track of which bytecode in the program is currently being executed.
- ○ `optop` The pointer to the top of the operand stack in the Java stack that is used when the program performs operations.
- ○ `frame` The pointer to the current execution environment of the current method in the Java stack.
- ○ `vars` The pointer to the first local variable of the current method that is executing in the Java stack.

The processor of your machine deals quickly with these registers.

The Java Stack

The Java stack provides the current parameters to bytecodes during execution of methods. Each method of a class is assigned a stack frame that is stored in the Java stack. Each stack frame holds the current status of local variables, the operand stack, and the execution environment.

The local variables for the method are stored in an array of 32-bit variables indexed by the `vars` register. Larger variables are divided across two local variables. When local variables are used, they are loaded onto the operand stack for the method. The operand stack is a 32-bit first in, first out (FIFO) stack that stores operands for opcodes in the JVM instruction set. These operands are

both parameters used in methods' instructions, as well as results of instructions. The execution environment provides information about the current state of the method in the Java stack. It stores pointers to the previous method, pointers to its local variables, and pointers to the top and bottom of the operand stack. It might also contain debugging information.

The Garbage Collection Heap

As you learned in Chapter 4, "Creating Your Own Objects," Java's garbage collector keeps track of references to objects allocated in memory using symbolic handles. When an object is no longer being referenced during the execution of the program, the garbage collector returns the memory used by the object to its garbage collection heap. This heap is a separate area of memory in Java that is allocated when the runtime system is started. It is provided specially for allocation of memory to new objects. If the system the interpreter runs on supports virtual memory, the size of the garbage collection heap can grow as necessary.

The JVM Memory Areas

The other memory areas provided in the JVM are for storing methods and the constant pool. All of the bytecode for Java methods is stored in the method area. It also stores symbol tables for dynamic linking of classes and additional debugging information associated with a method. The constant pool area encodes string constants, class names, method names, and field names for each class. It is created by the Java compiler. These memory areas are not required to be laid out in any particular location to avoid exposure to hackers who would be able to find their code if they knew the memory map before runtime.

Limitations

The JVM in JDK 1.01 has a few limitations due to its fixed operand and stack sizes that may be resolved in future releases of the JDK:

○ Stack width of 32-bits limits the JVM's internal addressing to 4G of memory.

○ 8-bit offsets into objects limit the number of methods in a class to 256.

○ 16-bit offsets for branching and jumping instructions limit the size of a method to 32K.

○ Unsigned 16-bit indexes into a constant pool limit the number of constant pool entries per method to 32K.

○ Unsigned 8-bit argument counts limit the size of an argument to 255 32-bit words (only 127 long or double words).

These limitations are not issues today because 4G of internal addressing space is not necessary on today's machines that typically have 16 or 32M RAM. However, technology advances quickly, so this limit could conceivably become an issue in the near future. Keep in mind that these limitations might be relaxed in later releases of Java.

Known Bugs

It is important that you are aware of the bugs in Java that have already been discovered and reported before you spend time and energy struggling with them. The latest release of the Java Developer's Kit is version 1.0.1. You should be aware of several bugs that exist in this release. This section lists the open bugs in the JDK 1.0.1 as reported by Sun Microsystems, some workarounds and patches that Sun suggests using, the JDK 1.0 security bugs that have been announced by Sun as fixed in JDK version 1.0.1, and some newer security bugs that have not yet made it to Sun's official list of open bugs.

Additional bugs will be discovered as Java is used by an increasing number of programmers in increasing capacities. It is important that you regularly check Java's Web site for bugs that Sun confirms, and additionally, unofficial Java Web sites, like Digital Espresso, report bugs that have not yet been confirmed by Sun.

Keep in mind that the bulk of these bugs address minor problems with the functionality of Java, and not with Java's security.

An updated list of the open bugs in the JDK can be found at `http://java.sun.com/products/ JDK/1.0.2/KnownBugs.html`.

Future Java Security

Many organizations are currently racing to produce tools that will improve Java security. These organizations are creating their own bytecode verifiers, runtime environments, compilers, and virus scanning software. They are working on providing encryption of binaries that will make it difficult for hackers to reverse engineer Java code. They are developing internal versioning systems and object directory services that will allow for authentication of applets.

Two examples of such organizations are Symantec, which has recently announced its virus scan software package for Java, and The University of Illinois Systems Software Research Group, which has recently announced the release of a package that gives the Java programmer access to a security API. The details as announced are as follows in this excerpt from Symantec Corporation's home page:

> *"Symantec Corporation, a leading supplier of utilities software products, today announced the development of new technology that lays the foundation for delivery of leading edge antivirus solutions. The Symantec AntiVirus Research Center (SARC) has developed the first native-Java virus scanner for Java applets sent over the Internet. In addition, SARC has also designed an in-house automation technology that can be used to analyze, replicate, detect and define a large subset of the most common computer viruses.*

One of the fastest growing development environments is Java. While no current Java virus threats exist, there is a possibility that a virus could be written. In addition, due to Java's inherent portability, a virus of this type could spread over a wide variety of platforms. To address this possibility, SARC has produced a Java class file scanner extension for NAV. This will enable NAV to provide real-time protection and monitor for Java virus activity within Netscape or any other Java supported Web browser.

The current AutoProtect capability in Norton AntiVirus (NAV) is configured to scan Java applets sent over the Internet in .CLASS files, and can detect a potential type of Java (Java Type I) virus that can be propagated by modifying HTML pages.

The new Java scanner technology can detect another, more complex, type of Java virus (Java Type II) that parasitically infects .CLASS files. The Java .CLASS file scanner provides a much faster and more efficient scan than that achieved with conventional brute-force scanning technology and represents the best scanning technology available today for the Java environment. At the first sign of a Java virus threat, Symantec will make this technology available to customers via an immediate virus definition update."

http://choices.cs.uiuc.edu/Security/JGSS/jgss.html

Caution:

This is a press release by the University of Illinois from the Digital Espresso home page:

"The University of Illinois Systems Software Research Group has released the first alpha version of their JGSS Java package. This package provides Java programs access to the Generic Security Service API defined in RFC-1508 and implemented by MIT's Kerberos system. The package is available for download for personal, educational, and research use at the following address http://choices.cs.uiuc.edu/Security/JGSS/jgss.html."

Summary

The status of security in Java is ever-changing. This chapter has provided you with a solid comprehension of the inner workings of Java's security structure as it exists today. To remain informed of the state of this structure as it grows and changes, and to be sure that you are effectively protecting your code and your computer environment from hackers, you must be sure to regularly check Java's Web site, other Java sites, and magazine articles for announcements of new changes, additional functionality, patches, and bugs as they arise.

Index

477

Tricks of the Java Programming Gurus

—Glenn Vanderburg, et al.

This book is a guide for the experienced Java programmer who wants to go beyond simple animations and applets. This book shows the reader how to streamline Java code, how to achieve unique results with undocumented tricks, and how to add advanced level functions to existing Java programs. This book provides a fast-paced guide to advanced Java programming.

$39.99 USA, $56.95 CDN, ISBN 1-57521-102-5,
888 pp., Accomplished—Expert

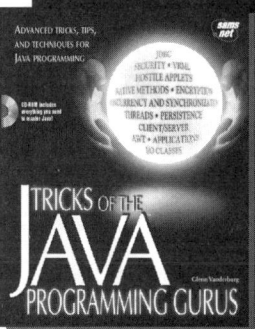

Programming Windows NT 4 Unleashed

—David Hamilton, Mickey Williams, and Griffith Kadnier

With this book, readers get a clear understanding of the modes of operation and architecture for Windows NT. Everything—including execution models, processes, threads, DLLs, memory, controls, and security—is covered with precise detail. This book teaches OLE, DDE, drag and drop, OCX development, and the component gallery.

$59.99 USA, $84.95 CDN, ISBN 0-672-30905-X,
1,200 pp., Accomplished—Expert

Peter Norton's Guide to Java Programming

—William Stanek and Sam DeWolfe

Peter Norton's Guide to Java Programming is a guide for Web developers. The highly qualified authors dispense their knowledge of Web programming with Java in an easy-to-understand format. The book explains threads and exceptions, Java tools, the Java API, applet re-use, and it provides the most extensive coverage available on how to enhance Java.

$39.99 USA, $56.95 CDN, ISBN 1-57521-088-6,
800 pp., Casual—Accomplished

Programming Netscape Plug-Ins

—Zan Oliphant

This book provides the reader with an understanding of what plug-ins are and how they should be used. Design information is discussed in detail, giving the reader the knowledge to program and design effective Web pages with Netscape.

$39.99 USA, $56.95 CDN, ISBN 1-57521-098-3,
448 pp., Accomplished—Expert

Web Programming with Visual Basic

—Craig Eddy and Brad Haasch

This book quickly shows the experienced developer how to develop Web applications using the 32-bit power of Visual Basic. It includes an overview of Web programming and delves into specifics, teaching readers how to incorporate animation, sound, and more in Web applications. This book includes coverage of Netscape Navigator and how to create CGI applications with Visual Basic, and it discusses spiders, agents, crawlers, and other Internet aids.

$39.99 USA, $56.95 CDN, 1-57521-106-8,
400 pp., Accomplished—Expert

Teach Yourself Internet Game Programming with Java in 21 Days

—Michael Morrison

Game developers can turn to this book for the latest information on game programming technology. This book shows in detail how to use Java to program games for interactive use on the Internet and World Wide Web. This book details information on the Java Developer's Kit, class libraries, and mulitplayer gaming, and it discusses Java's SDK and teaches ways to exploit its power in game programming.

$39.99 USA, $56.95 CDN, 1-57521-148-3,
456 pp., Accomplished—Expert

Teach Yourself SunSoft Java WorkShop in 21 Days

—Rogers Cadenhead, Laura Lemay, and Charles E. Perkins

The Java Workshop included with this book is a cross-platform tool that provides a rich set of tools for the beginner or the professional Java programmer. The book provides a comprehensive way to learn SunSoft Java Workshop. It teaches you how to quickly create Java applets with easy-to-use visual development tools and explores the advanced features of the Java Workshop.

$39.99 USA, $56.95 CDN, 1-57521-159-9,
600 pp., Casual—Accomplished

Java Developer's Guide

—Jamie Jaworski and Carie Jardean

Java is one of the major growth areas for developers on the World Wide Web. It brings with it the ability to download and run applets from a Web server. *Java Developer's Guide* teaches developers everything they need to know to effectively develop Java applications. This book covers Java interface, VRML extensions, security, and explores new technology and future trends of Java development.

$49.99 USA, $67.99 CDN, ISBN 1-57521-069-X,
768 pp., Accomplished—Expert

Add to Your Sams.net Library Today
with the Best Books for Internet Technologies

ISBN	Quantity	Description of Item	Unit Cost	Total Cost
1-57521-102-5		Tricks of the Java Programming Gurus (Book/CD-ROM)	$39.99	
0-672-30905-X		Programming Windows NT 4 Unleashed (Book/CD-ROM)	$59.99	
1-57521-088-6		Peter Norton's Guide to Java Programming (Book/CD-ROM)	$39.99	
1-57521-098-3		Programming Netscape Plug-Ins (Book/CD-ROM)	$39.99	
1-57521-106-8		Web Programming with Visual Basic (Book/CD-ROM)	$39.99	
1-57521-148-3		Teach Yourself Internet Game Programming with Java in 21 Days (Book/CD-ROM)	$39.99	
1-57521-159-9		Teach Yourself SunSoft Java Workshop in 21 Days (Book/CD-ROM)	$39.99	
1-57521-069-X		Java Developer's Guide (Book/CD-ROM)	$49.99	
		Shipping and Handling: See information below.		
		TOTAL		

Shipping and Handling: $4.00 for the first book, and $1.75 for each additional book. If you need to have it NOW, we can ship product to you in 24 hours for an additional charge of approximately $18.00, and you will receive your item overnight or in two days. Overseas shipping and handling adds $2.00. Prices subject to change. Call between 9:00 a.m. and 5:00 p.m. EST for availability and pricing information on latest editions.

201 W. 103rd Street, Indianapolis, Indiana 46290

1-800-428-5331 — Orders   1-800-835-3202 — FAX   1-800-858-7674 — Customer Service

Book ISBN 1-57521-113-0

CD-Rom Install

What's on the Disc

The companion CD-ROM contains an assortment of evaluation versions of third-party tools. The disc is designed to be explored using a browser program. Using the browser, you can view information concerning products and companies, and you can install programs with a single click of the mouse. To run the Guide to the CD-ROM, here's what to do.

Windows 95 Installation Instructions

NOTE:

If you have the AutoPlay feature of Windows 95 enabled, the Guide to the CD-ROM program starts automatically. If you have disabled the AutoPlay feature, please follow the instructions below.

1. Insert the CD-ROM disc into your CD-ROM drive.
2. From the Windows 95 desktop, double-click on the My Computer icon.
3. Double-click on the icon representing your CD-ROM drive.
4. Double-click on the icon titled setup.exe to run the install program for the Guide to the CD-ROM program.

Windows NT Installation Instructions

1. Insert the CD-ROM disc into your CD-ROM drive.
2. From File Manager or Program Manager, choose Run from the File menu.
3. Type <drive>\setup and press Enter, where <drive> corresponds to the drive letter of your CD-ROM. For example, if your CD-ROM is drive D:, type D:\setup and press Enter.
4. Follow the on-screen instructions to run the install program for the Guide to the CD-ROM.